MW00445033

John Gray

❧[*John Gray*]❧

Poet, Dandy, and Priest

Jerusha Hull McCormack

BRANDEIS UNIVERSITY PRESS
Published by University Press of New England
Hanover and London

Brandeis University Press

Published by University Press of New England, Hanover, NH 03755
© 1991 by Trustees of Brandeis University

All rights reserved

Design and production: Christopher Harris,
Summer Hill Books, Weathersfield, VT.

Printed in the United States of America 5 4 3 2 1

CIP data appear at the end of the book

Grateful acknowledgment is made for the following materials:

Papers, correspondence, holographs, typescripts, and other unpublished material by John Gray and André Raffalovich in the following locations: Dominican Chaplaincy, Edinburgh; National Library of Scotland, Edinburgh; John Rylands University Library of Manchester, England; Donald Hyde Collection, New York, New York; (letters from John Gray to John Lane, 27 May 1892 and 18 June 1892), Henry W. and Albert A. Berg Collection (Astor, Lenox, and Tilden Foundations), The New York Public Library, New York, New York; (3 letters from John Gray to Edmund Blunden—21 July 1929, 20 February 1933, and undated), Harry Ransom Humanities Research Center, The University of Texas at Austin; Princeton University Library, Princeton, New Jersey; The Beinecke Rare Book Room and Manuscript Library, Yale University, New Haven, Connecticut; The Houghton Library, Harvard University, Cambridge, Massachusetts; the Paulhan Archives, Paris, France; and photographs, prints, copies of prints and/or paintings, or other graphic representations from the estate of John Gray and André Raffalovich in the Dominican Chaplaincy, Edinburgh, or any other locations, all used by permission of their respective repositories and of the Prior Provincial of the English Province of the Order of Preachers, St. Dominic's Priory, London, England.

Manuscripts and correspondence of John Gray and André Raffalovich, including: Gray/Raffalovich correspondence; letters to and from Gray and Raffalovich from various correspondents; correspondence from Raffalovich to Charles Ballantyne and Norman Wright; holograph of John Gray's *Spiritual Poems* and manuscripts of other original work, all used by permission of the Department of Manuscripts, The National Library of Scotland, Edinburgh.

The journals and papers of "Michael Field" (Katherine Bradley and Edith Cooper) in the British Library Manuscript Collections, London; the letters of "Michael Field" to John Gray, willed to the Dominican Chaplaincy, Edinburgh, and now in the archives of the National Library of Scotland, Edinburgh, and (John Gray to "Michael Field" 20 January 1908, 24 July 1907, 14 November 1909, 24 November 1908, 3 August 1908, 29 January 1909, 24 October 1908, 29 November 1908, 10 June 1909, 17 April 1907, 1 July 1908, and 7 November 1910), in the Henry W. and Albert A. Berg Collection, The New York Public Library (Astor, Lenox and Tilden Foundations), New York, New York; letters from Charles Ricketts to John Lane, and from Max Beerbohm to Reggie Turner, in the Houghton Library, Harvard University, Cambridge, Massachusetts, and from Charles Ricketts and Frank Harris to John Gray, and from John Gray to Francis Vielé-Griffin, no date, The Beinecke Rare Book Room and Manuscript

Permissions continue on p. 319

For Dara, David, and Thomas

Contents

CONTENTS

Illustrations follow page 224

❧ *Acknowledgments* ❧

This book owes its genesis to Professor Edward Engelberg of Brandeis University. It was he who, having just edited *The Symbolist Poem,* drew my attention to the rich material there: many (then) obscure minor poets who made their work domesticating the French *symbolistes.* Without his skill in guiding me through an early draft of this book, or his confidence in its worth, it would have died an early (and unmourned) death.

From an early phase, the work was sustained by the extraordinary generosity of Father Brocard Sewell, O. Carm. Although working on his own study of John Gray, Father Sewell took a keen interest in my research, sharing leads, information, speculations. On my first visit to London, he arranged introductions to several people who had known Father Gray. Finally, we exchanged early drafts of our respective books. If readers note an occasional similarity of phrasing and argument, or a convergence of sources, it is due to this collaboration, which if not unique, is certainly unusual in a world of proprietorial and secretive scholars. I pay tribute to Father Sewell not only as a scholar but also as a comrade and friend. He has refreshed my sense of what intellectual endeavor can be. I only regret that, in my own biography, I may have caused him sadness in discussing subjects that he feels, in all honor, should be dealt with more circumspectly.

The book's center of gravity rests on a collection of manuscripts—both of letters and texts—which, in the early days of this project, resided in the Dominican Chaplaincy, Edinburgh. The collection was something of a legend among Gray scholars, as it had been regarded as inaccessible—with little justification, as it turned out. On enquiry, Father Anthony Ross, O.P., then in charge of the Chaplaincy, granted me the privilege of reading—and copying—the contents of this collection. His interests were those of the scholar, that Gray's story be told in its entirety; he gave his own version of it, referred me to past parishioners of Gray's, read and commented on an early draft of the manuscript. No standard expression of thanks is in order here: there would simply have been no book without his crucial intervention, and certainly no book that could attempt to approach the truth of another person's life.

That generosity has been sustained by Father Ross's successors at the Dominican Chaplaincy; in particular, I wish to thank Father Bede Bailey, whose prompt and knowledgeable assistance in locating items in the Gray archive has more than once saved me from despair. To the present Prior Provincial of the Dominican Order I am indebted for permission to use these and other documents relating to John Gray.

On my first visit to Edinburgh, I met Charles Ballantyne, an acquaintance of John Gray and a friend to André Raffalovich. He gave me permission to read his correspondence, shared his opinions, and proved, in the end, a valued friend. Alan Bell, then senior librarian at the National Library of Scotland, helped in tracking down several obscure items, and, before his departure, became instrumental in establishing a Gray Archive to which various manuscript collections, including much of that from the Dominican Chaplaincy, have since been transferred. He proved the first of many curators who have cunningly traced documents within their holdings, or copied correspondences whole. For their able assistance, I thank them. To the libraries in which they work, I also owe thanks for permission to use their collections, among them: the British Library, the Houghton Library, The John Rylands University Library of Manchester, the Library of the University of Texas at Austin, the National Library of Scotland, the New York Public Library, the Princeton University Library, the University of Iowa Library, the University of Reading Library, the William Andrews Clark Memorial Library, and the Yale University Library. The photographs are reproduced by courtesy of The Fitzwilliam Museum, Cambridge; the Greenwich Local History Library; Michael Maclagan and Sir Rupert Hart-Davis; and the Royal Commission on the Ancient and Historical Monuments of Scotland.

There are other debts of substance. Peter Vernon, a fellow Gray scholar, arranged for me to see the letters from Gray to Louÿs before they were published. His dissertation for London University on "The Letters of John Gray" proved invaluable in ordering Gray's scattered correspondence. From the first, the late Ian Fletcher kept me current with his work, which issued, three years ago, in *The Poems of John Gray.* Allan Campbell of Edinburgh, whose interest in Gray is as keen as my own, has been generous in too many ways to enumerate, both as scholar and host. His sharp detective work has unravelled several Gray conundrums. Professor Joan Halperin directed me to a correspondence between Gray and Félix Fénéon in a private archive in Paris. The story of Gray's early life would have been impoverished without Heather Coltman's long, fascinating letters about her great-uncle, her family photographs, and finally, those of the Woolwich Arsenal, which she tracked down. In granting permission to read the "Michael Field" journals and letters, Riette Sturge-Moore helped enliven an otherwise very formal version of the friendship with Gray. Similarly, the late Sir Norman Wright's permission to read his correspondence gave vivid detail to Gray's later years. Brian Reade was likewise helpful in his forthright version of several episodes in Gray's life. Sadly, many of those I must thank are dead: in particular, I wish to name Mrs. Richard Cammell, James Langdale, Kathleen O'Riordan, and Father John Baptist-Reeves, to whom I am indebted for copies of correspondence, information, insights.

I have been lucky in my readers. I must thank, above all, Dr. Isobel Murray for her tough criticism and warm encouragement. My debts to her formidable scholarship may be only partially estimated from the notes. Professor Ruth Temple, the late Richard Ellmann, and (in particular) Professor Laurence Davies provided notations, in every instance exact and helpful. The pencil of Dr. Laura Nagy has relentlessly improved the manuscript. Three translators have, on different occasions, limped with me through Gray's painful French: Dr. Caroline Karcher, Ghislaine Muchmore and Dr. Yolande Sexton. Finally, I must thank Gonny Vanderbroek for rescuing this book from the jaws of the computer, to which I had fed the manuscript in one large unmanageable meal (it was almost devoured entire).

Even with such comradely aid, nothing would have been accomplished without an initial travel grant from Brandeis University nor without a timely grant of leave of absence from University College, Dublin.

Those who have been around before the book deserve mention

for seeing me through. In particular, I wish to thank my parents, Drs. Gordon and Mona Hull, for the support they have offered over many years and in many forms. I must also thank David Hull, my brother, who took time out from his postgraduate work to do some crucial research for me in London. Of debts to my more intimate family, it is harder to speak. To David, for not interrupting me when I am juggling sentences in mid-air. For Thomas, for interrupting me when he felt it imperative. To both boys, who in every way counteracted the potential sterility of my work; who gave chaos to order, and urgency to ideas; who made me redefine my own sense of life. To Dara, my husband, for prodding me to finish and looking after the boys so I could do so, and for believing it would actually be finished. I hope that this book, dedicated to you and our sons, will be a worthy addition to your collection.

J. H. McC.

John Gray

❦⟦ *Introduction* ⟧❧

If the reader opening this book has heard of John Gray at all, it is probably as the putative model for the hero of Oscar Wilde's novel, *The Picture of Dorian Gray*. He might even know him as the "Dorian" Gray once acclaimed "the incomparable poet of the age" whose first book, *Silverpoints* (1893), was regarded as an epitome of frenchified decadence.[1] That reader would, almost certainly, be one who had studied the 1890s; to such an extent has scholarship reversed life. For until comparatively recently, most readers who knew of a John Gray who resided, at the turn of the century, first in London and then in Edinburgh, would assume that they were to read about the formidable Canon of St. Peter's, Edinburgh; and if they pursued the book, would be surprised, probably painfully, to find any connection between their sedate priest and the controversial nineties poet. They may have known their Father Gray to be aloof and at times puzzling; they did not imagine him a man with a past.

Canon Gray did much to distance himself from his history. He is not known to have referred to his childhood, although one priestly colleague noted "distinct undertones" of a Cockney accent in his otherwise carefully modulated speech.[2] On rare occasions the Canon might intrigue his company with an anecdote about Lionel Johnson or Ernest Dowson—and then firmly change the course of conversation.[3] Clues were dropped, but pursuit discouraged, not merely by silence but by an active policy of obstruction. From the mid-nineties on, it appears, John Gray began to buy up copies of *Silverpoints* in order to "immobilize" or destroy them.[4] Shortly after Gray's death, William Butler Yeats was refused permission to reprint poems in *The Oxford Book of Modern Verse* by Gray's executors, acting, apparently, on what they interpreted to have been Gray's wishes.[5] And when a friend of many years standing, Peter Anson, proposed a memoir, he came up against what he described as the "strong & determined opposition of the Canon's two sisters who feel that their brother would 'wish to be forgotten.' "[6]

Should this imputed wish have been honored? Certainly, if the silence had been complete and deliberate, if Canon Gray had so requested and ensured compliance by destroying all documents in his possession that spoke of his past before he entered into holy orders. But no such clarity of intention prevails. Quite the opposite: at his death Gray left to the Dominican Order a legacy of letters and manuscripts dating back to the mid-eighties as part of his (and his close friend André Raffalovich's) estate. Although not put in any great order, they showed clear signs of having been sorted through. The correspondence from Pierre Louÿs, a French poet and mutual friend of Oscar Wilde, for instance, had been preserved—with the notable exception of those letters for the years 1894 and 1895, the years leading up to and including Wilde's trials.[7] Another letter, from a close friend of Wilde's, Robert Sherard, suggests some complicity in a mysterious, perhaps illicit, transaction in France. These letters provoke leading questions; others are more circumspect. The six-year correspondence, from both sides, of Gray and Raffalovich speaks occasionally of their shared past, although only in veiled—usually remorseful—terms.

And then there are the manuscripts: the most significant being the text of a short story, "The Person in Question," carefully preserved in typescript.[8] It is about a haunting: of the young "Dorian" Gray by a person who appears, in some sense, to be himself—a hallucination so vivid that it makes the protagonist doubt his own reality. In this apparition, Gray comes to recognize an image of himself as he may become, an admission of identity that leads him near madness. As a story that has the feel of autobiography, it was perhaps too intimate in its implications about Gray and his relationship with Wilde to be publishable. Nevertheless, it was left to the Dominicans in a form which made its posthumous publication possible if not inevitable.

The legacy, then, has a certain ambiguous intention; it seems to invite speculation while at the same time making conclusions impossible, wholly in character with the Canon's tantalizing reserve. For if he genuinely did not wish speculation about his past, why preserve the letters and manuscripts at all? Why not simply build an immense bonfire and have done with it? It is obvious Canon Gray could not bring himself to do so. Nor did he himself ever place any prohibition on an account of his life. Hence in 1946 Father Bernard Delany, the then Prior Provincial of the English Dominicans, commissioned an official biography from Dr. Helen Trudgian, a lecturer in French language and literature at Durham University and later at the University of Exeter.[9] He did so, it is said, to protect the reputation of the priest whom he had known and admired.[10] With his backing, Trudgian began the daunting task of collecting material, despite failing health and heavy academic commitments. The projected biography, however, was never completed.

It was not until 1961 that *The Aylesford Review,* under the editorship of Brocard Sewell, devoted its spring issue to several articles on John Gray and his friend, André Raffalovich. Printed two years later under the title *Two Friends: John Gray and André Raffalovich,* it is, of its kind, a model of elegance and *élan.* An astute essay on his poetry (by Ian Fletcher) also placed John Gray securely on the literary map. Henceforth, he could confidently be assigned a place among the minor poets of the 1890s, in the company of Arthur Symons, Ernest Dowson and Lionel Johnson, who were also his poetic colleagues, a place since confirmed by Ian Fletcher's recent edition of *The Poems of John Gray.*

Most of the essays of *Two Friends* were written by the acquaintance of his later years and thus concern themselves with Canon Gray. "Dorian" Gray remains a shadow, if only because so little is actually known—of his origins, his early life, his relationship with Wilde, and his dramatic conversion to Catholicism and later to the Catholic priesthood. Using the material from *Two Friends,* Father Sewell constructed a sustained narrative of Gray's life in *Footnote to the Nineties,* published in 1968. A more coherent account (particularly in discussing Gray's relationship with Wilde), it was also a franker one, as Gray's youngest sister, alive when *Two Friends* was published, had since died. This was followed in 1983 by a longer study, also by Sewell, *In the Dorian Mode: A Life of John Gray, 1866–1934,* which incorporates more primary sources into the account of the life and also extends its scope to include commentary on Gray's work. Still, the latter book, like its predecessors, remains very much a memoir. The hard questions (about Gray's affection for Wilde, for instance) are still regarded as matters of tact: the book never forgets that Gray was to become a priest, and it is in the account of Gray's life as a priest that Father Sewell, himself a member of the Order of Carmelites, excels. To these accounts has been added G. A. Cevasco's *John Gray,* in the well-known (and uneven) English Authors Series. While it is the first to attempt a literary/critical appraisal of Gray, it finds little time to devote to analysis, assessment or further insights; the result is to a large degree both derivative and disappointing.[11]

Thus John Gray remains very much an elusive figure, despite these studies—or perhaps because of them. For, to a large extent, scholars found themselves collaborating with a conspiracy of selective silence initiated by Father Gray himself. It has been difficult to reconstruct a history which had been deliberately suppressed or destroyed. The facts of Gray's family background have to some extent been resurrected; but those concerning Wilde survive only in fragments which must be painfully pieced together. In the years immediately after Gray's death, many obstacles prevented a full accounting of his life. As already mentioned, Gray's family blocked efforts to write a biography at a time when many who knew him were still living; his sister Beatrice Hannah, now a nun, cooperated only at the very last, reassured by the Dominican's choice of a biographer in Trudgian. And for many years the Dominican Order was very protective of its legacy, although it did sell some of the more valuable correspondence.[12] Not until Father Anthony Ross threw open the doors of the Chaplaincy to Gray scholars were the bulk of his papers available; and it speaks well of the Order that they have now turned these over to the custody of the National Library of Scotland.

Always implicit in these attempts at biography was the understanding that Father Gray should be protected. When Oscar Wilde wished to deny that he was Gray's patron, he wrote that Gray would find such protection "not in Prince, or Pope, or patron" but in his own aesthetic temperament, which would "see how vain and foolish is all popular opinion, and popular judgement. . . . He needs no other protection, nor, indeed, would he accept it."[13] A man may seek to protect himself, as Gray has done, but it is folly for another to protect him from himself. In the case of a biographer, that folly would be compounded by a denial of the evidence, whatever it might be. I have tried to let the evidence speak for itself, and where Gray has suppressed it, to speak of the price of its suppression, not only to our sense of him, but to his sense of himself.

It might, then, be the grand, and inevitable, claim that this is the biography that tries to set the facts straight. It does certainly aim at setting whatever facts there are on the record. Whenever possible, I have tried to use original sources, particularly letters and holograph manuscripts.[14] I have also tried to give due weight to Gray's "past," which he himself sought to bury. Thus—unlike previous accounts of Gray's life—the focus of this biography is on Gray's career during the 1890s. Far from detracting from the merit of Father Gray, it is, as it has been with other good men, to his honor that with such a past, he made himself into what he became. The emphasis is also true to his sense of himself. Without his past, he would have been "Dorian" Gray without the picture in the attic. With no conscience to torture himself, he would not have achieved the rueful virtue of his later years. Father Gray needed his past to keep himself straight, to remind himself, as he relentlessly did, what one moment's inattention might unleash. He kept enough evidence for us to surmise what might have, except for his vocation, happened to him; but he also left us no more than enough.

Partly for that reason, there will never be a complete account of "the real John Gray." But that impossibility remains for a more cogent and disturbing reason. If "the real John Gray" ever existed, he did not do so in the mind of the actual John Gray; he was, in a radical way, not available to himself. And his sense of himself as a person in question, haunted by a self either displaced or lost, is reflected in the remarks of such others as Arthur Symons, who called him an "apparition."[15] Gray lacked the ballast of a known background. In a radical sense, he was a self-made man, a man who remade himself as a dandy. Today the equivalent might be someone made over in a certain "image." In Gray's time, the image was less facade than icon. As Baudelaire describes him, the dandy is a soul in revolt, fired by a "burning desire to create a personal form of originality within the external limits of social conventions." At a time when democracy had not yet become all-powerful and the aristocracy was only partially discredited, the dandy emerged as an "outsider" who, out of sheer superiority of mind, fashioned himself into a new kind of aristocrat: a hero of taste.[16] Thus, although by origin working-class, Gray chose to remake himself initially as the aristocratic "Dorian" Gray. Later, after the rupture with Wilde, he reinvented himself as a patrician priest. Those who knew Father Gray recognized that the priest preserved much of the dandy, and that his manner, intensely artificial, as intriguing as it was forbidding, never permitted them to know who was "the real John Gray."

This puts the biographer in the awkward position of accounting, almost by default, for "the real John Gray," since he in no way accounts for himself. It also, to some extent, puts the biographer in the wrong. John Gray, like Wilde his master, would contend that one's mask, as the mark of an achieved self and not its residue in the given self, is prior in terms of reality and significance. Thus, if Gray largely abandoned the self as given, he did so deliberately. Only then could he live the role of the moment, and perform its prerequisites with all the energy available to him. For it was, as he knew, a performance. In a speech which has the ring of a manifesto, Gray defended the actor as the paradigm of the modern artist. At the same time, he understood the implications of the life lived as role. Twice—once as "Dorian" Gray and later as Canon Gray—he wrote stories which center on an investigation into a self which passes as his own, but which is an imposture, a surrogate self, referred to (in the title of the first) as "The Person in Question." It is as a person in question that Gray will always remain, never more fully available to us than he was to himself, and available to us only as he understood himself: as a case, as a matter of inquiry, as a psychological conundrum.

"I am thoroughly sincere as a student of psychiatry," wrote the narrator of "The Person in Question" when accounting for his hallucination of himself.[17] And it is as a student of psychology that one must, however tentatively, approach the history of John Gray. Thus it seemed best in this book to take Gray's history literally—on his own terms—according to the names by which he identified himself and under which he lived. Chapter One opens with John Gray, tracing his self-transformation from a Cockney apprentice in the Woolwich Arsenal to John Gray the civil servant and "disciple" of Charles Ricketts, the man who dominated the artistic community of the Vale. Gray re-made himself not by means of mere ambition or taste (although he clearly had both), nor solely through his mentor Ricketts, but by converting to the Roman faith, from which he immediately, as he himself confessed, lapsed. The nature of his subsequent "course of sin" will never be known, but it would always be associated with Oscar Wilde, whom Gray, now known everywhere as "Dorian," addressed as his "beloved master, my dear friend."[18] Chapter Two observes "Dorian" Gray's performance of himself as he makes strategic appearances at the Rhymers' Club, reciting what Ernest Dowson describes as "beautiful & obscure versicles in the latest manner of French Symbolism."[19] Later he literally appears on stage, to read a lecture to the Playgoer's Club in which he defines the modern actor as the paradigm for the modern artist. Then, just as he is becoming popularly known (i.e., beginning to figure in the newspaper gossip columns) as a dandy, "decadent" poet and disciple of Wilde, Gray attempts—too late—to extricate himself from the role of "Dorian" Gray. The course of his disillusionment is recorded in his short story, "The Person in Question."

By the end of 1892, Gray's ambivalence toward this role becomes explicit in the history of his first book of poems, *Silverpoints*. Chapter Three considers contradictory evidence: how, on the one hand, Gray appears eager to exploit his pose as "decadent" poet while, on the other, trying to avoid its by now obvious implications. The chapter ends with Gray's final rupture with Oscar Wilde, who had originally offered to pay the costs of publication, and hereafter *Silverpoints* for Gray comes to symbolize his "sinful" past. In the midst of this crisis, Gray turns back to the faith he embraced as a young man and within its terms is again transformed. Chapter Four, "The Prodigal Returns," tells of Gray's discovery of vocation and the dedication of his art to spiritual ends. From Wilde he turned to another mentor, a young, wealthy Parisian Jew named André Raffalovich. Their history, for the most part suppressed, is one that evolves into a chaste intimacy, in its duration and commitment comparable to that of brothers.

Central to Gray's reconversion is their mutual involvement with the dying Aubrey Beardsley, who in his last months was received into the Catholic Church. With Beardsley, Gray's past finally died; he knew he must change his life. He found too that his poetry, which he now regarded as a spiritual instrument, must also be set aside to achieve complete commitment to his faith: after 1905, Gray was not to publish poetry for almost twenty years.

In the final chapters history comes full circle. Gray enters the Scots College, Rome, in 1898, and leaves as Father Gray. From his initial posting as curate in the Edinburgh slums, Gray retreats into a world defined by the beautiful church and presbytery built for him largely from the resources of André Raffalovich. Gray comes to be regarded as an enigmatic and aloof priest. Yet his kindness to individual parishioners, his efforts to rescue members of his own family from their difficulties, as well as the turbulent friendship with the "Michael Fields," do not wholly sustain his reputation for coolness and restraint. But that impression was true to the way he imagined himself, as being one of the fictive dead. It may be that Father Gray was playing imaginatively on the priest's necessary death to the world. But in Gray's case there is also a sense in which he has died to himself. The implications of that "death" are explored in his one extended prose work, the novella *Park* (1932), to which the only key seems to be autobiographical. This return to the problem of role and self is paralleled by a return to writing poetry, now in a recognizably "modern" style.

In standard histories of English literature John Gray is rarely accorded more than the status of a footnote: at best, he is included in a list of more significant figures—Wilde, Johnson, Dowson, Symons, Yeats—as a minor member of "the tragic generation." This account is not grossly unfair: in one degree or another his work, if not his life, has the significance of failure, the failure of grand intention. But in other respects the standard account is seriously misleading. One of the aims of the present study is to approach the true meaning of Gray's work.

I have proceeded upon certain assumptions: first that Gray belonged to a generation of poets who thought of themselves as constituting a generation, a period, an era in the history of feeling; second, that such poets, seeing themselves in a dramatic light, thought that their particular form of drama was tragedy, that they were fated or doomed; third, that even when Gray established relations with others he was, in effect, defining in more complex terms a relation to himself. Thus his life and work run together, and are inextricably bound, making for the most part a double imperfection. An attempt will be made here to show, however, that this imperfection in the general pattern of Gray's work allowed for occasional perfections, minor if judged by the highest criteria, but nevertheless genuine and secure.

The method I have adopted depends upon establishing a continuous relation between the life and the work. It is a measure of Gray's achievement, perhaps, that relatively few of his poems and little of his fiction stand off from his life with complete autonomy; much of the work seems incomplete, and demands to be completed, and often extended in its implications, by reference to the life. It should be said, however, that the present study concerns itself with Gray's life not solely as a continuous gloss upon the poems and fiction but as providing an interest to a large extent intrinsic and exemplary. Granted that John Gray was a minor artist: nevertheless, he casts light, and often intense light, upon an entire generation of writers. In that sense, it is valuable to establish his presence—as a genuine poet, as a man whose life read, even to himself, as a kind of moral tale—within that generation which flourished during the last years of Queen Victoria and before the Great War.

❧ John Gray, 1866–1890 ❧

Then did I seek to rise
Out of the prison of my mean estate;
And, with such jewels as the exploring mind
Brings from the cave of knowledge, buy my ransom
From those twin jailers of the daring heart—
Low birth and iron fortune.

> Bulwer-Lytton,
> quoted by Charles Dickens,
> *The Letters of Charles Dickens,*
> ed. Walter Dexter, 3:550.

John Gray's obituary in *The Times* of 19 June 1934 commented only on the loss of a notable figure in the ecclesiastical and social life of Edinburgh. The tribute to Canon John Gray left out perhaps his most remarkable achievement: his creation of himself as Canon Gray. Of the humble origins of John Gray or his later notoriety as "Dorian" Gray, the reputed model for Oscar Wilde's novel, not only *The Times* but most of Edinburgh remained happily ignorant.

Today, many of the facts of the first thirty or so years of Gray's life are still uncertain, as Gray himself wished, for he seldom spoke of the past except briefly and with circumspection. On his death, Gray left behind him a minor legacy of poetry and prose, distinguished in its own right. But his real achievement was of a self, in its own terms as perfect and as laboriously constructed as a work of art. For "Dorian" Gray was not born, but made. It is significant that most who met John Gray from the early 1890s onward would have assumed that he came from a middle-class background or one that was at least genteel; that he had been to a university, albeit not Oxford or Cambridge; that his manners, dress, and mode of address were acquired almost as effortlessly as his striking profile. They would have been mistaken. A few, alerted by traces of a Cockney accent—which Gray retained into later life—or some marked reticence, may have surmised that his origins were in fact quite otherwise.

Even the official records are unclear. According to the Register Office, John Henry Gray was born, the first of nine children, on 10 March 1866.[1] His mother was twenty-one; his father, twenty-three. In fact his parents, "weak in astronomy and novices in their character" (as Gray described them years later) registered the birth of their first child as being a day later than the actual event—a suitable beginning for a life in which crucial facts were to be obscured or suppressed.[2] Gray was born at home, Number 2, Vivian Road, Bethnal Green: a working-class suburb of terraced red-brick houses built, apparently, only a few years previously. A large house, with basement, ground and upper floors, Number Two was probably rented out in flats.

What little else is known or may be surmised about Gray's childhood must be inferred from family reminiscences. In later life, Father Gray proved "very shy" in speaking about these years, except to indicate that his origins were "very simple."[3] The only account of substance is that given by Gray's youngest sister, Beatrice Hannah. Born when Gray was twenty-one, she came to idealize the older brother who had virtually brought her up. As her godfather and later, spiritual adviser, he encouraged her in her religious vocation. Her memories of "this god who dominated my entire childhood," written years after his death, are inevitably highly selective.[4]

Of their ancestry, Beatrice recalls that their maternal grandmother, Sarah Harris, was a gypsy. The paternal grandfather was also said to have been one too, but this is less certain.[5] Beatrice may have thought such an ancestry vaguely romantic; in actuality it might have been rather a grim one. From an early age, Gray was inclined to go on long walks. Beatrice remembers her mother telling her that "as a boy John was fond of wandering about and exploring districts in and near London. When he was older he would often get up very early during the holidays, take some food from the larder, and leave a note" for his mother saying he would be out for the day. If (as Beatrice conjectured) the young Gray joined up with the gypsies on these excursions, he could not have avoided the discovery that his family was related on both sides to the lowest stratum of society.[6]

Certainly the Gray family did move around a good deal, although they kept within his mother's territory, she being a native Londoner.[7] Their second child (two years after John) was born in Islington; their third, just over two years again, in Lambeth. This kind of mobility, however, probably had nothing to do with gypsy blood; it was in fact quite common in London at that time among working-class families living in rented rooms. Nor would any stigma attach to it. After all, the senior John Gray—for whom his first-born was named—was an artisan, one of the aristocracy of labor. His own father, William, had been a soldier, while he himself had risen, by the time of his marriage, to the position of merchant's clerk.[8] Afterwards, he worked for a time as a wheelwright and journeyman carpenter in the Woolwich dockyard, later becoming Inspector of Stores at the Woolwich Arsenal, a position of some responsibility.[9]

From his only extant photograph, it would be difficult to place the senior John Gray as a laborer at all. Presumably taken for his wedding, it shows a slight, very youthful figure leaning on one elbow. His curling hair falls below the ears and he wears over his winged-neck shirt an over-large, black bow tie to match his best frock coat. In the other hand he holds a malacca cane. He looks extremely boyish—a trait he was to bequeath to his eldest son. But his apparent age is belied by a certain air of assurance, even coldness; this pose in turn subverted by a slight weakness about the mouth and the newness of his coat and tie, both a bit too large and worn as if borrowed.

The photograph is the only evidence we have of his history and character. But something may be inferred from the nature of two of his sons. In a series of fascinating letters, Heather Coltman, the granddaughter of the third boy, William Thomas, recalls that he was known as "a worldly (and rather spoilt) man who enjoyed good living, elegant clothes and attractive surroundings." In these traits, Coltman found several points of resemblance between her own grandfather and his eldest brother, although she considered that her Grand-Uncle John's later spiritual asceticism made him appear, in contrast to William, like the other side of the coin.[10]

Perhaps these qualities speak more of the mother than father. In her account, Beatrice commented that Hannah Mary Williamson Gray "never worried about [the young John]; in her eyes he could do nothing wrong or foolish."[11] From a very early age, it seems, John Gray mixed a fierce independence with an equally fierce dependence. He knew it of himself, once recalling that "after cutting up my apple, my mother used sometimes to remark: perhaps you would like me to eat it for you."[12] Such conflicting impulses (so characteristic of his later intimacies) grew, perhaps, as a reaction to his mother's forceful character. Heather Coltman remarks that, although Gray's mother "must have been what might be described as a 'tough cookie'—she adored and spoilt her sons, particularly John."[13] From Gray's own letters, one gains much the same impression: that his mother was a strong if not overbearing woman with whom her eldest son was to be periodically involved in a struggle of wills, at least during the last decade or so of her life.

But the primary conflict was between mother and father. As a young man, Gray wrote of hatred within marriage with a ferocity that could only come of intimate experience; not surprisingly, these pieces were never published.[14] In "Their Mothers," which tells how each partner discovers the satisfaction of hating the other while playing the games necessary to sustain a fashionable marriage, Gray analyzes sexual politics with a ruthless, neutral precision. Similarly, in the typescript for the last act of a play, "The Blackmailers," Gray has the hero indulging in a little moral blackmail of his own, reminding his mother of how

you never disguised from us your dislike of our father. You drew our attention to his bullying vulgar voice, his heavy tread, his untidy moustache, his physical delinquencies, his moral deficiencies. You sapped his power, and our love at the same time, and when we were older, and you needed his authority as a weapon against us, you called us unnatural because we despised him.

Such accusations have the trenchancy of actual experience. So do the notes of many years later that Father Gray made for a sermon on marriage, which converge on a vivid exemplar he calls simply "this man," a type of the "unskilled, uneducated, irreligious, labouring man." Of all the classes in English society, Gray observes, this man is alone in being a pariah, not having even the claims on society that belong to the criminal. The marriage he makes is a

daily debasement of two bodies. The prospect of family is at first kept out of thought, then hated. The wife is hated, for this man does not accuse himself on the cause of his wretchedness. It is not lack of affection, incapability of feelings of fellowship. This man is never so sullen but he has some vibration of warmth, however low, towards the men he sees every day, by the mere fact of seeing them; but with his wife, not at all. . . . It is conduct minutely parallel to his sexual conduct if this man should drink one third of his earnings; it is the same conduct expressed in two different sets of terms.

In sum, all the available evidence suggests a household which might have come from early D. H. Lawrence: one in which the "intellectual" mother with middle-class aspirations for her son is at odds with a father battling to keep him among his own, even at the price of his education and chances of betterment. It had the signs of bitter warfare, and it left its scars.

The deepest was a profound sense of alienation. From a very early age, it seems, Gray thought of himself as an outcast, even against the facts. Did it have to do with the family stories of their part-gypsy origins? Their somewhat uprooted existence? Gray's father, for instance, claimed Scots ancestry, although he actually came originally to London from Kent. It was an affectation that passed to his son, and became so pronounced in his later years, that, when settled in Edinburgh, Father Gray used to refer to England punctiliously as "your country."[15] Long before that, a few years after he had left home, "Dorian" Gray called England "my adopted country": then it was France, and not Scotland, which he regarded as his spiritual home.[16] But Gray's sense of dislocation cut deeper than that: even as a boy, apparently, he felt himself to be alien and doomed. "The first song I ever knew was Peter Gray," he once told Sarah, a younger sister: "He finished in the company of Indians (who scalped him)."[17] Peter Gray proved the first of several identifications with figures who met a bad end: the second was to be Dorian Gray.

There were also, as Gray confided to an acquaintance in the autumn of 1890, "some horrid family troubles."[18] What exactly these were is never disclosed, but it is clear that they were several and severe. More than a decade later, remarking on how his sister Sarah (then at school in Germany) had received the news of their mother's death, Gray remarked: "she must have had an unpleasant moment, poor girl; for all the miserable island history must have come back to her memory."[19] Gray coped by distancing himself, first physically, then emotionally. In later years, although he was the dutiful son, his mother was one of the few people who caused him to lose his temper violently. It seems he avoided her except when absolutely necessary. Of the entire family, Gray remained close only to the two youngest sisters, Sarah and Beatrice; the rest were a duty. He did assume responsibility for his youngest brother, Alexander, and later, after Alexander's death, for the schooling of his two young sons. As for his own father, Gray learned to hate him.

Gray's confrontation with his father can be dated precisely. This event, above others, crystallized Gray's relationship with his parents and clarifies theirs to each other. It had to do with school. Gray's mother, Heather Coltman writes, "was seemingly the parent with the intellectual abilities; capacities which she recognized in her first born at least, as she seems to have actively encouraged him in his endeavours at self improvement."[20] At first, it appears, Gray was educated at home. Then, when the family moved yet once again, to 97 Eglinton Road, Plumstead, Gray attended Mr. Nicols's Wesleyan day school in Plumstead Common Road.[21] No definite records of his schooling can again be traced until, at age twelve, Gray won a scholarship to the Roan School at Eastney Street, Greenwich. His great-niece recalls that he was known as that "clever man Uncle John"; and it was not mere family mythology. When he was still a boy the older lads at school would drop by the house to ask for help with their lessons.[22] The school, a long-established one, had an excellent record of scholarship and Gray distinguished himself there. He won an award from the Royal Humane Society for an essay on cruelty to animals. His character and conduct were recorded as being "excellent."

Gray's academic success should have been the first step in gaining entrance to the civil service or even toward a university degree. Instead, this promising start was brought to an abrupt halt. After only one year, Gray was summarily removed from school by his father to be apprenticed as a metal-turner at the Woolwich Arsenal, where he himself now held a job. Gray was only thirteen. Another thirteen or so years later, shortly after his father's death, Gray wrote a poem in which a passage—penned, then cancelled—assigns a motive for his father's action: he felt his eldest son should "learn to use his hands." Certainly a heightened, even exaggerated, respect for manual labor entered into it—the kind of respect the son was eventually to share for those "whose art it is to make a useful thing." At the same time, his father may have regarded his eldest son as getting a bit above himself; he should be brought down to earth by a stint of work among his own kind.

Realistically, as the eldest of (then) five children of a working-class family, Gray could have expected to be put to work, if only to help provide for the others. It should not have come as a shock, as it did for the young Charles Dickens, who suffered in part from a demotion in class. But John Gray was ambitious as well as bright. With his mother's encouragement, he had been set on a course which would bridge the great divide in Victorian society between those who worked with their hands and those who did not. His removal from school must have been the source of a bitter difference between father and mother, father and son. Gray took up the job but there is evidence that his resentment sharpened into hatred. In his only known reference to his father, Gray wrote on 24 November 1892, announcing his death to a friend: "I have lost my father. I am well pleased with the loss."[23]

Despite this stark and brutal rejection of his father, Gray was able in retrospect to give credit to his father's intentions and confess to his own mixed reaction:

> They [the parents] fed my infant brain,
> They set therein with little pain
> Some ancient smattering of strange alphabets
> Whereon I gave away my toys
> And went to school & mixed with other boys
> Learnt what, the test of which is that the boy forgets.

{My father then commands
That I must learn to use my hands
Thinking (?) that use is (?) everything.}
Then and still being young
Ill liking it I went among
Whose art it is to make a useful thing.
There many a long year I learnt
To make a thing; where living is well earned,
Where men set up the engines of their suffering.

A certain time expired
I dared confess that I was tired
Of whirring {lathe} and rank machine-oil's smell.
I lied; I loved them one & both;
Truth being vanity in me was loth
That wit like mine should cut no harder stuff than steel.

{I left the shop; & thence
Addicted me to pens & pence.}
Ah, that I thought to face
The world! To elbow me a place!
Ah Lord! I thank thee for that chastening.[24]

As he acknowledges here, Gray did learn to love the "whirring lathe and rank machine-oil's smell." Other poems, springing from the experience of these years, are eloquent with this love. In a piece not published during his lifetime, "The Wheel," Gray details each painstaking step of the making of a wheel. It might almost be used as an instruction manual if it were not so turned as to illustrate not how the man makes the artefact, but what the artefact makes of the man.[25] Indirectly, the poem might also be read as a tribute to his wheelwright father, as might another poem from the mid-nineties, "The Forge," which details vividly the young Gray's own experience as a metal-turner at the Woolwich Arsenal:

A long and narrow shop, magenta black
Mottled with rose; ten fires along one wall.

Faint day comes through the skylight overhead
Smoke-grimed to orange, when it comes at all.
The blast shut off for breakfast, fires are slack.

The buzzing neighbouring engine quieted,
You hear the mates talking from berth to berth;
The silence is complete. The seldom noises
Reverberate as, quaintly, under earth
The graves repeat the sayings of the dead.

In the quiet, human voices, "hoarse and soft, as out of hollowed wood" resound as the workers sear their bacon on the anvil. Then, with a hum, "the blast comes back":

Shadows on wall and roof start forth and die.
Rattle of tongs, slosh, fume; unlovely night
Grown Chinese hell, to seeming, suddenly,
Where strange gods heap the fire and trim the rack.

Half shapes of light leap higher than man's height
Out from the blackness and as soon subside.
Flame-flesh-shapes, sweat-swamped clinging cotton swathed,
In violent action, following the guide
Of the smith's gesture bidding where to smite.

The smitten steel complains, all bruised and scathed,
From thud to bark, from bark to metal scream;
Through ordeal of the fire and scaling trough,
To wake it from its long-embowelled dream,
To uses brought, flame-licked and torture-bathed.

This the arena wherein stubborn stuff
With man locks strength; where elements dispute
The mastery, where breath and fire bear blaze,
Where sullen water aids, to quell the brute
Earth into shape, to make it meek enough.

And this day is the type of many days.[26]

The poem was, in detail, the "type" of Gray's days at the Arsenal, but also the archetype for the heroic struggle whereby man shapes brute matter, and is as brutally shaped by it. The smith is broken by his work, "maimed in his poor hands, wry, with crooked back." Perhaps in his youth a paradigm for artisan and artist, for the older Gray the smith may have signified the man who must, spiritually, be broken and made again. The Arsenal was the arena, he knew, of his own remaking.

Looking back, Gray attributed his motive in escaping the Woolwich Arsenal to "vanity": to the fear that "wit like mine should cut no harder stuff than steel." He began to study at night, teaching himself the rudiments of French, German, and Latin within five years. He also began experimenting in the arts, at first haphazardly. He took up the violin, then lost interest. He taught himself to draw.[27] Probably on his own initiative, after three years in the machine shop he was promoted to the drawing room at the Arsenal. Although he never drew with any fluency, Gray had learned in the company of those "whose art it is to make a useful thing" a sense of pride in craftsmanship which, as the rightful legacy of an artisan's son, never left him. His eye had become educated to the beauty of machines and tools (a taste which later extended to aboriginal weapons and children's toys); he would come to the fine arts with a keen appreciation of the value of technique.

Now at his first desk job, Gray began to write seriously. Among his manuscripts there is only one poem from this period, a sonnet which Gray had carefully annotated, "writ by me when I was sixteen."[28] It is a self-consciously "literary" poem, a kind of Keatsian daze embellished with Pre-Raphaelite detail: a snail, a spider, the petal of a lily. Gray plays with eye-rhymes and non-rhymes. But the languor is his own. Beneath the lines, perhaps in the deadness of the meter, one senses an enormous weariness, a longing to come to rest. Was this the price of the frenzied activity, both public and private, of the next crucial few years?

By his own confession now "addicted . . . to pens & pence," Gray took the first of a series of open competitive exams which had recently made it possible for a boy of Gray's station to enter government service. At sixteen, the year he wrote his first known poem, he took the Civil Service Certificate exam, and on 29 September 1882, qualified as a boy clerk in the Post Office Savings Bank, a position he took up a few weeks later. Within the year, he moved to the Confidential Enquiry Branch, a job in which he dealt with questions of crime against the Post Office, such as theft or fraud.[29] There he became close friends with Arthur Edmonds, to whom Gray would later dedicate a poem in *Silverpoints*. Aside from his official record, which notes that he joined the service as a writer in the India Office, little else is known about the elusive Edmonds. It is possible that he is the author of the strange letter signed "Parent" from the Bedford Post Office (it is palpably *not* by Gray's father), thus becoming the first of Gray's father-substitutes, a role later filled by Charles Ricketts, Oscar Wilde, and André Raffalovich.[30]

Two years after entering as a boy clerk, in December 1884 Gray climbed the next rung of the Civil Service ladder by passing another competitive exam which qualified him as a Lower Division Clerk. Immediately after promotion, he transferred back to the Post Office Savings Bank. In the same year Gray, now eighteen, registered as a private student (i.e., with no collegiate affiliation) at the University of London, passing the matriculation exam in June of 1887. The matriculation requirements offer some evidence of the extent to which Gray had succeeded in educating himself. He had to pass exams in: Latin and either Greek, French, German, Sanskrit, or Arabic; the English language and history; mathematics; mechanics; and one science subject, either chemistry, heat and light, or magnetism and electricity.[31] Having thus qualified for entry, however, Gray did not choose to continue at university. Instead, he transferred fourteen months later (on 16 November 1888) to the Foreign Office, working initially in the Post Office Section until he moved in 1893 to the Foreign Office Library.

The six years thus accounted for by the official records show how in this short space, virtually by his own efforts, Gray had raised himself from metal-turner's apprentice to a respectable middle-class position with the rough equivalent of a middle-class education. From 1888 on, however, the achievement takes another form, as Gray begins to cultivate both his own artistic gifts and the friendship of artists and *literati*. Gray's new life now involves an aspect that is unofficial, even at times illicit. Lived outside office hours and largely unrecorded, it is the life that is to become identified with that of "Dorian" Gray: dandy, poet, and friend of Oscar Wilde.

Gray and the "Valistes," 1888–1889

Until this time John Gray was defined by a birth certificate, a brief school report, an entry regarding his matriculation at university and a dry civil service record. When we next hear of him, it is from memoirs and letters. He has entered at last into his private history, as a writer, in the company of two art students, Charles Ricketts and Charles Shannon. How they first met is unknown. Gray had obviously learned enough of the London art world to know that Ricketts and Shannon were young and enterprising, the center of a growing circle of influence. Ricketts was known to be generous to a fault with young artists, a kindly if formidable mentor. Shannon, although the older, quietly deferred to Ricketts's benevolent dictatorship.

At the time they rented a picturesque old house recently vacated by Whistler, The Vale. One of three situated in a cul-de-sac off the King's Road, Chelsea, it literally was in a vale, or (more accurately, according to one visitor) a "muddy retreat from the highway, edged by gardens in which . . . one expects to see dead cats mouldering."[32] The setting was certainly improbable for what was to become one of the centers of the new artistic movement in England, hardly the place to set in motion a revival of printing or disseminate the new aesthetics of France.

Ricketts and Shannon were young; they were poor. They had exact (and exacting) taste, impeccably catholic in terms of period, genre, and medium. Both were relentless and energetic in asserting it. Although artists themselves, they are best defined as connoisseurs: Shannon and Ricketts *knew* about art, and their definition of it extended from the Greek and the Old Masters to the Japanese print and the latest Impressionist. In their collecting, as in their own work, they ranged from painting to book design, from stage design to jewelry. "They were so different from any artists I had met hitherto," one of their disciples, William Rothenstein, wrote.

Everything about them was refined and austere. Ricketts, with his pale, delicate features, fair hair and pointed gold-red beard, looked like a Clouet drawing. Half French, he had the quick mind and the rapid speech of a southerner. He was a fascinating talker. His knowledge of pictures and galleries astonished me; he had been nowhere except to the Louvre, yet he seemed to know everything, to have been everywhere.[33]

Gray quickly became an intimate. Although other, already recognized, artists (Oscar Wilde, William Butler Yeats, and Roger Fry) as well as the more obscure (Charles Condor, Reginald Savage, Charles Holmes, and that aunt and niece, Katherine Bradley and Edith Cooper, who wrote as "Michael Field") would eventually gravitate to the Vale, few were admitted to the inner circle of the faithful, Rothenstein recalls. The friendship of Ricketts and Shannon, "rarely given," was, however, extended to Gray. Whether it was because he was so obviously homeless, spiritually as well as artistically, or so painfully young, poor, and eager: for whatever reason, they took him in. Rothenstein remembers Gray, "then a fastidious young poet and something of a dandy," as a habitué of the Vale and Ricketts's "disciple."[34] Gray did not dispute the title; indeed, in later life, he would confess that the Vale was the making of him. To what extent may be judged by Gray's first published literary work, by his new friendships and his new enthusiasms.

Ricketts, having been brought up on the Continent by a French mother—French being literally his mother-tongue—regarded himself equally at home in Paris and in Chelsea. Although only twenty-two the year he met Gray, he had "canvassed" the work of Rimbaud, Mallarmé, Cézanne, Gauguin, Van Gogh, and other painters and poets at the time virtually unknown in England.[35] He did more than introduce Gray to this world; his enthusiasms led Gray to get in touch with two of its leading critics, Félix Fénéon and Francis Vielé-Griffin, and may also thus have been indirectly responsible for Gray's meetings with Verlaine and Mallarmé. Ricketts also gave Gray a chance, his first, to write seriously as a critic of the new literature.

Gray found himself among this circle just as Shannon and Ricketts were to launch their first venture, a hard-cover magazine called *The Dial*. Today its pages may seem garish and cluttered; yet in

England *The Dial* was revolutionary as one of the earliest of the small literary journals which set new standards for typography, illustration, and binding. Ricketts tended to underrate *The Dial*'s achievement, calling it "one of those juvenile ventures common enough in France, but, at the time, rare in England."[36] At the time, its only competitor was the Century Guild's *Hobby Horse,* put out by another artistic community, the Fitzroy Settlement. But the impulse to make beautiful books was gathering impetus; a year later, William Morris would found the Kelmscott Press.

The first issue of *The Dial,* appearing in August 1889, was composed almost entirely of work by Shannon and Ricketts, Reginald Savage (an artist who moved in next door at No. 1, The Vale), and John Gray. In his initial contributions, a literary essay and a fairy story, Gray chose his masters: the new writers of France, and Oscar Wilde.

It was in an essay entitled "Les Goncourt" that Gray made his debut as literary mediator between France and England. Undoubtedly, Gray's attention had been drawn to the Goncourt brothers, Edmond and Jules, by Shannon and Ricketts. But he did not draw out the obvious parallels between them: the extraordinarily congruent mentality by which these two sets of collaborators worked or the absoluteness of their dedication to an ideal of Art. What intrigued Gray was the inimitable Goncourt style. It was, he concluded, less a literary experiment than a sign of a unique consciousness. He rationalizes their disintegration of classical French prose into meticulous detail by arguing that "where there is unusual insistance [sic] over trivialities, it is merely nature seen by two exceptional organisms of peculiarly rare culture." These "exceptional organisms," he concluded, were also hopelessly neurotic. Or (since the condition had yet to be invented) the Goncourt followed the type of the true artist who is "always an abnormal creature, a being with an overdeveloped brain, or diseased nerves. . . ."[37]

In the Goncourt style, Gray also discovers an analogy to the technique of the Pre-Raphaelites, whose influence, "at the present moment . . . seems to have died down in our midst." But when it returns, he predicts "it will be through France. In moments of supreme emotion, a trivial or irrelevant fact, a strange shape, an unexpected sound, have a value the artist cannot afford to neglect. If the Goncourts were not the first to discover this principle, at all events no one hitherto has so thoroughly understood and consciously applied it as they."

In short, Gray locates in the Goncourts an æsthetic program which could win for English art "freedom from the trammels of tradition." He points to several paths of deliverance: their discovery of the Japanese print, which during the decade had "so improved the best modern art," and the revival of interest in "the youthfulness in the art of the last century; a truth yet to reach us." Here Gray's discrimination is exact, if not prophetic; in Beardsley's art, these were to become the two main routes of a new "decadent" style. Finally, Gray argues, the example of the Goncourts is valuable, not only as connoisseurs, but as an instance of literary men being influenced by, and in turn influencing, "the manner of seeing, not thinking, of contemporary painters." Such interplay between poem and picture was to become an important resource not only for the 1890s but also for the modern poet.

In style, Gray's review even goes so far as to imitate the rather bizarre Goncourt prose: the contorted syntax, obliqueness of reference, and purple patches of accumulated epithet and exclamation. Indeed, so consistently does Gray write against the grain, that one may legitimately ask whether he could really write at all. The question, raised explicitly by his early critics, is unavoidable when one is faced with such a sentence as: "If the Goncourts not only announce, but also give effect to, their intention to war with conventionality, no exception will be made in their case, that those whose united tastes and opinions makes conventionality should be defeated at the challenge only—on the contrary" (p. 10).

More arresting is the tone of the article: Gray speaks as a disciple, fired by missionary zeal, vehement and contemptuous of the false standards which have prevented the recognition of such as the Goncourts:

And what shall we, we English, say? we the chosen? we who understand so well that a book, to be good, must recount a series of good actions? . . . Germinie Lacerteux stayed out late at night? stole from her mistress? Manette

Salomon was not married to Coriolis? Put it away! put it away! Dear me! if Freddy should get hold of it! Shocking blemishes, happily so soon discovered. Let us beware of the glittering poison. (P.12)

Much the same humor, but gentled into whimsey, marks Gray's second contribution to that first number of *The Dial,* "The Great Worm."[38] It is a story of a dragon who dies from unrequited love; its silliness is so precisely balanced with pathos, its parody by bemused self-parody (the worm turns out to be the dreamer of the tale), that one must suspend judgment about its success. The risks alone are worth the reading of it, as if a rococo artist had painted (say, in gold and white) one of Oscar Wilde's fairy tales.

By the time *The Dial* appeared, in August of 1889, we know that Gray had already met Wilde, for he is reported to be in Wilde's company at a small dinner party in the early summer of 1889.[39] If they were on intimate terms (as the report implies) Gray would certainly have told him about the Vale. But it was not until Shannon and Ricketts sent Wilde a gift copy of this first issue that Wilde dropped by the Vale to thank them and, finding Ricketts "very cultivated and interesting," soon became a frequent visitor.[40] It was the beginning of a long and fruitful friendship. Over the next ten years, Shannon and Ricketts were to design, either separately or together, almost all of Wilde's books and the binding of the Collected Edition of 1908. After Wilde's infamous trials, they were among the few who would still acknowledge him. All of this was to come; what Wilde discovered at the first was immense intellectual stimulation. To others he brought to the Vale he used to boast, "I am taking you to the one house in London where you will never be bored."[41]

And, despite the cocoa and less-than-fresh eggs dished up by Shannon after all-night conversations, the company of the "Valistes" (as Wilde was to call them) began to expand. Walter Sickert leased No. 3 on several occasions, and T. Sturge Moore became known as an adopted resident of the Vale, for although he lived at home, he spent most of his working hours there. They were joined, too, by Yeats and George Bernard Shaw and (occasionally) by Aubrey Beardsley and even Whistler himself. It was particularly on the young that the Vale had its impact. As an old man, Yeats wrote that Ricketts was "one of the greatest connoisseurs of any age, an artist whose woodcuts prolonged the inspiration of Rossetti, whose paintings mirrored the rich colouring of Delacroix. When he studied his art we studied our double." Yeats further declared that Ricketts had made him, as an artist who confessed to be in all things Pre-Raphaelite, conscious of the aesthetic in which he was working, one "proud of its ancestry, of its traditional high breeding" in which "an ostentatious originality was out of place."[42] The Vale, as he implies, was more than merely avant-garde: it sought by means of the avant-garde to realign the tradition of English art, both visual and literary.

For Gray, who came to him without artistic alliance, Ricketts did far more: he taught Gray to see, to discriminate, to explore. Almost twenty years later the poet recalled, "It has struck me often that Ricketts is able to show things as wonderful now as things were in childhood. How many a time did I walk home to the Temple in the small hours, dreaming sunnily all the way from the palace of enchantment which the old unhygienic Vale already was."[43] To their circle, Ricketts ("Prince Charles" as he was called) became almost a paradigm of The Artist. But for Gray, he took on a larger role: that of the father who was to take the place of his own, and that of the artist who was to beget the poet "Dorian" Gray.

If, shortly after the appearance of the first *Dial,* Gray began corresponding with several leading critics of the new movement in France, Ricketts's enthusiasms had undoubtedly pointed the way. Gray made his first foray into literary Paris in mid-July 1890. He was anxious to become better acquainted with the *symboliste* poets whom he and the other Valistes had discovered in some copies of *Vogue* that had made their way to London. On arrival he asked at Leon Vanier's bookstore how he might contact Félix Fénéon, a leading critic of the *symboliste,* Impressionist, and Neo-Impressionist artists in France and the earliest to recognize their importance. In painting, he was friend and promoter of Georges Seurat, Paul Signac, and Camille Pissarro, among others. In literature, it was Fénéon who rescued the circulating manuscript pages of Rimbaud's prose poems, "Les Illuminations," and edited and published them—posthumously, as he thought, although Rimbaud was actually then living the life of a trader and adventurer in the British protectorate of Aden. And it was also Fénéon who begged money for the ailing poet Jules Laforgue, arranged for his burial, and saw to it that Laforgue's work was published in the decade after his death.

In Varnier's bookshop, Gray was given Fénéon's work address at the War Office but, finding that he was out, Gray returned to the Hotel Continental on the Rue Castiglione, where he wrote a note introducing himself as "the last of a little band of artists, painters and men of letters in London which, like yourself, care about nothing except art."[44] Fénéon responded immediately, setting a time for Gray to meet him at his office, then inviting him for a more leisurely talk over dinner at home. With typical generosity, Fénéon arranged for introductions to all the "notables" of symbolism, even sending Gray to visit Verlaine in the hospital. Since Gray's civil service job allowed him only a few days abroad, Fénéon prepared a package of books and reviews for Gray to take home. At Gray's request, Fénéon also gave him a lithograph he had done of himself, one of his self-portraits resembling Mephistopheles.[45]

Events, however, took an unexpected turn. Two days after his initial letter to Fénéon, Gray wrote again on 20 July and, after thanking Fénéon for his kindness and "this big pile of decadent literature" in which he took "great pleasure," confided that he had stopped over in Switzerland because of a "bout of fever. The result, I think, of the insomnia from which I've been suffering for a while. . . . I am very ill unfortunately." When he felt a bit better, Gray proposed to join some friends at Interlaken, then to return to London as soon as possible to find his usual doctor. He planned to stop in Paris and, if possible, to see Fénéon again. He particularly wished Fénéon to accompany him again to the hospital where Verlaine lay ill, as the previous visit had proved a disaster: the servants had so irritated him with their "ridiculous questions," Gray confessed, "that I abandoned my quest out of fear of becoming violent (It is so annoying to think that this great poet is in the hands of such pigs.) But I'm going to make another attempt when I go by there on my return."[46]

Upon reaching London, Gray wrote that in the confusion of his sudden departure, a tragedy had occurred: he had lost the wonderful self-portrait of Fénéon as Mephistopheles; he begs for a signed replacement, dedicated to himself.[47] Subsequent letters throughout the late summer and autumn circle about three topics. Gray repeatedly apologizes for his execrable French (apologies are certainly in order); presses Fénéon for news of the new artistic and literary schools, sometimes requesting actual books or articles and posing specific questions. And he urges, fervently, that Fénéon come to London, to meet his friends, to stay with Ricketts and Shannon. To one such invitation, Fénéon replied that, while he could not come immediately, he would try for 1891; Gray immediately began to make enthusiastic plans:

> We shall see everything there is to be seen in London; we shall seek out drawings by a fellow named Simeon Solomon, a pre-Raphaelite, but also something else—somewhat like Verlaine, if what they say is true. [Solomon was a homosexual whose erotic drawings of boys were known among a certain set.] People no longer speak of him, except in whispers, but he was one of the great artists of that School (sometimes)—we shall go to Hampton Court, all the art galleries, and drive from one end of London to the other. Ricketts will decorate a room for you in Whistler's old house with mystical, sweet arabesques and decadent colours, the faint glimmer of gems on a tray of jade.[48]

It is not known whether Fénéon ever arrived in London to take up residence in the Vale.[49] He did give Gray's address to a young French artist bound for London: Lucien Pissarro, the son of the painter Camille Pissarro, in defense of whose art Fénéon had spoken many times. When Lucien left Paris in November 1890, Fénéon gave him letters of introduction to Shannon and Ricketts along with instructions to look up Gray at his lodgings at Number 1, The Cloisters, Inner Temple.[50] Lucien found Gray to be "un charmant jeune homme, tout jeune"; he was taken immediately to the Vale, portfolio under arm.[51] Ricketts and Shannon were so impressed with Lucien's drawings and engravings that they insisted he submit work for the next issue of *The Dial*. This proved to be the genesis of a long partnership (Lucien was to contribute also to the third issue of *The Dial* in 1893 and to *The Pageant,* another "Valiste" production). But at that first meeting, Lucien was surprised by the homage paid to the new artists of France: "There is a whole troupe of young people here," he wrote his father, "who follow this new movement [of symbolism] ardently. Parisians have no idea of the influence abroad of certain writers they despise."[52]

In this early correspondence, Fénéon, in his affectionate, avuncular manner, undertook to educate Gray to the contemporary French poets, providing him with information on Verlaine and Laforgue, advancing him copies of their latest books and providing him with the addresses of editors of esoteric reviews in Paris and Brussels.[53] He encouraged Gray to undertake his translations of the new poets of France. Gray reciprocated by sending Fénéon lithographs by Whistler and Ricketts; at one stage, Fénéon was acting virtually as the Vale's ambassador to literary Paris. He arranged for Ricketts to illustrate several of the new avant-garde journals, also soliciting articles as well as notes from Gray (which he proposed to intercalate in his own pieces for *Le Chat Noir*) on the new art in London and Paris. To write these notes, Gray eagerly devoured whatever material he could solicit from Fénéon: his obituary for Dubois-Pillet, a Neo-Impressionist of the group which comprised Signac and Pissaro, demonstrates just what a command of the technical idiom Gray had absorbed under Fénéon's tutelage.[54]

Fénéon's generosity toward Gray and his artistic perspicuity, so evident in his letters, justify his characterization by Mallarmé as "a man beloved by all; a meek and upright man with a finely penetrating mind." He was certainly beloved by Gray with an intensity he could only convey in a poem (to appear in *Silverpoints*) dedicated to Fénéon:

> Men, women call thee so or so;
> I do not know.
> Thou hast no name
> For me, but in my heart a flame
>
> Burns tireless. . . .[55]

Fénéon for his part called Gray his "dear," his "lovely friend." He hinted at an erotic interest ("You have told me that Ricketts intends to do your portrait in lithograph. That is a very seductive project. Has he carried it out?"). Gray proposed another visit to Paris in early 1891, and Fénéon, while regretting that he could not afford to help Gray materially, added, "I would like very much to receive you in an intimate apotheosis, esoteric and enchanting."[56] But his feelings for Gray were well within the bounds of propriety. Primarily they were those of a mentor; he showed Gray's work around, even had one sonnet ("Poem") translated into French (in response to Gray's own attempt), and needled him about a project to translate all of Rimbaud's *Illuminations* into English: an enterprise that Gray was, regrettably, forced to abandon. Such was his admiration for Gray's work that, some years later, when Fénéon became editorial secretary for the prestigious *Revue Blanche,* he again got in touch with the poet to ask him to contribute.

During these crucial early years of Gray's poetic career, Fénéon acted as intermediary in introducing Gray to Francis Vielé-Griffin, an American of French descent who had taken up permanent residence in Paris. Writing in late August of 1890, Fénéon suggested to Gray that a new journal, started in May by Vielé-Griffin with two other poets, Paul Adam and Henri de Régnier, under the quaint title, *Entretiens politiques et littéraires,* would be open to his contributions: Vielé-Griffin, he wrote, "would be happy to have some articles from you and your friends about artistic and literary issues in England." And added, as a concession: "You could write your articles in your own language. Francis Vielé-Griffin (who has translated Walt Whitman and Swinburne) will translate them with great precision."[57] Fénéon adds that Vielé-Griffin translated, at his request, Gray's recent sonnet (later to be published in *Silverpoints*), the one opening "Geranium, houseleek, laid in oblong beds," which he sent to Gray as evidence of Vielé-Griffin's skill.

Shortly thereafter, in a letter dated 5 November 1890, Vielé-Griffin himself wrote to Gray, saying that he had come to hope, from their common friend, that Gray would contribute an article on Rossetti for their new magazine. He continues:

I had in my hands your magnificent *Dial* and the pleasure—which I took equally in the text and illustrations—is of the most exquisite kind; having been informed by M. Fénéon of your intention of publishing a second number before long, I have taken the liberty of announcing the fact to the readers of our own review—we only hope that it isn't a false report.[58]

Gray replied promptly from his residence at 62 Chancery Lane:

Dear Griffin

I am very pleased to be at last in actual communication with you. You are right so far about the Second *Dial;* it will be out before long, though, its appearance depending, apart from ordinary difficulties, upon money, it might be a month or two before the babe actually sees light.

As to my Rossetti article for the "Entretiens" I suppose you will like me to promise it for a given date. I could promise it to be in your hands by Christmas I think. I feel ashamed to name such a distant date but I am very full of work, I have some horrid family troubles, and I want to do the article for you nicely. Indeed you are most amiable to undertake to translate it. I only hope it may be worth the trouble it will cost you. Your version of my geranium prattle was quite charming; we all liked it very much. Have you heard anything from Ricketts about designs for the Extraordinary number of the "Entretiens." He will write to Fénéon, but I had better give him your address. . . . I write English because I can't write French—I read it quite well however—so does Ricketts.

Yours ever

John Gray[59]

This letter is extraordinarily interesting because it records in its some-what rough English and uneasy social poise the early John Gray. One cannot miss the ambition: here is a man attempting to master French, which so far he reads but cannot write with any confidence (his letters to Fénéon are full of excuses for his "painful" French). Yet he is deter-mined to publish articles in leading French literary reviews and to translate the new French poets. This year had seen his first effort, a translation of Verlaine's "Beauté des femmes, leur faiblesse, et ces mains pâles," published in the August 1890 issue of *The Artist and Journal of Home Culture.* Its innocence of the poem's major thematic contrasts gives further support to the judgment that in these early years (1889–90) Gray had only an amateur command of French and of the new French poetry.

As Gray had anticipated, the second number of *The Dial* faltered because of insufficient funds (Shannon and Ricketts were underwriting it themselves out of meagre resources). Nor did his Rossetti article ever appear, perhaps victim to the "horrid family troubles" cited by Gray. But by the time the *The Dial* returned, in 1892, Gray had some claim to the office of poet and translator. That issue published two recent original poems and a very competent translation of Verlaine's "Parsifal," which stands as an excellent poem in its own right.

Thus, in three years under the tutelage of the "Valistes" and of Ricketts in particular, John Gray was to be transformed from an ambitious civil servant into a genuine poet, an early and noteworthy translator of Verlaine, Rimbaud, and Mallarmé, and a stylish writer of prose. The Vale proved itself the doorway to the circle of Mallarmé in Paris and the circle of Wilde and the Rhymers' Club in London. It had initiated Gray into the company of poets and exposed him to the literary revolutionaries of Paris who, not without dust and heat, were forging a new aesthetic. Without the Vale, it is safe to say, John Gray would have been little more than another Second Division Clerk.

In retrospect, John Gray himself went further. A few years after the death of Charles Ricketts and in the year before his own, Gray confessed to a fellow poet, Gordon Bottomley, that "I am able to say to you alone that, with my little talent, I was an invention of Ricketts. He used to set me tasks to perform; he was infinitely patient with the performer and very hard upon the performance." Gray recalled how Ricketts "was to me the kind of tyrant I have always approved of— and meet in my present profession. No more than the Pope would he ever have told me what he intended." And Gray returns again, wonderingly, to the richness of spirit sustained in the "old, unhygienic Vale":

In the midst of want, I mean of the necessities of life, there were the richest projects abounding; series were without hesitation planned which it would have taken a life-time to carry into being: volumes, palaces, statuary. There used to be word of a volume of Songs of the Flesh (which, need I say, were never sung); and the Spirit may have received a like attention. Prince Charles was fully capable of designing what would never be, as he was of drawing copies of Hokusai prints and Dürer engravings. I have heard him curse fir trees, and I handled the Melancholia.

Of his mentor Ricketts, Gray concluded, "Knowledge was what he had. But how he had it. It made him like the giants of the Renaissance."[60]

This might seem extravagant; it is not so. As artists, the work of Shannon and Ricketts remained a minority taste, at times perhaps too allied to the craft movement to win the recognition it might otherwise have commanded. Their innovations in book and stage design proved startling and influential both in England and abroad. But it is as connoisseurs and collectors that Ricketts and Shannon excelled. In their time they were among the most knowledgeable judges of Oriental, particularly Japanese, art; most of their Oriental collection was left to the British Museum, while their Old Master drawings and many other items in their collection were bequeathed to the Fitzwilliam Museum in Cambridge. Such was Ricketts's reputation that he was offered, and turned down, the position of director of the National Gallery in London, although he was later to become advisor to the National Gallery of Canada in its formative years.

But it is their influence over the younger generation, as critics and collectors, to which the history of John Gray testifies. Gray probably realized that Ricketts had, single-handedly, formed his taste. And there are very few of Gray's discriminations—from his admiration of Japanese prints to his appreciation of Nietzsche—that cannot eventually be traced back to one of Ricketts's enthusiasms. But, of course, in forming the taste, Ricketts shaped the man. To say that one's self is an invention at all is to acknowledge that the self is made, not born; that the psyche is a simulacrum, a creation not so much from the will as from the willfulness of the artist, who must revolt against his given history and character in order to create himself again. Charles Ricketts, not Oscar Wilde, proved the first, if not the only, begetter of "Dorian" Gray.

Toward Conversion, 1889–1890

Up to this point Gray had been leading a splintered life. While still living at home and working in the Arsenal, he passed examinations that would forever divide him from his class, if not his family. As a

very junior civil servant, he began to frequent the London bohemia of
the Vale and, in Paris, the *Quartier latin*. He was really neither middle-
class nor wholly respectable, appearances to the contrary. Nor did he
wish to be. He proceeded, almost instinctively, by antithesis. He
trusted himself, and if he was pulled in opposite directions, so be it.
He had not merely a tolerance, but a taste for contradiction; it was
later to be the method by which he created his poetry. But it leads to
narrative confusion.

In retrospect, Gray's history appears to have a satisfying symme-
try: his rise from poverty to fashionable notoriety, his realization of its
emptiness, a return to work with the poor as a priest after the turn of
the century, and, finally, to a renewed creativity. Its grand design,
however, simplifies the complexity of his story, particularly in these
early years before *Silverpoints*. His actions during 1889 and 1890 illus-
trate the problem. While ascending the ranks of a "respectable" career
in the Civil Service, Gray is also being initiated into the company of
the Vale and literary Paris. A similar pattern appears in his conversion
to Catholicism. While his attraction to the Church was prototypical
of the nineties aesthete, Gray's experience is anything but straightfor-
ward. It actually involves a double conversion: first, an impulsive de-
cision while in Brittany in 1889, formalized the following February;
then a deliberate lapse, a kind of apostasy *à rebours* during the years
1890–92. By late 1892 this revolt, a self-conscious cultivation of "sin"
symbolized by his life as "Dorian" Gray, precipitated a spiritual crisis
that was not entirely resolved until Gray decided to enter the priest-
hood.

While Gray was obviously acting out of a good deal of confu-
sion and anxiety, there appears to be something willful about these di-
lemmas. Reflecting on his "wasted years," Gray admitted as much,
commenting how common sense, "after the years of *voulu* non-
sense, . . . looks like the very way to God."[61] All that is known about
his conversion and his immediate lapse into "sin" points to such de-
liberation, as if he were pursuing paradox as a method, or trying ar-
tificially to induce those exacerbations of temperament which, in his
essay on the Goncourts, he identified as the mark of the true artist.

But perhaps it is misleading to talk of motive here; John Gray's
perversity was not unique, and was in fact typical of his generation. In

an essay which appeared only slightly more than a year after Gray's conversion, another young poet, Lionel Johnson, analyzed the maneuvers of the self-alienating aesthete (which he called "The Cultured Faun"). "You breed it this way," Johnson directs: "Take a young man, who had brains as a boy, and teach him to disbelieve everything that his elders believe in matters of thought, and to reject everything that seems true to himself in matters of sentiment." It is not difficult, he adds; most clever youths will discard their natural or acquired convictions, and it is unlikely they will replace them with dogmas of high Victorianism: "Carlyle is played out, and Mr. Ruskin is tiresome." Instead, such a youth will develop a genius for the absurd, for the gorgeous nonsense of "a really promising affectation, a thoroughly fascinating paradox." Here is where art and religion (or the religion of art and the art of religion) come in:

Externally, our hero should cultivate a reassuring sobriety of habit, with just a dash of the dandy. . . . Externally, then, a precise appearance; internally, a catholic sympathy with all that exists, and 'therefore' suffers, for art's sake. Now art, at present, is not a question of the senses so much as of the nerves. Botticelli, indeed, was very precious, but Baudelaire is very nervous. Gautier was adorably sensuous, but M. Verlaine is pathetically sensitive. That is the point: exquisite thrills of anguish, exquisite adoration of suffering. Here comes in a tender patronage of Catholicism: white tapers upon the high altar, an ascetic and beautiful young priest, the great gilt monstrance, the subtile-scented and mystical incense, the old world accents of the Vulgate, of the Holy Offices; the splendour of sacred vestments! We kneel at some hour, not too early for our convenience, repeating that solemn Latin, drinking in those Gregorian tones, with plenty of modern French sonnets in memory, should the sermon be dull. But to join the Church! Ah, no! better to dally with the enchanting mysteries, to pass from our dreams of delirium to our dreams of sanctity with no coarse facts to jar upon us. And so these refined persons cherish a double 'passion': the sentiment of repentant yearning and the sentiment of rebellious sin.[62]

Johnson's wit was not merely cynical: he himself was received into the Catholic Church in June of 1891, three months after this article was written, more than a year after John Gray. Yet a certain cynicism—

and its concomitant self-mockery—placed the necessary quotation marks around the aesthete's commitment to the Church. Perhaps it deflected him from the despair which would otherwise follow the inevitable failure to match its ideal. Or perhaps it simply reflects the strenuous willfulness by which he made himself into a convert in the first place. He who made himself, could as easily unmake himself: one was the condition of the other.

Far more than Lionel Johnson, Gray was aware of the precariousness of his spiritual state. When he later compared his poetry of the early nineties to a performance on the edge of a precipice, he spoke as truly of the sensibility which had produced it. Yeats had a similar metaphor. Rereading *Marius the Epicurean* after the turn of the century, he commented that Pater had "taught us to walk upon a rope tightly stretched through serene air." He wondered aloud if its great prose, "or the attitude of mind of which it was the noblest expression, had not caused the disaster of my friends."[63] Yeats here was speaking of Lionel Johnson, Ernest Dowson, Arthur Symons—poets of the nineties who were to become friends of John Gray. For Yeats, these were "the tragic generation," whose lives ended in disorder and premature death. If he envisaged their lives as stretched between antitheses, suspended in mid-air, it was not to detract from the gravity of their situation: but they took, as did Johnson and Beardsley and Dowson, their fate not without a certain mockery: theirs was, after all, a "double passion." They cast themselves as tragic actors, and Hamlet-like, watched themselves perform.

As a high-wire artist, Gray found the vacuum more intense and the line less securely taut. Unlike Johnson and Symons, he was not born middle-class, so its rejection, as a typical young man "who had brains as a boy," was more problematical. He had first, by dint of extraordinary effort, to *gain* the middle-class position from which he would subsequently defect. He first had to convert to the religion against which he intended to sin. In short, John Gray's task was more arduous, as he had actually to create the conditions which he, as poet, was to parody and subvert.

Gray's career in paradox, the chain of action and reaction, of turning and returning, seems to have started with Gray's meeting a certain Marmaduke Langdale, a young man about town with an im-

pressive ancestry, known in the nineties as a drifter, an "ardent Swin-
burnian" in verse, and a lady-killer.[64] Langdale and Gray apparently
became immediate and fast friends, for in the summer of 1889 he ac-
cepted an invitation to accompany "Marmie" to his home in the
Breton fishing village of St. Quay-Portrieux.[65] There Gray entered a
household beset with misfortune. Langdale's family had suffered se-
vere financial reverses. About a year and a half previously, the father
had died, leaving his wife with five children, several of whom were in
poor health. Yet Mrs. Langdale persisted in an unquestioning faith
which made an indelible impression on the young Gray. "I was very
lonely and not particularly happy when I had the good fortune to
spend that time with you at St. Quay," Gray wrote to one of Mar-
maduke's younger sisters, Fanny, in 1908: "consequently it has left a
deep mark upon my affections."[66]

At this time, Fanny was not given more than six months to live.
Her nephew, James Langdale, the source of this family history, writes
that he believes Fanny had a great influence over Gray:

She was only about 18 when Gray met her (I believe for the one and only
time) and she must have struck him as being so very different from the ordi-
nary girl of that age. There was never any trace of frivolity (one might almost
say of femininity) about her nature. She was, I believe, quite indifferent to
men as such (she once confessed to me that she had never in all her life felt the
slightest sentimental interest for any man). She was very strict, austere, and
she possessed the sort of faith that will move mountains. She had a very capa-
ble head for business, she was very level-headed, and she had a will of iron.
Poor Marie Caroline was no match for her formidable sister who dominated
her completely.[67]

Theirs was not the only influence at work on Gray. During his
stay in France, the Langdales introduced him to another Catholic
family, the Lenoirs. Gray struck up a correspondence with one son,
Louis Lenoir, and repeated a visit to the family in Versailles in July
1890.[68] At the turn of the century, at the same time Gray was at Scots
College, Louis was to become a Jesuit. He subsequently served as one
of the most celebrated army chaplains of the Great War, and for this
work, was later considered for beatification.[69] When Gray met them,

they were a family (James Langdale writes) so representative of the
"'bourgeoisie bien-pensante' of the last century—the sort of family in
which the Catholic faith was deeply lived by all its members."[70]

But all radiated from that first visit to the Langdales. It changed
Gray's life profoundly, in ways that he could only appreciate during
the fullness of a lifetime. In 1929, forty years afterwards, Gray wrote
to Fanny, with whom he kept up a lifelong correspondence, "I like to
repeat what I am sure you like to read that whatever I do at this pres-
ent day goes back in an unbroken chain of events to the weeks I spent
with you at St. Quay. The reality of religion there seen was the invisi-
ble seed of God's mercy from which all grew."[71]

Of the actual moment of his awakening to "the reality of re-
ligion," Gray is known to have spoken only once, to an old friend,
Father Edwin Essex, who recalled that Gray said he

had been walking abroad, I think he said in Brittany, when the faith finally
came to him. Early one morning he found himself at Mass in a small, way-
side chapel, with half-a-dozen peasant women. It was an untidy, neglected
place, and the priest an unshaven figure at the altar, slovenly, and in a hurry.
Vividly and slowly, as if savouring afresh each tiny detail, Canon Gray recon-
structed the scene, without a hint of criticism, leaning forward in his chair,
hands on knees, and, in his grave eyes, a look of brooding wonder even after
so many years. "Yes, Father," he said, with a slow turn of his head in my
direction, "it was then that it came to me. I said to myself, 'John Gray, here is
the real thing.'"[72]

Father Essex seemed surprised at the Canon's retelling of the story of
the slovenly Mass "without a hint of criticism." The Canon was fas-
tidious about his own church and saw all untidiness either in the chan-
cel or the sermon as a sign of disrespect toward God. To the young
Gray's love of the delicate and exquisite, the "real thing" was equally
an offense and a contradiction: perhaps, one suspects, that is why
Gray found it "real."

In later years, others who were to become friends—Ernest
Dowson, Lionel Johnson, Robert Sherard, and Oscar Wilde—all be-
came converts to Catholicism: "that too was a tradition," as Yeats re-
marked.[73] Arguably, they followed their master, J.-K. Huysmans,

into the Catholic faith for his reason, that "the Church was the only body to have preserved the art of past centuries, the lost beauty of the ages."[74] In her they found a continuity of culture, which (as T. S. Eliot complained of Arnold) they identified with religion. But it was, as usual, Walter Pater who gave this sensibility not only a language but also a form. In the very structure of *Marius the Epicurean* he explicated this equation, as personal ontogeny repeats religious—and cultural—phylogeny. Marius's progression through Epicureanism to Stoicism and finally to Christianity is not only a narrative of his personal spiritual development but a historical account of the origins of primitive Christianity. At the climax of the novel, Marius is welcomed to Cecilia's house, there discovering "the charm of its poetry, a poetry of the affections," a scene that signifies an epitome of personal, cultural, and theological development.[75]

Gray tacitly accepted this identification. His laborious self-education, the mastery of circumstance in his pose as dandy, had their transcendental aspects. Yet the vision in Brittany of a slovenly priest saying Mass to simple peasant women was far from the charm of Cecilia's house; distant even from the entranced peasants of the Brittany of Gauguin, translated from the ordinary by sheer force of style. The dirt, the disorder belonged to another world: the world of Woolwich which Gray wished to escape; the world of the poor Irish immigrant laborers to which he later came as curate as if in symbolic expiation for his life as a dandy. But in 1890, it was a world he seemed determined to leave behind; one from which the distance would be measured by the scrupulous dress and exquisite manners of "Dorian" Gray. By this strategy he would master circumstance, and would, in turn, be mastered.

Metamorphosis: John Gray/"Dorian" Gray: 1890–1891

On 14 February 1890, John Gray was received into the Roman Catholic Church as a convert, with conditional baptism, at Saints Anselm's and Cecilia's, Lincoln's Inn Fields. Soon afterwards he was confirmed at Saint Mary's, Cadogan Gardens.[76] This event more than any other marks the beginning of Gray's double life, the metamorphosis of John into "Dorian" Gray. For, as Gray recognizes in a letter written nine years later on the anniversary of his formal conversion, he made this act thoughtlessly and at once set out to deny it in his life: "I went through instruction as blindly and indifferently as ever anyone did and immediately I began a course of sin compared with which my previous life was innocence. The sequence of miracles which has brought me where I now am is beyond my comprehension."[77] The older Gray was a moralist. His Olympian overview of the "unbroken chain of events" from the vision in Brittany to his ordination is the simplification of a man who has divided his life into two parts, the evil past and the redemptive present. Unlike such fellow artists as Ernest Dowson, who glorified sin as part of their aesthetic attraction to the Church, Father Gray did not acknowledge that the same emotional adventurousness which led him to the Church also drew him to test more worldly pleasures.

It is too easy, however, to identify what Gray called his "course of sin" with an initiation into sexual activity. About the "overwhelming, superabounding-and-all-that-is-superlative-importance of the first sexual act," the older Gray once remarked: "All the passion of making the discovery that man is naturally chaste comes to me."[78] Sexuality—and particularly feminine sexuality—seems to have left him with a sense of revulsion.

But if Gray was so repelled by sex, in what did his "course of sin" consist? As he implies in a conversation with his intimate friend, Katherine Bradley (or "Michael" as she called herself) some twenty years later, his "sin" was largely a matter of guilt by association. In a diary entry, Bradley's niece Edith Cooper records how, on a visit in 1908, Father Gray encounters in their house a picture of himself as a seminarian in Rome. "The photograph is a shock," Cooper writes; "the wall that had been between us all the past heaves & falls." Bradley and Gray leave for a long walk and

As soon as they are out of the house he makes confession of the old days— their reckless destruction of health by exotic habits—their low company: their idle hours at the Foreign Office—their long nights of vain pleasure (Michael gathers in the haunts of the world & the devil not in sin—a conversing with sin not so much sinning). . . .[79]

By "the haunts of the world & the devil," Gray was probably refer-
ring to the London demimonde of music hall and brothel which he
frequented during the early nineties. But in stressing that he was
"conversing with sin" rather than actually "sinning," Gray was being
more than pedantic. Speaking in the aftermath of the Wilde scandal,
Gray is implying to Bradley that his association with the various artis-
tic circles of his time—and with Wilde himself—did not involve him
directly in homosexual activity.

In the case of Wilde, such a disclaimer must, in retrospect, have
seemed necessary. But this was not the only instance of Gray's being
involved with men of unorthodox sexual orientation. As we have seen,
Gray was deeply involved in the affairs of the Vale, and was regarded as
a "disciple" of Charles Ricketts. After he broke with Wilde, he entered
into an intense and lasting relationship with André Raffalovich. All of
these men were either suspected or declared homosexuals. Shannon
and Ricketts, so obviously and fortuitously "married," were generally
regarded as celibate; Bradley, in noting their devotion to Wilde, hoped
"they don't imitate their idol in more than conversation."[80] At the time
Gray first met him, in late 1888 or early 1889, Wilde was secretly a
practicing homosexual, although to the world, a happily married fami-
ly man with two young sons. Gray's last and most enduring rela-
tionship was with Raffalovich, who during the eighties was writing
discreetly "Uranian" poetry and during the nineties publishing "scien-
tific" treatises on homosexuality.

The only evidence as to whether or not Gray was a practicing
homosexual is literary: a recently recovered manuscript of a poem in
Gray's hand, "Passing the Love of Women." Its title, from David's
lament for Jonathan, was at the time regarded, one commentator on
the period observes, as "well-nigh a fiat for paederasty." For all its
high romanticism, there is no other way to read its fourth and fifth
stanzas:

> In the twilight darkling
>   When the sky was violet
> And the stars were faintly sparkling,
>   Thus it was we met,

In a lonely meadow
    Carpeted with crocuses
Underneath the tangled shadow
    Of the apple-trees.

Long and fain we lingered
    Whilst the world lay hushed in sleep.
Till the dawning rosy-fingered
    Clomb the eastern steep.

Priest nor ceremony
    Or of Orient or Rome
Bound to me my love, mine honey
    In the honey-comb,

Who albeit of human
    Things the most sublime he knew,
Left me, to espouse a woman
    As the people do.

Though he wind about her
    Those dear arms were holden in mine
He shall only reach the outer
    Precinct of the shrine;

For, when the pale stars shimmer
    In the vault of violet,
As far gleams of memory glimmer
    He will not forget.[81]

The poem clearly speaks of homosexual experience. But were there even more concrete evidence, it would be misleading to chart Gray's path during these years as a series of homosexual "affairs"; of itself, sexual attraction is only part of the story. Aside from their homosexual orientation, Ricketts, Wilde, and Raffalovich had another thing in common: they were all dedicated artists (although one might argue the case of Raffalovich, but only on the basis of artistic merit).

Their relationships with John Gray also show an arresting similarity: each, in the wake of his rejection of his own father, was to assume in his separate way a paternal role. Perhaps more: as we have seen, Gray went so far as to claim that he was an "invention" of Ricketts; Wilde was to become his "loved Master"; Raffalovich referred to himself not only as Gray's brother but as his "father & mother." The pattern is, again, made explicit in Pater's Marius, whose relation to the poet Flavian and later to the Emperor Marcus Aurelius is that of younger to older brother, son to father: "Platonic" in the exact sense, that is, erotically charged but also fraught with the spiritual destiny of Marius's soul. Its medium is not sexuality, but art. In Flavian's exquisite poetry no less than in the meditations of Marcus Aurelius, and finally in the dying fall of Pater's own cadences, Marius's soul seeks its own speech.

The connection between art, spirituality, and homoerotic feeling is as explicit here as it is implicit in the artistic sensibility of the English 1880s. Indeed, homosexuality among artists at the time was a kind of vogue.[82] In part, it attested to the illicit nature of the "new art" and its status as an underground cult. For Gray, as a self-consciously avant-garde poet and critic, it may have been difficult to escape the pressure of the homosexual clique.

One clique that was typical of its time gathered around Charles Kains Jackson. A London lawyer by profession, he worked as editor of the outwardly respectable magazine, *The Artist and Journal of Home Culture*. From 1888 until he resigned as editor in 1894, Kains Jackson used the magazine as a front for purveying "Uranian" material, i.e., material about the love of boys. Yet "only among the initiated," one commentator observed, "would the magazine be purchased for its advocacy of Uranian love. Jackson, using the discretion expected from a London solicitor, was tactful in the extreme, closely respecting pseudonyms and refusing to allow more than a thin scarlet thread of questionable literature to weave its way through the homespun of the monthly columns."[83] Gray's first translation of a Verlaine poem appeared in *The Artist* in August 1890. Although it is a poem that reflects Verlaine's ambivalence and remorse over his estranged wife, it would hardly qualify as "questionable literature"—unless contemporary French poetry was itself deemed questionable, which to some

extent it was. Some three years later, *The Artist* was the only maga-
zine to publish a sustained and serious critique of Gray's poetry.[84]

How well Gray knew Kains Jackson is hard to say. By 1891, rec-
ords show that Gray had moved from his rooms at the Inner Temple
to 62 Chancery Lane, a few doors away from Jackson's residence. But
he was to remain there only a year; so it is probable that his involve-
ment with this particular circle was merely tangential, or so discreet
that it would appear so.

Discretion was the password of this school, and it is exemplified
in the kind of cat-and-mouse game that Kains Jackson played with his
public by publishing poetry that could be read as "respectable" by
one reader and "Uranian" by the initiated. Another played it even
more daringly than he: a new arrival on the London scene, an émigré
Russian, André Raffalovich, who made his name in the 1880s as a
poet and socialite and wealthy young man about town. He would
share more than half of John Gray's life on the most intimate terms.

John Gray was not introduced to Raffalovich until November
1892, but by that date Gray certainly knew who he was (Raffalovich
had written at least one caustic review of Gray's poetry) and perhaps
something of his history. Raffalovich had arrived in London, not yet
eighteen, in 1882. He came from Paris, where his family had moved
in 1863, a year before his birth.[85] They were not willing exiles;
Raffalovich's father, Herman, a banker, had left Odessa when it was
decreed that all Jews in Russia must either become Christian or leave
the country. Raffalovich started life over again in Paris, where he
prospered, becoming a banker of international repute. Some years
earlier Herman had married his niece, Marie, who had been betrothed
to him for financial reasons while she was still in the cradle. She grew
into a woman of singular beauty and remarkable intelligence. A lin-
guist (she is reputed to have mastered eight languages), writer, and
connoisseur of the arts, Madame Raffalovich contributed regularly to
the *Journal de Saint-Pétersbourg* articles on current Parisian art exhibi-
tions. Her home on the fashionable Avenue Hoche became the venue
for a brilliant *salon* which included scientists, *savants,* and politicians
as well as artists. Only a woman of fierce determination—as well as
considerable wealth—could accomplish all this and still have three
children, each of whom distinguished themselves in their own way.

Her eldest son, Arthur Raffalovich, became a celebrated international economist, receiving decorations from more than one European sovereign. Sophie, her second child, married the Irish nationalist leader William O'Brien, having become a convert to Catholicism; Parnell made the wedding speech.

But with her last and third child there was always some painful constraint. It is said that she regarded the infant she had christened Marc-André with some distaste because he was so ugly. André, as he came to be known, was devoted to his mother but became rather sensitive about her; in his Edinburgh years, her portrait hung in his dining room, but it was understood among guests that it must never be mentioned in conversation. Madame Raffalovich did, however, recognize that André was precocious and took pains to introduce him early to the company of her *salon:* to such figures as her close friend the celebrated *savant,* physiologist, and senator Claude Bernard; to Henri Bergson, Ernest Renan ("one of my family's pet lions," Raffalovich remarked), Gustave Moreau, and J.-K. Huysmans.[86] While still an adolescent, Raffalovich began to cultivate his own "lions." It became his practice while still in Paris to compose articles (for the *Journal de Saint-Pétersbourg,* where his mother had some influence) on such English authors as William Morris, George Meredith, and James Thompson (author of "The City of Dreadful Night") and then send them copies. Often a correspondence would ensue.[87]

Thus by the time Raffalovich left Paris for London, he was already in touch with many of the key figures of English artistic life. At first his intention had been to enter Oxford; he certainly stayed there long enough to be warned by Professor Keats "to avoid the acquaintance of Pater and Symonds. The latter I did not admire, and was not curious about, too inexperienced to be excited by so clinical a case. . . . I, of course, made a point of knowing Pater." In later life, Raffalovich recalled "I had only kindness from him and his sisters. I fancied at the time that he treated me as if I were a friendly kitten."[88] That friendship survived Raffalovich's departure from Oxford to London, ostensibly for reasons of poor health, although the health of his morals might also have been, in such company, under question. There Raffalovich settled in quarters at Albert Hall Mansions, off Kensington Road (later moving to the more fashionable address of 72 South Audley Street, near Park

Lane) with his mother's trusted *dame de compagnie,* Miss Florence Truscott Gribbell.

Of Scottish origin, a bank manager's daughter, Florence Gribbell had entered Madame Raffalovich's Paris household as a governess to André, "whom she found to be a shy but very intelligent little boy, rather neglected by his mother who was too busy being a great hostess to give him much attention." Apparently the governess "understood the situation from all points of view, and quickly became the friend of both the mother and the child."[89] To André she was not only an efficient housekeeper; her stern sense of propriety safeguarded him from the excesses of his inclinations, which by late adolescence were overtly homosexual, while her devotion gave him the emotional security he so acutely needed. In time, she became no less than a second mother to him, and from his middle age onwards, the presiding hostess of his elegant dinner parties. Within a short time of his arrival in London, Raffalovich had established himself as a kind of professional guest of such celebrities as Browning, Whistler, Swinburne, Burne-Jones and Pater.[90] Because of his age—he was closer in years to his host's children—and his considerable charm, Raffalovich became in some cases (as with the Huxleys), a friend of the family. Others, like George Meredith, valued him also as a serious writer, since he had begun to publish poetry.

One cannot escape the impression that Raffalovich was out to conquer literary London. Wealthy and socially ambitious, he was an assiduous host; yet his foreign accent, the guttural tones of which never left him, and his Jewishness both proved a barrier in the anti-Semitic and xenophobic London of the eighties. He attracted the spite in particular of two of his guests: Irene Paget (Vernon Lee) and Oscar Wilde. It is Wilde's snub that reflects most sharply on the attitudes of the day and on the flaws in Wilde's own character. Of Raffalovich Wilde was purported to have said that "He came to London with the intention of opening a *salon,* and he has succeeded in opening a saloon," a remark he thought so well of that he used a version of it to describe the ambitious Lady Brandon in *The Picture of Dorian Gray.*[91] On another occasion, when the door of Raffalovich's house opened to Wilde and five other dinner guests, Wilde stepped forward saying,

"We want a table for six for lunch today."[92] Obviously he thought of Raffalovich as an objectionable *parvenu,* although that did not stop him from taking his dinner.

But Raffalovich did gain entry to these circles, and not merely by dint of his wealth and ambition. He proved a charming and tactful guest who, in matters literary, could be enthusiastic (sometimes too enthusiastic) and knowledgeable about both English and Continental literature. He also showed a talent for friendship, particularly "romantic" friendships with older men and younger boys; it is fitting that his first book, published in 1884—two years after his arrival in London—was entitled *Cyril and Lionel and Other Poems: A Volume of Sentimental Studies.* One critic calls its first poem an "almost flawless Uranian piece"; its questionable emotions were not missed by the reviewer of the *Academy,* who commented that "It is hard to say from internal evidence whether the poems are the work of a man or of a woman, the male and female attitudes of mind towards love and nature being exhibited on all but alternate pages."[93] Raffalovich's second book of poetry, *Tuberose & Meadowsweet,* appearing a year later, was reviewed anonymously in the *Pall Mall Gazette* by Oscar Wilde, who commented on its disturbing quality: "To say of these poems that they are unhealthy and bring with them the heavy odours of the hothouse is to point out neither their defect nor their merit, but their quality merely."[94] He disputed, however, the scansion of the word "tuberose"; none other than Robert Browning gave Raffalovich ammunition for his defence. It was Browning again who wrote Raffalovich that he had read his third book of poems, *In Fancy Dress,* "twice attentively over."[95] In doing so, he could not have failed to notice the unusual fact that in this book, as in its sequel, *It Is Thyself,* "no third person possessive pronoun occurs at all and nowhere is the sex of the object of the author's deep passion mentioned."[96]

The same flirtatious, disturbing quality that characterizes Raffalovich's poetry infects his relationship at this time with Oscar Wilde. In the last years of his life, Raffalovich would write pseudonymously about Wilde, confiding elsewhere to a friend, "It is an account of a dislike, not of a friendship."[97] Amy Renan, a friend of the family, had written to Wilde about Raffalovich before he had arrived in London in

1882.[98] Some time afterwards, he and Wilde took lunch together; Wilde "bullied the waiter and then took me to call on Speranza, his tall mother, in her darkened rooms in Park Street." Raffalovich reciprocated with a dinner invitation; they later went to a play. Years passed: Wilde went to America, married, became a father. Raffalovich could not recall how they were brought together again, perhaps by Whistler. Wilde had changed. Raffalovich remembers him confessing, "'You could give me a new thrill . . . you have the right measure of romance and cynicism,'" but adds, "that must have been towards the close of our friendship." Wilde would tease "Sandy" (as he nicknamed André) about the questionable company in which they found themselves. At a musical club, Wilde offered, "'My dear Sandy, come with me, and I will look after you there, and see you do not get introduced to any dangerous characters: the place is full of them.'" On another occasion, after Wilde had finished reading *Monsieur Venus* by Rachilde, in a state of visible excitement, "he once talked to me for several hours about the more dangerous affections." It must have been soon afterward, Raffalovich recalls, "that his wife Constance, who had always befriended me, estranged us. She said to me: 'Oscar says he likes you so much—that you have such nice improper talks together. . . .' I was furious: never again did I speak with him without witnesses." The final break did not come until 1892, however, incited, apparently, by jealousy over Wilde's attachment to a young, beautiful poet of their mutual acquaintance: John Gray.

For how long and on what terms Gray had known Wilde before Raffalovich entered the scene is not necessarily clear. No evidence supports the allegation that Gray was "picked up" by Wilde in a bar near Shaftesbury Avenue one night in 1889, but the date fits.[99] The first definitive report places them together as dinner guests in the early summer of 1889, a full year before *The Picture of Dorian Gray* first appeared in print in *Lippincott's* of June 1890. It was "at one of those Soho restaurants that furnish private rooms for supper parties," Frank Liebich, a popular concert-pianist of the day, recalls in an unpublished reminiscence; he had been invited by a young poet, John Barlas, together with John Gray and John Davidson. Wilde bantered with Barlas, "full of lively trivialities in which Davidson joined occasionally," but, Liebich remembers,

John Gray and I talked but little,—Gray seeming bored and tired. . . .
Whether Gray's mood affected him or whether his old-time friendliness for
Barlas had died, I could not judge,—but I found nothing memorable in his
[Gray's] speech nor in his manner, which seemed tinged with condescension.
I thought him a thoroughly blasé worldling,—a type which I could neither
understand nor admire. Barlas seemed to me the wittier talker of the two,—
but then, I admired Barlas more than any man I knew, apart only from my
musician-idols.

Barlas was a known homosexual and "had hinted" to Liebich, "rather
vaguely, of the (alleged) intimacy between Wilde and Gray, so that I
was really rather more curious about the latter, an extraordinarily
good-looking youth . . . but severely conventional in both speech
and behaviour."[100]

The date, if correctly remembered, and the nature of Gray's rela-
tionship with Wilde certainly allow for the possibility that Gray
might have acted, in some sense, as a model for the hero of *The Picture
of Dorian Gray;* certainly he acknowledged it in allowing himself to be
called "Dorian," and on at least one occasion signed himself by that
name in a letter to Wilde postmarked 9 January 1891.[101]

Yet in personal circumstance, history, and class, John Gray is far
removed from the self-assured, wealthy, and sophisticated "Dorian"
Gray. And probably no one would have thought that the beautiful
youth with the discernible Cockney accent could in these respects
have offered "the" model for Wilde's hero. What the nickname con-
fessed was the quality of the relationship with Wilde. To the initiated,
it must have been a code name, certainly, for a "Uranian" relation-
ship. Could anyone as conscious of words as Gray use the name
"Dorian" without a sensitivity to the nature of love among the Dori-
ans in early Greek history? Wilde claimed that Lord Henry Wotton
was "what the world thinks me."[102] The initiate also read Lord Henry
Wotton as a portrait of the notorious Lord Henry Somerset, friend of
Kains Jackson and later of Lord Alfred Douglas, who fled to the Con-
tinent in 1879 as the result of a public scandal involving his liaison
with a youth, Henry Smith.[103] Lord Henry Wotton's predilections
mirrored Wilde's. We know that Wilde was attracted to young men of
strikingly boyish appearance, such as the diminutive Lionel Johnson

and, somewhat later, to Lord Alfred Douglas, known significantly as "Bosie," a corruption of a pet name, "boysie." It was Lionel Johnson who, on first meeting Gray in 1891, described him as "aged thirty, with the face of fifteen."[104]

But unlike Johnson and "Bosie," Gray was not Wilde's social equal. Nor is it clear that Gray was a practicing homosexual, though he was deeply attracted to men who were. The pedantries of the situation are obvious, and I have no wish to indulge them, except to say that Brian Reade is probably closest to the truth when he claims that "the probability is that Gray had no strong sexual inclinations at all, and that by his subsequent chastity he exploited what was already there—a kind of incipient sexual anaesthesia."[105] Reade goes further in suggesting that it was under the influence of a certain environment—not of school or university, "but of literary suggestion and association, followed by the effects of flattery and affection from a dedicated homosexual"—that Gray became involved in a homosexual relationship. Whereas Reade identified that "dedicated homosexual" as Raffalovich, it is clear that Gray's first such attachment was actually Oscar Wilde.

However, I believe that only in a superficial way was the tragedy of his life as "Dorian" Gray the direct result of an involvement in a "homosexual" affair. At least in part, Gray's sense of self-betrayal had to do with his conscious exploitation of Wilde's attraction toward him. In the opinion of one who knew him in his later Edinburgh years, Gray's homosexual history was inseparable from his drive for self-betterment.[106] Gray may have claimed himself an "invention of Ricketts," and certainly his taste and literary orientation were to a large extent set by the Vale. But his public self was invented by Wilde. It was Wilde who literally made his name, introduced him to fashionable society, and (judging from the one letter remaining of their correspondence) coached him in his poetry. It was Wilde who, in 1892, offered to finance the publication of his first book of poems, *Silverpoints*. Wilde lent him the polish and finesse that public school or university might otherwise have bestowed. After the fashion of the current Uranian myth, Wilde made the "pauper" into a "prince," intervening so crucially in Gray's life that he enabled him to override the iron conditions of his birthright.

In other words, Wilde, and to an even greater extent, Ricketts, were less friends (of whatever quality and intensity) than fathers, the begetters—albeit not the only ones—of the poet "Dorian" Gray. Seen in this light, the continuum between these crucial relationships becomes clear: the actual, rejected father is replaced by a series of surrogate father/mentors, whose relationship is not merely of older to younger man, teacher to pupil, but of master to disciple and finally, with Raffalovich, of parent to child. Ultimately, Gray's search—with the death of his actual father precipitating his break with Wilde—turned to a spiritual quest. In retrospect, Father Gray saw his association with Wilde as a "course of sin"; but if so, it was necessary, therapeutic sin: clarifying for Gray the distinction, as yet confused, between his drive for self-betterment and the achievement of selfhood; between sexual attraction and spiritual quest; between playing the poet and writing genuine poetry.

Unfortunately, in Wilde's *Picture of Dorian Gray,* John Gray was offered a ready-made self. The tragedy of Gray's early manhood is in large part the result of his adoption of this persona. In exploiting the popular notion that he was himself the model for the novel—by, for instance, allowing himself to be called and calling himself "Dorian"—Gray also exploited his relationship with Wilde. For several years, according to the available evidence, Gray played up to the role the public assigned him and, it seems, used it to become accepted into fashionable society. At the same time, he evidently tried to escape the consequences of this identification (which, with the growing indignation over Wilde's attachment to Douglas, was becoming troublesome) by the threat of legal action and by withdrawal from Wilde's circle.

The psychological consequences would perhaps have been less serious for Gray had he not acted in a social vacuum, cut off from his own family and class and even drifting away from the community of the Vale.[107] Nor was Gray's isolation alleviated by Wilde and his coterie. Wilde's aesthetic stance was based in part on the pretense that, as self-styled dandy, he was both outside and beyond class distinction. He thought of himself as an aristocrat of culture, an ornament to the tale of an earl, a Byronic explorer of the London underworld, a reproach to the middle classes. Wilde's perpetual evolution of himself as an object lesson to the bourgeoisie accounts for much of his melodramatics, his emotional posturing, and the fragmented, artificial personality that all of his friends observed. It was, in fact, Wilde's insistence on living in a kind of sociological vacuum that made this masquerade possible.

The position was specious, of course. It is tempting to forget the rigidity of the class lines in late Victorian society. Gray had been exceptional in breaking through the wall that separated the lower from the middle class, those who worked with their hands from those who worked with their heads. But, having broken through, he found himself in a void. How much was principle, how much pretense, how much actual exile is hard to say. But Gray's isolation was more keen than most, as was his nostalgia for the ordinary which Yeats identified in the young artists he found in the Rhymers' Club: "The typical young poet of our day," he wrote, "is an aesthete with a surfeit, searching sadly for his lost Philistinism, his heart full of an unsatisfied hunger for the commonplace. He is an Alastor tired of his woods and longing for beer and skittles."[108]

The dandy's pose of living aesthetically cultivated, then, a false freedom. It also had, for Gray, tragic consequences. In the artificial social vacuum that he shared with Wilde and his friends, his performance as "Dorian" Gray was accepted without resistance. This persona soon became so essential that his own resistance to it led to thoughts of madness and death. The history of the next two years is a document of Gray's experiments in dandyism and of the discoveries made in the wake of its failure.

❦ *"Dorian" Gray, 1891–1892* ❦

*This passion for beauty is merely the intensified desire
for life.*

Oscar Wilde
unpublished notebook
Princeton University

Fruit of a quest, despair.
Smart of a sullen wrong.
Where may they hide them yet?
  One hour, yet one,
To find the mossgod lurking in his nest,
To see the naiads' floating hair, caressed
  By fragrant sun-

Beams.

"Summer Past: To Oscar Wilde"
John Gray, *Silverpoints*, 1893

During the next two years, 1891–92, Gray began to appear in various literary circles, at the Rhymers' Club, among the playwrights of J. T. Grein's Independent Theatre, and at all such popular literary haunts as the Cock, the Crown, and the music halls. He dined often with Wilde at the Café Royal; he recited his poetry to Walter Pater and at the famous dinner party given by Frank Harris for the Princess of Monaco. The record of these years, however, has the jerky abruptness of an early film; Gray appears and disappears on the scene with a cinematic rapidity, and before we have time to wonder what he is doing there, he is gone. That was, it seems, part of his technique, to be seen but not to be involved; it was his way of establishing himself socially without putting his inner self in jeopardy. Hence the history of these two years is really a series of vignette performances—in pantomime—by "Dorian" Gray. If his gestures appear trivial and fragmentary, a wearying parade of social rituals (attendance at first nights and private views, at lunches, dinners, recitations of the Rhymers' Club, and at select entertainments)—a parade that does not seem less trivial by the inclusion of a brothel visit or what seems to have been a brush with a blackmailing scheme in France—it is well to remember Wilde's dictum that "folly in its exquisite modes of triviality and indifference and lack of care is the robe of the wise man."[1] Undertaken in this spirit, Gray's adventures reveal a certain cynicism about his performance as "Dorian" Gray, although it proved a performance in which he himself was to come, tragically, to believe.

Gray's involvement with such serious artistic enterprises as the Rhymers and the Independent Theatre was, then, exquisitely nonserious. Yet to say simply that he was a "peripheral" member of these circles is something of a falsification, for Gray absorbed many of their ideas with the facility of a man with few theories of his own but a great deal of artistic ambition. His early experiments found their audience in the Rhymers' Club. More obviously, the ideas of Wilde became part of his poetry as well as his pose; or, rather, helped conflate the two. For what seemed to interest Gray was not the working out in isolation of a new poetic, but the impact that, as poet, he could exert on an audience, so that, in many ways, playing the poet's role became as important as, if not more important than, *being* the poet.

Unconsciously, earlier biographies—in particular *Two Friends* and *Footnote to the Nineties*—have adopted this theatrical metaphor: "Dorian" Gray is consistently described through his relation to other groups and other people, and he completely pales beside the lively personality of André Raffalovich. Such obliqueness of approach seems inevitable, for what is being recorded is the death of a personality, the symptoms of which are Gray's domination by those around him; his passivity toward the role of "Dorian" Gray, which was largely thrust upon him; and the repeated description of Gray as a "protégé" or disciple, as if he were somehow not responsible for his own actions or thoughts.[2] If this is indeed the case, such an anecdotal history tends to lend his figure a false animation, thus evading the essential biographical problem: the conscious suppression of an autonomous, interior self. In sum, it is the necessity of accounting for the life of "Dorian" Gray in this manner that implies, more than any other evidence, the impoverishment of these two years.

The Poet as Dandy

On the last Thursday of January 1891, six months after *The Picture of Dorian Gray* was first published, John Gray attended an evening of poetry reading at Herbert Horne's house at 20 Fitzroy Street, where the Century Guild—an artistic colony similar to the Vale—had its headquarters. By this date, the Rhymers had been meeting at various venues for almost a year; Gray may even have attended previous meetings.[3] But on this, the first occasion when his appearance is noted, he is introduced as "Dorian" Gray, appearing in company with that work's author, Oscar Wilde.

In residence was a young poet just down from Oxford, Lionel Johnson, who recalled the evening as particularly dull: "We entertained the other night eighteen minor poets of our acquaintance: from Oscar Wilde to Walter Crane, with Arthur Symons and Willie Yeats between. They all inflicted their poems on each other, and were inimitably tedious, except dear Oscar." Still, all except "dear Oscar" were not irredeemably dull; in the same breath, Johnson records enthusiastically, "I have made great friends with the original of Dorian: one John Gray, a youth in the Temple, aged thirty, with the face of fifteen."[4] Gray was actually twenty-five at the time, but the impression of extreme youthfulness struck many who met him during these years. Like Gray, Johnson admired "dear Oscar" and, like Gray, was drawn to Catholicism—he would become a convert in June—and he and Gray did indeed become "great friends." Although the record of their friendship, some twenty letters from Johnson to Gray, is now lost, Gray spoke of two particular incidents in later life. On one occasion, Father Gray recalled "sitting all through the early hours of a Sunday morning by the side of Lionel Johnson, who, stretched on a chaise longue, was slowly working off the Café Royal potations. 'Time for Mass, Lionel.' 'Yes.' 'Now, Lionel, if you do not get up at once you will be late for Mass . . .' —and Lionel was very late." On the other occasion, "There was once a fine hubbub outside the restaurant door. 'Whatever's that?' someone asked. 'Only Lionel (Johnson) crying for his perambulator,' came the answer—from Gray himself, I was led to suspect."[5] Johnson was a diminutive man who drank heavily, and Gray apparently assumed the role of protecting Johnson from himself.

Similar, but more affectionate and indulgent, was the role Gray was to play toward Ernest Dowson. Dowson's account of the evening suggests that he already knew and admired Gray:

Thursday at Horne's was very entertaining: a most queer assembly of "Rhymers"; and a quaint collection of rhymes. Crane (Walter) read a ballad: dull! one Ernest Radford, some triolets & rondels of merit: "Dorian" Gray some very beautiful & obscure versicles in the latest manner of French Symbolism; and the tedious Todhunter was tedious after his kind. Plarr and Johnson also read verses of great excellence; and the latter, also, read for me my "Amor Umbratilis": And Oscar arrived late.[6]

Wilde seemed to dominate these early meetings. "And round Oscar Wilde," Victor Plarr wrote, "hovered reverently Lionel Johnson and Ernest Dowson with others. This must have been in 1891, and I marvelled at the time to notice the fascination which poor Wilde exercised over the otherwise rational. He sat as it were enthroned and surrounded by a deferential circle."[7]

Nearly two weeks before this January gathering, Gray had in fact sent Wilde a copy of a poem on which he was working, apparently for help in revision. Wilde may indeed have suggested a change of title and the rewriting of the first stanza.[8] Although the poem was not to appear in print for more than two years, Gray probably read some version of it to his fellow Rhymers on this particular evening:

MISHKA

Mishka is poet among the beasts.
When roots are rotten, and rivers weep,
The bear is at play in the land of sleep.
Though his head be heavy between his fists.
The bear is poet among the beasts.

The Dream

Wide and large are the monster's eyes,
Nought saying, save one word alone:
Mishka! Mishka, as turned to stone,
Hears no word else, nor in anywise
Can see aught save the monster's eyes.

Honey is under the monster's lips;
And Mishka follows into her lair,
Dragged in the net of her yellow hair,
Knowing all things when honey drips
On his tongue like rain, the song of the hips

Of the honey-child, and of each twin mound.
Mishka! there screamed a far bird-note,
Deep in the sky, when round his throat
The triple coil of her hair she wound.
And stroked his limbs with a humming sound.

Mishka is white like a hunter's son;
For he knows no more of the ancient south
When the honey-child's lips are on his mouth,
When all her kisses are joined in one,
And his body is bathed in grass and sun.

The shadows lie mauven beneath the trees,
And purple stains, where the finches pass,
Leap in the stalks of the deep, rank grass.
Flutter of wing, and the buzz of bees,
Deepen the silence, and sweeten ease.

The honey-child is an olive tree,
The voice of birds and the voice of flowers,
Each of them all and all the hours,
The honey-child is a wingèd bee,
Her touch is a perfume, a melody.[9]

Mishka, a diminutive of Michael in Russian, is a homonym, applied both to a man and to a little bear. It cuts two ways. When Mishka, "poet among the beasts," is lured into a state of entranced sensuality, the poet becomes pure beast while, bathed in this world of entranced sensuality, the beast becomes pure poet.[10] It is, of course, a comic self-portrait. But it is more: for all its delicacy, it echoes the one sentiment agreed by all the Rhymers: that of Keats's cry, "O for a Life of Sensations rather than of Thoughts!"

Certainly no one in the room that night would have regarded "Mishka" as a parody, however playful or oblique, of his own poetry. Gray himself would probably have denied it. Dowson, as we have seen, was of the mind that Gray's lines were "in the latest manner of French Symbolism": a manner in which he was, two months later, attempting to write himself, defining it as being "verses making for mere sound, & music, with just a suggestion of sense, or hardly that."[11]

He may well have taken Gray's poems for richly musical nonsense. Nor would that have offended the principles of the Rhymers' Club; for the truth is that they did not operate on principle, or at least on any explicitly agreed upon. The Rhymers were, essentially, less reformers of English poetry than the audience of their own, which was written for the most part in isolation and without reference to a conscious aesthetic.

Implicitly, however, most agreed with Keats. In fact it was precisely this cult of "impressions" and "sensations" Yeats encountered in the Rhymers that made him feel an outsider, although he was actually one of its founder members. He recalls that whenever he would begin to talk about some of his ideas of poetry, "a gloomy silence fell upon the room." A few years later, he was scolded by a fellow poet: "'You do not talk like a poet, you talk like a man of letters.'" Yeats felt that the "one conviction shared by all the younger men, but principally by Johnson and Horne, who imposed their personalities upon us, was an opposition to all ideas, all generalizations that can be explained and debated. Symons fresh from Paris would sometimes say, 'We are concerned with nothing but impressions,' but that itself was a generalization and met but stony silence."[12] In short, unlike the French *symbolistes,* the Rhymers were intensely anti-intellectual. Gray, in his dislike of thinking or even talking about poetry, proved typical of the Rhymers' circle. In the only recorded aside about his methods of composition, Gray confessed to clapping two often incongruous ideas together and letting them "bake," presumably in the furnace of the unconscious.[13]

Yeats and Symons gave a good deal of thought as to why these differences existed, why the Rhymers could or would not work together. In contrast to the orderly progression of schools and movements in France based on a continuity of admiration of disciple for master, they noted a tradition in England not of "schools," but of the isolated efforts of great men. "In England the writers do not form groups, but each man works by himself and for himself," Yeats explained, ending with the melancholy observation: "England is the land of literary Ishmaels."[14] Perhaps recalling the phrase, Symons later gave his own account of the strain among the Rhymers:

In England art has to be protected not only against the world, but against one's self and one's fellow-artist, by a kind of affected modesty which is the Englishman's natural pose, half pride and half self-distrust. So this brave venture of the Rhymers' Club, though it lasted for two or three years, and produced two little books of verse which will some day be literary curiosities, was not quite a satisfactory kind of *cénacle*.[15]

"Literary curiosities" these books certainly are. *The Book of the Rhymers' Club* (1892) and *The Second Book of the Rhymers' Club* (1894) have between them 130 poems, most of which "are admittedly bad to mediocre."[16] Yet they can boast some good poems by Yeats and several of the best of Lionel Johnson and Ernest Dowson.

To us they also act as admirable guides to the Rhymers' confusion as to what their goals should be. Many obviously supported the revival of archaic forms, such as the ballad, the sonnet, the virelay and rondeau. Others advocated a sharp perfection of form à la Gautier, or the blur of crepuscular landscapes in the Verlaine mode. To add to the confusion, the Rhymers were themselves in open disagreement as to their masters. Symons and Gray were passionate converts to the *symbolistes*, having discovered Verlaine and Mallarmé by 1891. Independently, as we have seen, Gray had come upon the poetry of Rimbaud and Laforgue. On the other hand, Lionel Johnson, although well-versed in *symboliste* technique and theory, tended to parody it, while writing his verse in a strictly traditional form. At the same time Yeats, then working in the ballad form, was also writing exquisite pieces in the deliquescent mode of "The Lake Isle of Innisfree." But the *maladie fin de siècle* irritated John Davidson, a poet of the rough and direct school of Kipling and Henley, to the point of refusing membership, saying "he did not care to be ranked as one of the coterie."[17]

Thus the Rhymers provided John Gray less with a direction than, for a short time at least, with a milieu. If the aesthetics of the Rhymers were muddy, at least they were rich; in fact, their eclecticism was itself later to become a modern mode. More important was the fact that, between the puffs at the long clay pipes and the deep drafts from tankards of ale in the Rhymers' later venue of the Cheshire Cheese, the group offered Gray an audience ready to take his poetry seriously, a chance to encounter working poets on common ground. It was there that he became acquainted with Lionel Johnson, Arthur Symons, William Butler Yeats, and (probably) Ernest Dowson. From the perspective of the new century, Gray later named these as the poets who would last: "the rest," he proclaimed, "were preposterous."[18]

Gray himself never published in the books of the Rhymers' Club, a fact that may have defined his status as "permanent guest" rather than member.[19] But we find in his poetry the same eclecticism, the same conscious archaism and concern for the shape of the poem. These are the values of another early poem, "Heart's Demesne," (published in *The Dial* of 1892), in which Gray puts a well-worn poetic formula into reverse, with rather startling results:

> Listen, bright lady, thy deep Pansie eyes
> Made never answer when my eyes did pray,
> Than with those quaintest looks of blank surprise.
>
> But my lovelonging has devised a way
> To mock thy living image, from thy hair
> To thy rose toes; and keep thee by alway.
>
> My garden's face is oh! so maidly fair,
> With limbs all tapering and with hues all fresh;
> Thine are the beauties all the flourish there.

Amaranth, fadeless, tells me of thy flesh;
Briarrose knows thy cheek; the Pink thy pout;
Bunched kisses dangle from the Woodbine mesh.

I love to loll, when Daisy stars peep out,
And hear the music of my garden dell,
Hollyhock's laughter and the Sunflower's shout.

And many whisper things I dare not tell.[20]

Rejected by his lady, the poet revenges himself with the witty notion that, by planting a garden which mimics her living image, he will thus keep her "by alway." Not that it will be more permanent; the cruel suggestion is, in fact, that the garden is the more natural (her false soul speaks in "those quaintest looks of blank surprise"). Its very abundance parodies her hoarded virtues; the Amaranth and Briarrose, unlike her skin, will not fade, and the Woodbine surrenders the kisses she would not give. In the extreme pathetic fallacy of the last lines, the poem turns its mockery on to itself, neutralizing its intention into mere playfulness. If Wilde was to perfect this form of self-cancelling wit, his dandies rarely to this degree outraged sense or toyed with self-parody.

Another poem by Gray, certainly also read to the Rhymers and to appear in the 1892 *Dial,* "Les Demoiselles de Sauve," anticipates that formula to be devised by Beardsley, a kind of Burne-Jones medievalism *à la Japonaise:*[21]

Beautiful ladies through the orchard pass;
Bend under crutched-up branches, forked and low;
Trailing their samet palls o'er dew-drenched grass.

Pale blossoms, looking on proud Jacqueline,
Blush to the colour of her finger tips,
And rosy knuckles, laced with yellow lace.

High-crested Berthe discerns, with slant, clinched eyes,
Amid the leaves, pink faces of the skies:
She locks her plaintive hands Sainte-Margot-wise.

Ysabeau follows last, with languorous pace;
Presses, voluptuous, to her bursting lips,
With backward stoop, a bunch of eglantine.

Courtly ladies through the orchard pass;
Bow low, as in lords' halls, and springtime grass
Tangles a snare to catch the tapering toe.

Beardsley's women, too, were to deploy the same aggressive artifice. Here Gray's engage in an elegant, if somewhat empty seduction of the masculine garden. As naive Nature, he blushes for their practiced stratagems, provoking Berthe to a show of specious innocence, locking "her plaintive hands Sainte-Margot-wise." Finally Ysabeau, the last, abandons all pretense, launching a sexual assault to which her lover responds with a feeble protest, as the "grass / Tangles a snare to catch the tapering toe."

Feminine insolence, masculine impotence: Gray's ambivalence toward the other sex is, typically, exaggerated. More pointed than either "Mishka" or "Heart's Demesne," this poem has the same design of neutralizing a feared woman, whether mistress or seductress. Gray (as he himself confessed) did not "credit women with any of the perfections."[22] In these poems his personal distaste found its embodiment in a distinctly period figure, the *femme fatale*.

With conscious irony, Gray dedicated "Les Demoiselles de Sauve" to a formidable woman, H. S. H. Alice, Princess of Monaco, when it was reprinted in *Silverpoints*. A grandniece of the poet Heine, widow of the Duc de Richelieu, and now, in her mid-thirties, married to Prince Albert Honoré Charles of Monaco, she was a great patron, in the rather gushy style of society ladies, of art and artists. During the famous dinner party held in her honor by Frank Harris, Gray rose to recite the poem he was later to dedicate to her. She wrote him, telling of "what intense pleasure you gave me in repeating to me your strange, weird, fascinating verses."[23] When *Silverpoints* appeared, he sent her a copy along with a photograph.

A similar kind of "literary" friendship, with all its dreary and somewhat regressive innocence, is chronicled by Brocard Sewell in the history of poetic exchanges between the young Gray and the aspiring poetess, Olive Custance. Custance, who called herself "Opal," developed a very adolescent infatuation for Gray, addressing him as her "Prince of Poets," writing him poems and inviting him to tea; "And very soon he came and brought me 'Silverpoints' and was so kind and talked so beautifully—and looked so nice."[24]

What these episodes suggest is that Gray's poetry at this time was neither merely a craft nor a form of "art for art's sake." Rather, it may be argued that the poetry was conceived, recited, and later published with the intention of making poetry but also of literally making himself. In this sense, his art may be called a mask, in that it did have a use that was politic. It allowed Gray to play the requisite social games, like the flirtation with Olive Custance, while deflecting attention from his actual class, status, and personality. It gave him a role, a mode, and a manner. Gray's own sensitivity to its uses as a social instrument, almost a form of etiquette, may be judged from this clever *vers de société* published in a fashionable magazine during 1891:

VAUXHALL. 17—

Peerless ZELINDA, Can I fitly write
The joy still lingering of Yesternight?
You dined with LADY CAROLINE, and I
In the adjacent Bower. Though so nigh
To all I worship that the World can give—
But for your Charms, ZELINDA, need I live?
You seemed, for me, more distant than the Stars.
I hazarded and lost, while you waged Wars
of Ombre. Later, on the Promenade,
Among the Throng we passed, Your fan kept guard
Upon your Glances; then you dropped your Mask.
ZELINDA, it was mine, oh, grateful task!
To snatch it from the Ground, ere PETERHAM stoops—
And tangles his red Heels with CELIA's Hoops—
And kiss the Hand that takes it. Not your Glove
You dropped, nor Fan, nor Kerchief. For my Love
Your Mask you dropped, that all Vauxhall might see
It was ZELINDA threw her Gage to me.
What I have else to tell you will be soon;

I'll see you at the Play this afternoon,
Or in the Park.
ZELINDA, credit me,
Your humble Servant, and Eternally,'

JOHN GRAY[25]

Who would have thought this was written by a Cockney metal-turn-
er's apprentice from Bethnal Green? Its ease and elegance, its mastery
of eighteenth-century idiom, speak of Gray's own mastery of circum-
stance, a mastery won in part through just such literary ingenuity. If it
is superficial, if derivative, that attention to surface, that accomplished
mimicry, serves to deflect the reader from emotion or engagement. In
evolving a poetry that thus serves as an elegant carapace, Gray's early
poetic strategies cannot ultimately be divorced from the strategy of
other performances, on stage and off, by which he himself evolved as
the dandy, "Dorian" Gray.

Literary Society

Between 1890 and 1893, with an interlude of one year, Gray took up
lodgings in the Temple, a complex of rambling old buildings sloping
from the south side of Fleet Street down to the Thames embankment.
A picturesque haven from the roar of city life, with quiet squares and
winding passageways, the Temple was virtually unchanged since
Dickens described it in *Great Expectations*. Among its narrow streets,
Arthur Symons thought he could find the exact window at which
William Blake worked, looking from Fountain Court down through
an opening between the houses, sharing the river and the hills be-
yond.[26] Such associations made the area ideal for the literary man,
although it was rightfully the residence of lawyers, the Temple being
one of the Inns of Court. It was convenient (ten minutes from the
theaters and restaurants of the Strand) and relatively cheap, but, ac-
cording to Max Beerbohm, who was vehement in persuading his
friend Reggie Turner not to move there, it lacked every modern con-
venience: "People living there," he reported, "spend their time in
prolonged gloom & discomfort & despair: . . . they can think of
nothing but food decently cooked and decently served, and have a

perpetual craving for hot-water laid on, which never leaves them even in after-life."[27]

In fact the rooms, while spartan, varied from the miserable garret rented by George Moore to the sunny rooms overlooking Fountain Court taken by Arthur Symons, who found "that when I entered it for the first time in my life, to call on [George] Moore, I was seized by a sudden fascination which never left me."[28] At this date (March 1891) Gray lodged in a private house across from the Temple, at 62 Chancery Lane, but a month later, when he moved to No. 3, Plowden Buildings, the Temple was becoming known as another literary gathering place.[29] In 1892, Joseph Hone (Yeats's future biographer) left the Fitzroy Settlement to live there, and in 1895 Yeats himself moved into a set of rooms which led, by a narrow corridor, to those of Arthur Symons. Ernest Dowson would often come to visit and sometimes stay for the night, although he was still working at his family's dock on the Thames. Even Wilde, who despised Bohemia, was recorded to have been lured to the Plowden Buildings, the Temple, in the spring of 1893 to sit for a bust.[30] It was to be sculpted by Henri Teixeira de Mattos (Gray was later to dedicate "Mishka" to him in *Silverpoints*) and was, reportedly, a complete disaster.

In short, the sedate Temple, home of the dry legal quibble, had become nothing less than a place of literary ferment. The fragmented, transient circles that gathered as the Rhymers' Club and in the various pubs—the Cock and the Crown, as well as the splendid rooms of the Café Royal—here took a settled form, perhaps not as organized as a colony but certainly having the rudiments of an intense, even ingrown, little society of like minds. Gray knew most of its inhabitants from the Rhymers. But after his move back to the Temple he drew particularly close to Dowson, who had once spoken so warmly of his poetry.

By 1892, Dowson had discovered in a young girl his poetic ideal: Adelaide Foltinowicz ("Missy"), the daughter of the owner of a Polish restaurant in the West End. Her parents, for obvious reasons, did not consider Dowson a prudent match; and there is little evidence that "Missy" was other than naive and kind, an unwitting player in Dowson's own imaginative drama. In later life, Father Gray "would describe, but only when the humour took him, how Dowson scribbled verses on the tablecloth in a Soho restaurant, wooing his Cynara as she served the spaghetti; and what wailing and lamentation went up one day when Dowson was told she had eloped with a chef."[31]

Dowson's letters reveal that Gray had become confidant and ally in his anxieties over "Poland." In July 1891, Dowson describes dinner with a group of Temple inmates:

I have been dining in Poland recently with a host of people—Swanton; W. Hall and Gray ("Dorian" Gray); also with one De Mattos, a man whom I, & doubtless you? have known by sight for years: a long, pale man with a hawk like nose, who was inveterate at the Arts & Letters. And Dorian, who is charming, returns frequently to the veal cutlet and the dingy green walls of my Eden: in fact he promises to be one of my most enthusiastic Polonais![32]

In March of 1892, Dowson wrote to Victor Plarr: "I have seen scarcely anyone lately but Gray & Hall. . . . In effect I am become far too absorbed to do anything but sit, in Poland, & gather the exquisite moments."[33] Gray, as an "enthusiastic Polonais," sympathized with Dowson's infatuation. In other ways, as well, Gray understood the importance of being a faithful audience; he attended Dowson's verse play, *The Pierrot of the Minute,* not once, but twice—in November of 1892 and March of 1893. But he could only look on helplessly as Dowson committed "all the accompaniments of poetry," which included, according to Gray, taking hashish.[34] Dowson, for his part, genuinely admired Gray's literary work, addressing him as "Poeta Optime" and praising the berated "Modern Actor" lecture, which Gray was to give in the winter of 1892.

Their dining partner on at least one expedition to "Poland" and to both performances of Dowson's play was Alexander Teixeira de Mattos ("Tex"): as Dowson described him, "inveterate at the Arts & Letters" and a fellow dweller of the Temple, who was also to become a literary collaborator. At the time, he was London correspondent for a number of Dutch newspapers and editor of the magazine *Dramatic Opinion.* The story has often been told of how de Mattos, who had already decided to make his fortune translating, began to farm out assigned work among his friends at the Temple, to Dowson, Symons, and Victor Plarr. In the autumn of 1891, after Gray had apparently made a trip to Holland from which he returned enthusiastic about the work of the young Dutch *symboliste* writers, de Mattos suggested that they together undertake the translation of one of its better known novels, Couperus's *Ecstasy*.[35] During the winter, Gray also composed a preface defending the translator's work as no longer "hack-work for governesses"; in the light of this defense, it is perhaps ironic that de Mattos later alleged that Gray had not translated from the original text.[36] *Ecstasy* was published in 1892 to mixed reviews, one of which enquired, apropos the English, "Who translated Mr. John Gray's preface?"[37]

A more improbable literary colleague was the swashbuckling Frank Harris. An aggressive, unacademic American, Harris had made his name as the editor of *The Fortnightly Review*. Dark, thick-set, heavy-moustached, Harris had been a war correspondent in Russia, a traveller, and an adventurer. He was once described as looking "like a mixture of lion-tamer and pugilist, and dressed like a parvenu millionaire."[38] Wilde clearly enjoyed Harris's outrageous behavior; they met frequently during 1892 and 1893, and though a scoundrel and a romancer, Harris showed an almost unfailing kindness and generosity toward Wilde.[39]

Still, it is difficult to imagine Gray, by all accounts the most tactful and self-effacing of friends, in such company. Indeed, he was on occasion embarrassed by Harris. In the summer of 1892, Gray apparently promised to do some scavenging for articles for the *Fortnightly Review*. When he contacted Herbert Horne (of the Fitzroy Street settlement) to arrange, at Harris's behest, a meeting at the Café Royal, he added apologetically, "If you resent any or all of this pray forgive me my share in the offence."[40]

For his part, Harris regarded Gray as a man of "not only great personal distinction, but charming manners and a marked poetic gift."[41] As a letter dating from August 1892 makes clear, Harris interested himself in furthering Gray's literary career. At the time Gray was negotiating with John Lane over the publication of *Silverpoints,* delayed throughout the autumn and not, in fact, to appear until the next spring. In this instance, Harris took upon himself the role of critic, thus influencing the final form of at least one poem, Gray's translation of Rimbaud's "À la Musique." Gray apparently took the initiative by asking whether this poem could be published in *The Fortnightly.* "Now for your question," Harris replied,

If you can make the French-Square picture ["À la Musique"] right; that with "Beautiful Ladies" etc & the Flower piece could go in *The Fortnightly*, either next month (September) or October. I shall do my uttermost to get them in the Septr. No. But pray get the French piece right. I've thought much of it & feel sure that "I struggle to define / The subtle torso's hesitating line" should end the sensual note. Then the girls stop to give him an opportunity to speak—laugh with embarrassment & think him an idiot when he doesn't avail himself of the chance & then he passing on "feels faint kisses creeping on his lips." If I thought the stripping naked helped the poem I'd not ask you to alter it. Take what I say & weigh it for Art's sake. Don't take anything else I say more seriously. What makes for health is worth doing—but one man's food—

Then after the French scene is perfect don't forget *prose*—an article or two or twenty in the *F.R.* can only do you good.

So far as I can make the *entrée* easy to you I will. In all things believe me—not a monitor—my own conduct of life's anything but exemplary—but a sincere friend who feels greatly drawn to you.

Yours always, FRANK HARRIS[42]

But for some reason the *entrée,* at least to *The Fortnightly,* was not made at all. None of the three poems mentioned in the letter (although they appeared later in *Silverpoints*) were to be published there, nor was anything else by John Gray. Probably these plans were abandoned, with others, when Gray suffered a breakdown during late summer and autumn of 1892. Certainly their nonappearance had little to do with Harris's censorship of the two Rimbaud lines

J'ai bientôt déniché la bottine, le bas . . .
—Je reconstruis les corps, brûlé de belles fièvres

which Gray had originally rendered as

> I have stripped off the boots the stockings now
> Naked they stand my eyes embrace their hips

and which Gray "improved" (on Harris's advice) to

> Only my rustling tread, deliberate, slow;
> The rippled silence from the still leaves drips.[43]

Yet it is a rich irony that the "improvement" should be suggested by Frank Harris, of all people—the very man who enjoyed jolting his audience with obscenities, and author of that pornotopia, *My Life and Loves*. His rare show of propriety here may well have been dictated by a knowledge of what *Fortnightly* readers would and would not tolerate. It is simply another irony that, for all his literary caution, Gray was not to escape the reputation of a "decadent" poet.

But Frank Harris had, in a sense, already made Gray's *entrée* into polite literary society by inviting him as a guest to that famous dinner held at Claridge's in honor of Alice, Princess of Monaco, some time in 1891. To this party Harris also invited Oscar Wilde and another Irish writer, George Moore. Putting two Irish writers together at the same table is, it is generally conceded, a large social risk; a greater hazard in this instance, as Moore and Wilde, the arch-realist and the arch-formalist, had already clashed. To make matters worse, George Moore had the reputation of being at the mercy of his temperament. In the event, Wilde set himself to please. A fictive version of the evening recounts how Wilde's talk first intrigued, then charmed, the prickly Moore. What actually occurred seems to have been more in the line of a poetry reading. Among those who recited was "Dorian" Gray, his "strong, weird, fascinating verses" so intriguing the Princess that she later recalled their effect when writing from the Palace of Monaco to thank him for his photograph and the vellum-bound edition of *Silverpoints:*

My dear poet,

The photo has just come with the book and I can't say what pleasure both give me—Since I first heard you recite, that evening Frank Harris gave us a dinner. I was most enthusiastic. They carried me very far away. Since then, I saw you again, heard of more of that soft music & the charm was to me greater. Now I get that lovely work of art & am intensely grateful & happy.[44]

The Princess of Monaco, her dinner guests, the Rhymers—these were not Gray's only audience. It was with such a recitation, too, that Gray won Walter Pater's approbation. In a letter written to André Raffalovich after the turn of the century, Arthur Symons recalls the effect of the performance: "I remember meeting Pater at your house. He who was then John Gray repeated one of his poems. A certain expression passed over Pater's face and he asked Gray to say it over again. 'The rest was silence.' "[45] Pater appears to have taken a mild paternal interest in Gray's poetic career; when *Silverpoints* appeared, he was one of the first to praise it, but in private conversation, it seems, as no review of his has yet been found.[46]

These episodes indicate to what extent the impact of Gray's poetry depended on its performance and on the response of an audience to the sight of an exquisite young man reciting equally exquisite verse. Each of the several circles of which he was a member offered Gray an audience and, as often as not, the encouragement of such admirers as Wilde, Harris and Alice, Princess of Monaco. If Gray sometimes exploited the opportunities they offered, he could also be, as he proved with Dowson, a true friend. It was just such a literary friendship that would rescue "Dorian" Gray from the consequences of his performance as dandy when, in the autumn of 1892, Arthur Symons arranged for him to meet the poet and novelist, André Raffalovich. From the time of that meeting on, Gray would set his feet on the path of retreat from the Temple and its literary world, a path which, eventually, would become the road to Rome. But in 1891 and during the spring and summer of 1892, Gray was still seeking an *entrée* to that world of public performance which, as "Dorian" Gray, in imitation of his master Wilde, he pursued as "the intensified desire for life."

"My Life is Like a Music-Hall. . . ."

The young artist of the 1890s did not value experience for its own sake. On its own terms, life was too dictatorial: it was life that said we "ought" because we "can." Also, life was messy, unpredictable, and at times outrageous; fate could be mastered only by meeting its violence with a countering violence. Of itself, will was not sufficient; only Art could impose order where there was confusion; form where there was flux; intensity where there was dissipation. Pater was charged with preaching such doctrine in the subtle epilogue of *The Renaissance;* but it was Wilde and those caught in the wake of his influence who came to believe that experience could only be redeemed by an intensity artificially induced. Some took hashish; others drank; still others, like Lionel Johnson, tried to live only through their art, sleeping by day and waking at night to write. Yeats was fond of intoning a maxim of Villiers de l'Isle Adam: "As for living—our servants will do that for us."

For Gray, life at its pitch could be located as exactly as if it were a destination: first of all, in the "haunts of sin"; secondly, in the theater, which he, along with so many of his generation, identified with a kind of consummate vitality. The two were not mutually exclusive; indeed, when Gray located the "true theatre" in the music halls, he explicitly identified the two centers of "life" as being one and the same, music halls then being notorious as places of assignation. As if in imitation of his literary double, "Dorian" Gray visited this demimonde and entertained its occasions of sin. Such experiences confirmed him in his creation of himself through artifice, being neither truly "experience" (even Gray found the demimonde unreal in comparison with his ordinary life as civil servant) nor truly "art" (even Gray found it sordid). But these occasions were transformed by the spirit in which they were encountered, as part of the larger drama of "Dorian" Gray.

The spring of 1891 started quietly enough. Gray had made one, possibly two, appearances at the Rhymers. He was working away at his translations from the new French poets, and hoped to make another trip across the Channel. This desire was whetted when, in mid-March, Wilde returned from Paris full of the news of his encounters (as Gray reported to Fénéon) with Mallarmé, Verlaine, Jean Moréas, and Henri de Régnier. Gray confessed that he hoped "to visit Paris with [Wilde] in a little while."[47] But since early March he had been suffering from serious bronchitis, which now took the form of a recurrent fever, erupting every third day for a few hours. Gray had to take sick leave from work and leave London for the "watering-places" of the south coast of England. This disease, diagnosed by Gray's doctor as a "nervous fever," was apparently to recur at various intervals for the next year.

It was not until February 1892 that Gray had managed to reach France. Although our only source places Gray in Tours and not in Paris, other evidence suggests his presence there. Certainly by this time Gray was already acquainted with Marcel Schwob, a critic, translator, and collaborator on several *symboliste* reviews and a writer of considerable talent.[48] Gray wrote to Schwob in early 1892 about "Oscar, who will be in Paris at the same time as this letter," during the visit which was to become "the 'great event' of the Parisian literary salons" that season.[49] Schwob at first conceived for the visiting aesthete "a rapturous admiration," and was to act, in the words of Jean Lorrain, as Wilde's pilot and "cornac," i.e., elephant keeper. Although he quickly became disillusioned with Wilde, Schwob's admiration for Gray burned steadily. Meanwhile, Gray's introductions had been extended to at least another of the new poets he was then struggling to translate; he was initiated, most probably by Fénéon, into the set that gathered at Mallarmé's apartment on the Rue de Rome every Tuesday. There is only the bare report that he was considered very much one of the circle, Mallarmé having "a specially warm place in his heart" for Gray and Dowson.[50]

The only sure evidence of this second trip to France is that of an unpublished letter to Gray from Robert Sherard, who had been, for almost a decade, an idolatrous disciple of Wilde.[51] The great-grandson of Wordsworth and himself a writer, Sherard was to become Wilde's biographer not once but three times over. "A kind of god with straw-coloured hair, tired of his divinity" was how Gray described him to Fénéon in early January 1891, promising that, when he came to Paris soon, he would introduce his friends to each other.[52] But, as a long-term resident of Paris, it was Sherard, not Gray, who accompanied Wilde on his triumphal progress through the Parisian *salons* in November and December 1891.[53] As Sherard's letter makes clear, however, Gray *had* recently been in Tours with Sherard and, while there, became involved in some rather shady dealings with the editor of the local newspaper:

> Hotel de La Boule d'Or
> Tours,
> Tuesday night.

My dear John Gray,

I am back here for to-day & to-morrow as Franchet has not been loyal & I have had to see him again. I have had a long interview with him this afternoon & believe we shall at last get some satisfaction out of him. I came down by that same train, & in it [*sic*] as ever since I have been here. I have missed you sadly. At the same time I have had the comfort of missing somebody else—It is no compensation, however. The people here were most affable, though our obsequious old waiter has left. I am writing this in a room adjoining our apartment, which is in every way a more comfortable room. But in spite of Vouvray Mousseux, I am feeling very tired as, as last time, I came down after a *nuit blanche*.

How delighted Oscar must be. I devoured the notices. It is a perfect triumph. I am announcing it in the French papers. Schwob who dined with me & Philips a night or two ago was enchanté & so is everybody here. Schwob, by the way, asked to be remembered to you most kindly.

I hear from Davidson that Barlas proposes a fresh act of folly as soon as his bail expires. I do hope that this is not so, as it would be fatal for him. So far he has not done badly, for he has won much sympathy & a number of admirers who have written to me. One by the way was most anxious to know about your work. I wrote him about you. By the way I see the papers have been busy with your name of late. You ought to get your book out soon.

Rothenstein asked me to dinner one night about a fortnight ago & we dined together on the following night also. I am afraid I shall never like him at all. I have been but little in the Latin quarter of late & hope eventually to break myself of it altogether. Not because I regret my frequentations or conduct there, but because I want to work. I drew a vast inspiration & resolution from Balzac's statue this afternoon, but will it last?

Write to me when you have leisure & in your prayers wish me a safe deliverance from Franchet, Vincent & the rest. Que diable allais—je faire dans cette galère. There is one libel suit coming on for an article which Madame Vincent had inserted in the *Gil Blas* & I fear my name will be involved, & altogether I dread the future of this affair, which is not a creditable one. But we did not know this when we took it up & so neither of us is to blame. I say "we" & "us" lest you should think que je vous en veux in any degree. I shall stick to my last in the future.

Yours ever

—Robert[54]

The letter is identifiable as Sherard's from the handwriting; all the references point to a date of late February 1892. Wilde's "perfect triumph," *Lady Windermere's Fan,* first dazzled its audience on 20 February 1892. A letter of Dowson's dated 14 February clears up the reference to Barlas, a Rhymer whom he calls "a charming poet and anarchist, who was lately run in for shooting the House of Commons."[55] In the same postscript, Dowson adds that Gray was threatening one newspaper with a libel suit for being "busy" with his name.

This letter was received by Gray at a trying time. He had just given (on 7 February) a lecture in tandem with Wilde which had provoked reports that he was the "Dorian" of Wilde's sensational novel. He was about to enter into months of turmoil which would end with a rupture with his "loved Master" and thoughts of suicide. Sherard's letter indicates that Gray was also in trouble on the other side of the Channel. Sherard seems to be alluding to a complicated affair; he mentions no names, but says that it occurred in Touraine and that he had to return to "T—" to sort it out. It was a case of bribery and blackmail.[56] As so often in the history of Gray, we are reduced to conjecture, supported by a few tantalizing facts. However, it is clear from the letter that Gray with Sherard was unwittingly drawn into some distasteful and perhaps unlawful activity.

Gray returned to London some time in mid-winter. Early in the new year his name began to be associated with the director of a new artistic enterprise, the Independent Theatre. He was Jack Thomas Grein, a drama critic, playwright, and manager, who had come to England from Holland. In 1891 he set up an experimental theater, along the lines of Antoine's Théâtre Libre. He had two aims: to bring

Continental drama to the English stage, and to produce plays by new writers which were too risky for the conventional stage.

Grein launched the Independent Theatre with a production of Ibsen's *Ghosts*. Following on the heels of an earlier Ibsen production (*A Doll's House* in 1889) its impact has been compared to "the first performance of Wagner's operas, and the appearance of the Impressionist painters."[57] To the conventional, *Ghosts* was a symbolic outrage, an affront to all they held civilized, an embodiment of "decadence." Only thus can one account for the wild display of invective and vituperation, epitomized by the lead article in *The Daily Telegraph* (14 March 1891), which compared the play to an open drain, a loathsome sore unbandaged, a dirty act done publicly, a lazar-house with all its doors and windows open. Bestial, cynical, disgusting, poisonous, sickly, delirious, indecent, loathsome, fetid, literary carrion, crapulous stuff, clinical stuff: "It is difficult to expose in decorous words," the writer continued, "the gross and almost putrid indecorum of this play."

Charged with such crimes against public decency, the Independent Theatre was soon in debt and at odds with the censorship regulations. To circumvent both, Grein redefined his enterprise as "a private club" and put it on a subscription basis. Known officially as the Independent Theatre Society, it would rent various available venues for its productions. Slowly, Grein built up a circle of keen young playwrights, among them Bernard Shaw, Arthur Symons, George Moore, and Frank Harris, who were willing to risk plays for this, the second season of 1891–92.

Grein was not a man without a sense of humor. He decided to avenge himself on the critics with a "little joke": a spoof of the most advanced "decadent" drama. Entitled "In the Garden of Citrons," it was published under Grein's pen name, "Emilio Montanaro," and solemnly reviewed by another conspirator, Teixeira de Mattos, "from the proof sheets" for one of Grein's publications of the first week of January 1892. Its preface was fabricated by John Gray in his most archly precious, tangential style. This "'too-too' introduction" (as the *Star* was to call it) proceeds thus: "Whoso cares to do so will find in the *Garden of Citrons* naivety so naive that it is always blushing—at nothing—side by side with the most astounding precocity." To this, Gray adds a catalogue of nonexistent plays by the same author and a mock biography: "Once in the West Indies, in some moment of weary leisure and physical relaxation, the stifling air of Cuba, the fetid mist creeping up from the tobacco garden, ravished the soul of the young Italian planter, and the simple agriculturalist became the fantastic and complex poet."[58] Written in the new style of Maeterlinck, the play itself parodied the trivial dialogue, mysterious occurrences and elaborate synesthesia of the Belgian *symboliste*.

Predictably, the respectable *Theatre* took the piece at face value, and raged at the "veriest and tritest twaddle that ever came from the invention of anyone not a sentimental schoolgirl." For her part, Mrs. Grein recalls that, on the night of the play's first and final performance, the parrot, raising its voice in Italian, gave the show away, but "not before J. T. had his laugh and [the play] had enjoyed serious consideration in many quarters."[59]

None of this was calculated to allay the suspicions of the public. Was Grein serious or was he not? What was he about, if not to attack the inviolate prejudices of his audience? The uneasiness increased with his next production. Scarcely a month after this elaborate hoax, on 7 February 1892, Grein invited another *agent provocateur*, Oscar Wilde, to chair a meeting of the Playgoers' Club—a group Grein had organized to attend first nights and to hold a program of discussions.[60] Gray and Wilde were both members, and it was most probably Wilde who persuaded Gray to precede his remarks with Gray's on "The Modern Actor." That they conspired together is certain: Gray's paper introduces Wilde's by proposing their common theme, a radical redefinition of the nature of the actor. Wilde argued that, as performers, actors are less suitable than puppets; Gray, that the true actor is, in fact, none other than the performer of the vaudeville.

While Wilde contented himself with making debating points, Gray used the occasion to make a statement. He was entirely unsuited for the part of crusader. His voice, like Pater's, was a slow murmur: "A clumsy or ignorant person might have thought the voice was of a drunken man, or one half asleep," Gray later wrote in "The Person in Question." Yet the tone of his lecture suggests he was driven to make this statement out of a deep anger and frustration, even though the privacy of his temperament, his apparent aloofness, recoiled from such exposure. As if in self-protection, he veiled the lecture in metaphor and parable; but the ring of manifesto is not lost: "To spare any possibility of mystification, let me announce at once that by the modern actor I mean the Music Hall singer, the 'artiste' many estimable and rightly-inquisitive people have never seen, the 'professional' thought of by some only with horror and disgust."[61] Whereas by the nineties the actor of the legitimate theater had become a respectable and even idolized figure, the music hall *artiste* was regarded as degraded and vulgar, a concomitant of the halls' corrupt reputation. "Most, I suppose, look upon this person as more or less of a pariah," Gray continues: "those who so look upon him are perfectly right."

Gray goes further; to extremes, in fact. Not only the music hall *artiste* but "every actor, and indeed, every artist, is properly an outcast and unclassed person." For Gray, the lecture takes on the force of personal declaration: "England has been rich in singers; the best of these have been done to death. Give her the advantage of one or two doubtful exceptions; all the rest she has driven to exile and suicide and misery." Pure and childlike, the artist is tortured, not only by the Philistine but even by "those he would love," who "look upon him with dread and hate, or, taking courage from his harmlessness, try which of them can first draw from him a sob of pain. They mix ashes and offal with his food and his drink, and pretend themselves defiled by touching the thing that had left his hand, or by treading in one of his footprints" (p. 104). Gray, having noted the exaggeration, defends it as a "true description." The allure of such a picture, so reminiscent of Dickens's upholstered treatment of the prostitute and sinner, was for Gray the bad light in which the outcast places society as a visible emblem of its stupidity and cruelty. It was typical, a later friend said of Gray, for him to express himself exaggeratedly.[62] And it is true that the very extremity of the statement makes it difficult to take it with complete seriousness. How Gray regarded it is another matter. His histrionic manner suggests that, once again, in dramatizing his position, he was in danger of being taken in by his own performance; he was, in short, beginning to feel sorry for himself.

Such is the hazard inherent in his premise. If every artist is, first and foremost, an actor, there is always the moment that, as actors say, he brings the character home. In this case, the character is nearer home in the first place, no longer noble, no longer to be identified with the beautiful "mercenaries" of the conventional theater. The true actor is the juggler, the contortionist, the mime, the petticoat-dancer, the cloggie, and the magician: those who work in the world of trickery and suspect illusion; those who are drawn from the very streets in which Gray grew up. Gray would argue that they were the more authentic, not because they were, essentially, working class, but because nothing is done for them: even the music hall's "trashiest artiste has to face a difficult, a master feat—he must *act*," and by so doing, is able "to make something out of nothing, to so utter the words of his song as to give an illusion, to so dance that mechanical movements are rightly combined to a complete, a satisfying result in art."

The character that Gray "brought home" had a name: Albert Chevalier. Scarcely a year previously, Chevalier had left the legitimate (or, as Gray called it, the "dead") theater for the music halls, the theater which Gray predicted would be the theater of the future. In this claim Gray was not merely precocious but prescient: Beckett as well as Brecht (among others) were to exploit its routines, its patter, its clowns and bums. More significant is Gray's anticipation of what is now, in popular culture, the cult of personality. At a time when the actor of the legitimate theater was at last recognized as an artist, the music hall *artiste* was simply a celebrity, one who used the devices of his art to intensify his own eccentricities, to paraphrase a contemporary review in *The Artist and Journal of Home Culture*.[63] He made himself through his performances, as Gray recognized in a review remarkable for its hyperbole, praising Chevalier for an ability to reveal in the "single moment in the life of a single individual . . . all its human significance." Chevalier's was the spontaneous mastery of illusion which Gray hailed as "a key to all life and all emotion,"[64] and which marked him, through his "sure and supple intelligence as an artist," a "prince in the world of masks."[65]

In this "prince in the world of masks," Gray found an emblem, not merely fitting but disconcertingly apt, for his own performance as "Dorian." Chevalier, like Gray, rose from the working class. Both had Cockney accents, although Gray's was modulated and Chevalier's correspondingly exaggerated; Symons christened him the "Coster's laureate." Both had been taken up by the trendy fashion-setters of the day: Chevalier was even asked to read at the Playgoers' Club in 1893, now that a taste for the working class was part of the artistic revolution. As Symons and Gray understood, the actor of the music halls, although nominally "an outcast and unclassed person," was in fact the mocking image in the mirror, the double but the double disavowed. "My life is like a music-hall," Symons wrote:

> Where, in the impotence of rage,
>   Chained by enchantment to my stall,
> I see myself upon the stage
>   Dance to amuse a music-hall.[66]

This is not the work of magic; it is the effect of power. What counted to Gray was Chevalier's hold on the audience. In the music halls they were rowdy, rough, often drunk; they would cheer or boo, talk or simply walk out if they did not care for a particular "turn." While conceding that they were a much more difficult audience than that of the legitimate theater, Chevalier mastered them. He understood that the music hall artist's power was highly manipulative. Like the dandy, he seemed *sui generis,* entirely dependent on the energy of his own self-transformation. He appeared as in a vacuum, his outcast state being prerequisite, for anything less than a constantly changing audience might compromise illusion. He is, as Gray names him, a "prince in the world of masks," though for only that "single moment." His enchantment is, in part, in the very labor of its contrivance, its speciousness which, like *trompe l'oeil,* gives the viewer a sense of intense, consummate reality—until the second look.

Thus in the artifice of the music hall Gray sought, as did many others, a world outside that of Victorian earnestness and duty, a larger world of the imagination which was also inextricably mixed with the world of "sin." Symons confessed: "I lived in them for the mere delight and the sheer animal excitement they gave me. I liked that glitter, barbarous, intoxicating, the violent animality, the entire spectacle, with absurd faces, gestures, words, and the very odour and suffocating heat."[67] The animal excitement was explicit: a music hall such as the Empire, where Gray was to accompany Pierre Louÿs in July, was described by a contemporary as "the most popular whore market in London."[68] But if the search also led Gray to become actually involved in the demimonde of sexual encounter, blackmail, and brothels, this was not its most harmful effect. Rather, it is that it led Gray into taking his fantasy of himself as an "unclassed" person to heart, that it led him to destroy the only reality that could act as an antidote to his fictional pose. And, for the first time, the public also began to take his performance seriously with the appearance of the first reviews of the "Modern Actor" lecture.

At the conclusion of this particular evening, Wilde turned to Gray and congratulated him on being misunderstood, "a distinction he [Wilde] himself shared."[69] For his part, Dowson greeted the speech with enthusiasm. "*Mes compliments* upon your Paradox of Café concerts," Dowson wrote Gray. "I am quite of your advice, and hold that the artist should be too much absorbed in God, the Flesh and the Devil, to consider the World, quâ World, at all."[70] Wilde defended it in print as a "brilliant fantastic lecture."[71] But the newspapers were more taken by the mannerisms of Gray's delivery. *The Players,* surely as parody, reported, "Delicacy is developed to an extent almost abnormal in Mr. John Gray. . . . [He] has builded himself a world of strange féerie, wherein he dwells, anticipating the re-birth of the native drama within its limits. . . . His language is irridescent, or perhaps scented. . . . His method of delivery is very gentle. He ceased; he did not conclude."[72]

This was, without doubt, Gray's first real claim to public notice. And although he had been upset the day before this performance by the report of a gossip columnist that he was "said to be the original Dorian of the same name," it did not prevent him from appearing once more *devant le public* on 4 March.[73] The occasion was both more exposed and more momentous, a program of three plays for the Independent Theatre, one of which, Théodore de Banville's *Le Baiser,* Gray had himself translated. Once again, the Independent Theatre was in crisis. Their previous production, a dramatization of Zola's *Thérèse Raquin,* had been assailed almost as hysterically as the notorious production of *Ghosts.* This night, then, opening with Gray's reading and continuing with Gray's translation, was to hold a strategic importance in the future of the Independent Theatre.[74]

Grein realized that this was a last-ditch stand. But he knew how to pack an audience. In the house, fresh from his triumph of *Lady Windermere's Fan,* was Oscar Wilde, who had rented a box for himself and a "suite of young gentlemen," probably including a visiting French poet, Pierre Louÿs, and Edward Shelley, the office boy from the Bodley Head.[75] All were conspicuously wearing green carnations, the badge of Parisian homosexuals which Wilde had made his own, though most people, including those in Wilde's entourage, had not the faintest notion of what it stood for. Opposite, George Moore had rented another box. Below, decorously, were to be found Henry James and J. M. Barrie. Other loyal supporters and authors were either in the orchestra or behind the scenes. These measures together with the wider and less controversial appeal of the plays gained for the evening neither wild success nor wild rebuke. It was the first thaw in public opposition to Grein's theater and did much, in the opinion of critics, to justify its existence.

Reviews of Gray's little dramatic piece were mixed and even contradictory, noting on the one hand, the adroitness of the translation and, on the other, a certain clumsiness in the verse. One critic commented that "some Cockney rhymes occasionally offend the ear."[76] Another "dramatic critic" was openly hostile. In an attack on Gray's lecture in *The Players* about a month later, entitled "The Very Little Vance," the writer began by recalling "The Great Vance," a music-hall singer of a few years back, a flashy and conceited person of atrocious taste, a prop of the music hall at the most degenerate stage of its career. During his heyday the huge Vance often appeared clad in startling colors and gaudy accoutrements—a puce, lemon, and bottle-green suit, a gold-knobbed cane, huge diamond studs, the costume of a type known in the halls as a Heavy Swell. Now, the critic snorted, the music hall had found a new star, "whom by way of contrast I will call 'The Very Little Vance,' otherwise that music-hall champion and illiterate lecturer, Mr. John Gray." He ended by sneering at the "execrable English" of this "very silly youth."[77]

The savagery of the attack, not dissimilar from others which were to appear during the ensuing months, may have been prompted by what the reviewer saw as Gray's getting above himself, a working-class boy on the make. For him, the Cockney Swell, the Toff of the

music hall, was a fitting double for this "very silly youth." Gray's
hurt reply shows how vulnerable he had become. Confessing that he
"had rightly feared offence," he is bewildered as to why his words,
"blameless when they left my lips . . . were afterwards picked up in
gutters, soiled and distorted, and turned to all unworthy account, so
that I am hissed and brayed against in public places."[78] The naiveté
rings true. It is possible that, while defending his notion of the actor,
Gray had himself allowed the mask to slip. Or perhaps he did not re-
alize that the public had already cast him in the role of Wilde's pro-
tégé, as the disciple to fit the face of *The Picture of Dorian Gray*. The
critics had seen something arresting, an impeccably dressed, beautiful
young man reading, in an accent not entirely free of its Cockney ori-
gins, an affectedly avant-garde paper. But it was not Gray's English or
his dandified affectations alone that excited their hostility: it was di-
rected toward him as a creature of Oscar Wilde, in whose fate John
Gray had by now become almost fatally implicated.

A Picture of Dorian Gray

The crisis that overtook Gray in the autumn of 1892 was anticipated
by several episodes during the preceding spring and summer. Gray's
unease began when his "Dorian" nickname became public currency.
The Star of 6 February, the day before his reading of the "Modern
Actor" lecture, announced on its front page that

> Mr John Gray, who writes the "too-too" introduction to the latest dra-
> matic novelty, Emilio Montanaro's *In the Garden of Citrons,* is said to be the
> original Dorian of the same name. Mr. Gray, who has cultivated his manner
> to the highest pitch of languor yet attained, is a well-known figure of the
> Playgoers' Club, where, though he often speaks, he is seldom heard.[79]

Gray was so disturbed by the comments that he initiated legal pro-
ceedings; about a week later, Dowson was writing Victor Plarr the
latest news, "that Gray, of whom I am seeing a good deal just at pre-
sent, pursues the 'Star' for a libel asserting him to be 'the original
Dorian of that name.' This will be droll."[80] *The Star* was home ter-
ritory for the Rhymers, and certainly the whole episode may have

been originally intended as a joke; but Gray took it seriously enough to take out an injunction.[81]

In any case, the paper was put to full rout. Nine days later, on 15 February, *The Star* withdrew its allegation, adding, for good measure, a few tactful remarks about Gray's play:

Mr John Gray has done into graceful verse Théodore de Banville's pretty conceit "Le Baiser", a one-act piece produced at the Théâtre Français about four years ago. Mr Gray's translation, which preserves the characteristic delicacy and dexterity of the original, is to be produced by the Independent Theatre Society.

By the bye, we are told that some people have taken quite seriously a suggestion which appeared in this column a few days since that Mr Gray was the prototype of Mr Oscar Wilde's Dorian Gray. The risks of the New Humour could not have a more unfortunate illustration than the acceptance as serious of a statement that a skilful young literary artist of promise like Mr Gray could possibly be the original of the monstrous Epicurean of Mr Wilde's creation, and we greatly regret the erroneous impression that has been produced. Apart from the fact that Mr Wilde's acquaintance with Mr Gray did not commence until after the publication of this novel, Mr Wilde would be as likely to draw a character from life as to call a photograph an artistic production. Character sketching he regards as literary work, but not as literary art.[82]

This line of defense, clearly worded by Wilde himself, was not only untrue, but also ineffective, for by the time the retraction was published, the rumor had taken on a life of its own. Three days previously, in a squib for the forthcoming production of *Lady Windermere's Fan,* the *Daily Telegraph* referred to Oscar Wilde's appearance at the Playgoers' Club in the role of the "literary and dramatic godfather of a youth, who, with sublime assurance leaves Ibsen, Maeterlinck and Montanaro far in the shade of obscure Philistinism."[83] Gray clearly was upset by the passage, following as it did so closely on the heels of *The Star*'s "Dorian" remark. His reactions to both suggest that more than a pride in his independence as poet and critic was involved; he had never hidden the obvious influence of Wilde on his own work. Now the scene had changed and the implications were larger. Once the nickname had been flattering, a tribute to his success in inventing himself as a poet, a recognition of his discipleship to Wilde. But now there was a distinct danger in the assumption that literary *personae* are drawn from life. As Wilde's affair with Alfred Douglas became more flamboyant, even the most obtuse began to see in Dorian's seduction the truth of life imitating art.[84] In short, to be named in the spring of 1892 as Wilde's "protégé" or as the original of "Dorian Gray" was the equivalent of being named Wilde's lover.

What happened next is a matter for conjecture. The most probable explanation is that Gray acted quickly during the week following the *Telegraph*'s remarks. He went to Wilde, pointed out the dangers and consequences of such a rumor, and asked his help in writing a letter to put an end to speculation. While Wilde himself was indifferent to such dangers, he was generous to a fault with his friends; thus to the end of a long letter correcting the *Telegraph*'s version of his own contribution to the evening, Wilde added praise, not merely of Gray's lecture, but of Gray himself:

> Suffer me one more correction. Your writer describes the author of the brilliant fantastic lecture on "The Modern Actor" as "a *protégé*" of mine. Allow me to state that my acquaintance with Mr John Gray is, I regret to say, extremely recent, and that I sought it because he had already a perfected mode of expression both in prose and verse. All artists in this vulgar age need protection certainly. Perhaps they have always needed it. But the nineteenth-century artist finds it not in Prince, or Pope, or patron, but in high indifference of temper, in the pleasure of the creation of beautiful things, and the long contemplation of them in disdain of what in life is common and ignoble, and in such felicitous sense of humour as enables one to see how vain and foolish is all popular opinion, and popular judgment, upon the wonderful things of art. These qualities Mr John Gray possesses in a marked degree. He needs no other protection, nor, indeed, would he accept it.
>
> I remain, sir, your obedient servant,
>
> OSCAR WILDE[85]

It does not matter that the substance of this defense was untrue; for Wilde, lying was the necessary condition of all art, and in any case he was protecting a friend. But as already noted, Gray undoubtedly met

Wilde before the first publication of *The Picture of Dorian Gray* in July 1890.[86] There is little doubt that by the time *The Star* and the *Telegraph* reported on their acquaintance, it was neither "extremely recent" nor an "acquaintance" at all. Whatever had passed between them, it had a history sufficiently charged for both of them to wish to repudiate it.

What was that history? It is, for the most part, hidden, and, in the spring of 1892, was still to play itself out. Letters between Gray and Pierre Louÿs reveal that by summer 1892 Gray had become part of a homosexual circle centering around Wilde and including Edward Shelley, the office boy at the Bodley Head who had become one of Wilde's lovers. In an early letter to Louÿs, Gray speaks of this circle as Wilde's "school," and his own position as disciple had by this date its double entendre.[87] Max Beerbohm gave a public, if anonymous, opinion when he accused Wilde of "'corrupting the youth'" and John Gray of being "one of the corrupt."[88] Perhaps the nature of this circle can best be judged by an offhand remark of Wilde's. When in December 1894 a university magazine, *The Chameleon,* published a short, intense, and soon notorious story about the tragic love of a priest for his acolyte, Wilde casually wrote his confidante, Ada Leverson: "'The Priest and the Acolyte' is not by Dorian: though you were right in discerning by internal evidence that the author has a profile." In other words: Wilde found its author (as he found Gray) extremely attractive—"an undergraduate of strange beauty."[89]

Likewise, on "internal evidence," it seems clear that Dorian Gray had a precedent with a profile. Wilde was certainly taken with Gray's beauty. He may well have met him in an artist's studio (with Ricketts in the Vale?) as Lord Wotton first encounters Dorian in the book. And Lord Wotton's spiritual/sexual seduction rings true to the idealized tone of the actual friendship.

External evidence also implicates Gray. As we have seen, one memoir recalls a dinner with Gray and Wilde at a date before the first publication of *Dorian Gray.* To this may be added the observation of Arthur Symons (in 1903) that *The Picture of Dorian Gray* was "partly made out of Wilde himself, partly out of two other men, both of whom are alive."[90] Symons first met Wilde in October 1890, four months after the first version of *Dorian Gray* appeared in *Lippincott's Monthly Magazine* but seven months before it was published, in expanded form, as a novel. Sometime between these two dates, Symons records how "at a Private View in the New Gallery, as I came downstairs, I came on Wilde, in the midst of his admirers. . . . Seeing me he made a gesture, and as I went up he introduced me to John Gray, then in what is called 'the zenith' of his youth . . . I was not aware that he was supposed to be the future Dorian Gray of Wilde's novel."[91]

Additional evidence is Wilde's persistent habit of using the names of friends and acquaintances in his work. After falling out with his publisher, John Lane, Wilde created a champagne-swilling butler by the name of Lane in *The Importance of Being Earnest*. The name of another close friend appears in *The Picture of Dorian Gray*, when Robert Sherard makes his entrance as "Sir Anthony Sherard." Sherard objected vigorously to the use of his name in the original *Lippincott's* version, but it was not altered in Wilde's revisions for the book ten months later.[92] Nor was the connection between Lord Henry Wotton and the notorious homosexual Lord Henry Somerset lost on the reading public. Certainly the use of Gray's surname for the book's beautiful, boyish hero must be more than coincidence.

Apart from this evidence, there is an arresting similarity between Wilde's description of his fictional hero and John Gray. "Dorian Gray has not got a cool, calculating, conscienceless character at all," Wilde wrote, protesting a misinterpretation of his hero:

On the contrary, he is extremely impulsive, absurdly romantic, and is haunted all through his life by an exaggerated sense of conscience which mars his pleasures for him and warns him that youth and enjoyment are not everything in the world. It is finally to get rid of the conscience that had dogged his steps from year to year that he destroys the picture; and thus in his attempt to kill conscience Dorian Gray kills himself.[93]

This is both a perceptive and a prophetic account of the history of John Gray, who, "haunted all through his life by an exaggerated sense of conscience," sought as "Dorian" Gray to conceal his past, and as Father Gray, to destroy it.

That proleptic quality speaks less of Wilde's insight into John Gray, however, than of the power of his archetype. If John Gray, like

Dorian, was of arresting personal beauty, so were Alfred Douglas and others; if Gray, like Dorian, was infatuated with an actress and wrote her poetry, infatuation with actresses was the malady of the times.[94] If Gray had become, like his fictional counterpart, attracted to the Roman Church, that too, was part of the nineties ritual. Clearly Huysmans's Des Esseintes, the hero of *À Rebours,* was one major "model" for the novel.

Which is only to underline Wilde's contention that it is Art—not Life—that provides the models for our experience. And it should warn against thinking too simplistically about the *roman à clef.* Certainly Wilde took a mischievous pleasure in naming his fictions after actual people, and his actual people after his fictions. John Gray's name, his striking profile, his instinctive dandyism, may well have provided Wilde with flesh for his character. But in many points he is dissimilar: by birth, status, and class. John Gray may have been *a* model, but he was probably not *the* model for Wilde's Dorian Gray. What happened to Gray, however, was that, like Dorian, he was corrupted by a book in which he found "a kind of prefiguring type of himself." Dorian Gray was what John Gray was to become. In Dorian Gray, John Gray discovered less a pose than a fate, the shape that experience was to take for him.

How could a fictional *persona* come to exert such influence over Gray's life? It was, I believe, possible because Gray was to Wilde an extraordinarily submissive—Bernard Shaw unkindly added "abject"—disciple.[95] In one sense, Shaw was wrong; Gray was able to see Wilde objectively and, as a critic, to distinguish between the man and his work. Gray once stated that he was not in "any great sympathy with the methods and the feats of Mr. Oscar Wilde," since he had "always disclaimed respect for the forms of charlatanism in which it has pleased him [Wilde] to indulge, and which he would, we suspect, be about the first himself to admit." Yet even after that disclaimer, Gray could still judge *Lady Windermere's Fan* comparable to Swift's *Polite Conversation* and Sheridan's *School for Scandal* and, "as a specimen of true comedy . . . head and shoulders above any of its contemporaries."[96]

Yet Gray was dominated by Wilde in a way that other admirers were not, perhaps because the likes of Lionel Johnson and Alfred Douglas had no need to look to Wilde, as Gray did, for an education in how to live. They had ties of class, university, and family, while Gray apparently moved in a self-created vacuum. It is impossible to know whether Gray was Wilde's lover; that issue is of less importance than Gray's drive to efface himself in order to play out the dandified role of "Dorian," which, through Wilde, was his entrée into fashionable society and literary success.

Still, the relationship was not one of cool and calculated exploitation, but in character with "Dorian Gray" was in many ways "absurdly romantic," intense, and idealized. And so, despite Wilde's own infatuation with Douglas, Gray remained deeply attached to Wilde during the course of 1892. It says much about the nature of Gray's feelings that, in October 1892, when his translation of Bourget's *A Saint and Others* appeared, Gray inscribed his copy to Wilde: "To my loved master my dear friend Homage."[97] Wilde called him "the poet" and offered that summer to underwrite the cost of publishing his first book of poems. It was this romanticizing of the relationship to which Wilde paid homage when he wrote, years later, to Douglas from prison: "When I compare my friendship with you to my friendship with such still younger men as John Gray and Pierre Louÿs I feel ashamed. My real life, my higher life was with them and such as they."[98]

Thus during the first half of 1892 Gray was, as his friend Dowson teased, "incurably given over to social things."[99] In the small literary successes—the poetry published in the second *Dial*, the "Modern Actor" lecture, and the favorable reception of his translations of Bourget, Banville, and Couperus—Gray saw at last the fruits of his effort, in his own words, "to elbow me a place" in the literary and social world of London. But under the pressure of events over this summer and autumn, his frail confidence collapsed.

In early June, Gray received a letter in the form of a prose-poem. Written in an aristocratic hand on blue paper under an embossed yellow sphinx, it was posed as a riddle:

Sir,
    In Paris quite extraordinary things are taking place; naiads have been found seated upon the bed of the Seine, beside an old boat which one wanted to refloat; at the Bois de Boulogne a trampled clearing has been discovered, where fauns had certainly danced, for there were prints of goats' hooves

everywhere, and where they had been sitting, their little tails had made hollows in the dust. Lastly, Sir, the moon, which was last month like a Princess who wears a yellow veil and silver shoes (ask Oscar), is now just like a beautiful nymph who offers an iris to a small nymph who cannot be seen. I find this very frightening, Sir, because one must not see goddesses; one must only say that one has seen them, to people who do not believe you. Moreover I am about to leave Paris to go to London, if the fauns are not there already.

> I am,
>
> PIERRE LOUŸS[100]

The letter everywhere speaks of its source. Wilde used to say that there are actually two worlds, one the real one, so called because no words are required to make it visible, and the other, of which one must speak because without words it would not exist. He used a parable to illustrate his meaning. A storyteller who could spin wonderful fantasies about fauns and wood-nymphs, mermaids and sirens, one day met the creatures of his imagination in the flesh. When he returned to the village and was asked, "Now, then, tell us, what have you seen?" he replied, "Nothing."

As if to confirm the source, Louÿs speaks of the moon "which was last month like a Princess who wears a yellow veil and silver shoes (ask Oscar)," referring to lines in Wilde's *Salome,* a play Wilde had originally written in French during his stay in Paris and then asked Louÿs to check for solecisms. Wilde was thus Louÿs's passport to Gray's friendship; its nature may be judged from Gray's response. To a letter in code, Gray replied in code, but of another kind. Even for a letter from a young poet of twenty-six to another young poet of twenty-one, it takes large risks and makes large assumptions:

> 3, Plowden Buildings
> in the Temple
> *Whitmonday 1892* [6 June 1892]

Dear Monsieur Pierre Louÿs,

As thou dost me, I know thee beforehand by thy name from the telling of Oscar Wilde. With free and open speech I may tell thee of the denizens of the woods and rivers of this dismal country. Verily they are stuffed with sheep and fish and other such beasts, the most of these neither faunes nor nymphs, none having need of any such now-a-days. Come shod with light or straw, thou shalt be welcome. The school is at this present hour most shrunk in. Our Kit Marlowe is gone down to the shades, dispatcht thither by a scurvie poniard thrust through his eye. The froward Jehan Keats hath nought else in his noodle but to search out the grounds of gold and set there marygolds and greensward. Shelley is become a fisher for corals, and Shakesper doth busy himself about the putting-on of his plays. There, thou hast all our intelligence, and no more.

JOHN GRAY[101]

Gray was writing to a virtual stranger; but he must have known (certainly from Wilde) that Louÿs was learning English, for the Rabelaisian *double entendres* work only in that language (in such phrases as "les habitans des boys") or as French versions of English slang (as in "ils sont emplys de moutons et poyssons et aultres bestials" or the reference to "les fondes d'or"). All these are overtly homosexual; hence the further game of using disguised names. "Shelley" is Edward Shelley, already a lover of Wilde's, whom Louÿs was to meet during his London visit. After his departure in September, when Louÿs asked Gray for Shelley's address, Gray advised, "Only, if you seek the experience of Shelley, you must explain to him precisely that he should address himself to your interests and not fool around."[102] "Shakesper" is most probably Wilde himself, a pseudonym inspired by his piece on the young man of Shakespeare's sonnets, "The Portrait of Mr. W. H." and "Kit Marlowe" could be none other than Ernest Dowson, whose middle name was Christopher, and who signed at least one letter to Gray, "Kit Dowson"; when Gray inscribed a copy of *Silverpoints* to him, it was "To Kit Dowson the master singer."[103] Just as Marlowe was reputed to have died horribly of a stab-wound to the eye, Dowson was famously stricken in late 1889 with his infatuation for the Polish restaurateur's daughter.

The rest, even including the identifications above, must stop at surmise. All that may be said with any degree of certainty is that by June 1892 Gray was included in this group of young men who gathered around Wilde, and to whom he, in turn, introduced Louÿs after his arrival on 12 June. Not all were homosexual; Dowson certainly was not and Gray was probably more engaged in inventing his *double entendres* than in enacting them. Louÿs, in any case, would have taken only a voyeuristic interest; he had, after all, arrived in London with his mistress, Lucile Delormel. Nevertheless (as he confessed to his close friend André Gide) he was enchanted by the manners, the rituals, the charm of the English "school":

> It is not at all as one thinks it is here, he told me. These young people are most charming. . . . You cannot imagine the elegance of their manners. Well, then, to give you an idea: the first day I was introduced to them, X, to whom I had just been presented, offered me a cigarette; but, instead of simply offering it as we do, he began by lighting it himself and not handing it over until after he had taken the first drag. Isn't that exquisite? And everything is like that. They know how to envelop everything in poetry. They have told me how several days previously, they had arranged a marriage, a true marriage between two of them, with an exchange of rings. No, I tell you, we cannot imagine such a thing; we don't have any idea of what it is all about.[104]

From their first meeting, Louÿs was delighted with Gray, writing him with his usual affectionate childishness, "I am very pleased with your letter, with your invitation, and with yourself."[105] The invitation was for an expedition; on 15 June, Gray had written, "if it seems well to you to pass a few hours with me I should be filled with joy":

> I[t] happens that on Thursday and Friday the National Gallery is filled with students—all hideous. I think we might go into the city: there are some Pre-Raph. pictures at the Guildhall of entrancing loveliness among them the two best things Millais ever painted and probably therefore the finest modern pictures in existence. Or we could go to the British Museum together and see the Greek vases and mediaeval missals [.] Or again, for pleasaunce, we might go for a promenade on a River Steamboat *down* the Thames where all is filth and smoke the very hub of beautiful scenery[.][106]

To this Louÿs replied that he was not free until 17 June, but that he would call for Gray that morning at the Temple. He suggested they lunch at St. James's Hall, a restaurant where Wilde often dined and which he liked to recommend to his friends; then they would proceed to the Guildhall. There they viewed John Everett Millais's "Ophelia"; Gray was to commemorate their visit in a poem ("On a Picture") which he dedicated to Louÿs when it appeared in *Silverpoints*.

After this, the letters show an erratic pattern of meetings. When Gray was finally to say goodbye, he apologized for not seeking Louÿs out for three or four days at a time, writing that he feared Louÿs would accuse him of indifference. In fact, he confessed, "I am melancholy by temperament and take care to hide myself very often on that account." But evidently Gray also had other reasons for hiding: he had written earlier, "I hope I may see you very soon indeed but I am so bothered at a prospect of the huissiers [bailiffs] coming that I do not like to show myself."[107] Gray had told another friend he was so short of money during this period that he sometimes went without food for several days. Nevertheless, he adds, "I expect to be in the Café Royal for a few minutes this evening but the time is uncertain and I will take my chance of meeting you." It is also possible Gray exaggerated his retirement: the record shows that at least on one occasion, Wilde invited Louÿs and his mistress to dinner along with Gray, adding that he would be found in the Café Royal for an hour before they dined.[108]

Thus, for whatever reasons, there is a gap of almost three weeks in the letters. Then, shortly after Wilde left London in early July to take the waters at Bad Homburg, Gray issued another invitation. "My dear Pierre," he writes:

> I think I remember that your free days next week are Tuesday Thursday Friday Saturday. Alexander is writing for seats at the Empire for Tuesday and afterwards if you are agreeable we will go to a place called the Corinthian Club where most of the swell whores in London resort.
>
> Altogether it will make an interesting if not vastly amusing evening.
>
> Ever yours
> j.g.[109]

On this expedition, Louÿs's mistress was emphatically not invited. Its intention, which might be judged from its venues—the Empire was described by a contemporary as the "most popular whore market in London"[110] —was underwritten by an enclosure: a pornographic photograph of a black prostitute, young, naked, straddling a low stool, with the inscription: "The new mistress of Alexander." Alexander was of course Alexander Teixeira de Mattos, Gray's friend from the Temple and the Independent Theatre.

Whether this proposed visit reflected a genuine taste of Gray's or was an attempt to impress his Parisian visitor, it certainly implies that Louÿs had indicated no interest in becoming sexually involved with the beautiful young men to whom he had been introduced. He had, after all, pointedly proclaimed his preferences by arriving in London with his current mistress. These, as Gray may have discovered, also included a pronounced distaste for practising homosexuals; it appears that Louÿs later broke with André Gide when he discovered Gide's predilections, and it may certainly have been an element in his subsequent rift with Wilde in the coming year.[111] One wonders then, what he must have made of Gray's first suggestive note? Of the marriages between those men he mentions in a letter to Gide? For all his artful childishness, Louÿs was not naive about the circles in which he was mixing. The evidence suggests that it was Wilde's morals—and the pain he was causing his wife, the embarrassment to his friends—to which Louÿs apparently objected. Louÿs's interest in homosexuality was, as his books were to reveal, in any case, in lesbianism, not male homosexuality; his engagement there, channelled into his writing.[112]

In the event, Louÿs replied the next day to Gray's invitation with the news that he would have to leave London on Thursday morning in order to take his exams in Paris, which were to begin sooner than he had anticipated. Until then his three evenings were taken, but, "Sarah has given me two *stalls* to go hear her on *Tuesday* in Frou-Frou; there is one for you, of course. Come with me and afterwards we shall go to the whore-Club."[113] "Sarah" was Sarah Bernhardt, whom Louÿs idolized; the high point of his London visit had been his introduction to her at the end of June. On hearing he was a poet, she asked him to write a play for her, and, in feverish excitement, Louÿs began the text of what was to become the basis of his novel *Aphrodite,* which four years later was to win him international fame. Gray and Louÿs did attend this performance and later went together, it appears, to the Corinthian Club.[114]

It was to be their last meeting. Louÿs had come to London ostensibly to improve his knowledge of English for the *licence* exam which he now had to take in Paris. Gray, hearing of his imminent departure, wrote a rueful note:

12 July 1892

My dear Pierre,

A little farewell: although I hope to see you again before this beautiful sojourn is over—at least for your departure. There are a few small matters I must mention: in memory perhaps you will sometimes accuse me of indifference: you will recall stretches of three or four days when I did not seek you out and said nothing. But you must not hold it against me; I am melancholy by temperament and careful to hide myself very often on that account.

Also you will promise not to forget me; I do not insist on letters—that is too much—but I would like, when I see you again—be it after a twelve month, to find this friendship still warm, that has been so dear to me—do you not agree?

This is quite the letter of an irritated child, but all the same it represents my true feelings.

That is all my dear friend, I give you my hands.

always,

j.g.[115]

Gray had hoped to meet Louÿs again, however briefly. But four days later he wrote, "So you had gone and I did not see you again. It was unlucky: a godless cousin of mine arrived in London from Ceylon on Thursday evening without a shilling and almost without a shirt. Naturally I had no alternative to looking after him and getting the things he most pressingly needed."[116]

Louÿs had gone; Wilde was gone. In the void of London after the Season, Gray wrote plaintively, "I am really quite alone now among drunkards only." The emptiness was filled with mere acquaintances; his true friends had left. Louÿs acknowledged the rareness and intensity of their bond in a letter written just before leaving for Paris:

My dear John

When I told you last evening about a letter I had received from you, I meant only the first one and I did not know you had written to me such a beautiful second letter. I know now you are quite a *friend,* such a terrible word! how many have you? how many have I? Do we know? You shall go in Paris. We will meet again and often. I wish now one thing: to be for you what you have been for me during that short month.

> Give me your hand
> PIERRE LOUŸS
> Chelsea 18 July. [117]

Gray had promised to visit Louÿs in Paris that autumn, but over the next three months there were signs that something had gone wrong. On 2 October, Gray wrote Louÿs a distraught letter:

My dear Pierre

The other day, early in the afternoon, I received a telegram signed in your name: it read: "Good night." This was not a matter of indifference to me, but I instantly decided that, in a moment of agitation, you had committed suicide. And now, after such a long silence, this decision is more or less confirmed—and I am writing for news.

It is a case, clearly, of Gray's reading into Louÿs's silence his own morbid preoccupations. For more than a year he had not been physically well, and was now in the country (probably in Cornwall, a favorite haunt) for, he continues, "It is quite nice, the country, in its way, and thanks to its comfort, I am sorry to inform you that I am completely cured of my nerves and other vices."[118] The letter then breaks off; the rest is lost or, as in the letters of 1895 to 1896 in this correspondence, deliberately destroyed. But it is enough to reveal Gray's state of mind, one that becomes more distraught as the month wears on.

Coincidentally, Louÿs had written Gray on the very same day. He had just returned to Paris from the Bayreuth festival, where he was supposed to meet Wilde, but did not see him. From his breezy tone it is clear that it is not Louÿs, but Gray, who is in difficulties. "My dear and good John Gray," the letter opens: "Why aren't you already in Paris? I am waiting for you, hoping for you, you really ought to be here."[119] He asked Gray to come for Sherard's sake if not for his; and his account of Sherard's marital difficulties finally helped galvanize Gray into action. There must have been a second letter, for by the time Gray replied, Sherard's difficulties had transmogrified from troubles with his Polish wife to a challenge to a *duel à mort* with a Pole who lived in his village. Somehow Sherard, together with Louÿs, had persuaded Gray to act as his second.

Thus Gray wrote to Louÿs on 10 October saying that naturally he would come to Sherard's assistance in this unfortunate affair and laying out elaborate plans to get leave from his job: "I will ask for leave of four or five days to conduct my sister to Petersburg; and by means of this ruse I shall obtain a passport without arousing any suspicion. If it turns out badly in the end, I shall probably be prevented from returning to England, which is all the same to me, almost what I want."[120] He confides in Louÿs that he must make up some lie about being involved with another woman to escape from his mistress for several days, and then asks whether frock coat and top hat are the approved costume for French duels. The whole letter has such a hysterical ring that one wonders if Gray had already been overtaken by the nervous illness that apparently struck about this time and lasted throughout November. Certainly the humorous account Louÿs gave of Sherard's contretemps with his wife, who threatened to kill him with a hat–pin, or even the suggestion (not found in any extant letter) that Gray engage himself as Sherard's second in a duel, would not justify Gray's exaggerated response. Why should Gray lie to obtain a passport? Who is this mysterious "mistress" whom he has to deceive? Why should he be just as happy not to return to England?

The climax came in late November, when, on the twenty-fourth, Gray wrote Louÿs in more than usually imperfect French:

Silverpoints (my verses) is about to appear. I am occupied at the moment correcting the proofs which is very difficult the poems being printed in italics. . . . Besides this, I have as guides and peers companions who are a bit bizarre. Of late, I have consorted with the dead. Nowadays it is DEATH who loves me now. It is Folly and Calumny who keep me company. I am an heir. The rich ground which hangs between Life and Death is almost mine. I am going to enjoy my new estate presently. Write to me. That is what I need. I will write to you again about that. I am very unhappy. Some days ago I almost decided to leave England, to withdraw my poems, in order to become a

French citizen, never again to speak a word of English. . . . I have lost my father. I am well pleased with the loss. Write to me.

Always your

j.g.[121]

Gray was, as he himself realized, close to madness. With his disaffection with Wilde, his dismay over the rumors about their relationship, he is watching his whole world die, and with it the life he had lived as "Dorian" Gray. It is as well to consider, also, that during these months Gray was also broke and starving and still weakened from the illness of the previous year. But all these considerations are overshadowed by the brute fact of his father's death nearly three weeks earlier.[122] One can only speculate on the stark bitterness of the lines, "I have lost my father. I am well pleased with the loss." Thus the father who bullied his eldest son, named for him, to try to get him to meet his expectations, is now decisively rejected by the son, who has escaped him, his class, his aspirations. Perhaps it is not a coincidence that during these months of late 1892 and early 1893, Gray first began writing religious poetry, manifesting a new hunger for acceptance by another, more adequate Father.

As to his actual physical collapse, we have only two facts. First: that at some point in the course of the illness, Gray suffered from convulsions.[123] A *grand mal* seizure can result from severe psychic stress and it is clear that Gray was in an emotional and spiritual crisis. Second: that it lasted in its acute form only a matter of days, as few as four. At the end of that period, on 27 November, Gray was able to write Louÿs, in response to a sympathetic letter, "I am better today than since months," and the next day, "I am inundated by a surge of health and joy; I have become almost mad with it. . . . All that remains of my illness is a slight preoccupation with myself."[124] On 3 December he writes of the "furious impulse of high spirits which came to me with health—as I have never known it—suddenly returned to me—a true miracle. This access of joy has driven away all my fancies and worries and though it is alas a cold fact that they think that of me I cannot believe that they do."[125]

What "they" thought of him was that he was Wilde's lover,

Wilde's creature, Wilde's double. What he thought of himself he put down in a narrative that acutely and dispassionately charted his own disintegration during these final, climactic months of 1892.

"The Person in Question"

Gray's double life was falling apart. On the one hand, there was his appearance on the podium of the Playgoers' Club, along with his mentor Wilde, extolling the virtues of the music hall; on the other, the panicky denials of the rumor that he was "Dorian," or Wilde's disciple, in any sense of the term. The crisis of late 1892 might have been precipitated by his realization that a final rupture with Wilde was necessary. But there are signs that the intensity of the crisis grew from a larger and more final disillusionment with the world that he had created for himself as "Dorian" Gray.

Sometime in the heat of this conflict, probably in November, Gray wrote an almost clinical self-analysis of his state of mind. "The Person in Question" may have been inspired by one of Wilde's asides to Sherard, who noticed a man sitting alone at the Café Royal and asked who he was. "That is Frederick Sandys," replied Wilde, adding sorrowfully that he had been dead for some years.[126] The story also owes an obvious debt to *The Picture of Dorian Gray*. But whereas in Wilde's novel it is the dandy who is ageless and his picture that grows ugly and old, the hero of Gray's story sees a hallucination of himself as he will be in twenty-five years, a stout and affected old man. One theme is shared: the question of the reality of appearances and, in particular, the world of "pure" appearance and of the mask the dandy has fabricated.

"As well as I remember," the story opens, "the first time I saw— or to be quite accurate, the first time I observed—the person in question must have been in the last days of last August twelvemonth."[127] Oppressed by the late summer heat and a faint appetite, the writer takes himself to the Café Royal, where he overhears a customer summon the waiter in what he recognizes as his own slow murmuring voice. When the mysterious voice then asks for a certain Dutch paper that the narrator was accustomed to read "for the remotest of reasons," he turns to observe this disturbing stranger: "He was a man of about my own proportions; he might even once have been like me in face—for he was at least twenty five years older than myself, and bearded stragglingly; so that any existing likeness between us was well obscured" (p. 15). But the sense of mysterious resemblance persisted:

> My first emotion was fear. . . . Then I gave myself up to observe this so complete illusion; for such I supposed it to be. The coincidences offered me nothing new, unfortunately—in principle. I had for months been accustomed to see my own face suddenly, unexpectedly, younger and better looking, or quite old, looking into my own and very close to me, healthy or haggard, puffed and spotted, or pure and transparent like an angel's. (Pp. 15–16)

These hallucinations, which had been brought on by a fever the previous year, disappeared from this day forward. But the illusion of familiarity in the stranger's "distinctive gesture and turn of phrase" was now certainly beyond "safe and normal limits" (p. 16). With growing panic, the narrator observes that his identity is unquestioned by the *garçon*.

Months later the narrator reencounters the stranger, scrupulously dressed, at a large and fashionable party. The writer boldly points him out to the hostess, who gives his name, which the narrator instantly forgets. From that moment on, the apparition follows him in all activities, through the streets, to restaurants, first nights, and clubs. Then the revelation strikes; "In some near or remote sense *he is myself*"(p.20), a correspondence of identity that had already been psychologically conceded. Once the writer "accepted him, for whatever he might be," he feels a protective compassion for "the person" and even vague gratitude for unlocking a whole different world, one of doubles and mirror images: "I used to laugh sometimes, at the expense of the people with whom I supped or went to the theatre. 'There sit,' I would think, looking at the other table, or in the opposite box, 'themselves, or their parts or doubles (whatever they are) and *they don't know*.' I would try to *pair* the actual and phenomenal" (p. 21). At first the half-conscious accommodation of the figure is solicitous, then dependent. But at one luncheon, after an appearance at every evening of the season, the person in question is absent. The writer goes in desperate search for him to all his old haunts, locating him finally at the switchback at the Exhibition (a roller coaster at one of the trade fairs of the time). Carefully avoiding him, the writer chooses a seat; the apparition defers, and chooses one behind. Then something shocking occurs:

A sudden waft across the still dusty air, of foin coupé, made me turn my head with revulsion and hate. A strange woman sat beside him! You may guess I soon looked away again; only thankful I was to be windward of the hated odour. A natural, rational woman riding by herself on the switchback! Unheard of! I saw that this hateful accident, *that* man and such a woman, shadow, (what you like) beside him, was so full of possibilities that I *dared* not to dwell upon it. (P. 24)

Although the narrator never sees the apparition again, the horror of the scene, the ugly reality represented by the prostitute and her cheap perfume, recurs like a bad dream until the writer is driven to the verge of madness. His nerves have deteriorated; he is incapable of doing more than roving the streets, in continual disappointment, looking for this lost apparition. Only one friend might help, the writer concludes, and "he would never forgive my treachery in keeping my secret" (p. 26). "Infatuated wretch that I was to think that I could walk alone into the posses[s]ion of rare knowledge and experience," he is now locked into the nightmare of his own making, keeping, as the story ends, only the most precarious grip on his sanity.

As a narrative, as a dispassionate report of a certain type of psychic experience, the work is utterly convincing. Yet as a *doppelgänger* story, "The Person in Question" is quite odd. There is not the usual problem that we find in Poe's "William Wilson," for instance, of an apparition that is the offspring of private delusion. In Gray's story everyone except the author acknowledges the reality of "the person in question"; not his existence but the question of his *identity* is the crux of the narrative. The author is initiated into the secret of their shared identity only by dint of his pathological state: "It may be, probably is, that my nerves, quickened and refined by disease, and unable to return to their first insensate condition, put me in a position to appreciate a phenomenon perhaps of the most ordinary description, which those who can detect it do not think themselves bound to disclose to those who cannot" (p. 20). As the result of nerves "refined by disease," a condition that Gray may have been experiencing and certainly one he recognized in the case of the Goncourts as the mark of the true artist, the author is initiated into a second world, the actual, with which the phenomenal is at odds but may be made to correspond.

This state of heightened perception of correspondences describes accurately the consciousness which Pater had named as the "'imaginative reason,' that complex faculty for which every thought and feeling is twin-born with its sensible analogue or symbol."128 In this extraordinary ability of the mind to recreate the world in its own image, Gray finds its power as well as its danger, for its efficacy rests on the sheer manipulation of appearances. For Wilde, the dandy was a kind of supreme artist because he did not limit his manipulation to words or canvas; he was to be the artist of his own life. But in both Gray's and Wilde's stories, it is the aging of the dandy which threatens to crack the beautiful facade. If, as Wilde held, "not *doing,* but *being*" was the ideal of the dandy, one factor was neglected in his effort to transform life into art: the corrosions of time.129 Dorian Gray manages to sidestep that problem by a bargain with the devil; but Gray's story, more realistically, sees the pathetic absurdity of the aging dandy. In the story, the shock of recognition is that of a *potential* self, of Gray seeing in Wilde, then thirty-eight, what he might become in twelve years' time. In one way the story is about the impossibility of remaining a dandy and the failure of the dandy's goal of manipulating appearances to his own ends.

But as in *Dorian Gray,* the aging of the dandy stands as a sign of the underlying moral corruption which is only revealed at the end. When the "person in question" is joined by the prostitute on the switchback, the writer becomes hysterical, not merely because of the moral corruption that implies, but also because the *illusion* of identity breaks down.

The shock and panic of the narrator at this discovery has an obvious parallel in Gray's relationship with Wilde. The transformation to "Dorian" Gray the aesthete occurred under Wilde's influence, and the qualities which Wilde praised in Gray were tastes mutually cultivated. In their "masks," their stylized personalities, different as they were, both revealed a kind of fragmentation of personality. An air of unreality must have surrounded them both, for Symons was to comment on the society of the Café Royal (not coincidentally, the setting of Gray's story), "Nor must I omit to mention Oscar Wilde, an apparition; sometimes with John Gray, another apparition."[130]

This intense air of artificiality never left Gray's mannerisms or surroundings; that self-possession shattered in Wilde by his impulsiveness, his humor, became hardened and more precious in the older Gray. During the later months of 1892 and the beginning of 1893 when Wilde, now grown fat, appeared everywhere with Douglas, the discrepancy between his beautiful manners and his underworld company must have provoked a deep moral revulsion in Gray. The horror of the scene on the switchback is only accountable in these terms. Ultimately, it is the dissolute sexual proclivities that proclaim the moral bankruptcy of the dandy's cultivated appearance. The person in question pictured for Gray, as if in a mirror, not only what he *might* become, but what, in fact, he *had* become. Wilde could not have been far from his mind.

THREE

❧ *Silverpoints (1893)* ❧

> *Mrs. Windsor was not subtly happy. She never was.*
> *Sometimes she was irresponsibly cheerful, and gener-*
> *ally she was lively, especially when there were any*
> *men about; but though she read much minor poetry,*
> *and knew all the minor poets, she was not poetic, and*
> *she honestly thought that John Gray's 'Silver Points'*
> *were far finer literature than Wordsworth's 'Ode to*
> *Immortality,' or Rossetti's 'Blessed Damosel.'*
>
> Robert S. Hichens
> *The Green Carnation*
> London, 1894

In "The Person in Question," Gray had used a fictional mode to ana-
lyze a personal crisis, one provoked by an acute sense that he was in a
sense two people who, while sharing a curious dependence, were in-
imical to each other. The story crystallizes an insight into the pattern
of his actual life. By late 1892 and early 1893, the path of the punc-
tilious civil servant John Gray had almost entirely diverged from that
of the profligate "Dorian" Gray; it would seem that a kind of balance
was maintained by keeping the two lives reasonably distinct.

In January 1893 John Gray, now a junior Second Division Clerk,
transferred to the Foreign Office Library. There he worked at filing,
indexing, and retrieving the correspondence that came into its charge.
Although called a "library," it was apparently a general reference
room. Working conditions for the clerks were Dickensian: "The Map
Room where they are at present," according to one account, "is al-
most insufferable in winter because of smoke from the fire and if there
is no fire it is cold. The room is at a distance from the rest of the de-
partment and it is therefore difficult to exercise control over them."[1]
In theory at least, Gray was unable to leave during office hours (which
were from eleven to five o'clock, with an obligation to remain until

work was completed) without the express permission of the chief clerk. Such conditions led Gray to refer darkly to the Foreign Office as "the galley where life has chained me."[2] But since the distance of the map room from the other offices made surveillance difficult, "Dorian" Gray was able to write personal letters and take leisurely dinners at mid-day.

In some ways, then, the life of the civil servant did not seem to impose greatly on the life of the poet, although that of the poet came to pose problems for the civil servant. For instance, some time in 1893, after *Silverpoints* had achieved a certain notoriety, "an explorer" who ventured to the second floor of the Foreign Office there "discovered a second division clerk employed in the Library, who was also a minor poet. Delighted with his find, he was wont to escort parties of friends to the spot, who peeped at the poet one by one."[3]

This was a minor imposition. A much more acute problem was "Dorian" Gray's demands for money. John Gray's salary in 1892 was about £200 a year.[4] What otherwise was considered a good salary might have proved more than sufficient for a bachelor of modest tastes, but "Dorian" Gray evidently ran through it at an appalling rate. Elegant clothes were to him a necessity; he is, at this period, almost obsessively preoccupied with what he will wear, whether on an expedition with Louÿs down the Thames, or acting as a second in a duel in France. Tickets to theaters and the opera were another expense; in addition, he dined out regularly and obviously could not do without journals and books. His rooms at the Temple themselves cost £60 per annum. During the early nineties, he was often in debt and hungry, once having starved from Monday to Friday, and on at least one occasion he had to hide from debt collectors.[5]

Inevitably, hunger, debt, and anxiety took their physical toll. Gray spoke of his collapse only to a very few; the sole written record is that of a diary entry made by Edith Cooper recording how Gray confided in her aunt, Katherine Bradley, of his "reckless destruction of health by exotic habits": "A good Doctor, seeing death sure in two years if such life were continued, broke the spell & got the fair young wreck to eat meat at each meal & take sleep in nature's way. The beginning of redemption was made! The Doctor was preparatory master for the seminary & the priesthood."[6] The physical breakdown was as dramatic as the psychic; its nature is largely unknown, although Gray did write Louÿs in December 1892: "It is *impossible* for me to have convulsions again."[7]

Most probably the "Doctor" was André Raffalovich, who was referred to as such in an age when "scientific" was a term elastic enough to include his treatises on homosexual behavior in various journals of psychology. Raffalovich may also have figured as the "friend" mentioned in "The Person in Question" who brings the narrator to a Jewish eating-house and, later, becomes the "one person" in whom the narrator feels he may confide. Certainly it was Raffalovich who "broke the spell" which held "Dorian" Gray in thrall. In late 1892, he literally rescued Gray by providing him with an enduring and generous affection; an assured income; and, finally, by insisting that, as the one condition of his friendship, Gray make public and formal his disaffection with Oscar Wilde.

That estrangement was not sudden. Since February, when Gray took issue with the "Dorian" nickname, his disillusion had grown. Its course, meticulously recorded in "The Person in Question," was painfully underlined by the death of his own father in November. Now, as he wrote Pierre Louÿs, he was as one living among "the dead," tortured and disaffected.[8] It seems that during this crisis, Gray came to the decision to end his relationship with Wilde. The actual rupture, however, did not occur until March 1893. At that date, only two weeks after the publication of *Silverpoints,* Gray wrote Louÿs: "About the falling-out with Oscar. I say it to you only and it is absolute. It will suffice that I recount its origins when I see you in London."[9]

Louÿs, mindful of many favors and much hospitality, was slower to make the break with a celebrity who had introduced him to Sarah Bernhardt and honored him in the dedication of *Salome*. When Louÿs did come to London in April, he attended the first performance of *A Woman of No Importance* at Wilde's invitation. But Wilde's companions filled him with consternation; "London is charming," he wrote his brother Georges, "but I am in a group of people who make me a little uncomfortable." The decisive moment came one morning when Louÿs dropped by the hotel room Wilde occupied with Alfred Douglas, having moved out of the house he shared with his wife and two young sons. Louÿs noted one bed with two pillows, and, while he was there, Constance, Wilde's wife, who came daily to deliver his mail, arrived in tears.[10]

Given Louÿs's distaste for homosexuality, it was inevitable that he would have quarrelled with Wilde. Replying to Gray's news of his own quarrel, Louÿs wrote: "You know that I have completely broken with Mr. Wilde and that I can never meet him again anywhere."[11] According to Wilde, Louÿs told him in late May that "I would have to choose between his friendship and my fatal connection with A.D."[12] Wilde made the motive sound like sexual jealousy, but it was not. Certainly at this time others, from more disinterested motives, tried to dissuade Wilde from his flamboyant courtship of Douglas, if only because that relationship was becoming, in the context of the recent Criminal Law Amendment Act, which made such interactions between males a criminal offense even if practiced in private, nothing short of provocative.[13]

As for Gray's own reasons for falling out with Wilde, the burden of discipleship seemed finally to weigh too heavily on him. The price it exacted was large: the necessity of allowing himself to be passed off as another "beautiful soul," Wilde's protégé, his creature. These are deep waters, and by destroying records of this part of his past, Gray has reduced us to surmise. As we have seen, however, the essential dilemma, that threat of self-destruction by an alien, artificially cultivated personality, is quite apparent in the anguish of "The Person in Question." It is, moreover, a dilemma that Gray fails to resolve, and that will repeat itself in his effort to fulfill the role of a priest to such perfection that every gesture would become symbol. He himself made the distinction between "priest" and "man" only insofar as he thought of the inner self as an elusive thing lost inside the artifact of his "character": "I could not express any satisfaction at being what I am," he would write Raffalovich in 1898, after the first month of his stay at Scots College. "The inside of the Machine is so far beyond outside appearances."[14]

Paradoxically, what saved Gray from the posturing that came to characterize Wilde and his set[15] was exactly this sense of split consciousness, of a reflexive division into "true self" and "mask" with a resulting ambivalence over his role as "Dorian" Gray. His recognition of the distance between the two is most evident when he uses his mask to manipulate others, to charm them, occasionally to enlist their aid. In the early letters to Louÿs, one may actually distinguish between the voice of "Dorian," the clever, flamboyant boulevardier, and the plaintive, rather flat tones of John Gray, who in one letter excuses himself from seeing Louÿs in the following words: "You will recall stretches of three or four days when I did not seek you out and said nothing. But you must not hold it against me; I am melancholy by temperament and careful to hide myself very often on that account."[16] Gray obviously makes a distinction here between his mask and the temperament which threatens it; he is careful to hide himself away when he cannot keep up the performance.

Clearly Gray used his mask as a means of exploiting others; but then, his was a hard school. He was poor, obscure, ambitious; and, in any case, his exploitation took the engaging mode of charm and deference. More tragically, the mask became a form of self-exploitation. In particular, he used his art to create an artificial persona for himself; the *Silverpoints* poems cannot intelligibly be read apart from his life as "Dorian" Gray. As such they stand as an objective correlative to Gray's dilemma over his relation to this image, to the compromises and (in the end) the price that it exacted. In *Silverpoints,* "Dorian" Gray gives his final performance. Its history is intimately bound up with his relationship with Oscar Wilde. Immediately after publication, Gray broke with Wilde and began privately to rue the day that *Silverpoints* had seen the light.

Fashionable Decadence

Like its creator, *Silverpoints* was a creature of the hour. Had John Gray not arrived on the scene in the wake of Wilde's notorious novel, "Dorian" Gray would never have had to repent the purple passages of his life. Had John Gray's first book of poetry, *Silverpoints,* been published a few years earlier, it would probably have sunk with only the most modest ripples; published two years later, it would have fallen victim to the hysteria of the Wilde trials. As it was, *Silverpoints* appeared at exactly the right moment to crystallize in the public consciousness a vague new fashion which had attracted the name of "decadence."

The very vagueness of the term made it useful. Originally French, "decadence" could be securely located on that side of the Channel by reference to other literary movements such as Symbolism and Impressionism, or exemplified in Huysmans's *À Rebours* and the work of the Goncourt brothers. Across the water, what "decadence" lost in precision, it gained in resonance. In the two or three years after 1891, there was an explosion in the popularity of the word itself, with its usage ranging from scathing abuse to parody and even self-parody.[17]

In fact, for the first few years of the new decade, "decadence" was a catchword in search of authors, and in a far-reaching and influential essay, Arthur Symons obliged. "The Decadent Movement in Literature," appearing in *Harper's New Monthly Magazine* in November 1893, both defined and vigorously defended the Decadent movement as an innovation not solely in French, but also in European literature. Symons cites as its practitioners Verlaine and Mallarmé, the Goncourts and Huysmans, the Belgian Sensitivists (such as Couperus in *Ecstasy*), as well as the Ibsen of *Hedda Gabler* and *The Master Builder*. In England, he names as foremost Walter Pater, asking (rhetorically) of his *Marius the Epicurean* and *Imaginary Portraits,* "Have they not that morbid subtlety of analysis, that morbid curiosity of form, that we have found in the works of French Decadents?"[18] For Symons, "decadence" is a style that mimics a certain temperament—curious, over-refined, neurotic—which, in an insight anticipating T. S. Eliot's premise of impersonality, is an epiphany not of itself but of a certain epoch: the disembodied voice of *fin de siècle* sensibility.

Such subtleties were lost on most of the English reading public. At first the word had no particular focus and might be used equally to abuse an Ibsen play or a painting of Degas, each of which enjoyed a *succès de scandale.* By 1892, "decadence" began to pick up momentum as a term indicating a kind of counterculture, generally employed as a gesture toward anything that appeared to threaten the then quite monolithic conventions, moral and social, of the Victorian middle classes; "decadence," quite simply, applied to that which was deemed unhealthy, uncouth, and emphatically un-English. Such an atmosphere left no possibility for fine distinctions. It did not matter to the reading public that "decadents" themselves might not have confessed to the name or that they were, as artists, divided not only among themselves, but against themselves; in reality they were as capable of directing their irony toward their own work as toward their readers. They could do so because, as artists, to a large extent they conspired with their audience. Whatever their readers thought, these artists were not outsiders; shocking the middle class was itself very middle class.

One result of that collusion is that the public began to understand that the true Decadent is one who makes for himself a biography or, at the very least, what we would call an "image" that would fulfill his view of art. In short, "decadence" was to become largely a personality cult, and as such, it was virtually defined by two people: Wilde and Beardsley. The willful confusion of art and life which one observes in Wilde's dandyism, his creation of a persona on stage that he would begin to live out in his flamboyant private life, was intended to be provocative. Not less so were Beardsley's drawings, as perverse in their artifice as Beardsley was in life, "against nature" in his lonely battle with the critics and with his sickly body. When Wilde and Beardsley collaborated in the publication of *Salome* (which appeared just weeks before Gray's *Silverpoints*) their work was seized upon as the epitome of all that "decadence" represented. A year later, *The Yellow Book,* for which Beardsley acted as Art Editor, was again denounced as an instance of artistic violence. The hysteria of this reaction can only be understood if one tries to comprehend how profoundly middle-class England regarded decadence as a threat, and how relentlessly Wilde and Beardsley engaged in a kind of audience-baiting. Finally, in the spring of 1895, this sense of diffuse outrage found its theater at last in the drama of Wilde's arrest, two trials, and sentencing. The imprisonment of "the High Priest of the Decadents" played out the symbolic defeat of the movement in England.[19]

Such was the backdrop against which *Silverpoints* played, and in March 1893, for one brief moment of notoriety, it was greeted as "le plus décadent des décadents," the newest epitome of "the new."[20] To say that a book exemplifies a fashion is to confess that it became a classic largely by virtue of its context rather than by sheer force of content. That is not to say that *Silverpoints* does not contain poetry of some quality. Its best work easily bears comparison with that of Lionel Johnson and Ernest Dowson, and a handful of poems set a standard for the decade. But it is undeniable that the poems are, for the most part, period pieces, significant through the timing of their creation; some are, for instance, early and striking imitations of the "new" French poetry, or arresting critiques of the "decadent" aesthetic. Some are merely dated and one or two inept. Such unevenness of quality, however, is justified by the avant-garde role which Gray indicated in his choice of epigraph: a line from the Verlaine poem (". . . en composant des acrostiches indolents") which opens, "Je suis l'Empire à la fin de la décadence." Thus from its first utterance, *Silverpoints* proclaims itself an agent of the new movement, and every aspect of the book's production elaborates this gesture.

In physical and typographical terms, this new kind of poetry had a new kind of book: as dainty and delicate as its verse, as precocious in design as in poetic technique, as precious in its severe limitation of the edition (an edition of 250 ordinary copies and a deluxe edition of 25) as in its euphuistic style. Tall in proportion to its width (11 × 22 cm.), the book resembles a large checkbook stood on end and bound in vellum or green cloth stamped in gold. The design of flamelike leaves against a wavy latticework was by Charles Ricketts, who also dictated its "build," modelled, as he revealed, on "one of those rare Aldus italic volumes with its margins uncut."[21] Inside, the poetry, printed on expensive Van Gelder handmade paper, was set out in a delicate, almost unreadable italic, an island in a sea of margin. Its typographical extravagance did not escape the wit of Ada Leverson, a friend of Wilde's, who remarked after "looking at the poems of John Gray (then considered the incomparable poet of the age)" that Oscar's next book should be "*all* margin, full of beautiful unwritten thoughts."[22]

Certainly it marked a dramatic break with the cheap commercial books of the day, their inferior paper, cluttered type, and garish or dull bindings. Even today, the reputation of *Silverpoints* as a milestone in book production usually overwhelms its consideration as a milestone in the English poetic tradition. At the time, two critics complained that the poems did not come up to their binding.[23] Yet it is to the credit of its makers that such a distinction would not have occurred to them. *Silverpoints* was conceived as a work of total art, according to the Paterian ideal of art in which it is least possible to detach matter from form.[24]

When the book's publishers, John Lane and Elkin Mathews, first set up under the sign of the Bodley Head in Vigo Street (initially as booksellers, then as book producers) in 1887, they had no express intention to espouse a particular artist or literary cause. Yet the Bodley Head imprint was to become so identified with the "decadent" school that Richard Le Gallienne, looking back on the period, concluded that about the only thing the group of writers most closely associated with "decadence" had in common was a publisher, John Lane.[25] Within the space of six years, from 1889 to 1895, the Bodley Head brought out the works of Symons, Dowson, and Yeats, produced the two collections of the Rhymers' Club, and several key works (including *Salome*) of Oscar Wilde. Ricketts designed many of its books. Aubrey Beardsley worked for the Bodley Head from the later part of 1893. Perhaps its moment of keenest notoriety came with the publication of *The Yellow Book,* then regarded as the nadir of "decadence."

This reputation was largely due to John Lane, who made it his business to search out new authors and publicize the firm's activities. Yet the publication of "decadents" was actually resisted by the more cautious Elkin Mathews, who feared its repercussions. Nevertheless, the Bodley Head imprint was, in terms of its aesthetic stance, in as much disorder as the poets and the public itself. The tension between Mathews and Lane, between conservative and modernist, was only a reflection of the greater tension among the *literati* and their public.[26]

In John Gray's poetry, too, one notes a similarly bewildering mixture of traditional forms and avant-garde techniques: imitations of Tennyson side-by-side with imitations of Baudelaire and Verlaine. Indeed, if one takes the *Silverpoints* collection as a whole, one of its most striking features is its eager courtship of a "decadent" reputation while, at the same time, engaging in frantic efforts to avoid its implications. Was this the result of conflicting editorial policy? Was Gray caught between the conservative instincts of Elkin Mathews or Richard Le Gallienne, the Bodley Head reader who, at the time, was turning against "decadence," and the more adventurous ones of John Lane? We do know that one poem, "The Song of the Stars," was withdrawn at the publisher's request a day after the initial contract for *Silverpoints* was signed. Was the apparent double-bind the price of what has been called the "decadent dilemma," of failing to find forms adequate to the forces of disintegration, resulting in a kind of necessary, even obvious, failure?[27] Or, finally, was it the result of Gray's own personal double-bind, his attempt to disengage himself from the "beloved Master," Oscar Wilde, who initially offered to underwrite the cost of *Silverpoints,* and from the persona of "Dorian" Gray, whose studied dandyism the poems in many ways came to personify?

One can, by way of an answer, only point to the history of the suppressions and expurgations from the original manuscript of *Silverpoints,* a history in which Wilde played a part. Gray was almost unknown as a writer when Wilde, already a Bodley Head author, introduced him to Lane in the spring of 1892. On 27 May Gray called at the Bodley Head, leaving for Lane "the roll of my poems," and on 17 June, Wilde signed a formal contract to pay the cost of design, manufacture, and advertising for *Silverpoints.*[28] The book was due to come out in September; but the contract with Wilde was abandoned and on 4 January 1893 another drawn up which stipulated that the costs were to be paid entirely by the publishers, with a royalty of 20 percent for Gray. Wilde, for "the help we have received in this matter," was to receive one free copy of the special and of the ordinary editions.[29]

Why this legal turnabout? Clearly it was precipitated, in part, by Gray's disaffection with Wilde and introduction to Raffalovich, two events during the period between the two contracts that marked a personal crisis so critical, it was to change the whole course of Gray's life. This radical shift of direction is reflected in the state of the original *Silverpoints* manuscript. Over a period of some months Gray began systematically to expurgate questionable passages from the fair copy, withdrawing several poems completely. It appears that Gray was attempting to excise anything that might cause controversy, specifically, anything that might associate him in print explicitly with Oscar Wilde and the "decadent" movement with which he was becoming identified.

Most telling is Gray's suppression of the poem "Sound."[30] A *tour de force* of word-music, it might well have been read as an indirect adaptation of the passage on "barbaric music" from *The Picture of Dorian Gray.* Although it differs in the instruments named, the onomatopoeic technique, and mesmerizing monotony of the piece, work to ward the same effect.[31] Whether Gray took it from Wilde or Wilde from Gray is open to doubt. Though referring to another work, Gray once elaborated on such borrowing in later life. Walking with a colleague near Edinburgh in early spring, Father Gray remarked on the "shrill" green of the buds; his companion, Father Hart, said:

'I have just met that epithet in Oscar Wilde's *De Profundis*.' 'When we met in the terrible cenacles of poets,' he replied, . . . 'we used to recite our poems one to another. I remember having composed a sonnet on spring and reciting it duly, and, Father, . . . I remember that Oscar Wilde was one of the company. Would you like to hear it?' Abashed beyond measure, I murmured, 'Please'. And then without a falter he recited the sonnet which included the epithet 'shrill.' 'So, you see,' he concluded, 'Oscar Wilde may have been the plagiarist.'[32]

A second *Silverpoints* poem, "The Song of the Stars," was, as Gray carefully noted on the final draft of the manuscript, "suppressed from the volume on the ground of indecency" and removed at the express request of John Lane.[33] One can only guess at the offending phrases, perhaps those about "swollen women" or a "corpse lying naked and robbed." At the same time, Lane obviously permitted Gray's translation of Baudelaire's notorious "Femmes Damnées," although with the last verse left out. It is impossible to discern whether this is the result of some obscure compromise, naiveté about the nature of the "women damned," or latitude given a poem originally French which could not be extended to one in English. The effect is a kind of artistic confusion generated by a publisher and writer caught up in conflicting standards.

As the evolution of its content implies, what *Silverpoints* represents is an extraordinary compromise between the daring and the conventional. To some extent this may have resulted from the publishers' conflict between editorial prudence and commercial opportunism. Ultimately, however, it must be a sign of Gray's state of mind, torn as he was between aesthetic daring and self-distrust, between ambition and discretion. In its final form, the *Silverpoints* poetry, which shaped and was shaped by his pose as dandy, reflects in the mutilated state of the translations and the strategic omission of other poems the failure of Gray to come to terms with his posture, his desire to reap the rewards but to escape the consequences of his artistic audacity. They speak tellingly of a man divided against himself.

Making It New

In *Silverpoints,* Gray set out deliberately and self-consciously to write a new kind of poetry. In the course of a "Translators' Note" to Couperus's *Ecstasy* (1892), Gray defines the Dutch school of "Sensitivists" as "young men [who] are for beginning all over again; for finding out *the* principle, and applying it hot, as it were."[34] Neither critics today nor critics of the 1890s agree on "*the* principle"; the uneven quality of the *Silverpoints* poems as well as the difficulty of defining their style suggest that Gray did not have a very clear idea either. Yet he obviously felt that in his discovery of French poetry from Baudelaire to Laforgue he had a hold on something revolutionary.

Still, an attentive reader would be forgiven for thinking he was in fact in the hands of a poetic reactionary. Far from being "new," many of the original poems have their origins firmly marked: in the Elizabethans, Blake, Tennyson, the Pre-Raphaelites. Whether ingeniously assembled or boldly pirated, these ties are meant to be recognized. Indeed, *Silverpoints* seems to espouse a taste for pastiche as a literary form. In anticipation of the modern poetic/visual montages of the next generation, Gray employed borrowed technique and image, detached from actual or theoretical origins, in an obvious, naked way; they are brandished in the poems almost as trophies. One might compare such poetry to that of the cluttered Victorian interior, replete with souvenirs and curios and family pictures, allusive in every detail.

This was "decadence" in the mode Gray's audience understood it: an exhaustion of a culture marked by a style which could only turn back and in on itself, until it became overlaid, overelaborate, almost entirely self-referential and inevitably self-critical and self-mocking. For the late Victorian, the operative paradigm was of the decline of the Roman Empire, a decline most marked in the degeneration of Latin into the infantile lispings of the early Christian hymns or the precious extravagance of Apuleius. Once again, Walter Pater marked the hour most notably; *Marius the Epicurean* was to Gray, as to Dowson and Johnson, Yeats and Symons, their "golden book," its hero, the poet Flavian, their archetype. Flavian is drawn to the highly ornate Latin of *The Golden Ass,* "full of the archaisms and curious felicities in which that generation delighted, quaint terms and images picked fresh from the early dramatists, the lifelike phrases of some lost poet preserved by an old grammarian, racy morsels of the vernacular, and studied prettinesses:—all alike, mere playthings for the genuine power and natural eloquence of the erudite artist."[35] Decadence was above all a style: but a style achieved only through the force of a sensibility, one which could compel the disintegrating elements of the language into a coherence no longer validated by its culture.

In this sense, *Silverpoints* was very much the child of Pater's poet. Its archaisms, its racy innovations, even the extraneous, padded quality of its diction—as if words themselves were cut adrift and could no longer be securely anchored to things—Gray understood to be the result of a new way of seeing things. In his remarks on the "Sensitivists" he noted their chief virtue as "exact observation. . . . Most people, knowing that water is transparent, look *through* it: they see water, green, brown, or whatever may be in its density. Some, with a quicker visual sense, look at its surface, and almost always see beautiful colour."[36] Gray understood that words were used by the "Sensitivists" as the Impressionists used color—to catch the deliquescent flow of the senses, holding it at the moment of its dissipation. In "On a Picture," Gray imitates the method of his subject, the famous Millais painting of Ophelia that he and Pierre Louÿs viewed at the Guildhall:

> Not pale, as one in sleep or holier death,
> Nor illcontent the lady seems, nor loth
> To lie in shadow of shrill river growth,
> So steadfast are the river's arms beneath.
>
> Pale petals follow her in very faith,
> Unmixed with pleasure or regret, and both
> Her maidly hands look up, in noble sloth
> To take the blossoms of her scattered wreath.

No weakest ripple lives to kiss her throat,
Nor dies in meshes of untangled hair;
No movement stirs the floor of river moss.

Until some furtive glimmer gleam across
Voluptuous mouth, where even teeth are bare,
And gild the broidery of her petticoat. . . .[37]

This should have been a poem about madness and violent death. Instead, it is about order, pattern, stasis. Noting the exact, the superficial detail, Gray mimics here Millais's obsessive detachment (which in turn imitates the fatal distraction of Ophelia herself) by a systematic denial of emotion: the lady is not pale, or unhappy; the petals that follow her are "unmixed with pleasure or regret" and even Nature is lulled by her noble indolence. Sealed as picture within picture, the poem's own momentum is stilled by the frame of the sonnet, its drift dying at the strict limits of the line and held fast by the unusually restricted rhyme scheme. Only in the last tercet does some brief movement occur, as a furtive gleam glints across the surface, and, in the eloquent last four dots, breaks the spell of deathly stasis, presaging actual death, and, with it, the disintegration of the picture—and the poem.

Outside the picture, Gray lingers as a critical Hamlet, contemplating the "old abounding, nonchalant reverie" of death, the "old emotion" Yeats recovers, also standing before Millais's "Ophelia" almost twenty years later. Yeats recalls his youthful struggle to write a poetry which, like that of Keats and Shelley, was written "out of the impression made by the world upon their delicate senses." Yet, looking back on the work of his fellow poets of the Rhymers' Club, Yeats felt that the "casting out of ideas" had led to a dead end:

The manner of painting had changed, and we were interested in the fall of drapery and the play of light without concerning ourselves with the meaning, the emotion of the figure itself. How many successful portrait-painters gave their sitters the same attention, the same interest they might have given to a ginger-beer bottle and an apple? and in our poems an absorption in fragmentary sensuous beauty or detachable ideas had deprived us of the power to mould vast material into a single image.[38]

Yeats's comment is perhaps the best single critique that may apply to the *Silverpoints* poems. By attending to surfaces, Gray deflected the poems from engagement in passion. By employing detachable ideas or images, Gray borrowed his distance. But it was at the time a necessary distance and hard-won. If, like Hamlet, he stands outside the frame of his poem as he stood beside Millais's "Ophelia," he does not do so to contemplate her deathly reverie but to gain detachment from his own thoughts of his father's death, of the temptation to madness and suicide which, at the time he was writing the poem, threatened to engulf him. Poetically, these may seem desperate measures, until one understands that the poetry itself was a measure of desperation, an attempt to restore calm and order to a life on the brink of disintegration. Through the poem Gray constructed a distance from himself, regaining his self-possession by means of its voice.

The construction of a *Silverpoints* poem is almost always a fabrication. In fact, Gray liked "clever" poetry.[39] For him, poetry became a game, or a gesture: not entirely serious, indeed, at times tinged with self-mockery. If the poetry deflected passion, it paid the price for its cool self-sufficiency in appearing trivial or flat. On occasion, it has the fatal touch of a poetry that has been *learned*. One poem, dedicated to Félix Fénéon, has been called simply "inept":

COMPLAINT

Men, women, call thee so or so,
I do not know.
Thou has no name
For me, but in my heart a flame

Burns tireless, neath a silver vine.
And round entwine
Its purple girth
All things of fragrance and of worth.

Thou shout! thou burst of light! thou throb
　　Of pain! thou sob!
　　Thou like a bar
Of some sonata, heard from far

Through blue-hue'd veils! When in these wise,
　　To my soul's eyes,
　　Thy shape appears,
My aching hands are full of tears.[40]

This sounds as if it should be an emotional poem. Instead it is a poem that tries to catch the *effect* of emotion. Using it to project an apprehension of his own consciousness, Gray produces a poem that is not merely self-conscious, but consciously self-conscious, both affected and impersonal.

There is a point, of course, at which self-consciousness verges on self-parody, and "Complaint" is balanced on the edge (some would contend it had fallen over). Such risks are inevitable, given its intentions. Attempting to register effect, it shows how the senses are fused in the stress of utterance, the technique (used by Baudelaire and Huysmans, among others) of synesthesia. Here, unfortunately, it merely resembles hysteria, and exhibits in its taut frame the same terrible struggle for icy control so characteristic of the disease.

Again one notes, as in the poem on Ophelia, the disparity between the content and form: the forces of chaos, madness, and disintegration which are barely held in check by the rigidities of rhyme and shape, a duality Lionel Johnson seized upon in his own definition of "decadence." Writing in April 1891, at the time when he had made "great friends" with John Gray, Johnson meditated on this schizoid quality of the new poetry, to which he ascribed the quality of "reflection": "Hence come one great virtue, and one great vice: the virtue of much and careful meditation upon life, its emotions and its incidents: the vice of over subtilty and of affectation, when thought thinks upon itself, and when emotions become entangled with the consciousness of them."[41]

Johnson ascribes this schizoid quality to the poet's perception of the "double existence" of things: their existence in nature; their existence in the mind. What he failed to perceive was that this doubleness was of the nature of consciousness itself, and that, in decadent poetry, it had assumed the status of duplicity, of one part of the psyche betraying the other, of a kind of manifest poetic "bad faith," which is so obvious in the tonalities of several of the *Silverpoints* poems. It has been given several names—in the verse described, for instance, as ironic or affected—but essentially the tone is one which rings consciously and even embarrassingly false.

This is perhaps most exquisitely true of a poem which mimics early Blake, "Song of the Seedling":

> Tell, little seedling, murmuring germ,
> Why are you joyful? What do you sing?
> Have you no fear of that crawling thing,
> Him that has so many legs? and the worm?
>
> Rain drops patter above my head—
>   Drip, drip, drip.
> To moisten the mould where my roots are fed—
>   Sip, sip, sip.
> No thought have I of the legged thing,
>   Of the worm no fear,
>   When the goal is so near;
> Every moment my life has run,
> The livelong day I've not ceased to sing:
>   I must reach the sun, the sun. (P. 22)

The manner is that of the perfected *faux naïf,* the feigned innocence of Victorian sexuality, those "quaintest looks of blank surprise" encountered in other *Silverpoints* poems. Here, such is the patronizing intimacy of Gray's tone that, were the naiveté not so perfectly self-conscious, the poem could be read only as parody.

But we are always aware of the artifice, the forced quality of the voice: it seems always, well, performed. And this is the analogy I believe Gray had in mind throughout *Silverpoints.* With some deliberation, Gray had, as we have seen, included in his lecture/manifesto as "modern actor" (along with the mummer, the juggler, and the music-hall *artiste*) the poet as pictured by Baudelaire: an outcast and martyr, one defined by his role *as* poet, that is, one for whom his poetry has become part of his performance. It is to the point that many of the *Silverpoints* poems had, before they were published, actually been recited before audiences that included the likes of Walter Pater and the Princess of Monaco and her dinner guests.

Clearly the poems were the means by which "Dorian" Gray constructed a self. As such, the *Silverpoints* poems may be taken not merely as analogues to the dandy's stylized behavior, but as its purest expression. Just as the dandy's performance repudiates the notion that the self is single, continuous, and constant, Gray's poems here propose a radically "insincere" kind of poetry whose borrowed styles allow him a multiplicity of voices. These are not mere imitations. Nor are they masks, to be put on and off, in a kind of adolescent role-playing. Rather, Gray employs this kind of ventriloquism to comment, from a distance, on the aesthetic in which he is working. Sometimes this distance registers as wit, other times as irony, still others as humor or grotesquerie. But all take their tone from exquisite self-consciousness and steely intention. For it is only by an act of pure poetic will that Gray can hold together, within the tight frames of his artifice, the forces of dissolution.

That willfulness, however, did not proceed from theory. Quite the contrary. Gray employed in fact a bizarre method of composition, once described to Katherine Bradley, who recorded it in her journal: "He tells of how he did poems seven days alone before they went into proof, by getting 2 ideas (often incongruous) & clapping them to bake in his brain—repeating the process till the dish was single."[42] The method was, in short, the result of a certain sort of sensibility, one which tolerated incongruity even when divided against itself and whose tone was, inevitably, ironic.

In his double lives as convert and sinner, civil servant and dandy, Gray pursued much the same course of systematic contradiction. To adopt it as a poetic strategy argues the intimacy of his art and life, as does the dialectic, within his poetry, between commitment to art and passionate distrust of its terms. Gray understood the aesthetic in which he was working—that of the self-conscious registration of one's sensibility—to be dangerously exclusive, ultimately entailing a denial of the life of the imagination, a terror of feeling and a retreat from experience, even from the experience of art: for in such an aesthetic there is always the jeopardy of becoming the creature of one's creation.

That danger, which Gray half courted, half tried to avoid, is enacted in the most graphic of the *Silverpoints* poems, the melodrama of "The Barber."

I. I dreamed I was a barber; and there went
   Beneath my hand, oh! manes extravagant.
   Beneath my trembling fingers, many a mask
   Of many a pleasant girl. It was my task
   To gild their hair, carefully, strand by strand;
   To paint their eyebrows with a timid hand;
   To draw a bodkin, from a vase of kohl,
   Through the closed lashes; pencils from a bowl
   Of sepia to paint them underneath;
   To blow upon their eyes with a soft breath.
   They lay them back and watched the leaping bands.

II. The dream grew vague. I moulded with my hands
   The mobile breasts, the valley; and the waist
   I touched; and pigments reverently placed
   Upon their thighs in sapient spots and stains,
   Beryls and crysolites and diaphanes,
   And gems whose hot harsh names are never said.
   I was a masseur; and my fingers bled
   With wonder as I touched their awful limbs.

III. Suddenly, in the marble trough, there seems
   O, last of my pale mistresses, Sweetness!
   A twylipped scarlet pansie. My caress
   Tinges thy steelgray eyes to violet.
   Adown thy body skips the pit-a-pat
   Of treatment once heard in a hospital
   For plagues that fascinate, but half appal.

IV. So, at the sound, the blood of me stood cold.
    Thy chaste hair ripened into sullen gold.
    The throat, the shoulders, swelled and were uncouth.
    The breasts rose up and offered each a mouth.
    And on the belly pallid blushes crept,
    That maddened me, until I laughed and wept. (Pp. 24–25)

The dream, even at first, is less than innocent; we are allowed no illusions in any case. In the 1890s, decent women did not "paint," and part of the charm of this verse is its disingenuousness, a kind of mischief also at work in Max Beerbohm's "Defence of Cosmetics." As for the barber, he is nothing less than the decadent artist himself, who, in the manner of Wilde, prefers the artificial to the natural. An artist of surfaces, of masks, he pastes upon his client jewels, "Beryls and crysolites and diaphanes," the brilliance of which suggests her inner corruption, in a line that echoes one from Wilde's *Salome*.[43]

Content at first to "gild," to "paint," and to "draw," the barber begins to touch and mold (as "a masseur"); then, spellbound, watches in horror the flesh respond as "Suddenly, in the marble trough, there seems/. . . Sweetness!/A twylipped scarlet pansie. My caress/Tinges thy steelgray eyes to violet." Gray had originally written, "thy mouth a scarlet pansie," but the more ambiguous phrase prepares us for the jolts of the last stanza. He has altered more than he planned. What he was to "gild" has "ripened into sullen gold"; the breasts, "moulded with my hands," now aroused, "rose up and offered each a mouth." Before the voracious sexual energy of his subject, the barber grows more confused, more ambivalent, until he finally breaks down, crazed with fear.

Clearly the poem is climactic. Read against the events of the summer of 1892, one becomes aware of how it fuses associations: Gray's new and fervent friendship with Pierre Louÿs; his growing disillusionment with Wilde; his abhorrence of sexuality, particularly feminine sexuality. A central text might hold them all together: Wilde's *Salome*. It makes that symbolic equation of sexual arousal and morbidity enacted in Gray's own adventures with Louÿs during June, followed by Gray's breakdown that autumn, his thoughts of suicide, his talk of death. Indeed, Louÿs's first letter to Gray alludes to lines from *Salome*.[44] Eventually, even the publication of *Silverpoints* the next spring became involved with the fate of Wilde's play. His first book was delayed by some weeks because, as Gray explained to Louÿs, "The editors have the idea of having me appear on the same day as Salome—an idea which warrants as little wisdom as it does satisfaction."[45]

"The Barber" is thus summation, and indictment, of Gray's own art and the life from whence it sprang. Symbolically, it traces the artist's transfer of his own autonomy to his art; art revenges itself by destroying the artist. It is the double-cross found in the plot of *The Picture of Dorian Gray* or Thomas Beddoes's version of the Pygmalion myth, perhaps its closest antecedent. No such betrayal would have been possible had not the work of art, in a profound sense, appropriated part of the artist's psychic life and become a kind of alter ego, a disengaged fragment of consciousness which undermines his confidence in his own integrity; in other words, the work has become part of the artist's mask. In this poem Gray acknowledges the inherently cannibalistic nature of an art which feeds on its own sensibility. But he also explores the psychic dilemma of his performance as "Dorian" Gray. Inevitably, as he comes to see, his meticulous artefact—whether poem or mask, poem creating mask—will consume its creator.

"The Barber" may thus be read as a critique not merely of Gray's own poetry but also of the aesthetic in which he was working, one in which "art" and "consciousness" have become indistinguishable. Gray carried this equation to its logical extreme, and, at times, to its logical absurdity. His poems have certainly some claim to being the most precocious of those written during the nineties. Two qualities in particular stand out: extravagance and a corresponding hollowness of style, an alliance that implies the rococo. But, as in the late, elaborate manner of Beardsley, their extravagance becomes a kind of self-mockery which, not entirely self-contained, implicates its audience as well. Like the barber, we do not know whether to laugh or weep.

If, ultimately, this style may be judged (as Gray judged it) an artistic failure, it is certainly not a failure of artistic intention. Gray clearly succeeded in his aim of composing a decorative, imitative, charming, and clever kind of poetry, even though it may at times have undone itself through an excess of ingenuity. "New-found freedom," Gray remarks of the *symboliste* poets,

is apt to realize itself a little too vividly, and first experiments with a language loosed from the moorings of its tradition are like to be carried out with more impulse than balance. But the temerity of these forerunners has its immediate reward . . . in the inevitable youth and cleanness of their language; every word they write is with intention. [46]

In the final analysis, Gray's poetic experiments may be said to be re-deemed by their intense consciousness of themselves *as* experiments. After the turn of the century, meditating on his nineties poetry, Gray ruefully observed that "all I have done has been a performance on the edge of a precipice, usually rewarded as such deserves, and more for reproof than applause even when I did not fall over." [47]

Thus Gray acknowledged that he, too, committed his poetic ex-periments often "with more impulse than balance." But his temerity had less to do with actual technical innovation (as it did with the *sym-bolistes*) than with the bold importation of foreign elements, particu-larly those adapted from contemporary French poets. Valuing his native tradition, Gray nevertheless believed, as he stated in his article on the Goncourts, that it would be revived through congruent French technique. Thus the mellifluous word-music of Tennyson prepares for the subtle tonalities of Verlaine, the fragmented detail of Rossetti for the poems which imitated the Impressionists. And as Gray's poetry, by intention, elaborates the values of surface, it is not surprising that the version he adopts of the new foreign poetry is relatively superficial. Broadly speaking, what Gray neglects in his relations with the French is as significant as what he appropriates.

Poisonous Honey from France

"The book on its appearance was not treated fairly," one critic noted of *Silverpoints* some eight months after its publication. "The milk-maid school of poets and critics naturally could not appreciate the aims of a writer who went as far as possible away from the conventional style they delight in; while other critics attacked the volume through simple dislike of the egregious firm that published it."[48] In their eyes, both John Gray and John Lane had failed in some profound sense to be English, a deviation assumed to be "French." Gray, of course, overtly played to this expectation in his imitations and translations from Baudelaire and the *symboliste* poets; but the taint was assumed to be deeper than that. To most critics even the mock-Elizabethan sonnets, for all their quaintness and verbal embroidery, had the fatal Gallic affectation. The same critic who complained of the book's unfair reception notes in these mannerisms Gray's large debt to Mallarmé ("a much over-estimated writer by the way"): "Both are fond of labouring at conceits, both indulge in esoteric fancies, and both attempt to make up for lack of imagination and creative power by over-elaboration; Mr. Gray, however, has not yet followed his master into the absolute imbecility of his later productions." As Richard Le Gallienne put it in another review, Gray has demonstrated in *Silverpoints* "that if he would abandon the affectations of contemporary French verse, he might write excellent English poetry."[49]

This antagonism was not new; if anything, it was already part of the Victorian landscape. When in 1873 Alfred, Lord Tennyson, wrote scornfully of "Art with poisonous honey stolen from the flowers of France," he was, even at the peak of his influence, merely voicing the opinion of his time and place. By the early 1890s, that cultural antipathy had become so exacerbated that "French" was virtually synonymous with "corrupt."[50] What this meant in moral, and particularly, sexual, terms is fairly clear. What it meant in terms of poetry—to Gray, his audience and to us—is more problematic, partly because, as we have noted, "French," like "decadent," carried a lot of emotional baggage, not only poetic, but social, moral, and political. "French" was what the English did not wish to be or become.

Yet it is important to clarify the terms of this confusion, if only because the discovery of the *symboliste* poets, in particular, was to direct the course of that revolution which produced, for better or worse, modern poetry. In introducing this "new poetry" to England, in attempting to domesticate its technique, *Silverpoints* played a modest but crucial role. Yet the assimilation is now in so many ways complete that it is difficult to say exactly what role it played. What Gray's audience, for instance, considered "French" would not necessarily strike us as such; we have, through such poets as Pound, Eliot, and Wallace Stevens, come to think of many once novel techniques as indigenous, rather than new and shocking. Indeed, Gray was probably one of the first to recognize that many of the "imported" innovations, such as the *pointillisme* of the Sensitivist school, could already be located in the native tradition, as in the mannerisms of Rossetti.

At the same time, Gray also obviously agreed with his reviewers that the "over-elaboration" of a technical stunt, such as a typical Elizabethan conceit, did indeed make it new: not so much, perhaps, in keying up a tired cliché to a novel and impossible pitch, but in the preoccupations manifest in the exercise, in particular those involving technique and form. Yet in other ways, a poem such as "Heart's Demesne," a version of a sonnet, is a form almost ossified, one would have thought, by tradition. Choosing such a form, Gray demonstrated his high regard for the shape of the poem. A generation before, this might have been regarded as "French," when the English Parnassians, such as Gosse and Swinburne, made much of their admiration of Théodore de Banville and his master Théophile Gautier. Their influence lingered on into the new decade (one notes the various rondeaux, rondeaux redoublés, and triolets in the two books of the Rhymers' Club). But by the nineties, this was considered neither novel nor even particularly foreign: traditionalist "English" poets such as Watson or Le Gallienne were just as likely to turn out shapely verse.

Gray's poetry, early and late, always has a firm clear outline. No debt to France explains this; possibly no literary debt at all. *Silverpoints* by title invokes a craft of the clear, unhesitating line; in this artistic method, by which one draws with a silver stylus on especially prepared paper, there is little room for error or revision. Gray's first formal training was in the Drafting Room of the Woolwich Arsenal; he would have watched and may have learned actual silverpoint technique under the formidable tutelage of Charles Ricketts. Having been trained in a craft, Gray fervently believed that—as he wrote many years later to a fellow poet—"Poetry is an art and art is skill (and artificial is not a pejorative epithet)."[51] At times, indeed, Gray seems almost blind to the technical revolt of the *symboliste* poets, remarking instead on their craftsmanlike deliberation, observing that "every word they write is with intention."[52] For Gray, the poem should always manifest the poet's designs on it; or, as he observed to another poet, Olive Custance, about a year after the publication of *Silverpoints:* "At a certain time one is apt to want to live for grace. Soon the better ideal comes to live well and chance the grace. And is it not so with poetry? Have you come to the determination to write *well* at every risk? to put more fire into your work than anyone else could ever find out."[53]

Gray exercised this determination to "write *well*" through a fastidious attention to the formal elements of rhyme, meter, and rhetorical device. Many of the *Silverpoints* poems appear to have been assembled, as if they were artefacts. Such a poetic strategy often, however, numbed Gray's appreciation of such a poet as Mallarmé, whom he tended to imitate in terms of mere rhetorical manipulation, using (in "Sound," for instance) assonance, alliteration, and onomatopoeia to convey the "music" which for Mallarmé had assumed an entirely conceptual status.[54]

Numbed, too, was Gray's ear. He lacked the lyric grace of Ernest Dowson or the metrical virtuosity of Lionel Johnson. His poems do not sing; instead, as several critics complained at the time, they stumble.[55] When felicities do occur, they are the result not of a keen ear but of verbal patterning strongly reminiscent of Tennyson; one fictive account has Father Gray reciting "'Now sleeps the crimson petal, now the white' with the subdued relish of an epicure."[56] But the insistence of such word patterns often drags the line toward stasis, as in "How very pale your pallor is" or "And rosy knuckles, laced with yellow lace."

Patterning such as this tends to deaden the poem on the page. And, in fact, the resonances set up here are really effective only when the poetry is read aloud, as a late Victorian audience would tend to receive it. It is worth recalling that most of Gray's audience—the Rhymers, the guests of the Princess of Monaco, Walter Pater—*heard* Gray's poems before they ever appeared in print. Gray knew his audience and clearly intended to compose a poetry to be closely read, repeated, and reread for different levels of significance; for echoes, patterns of statement, and variation; for allusions to such other poets as Verlaine and Laforgue which would be grasped only by other initiates. Oblique allusion to private events (such as the viewing of Millais's "Ophelia," which inspired "On A Picture") would enhance their appeal to such a coterie. In this context, the "borrowed" quality of much of *Silverpoints* becomes part of its peculiar beauty.

However, despite Gray's scrupulous craftsmanship, there is much here that violates neoclassical decorum. The language, for instance, is often extremely mannered. It is true that Gray attributed to his models, the French *symbolistes,* a "claim to throw over, in the matter of expression, a considerable portion of the tyranny of the grammar book."[57] And it is clear that for John Gray, "to write *well*" did not necessarily mean "to write good English," or even "to write good poetry." From this angle, *Silverpoints* shows up rather poorly beside the work of, for example, Lionel Johnson, who was a serious and very competent technician, while Gray thought of technique as something of a trick, a kind of tinkering with imagery and syntax for unusual effect. At times, indeed, it is actually difficult to say whether an unusual construction is merely awkward or a deliberate attempt to write against the grain, as in the case of "A Halting Sonnet." This in itself indicates something about the quality of the verse.

Yet Gray's prose of this period is clear, fluent, forceful. "The Person in Question" and another (unpublished) short story, "The Yellow Princess," have some claim to being minor classics of the decade. Even in a space of a few years, Gray's prose has become plainer, flatter, a far cry from the tortured syntax of his article on "Les Goncourt." Its redeployment in *Silverpoints* thus must be from choice, perhaps an effort to so estrange poetic language from ordinary speech that even their craftsmanship seems a form of perversion. Art is art, as Yeats was fond of intoning, because it is not Nature.

Yeats wrote his own commentary on that conviction in "Sailing to Byzantium" at a time when Byzantium was commonly regarded as a symbol of a culture in decadence. Like Gray, Yeats suffered for a time from an identification of art with artifice, although the most self-conscious advocate of that view was always Wilde. In this presumption, Gray followed his mentor, remarking of the Sensitivist poets that "in the end, the language they play tricks with thanks them."[58] Yet in exploiting so heavily the tricksiness of language, Gray became indifferent to, or simply did not comprehend, the radical style of Baudelaire and those *symboliste* poets whom he translated. Each regarded the symbol as arising ineluctably from concept and/or feeling: Gray employed imagery to neutralize both. Take, for example, the last two stanzas of "Complaint":

> Thou shout! thou burst of light! thou throb
> > Of pain! thou sob!
> > Thou like a bar
> Of some sonata, heard from far
>
> Through blue-hue'd veils! When in these wise,
> > To my soul's eyes,
> > Thy shape appears,
> My aching hands are full of tears. (P. 23)

The images have, obviously, no conceptual value; in fact, Gray's approach to writing poetry was, as his "method" of composition suggests, aggressively anti-intellectual. As for emotional value, this has been short-circuited by Gray's use of imagery for the purpose of emoting; it has become part of a histrionic display.

It is not, then, that Gray merely misunderstood Baudelaire and the *symbolistes;* the issue, as we shall see, is more complicated than that. He misunderstood them for his own ends. There is a certain willfulness in the way in which he turns their techniques (as, above, synesthesia) into tricks, escaping emotion by its very exaggeration, turning it back on itself in a kind of grotesque self-parody. Gray did not aim to embody the inner life. On the contrary, it was precisely from the inner life that he sought to distance himself, seeking in his poetry a refuge in what Wilde called "beautiful, sterile emotions."

The irony of his position was not lost on Gray. Nor on Yeats, who, praying for release from the form of "any natural thing" into the "artifice of eternity," found its epitome in the mechanical golden bird whose song serves only to "keep a drowsy Emperor awake," its passionate music trivialized and despised. Gray's "Poem" is both a more ruthless and a funnier version of such betrayal of artist by artifice, of the poet by his poetry, the fate, here, of that ardent singer, Robert Burns:

> Geranium, houseleek, laid in oblong beds
> On the trim grass. The daisies' leprous stain
> Is fresh. Each night the daisies burst again,
> Though every day the gardener crops their heads.
>
> A wistful child, in foul unwholesome shreds,
> Recalls some legend of a daisy chain
> That makes a pretty necklace. She would fain
> Make one, and wear it, if she had some threads.
>
> Sun, leprous flowers, foul child. The asphalt burns.
> The garrulous sparrows perch on metal Burns.
> Sing! Sing! they say, and flutter with their wings.
> He does not sing, he only wonders why
> He is sitting there. The sparrows sing. And I
> Yield to the strait allure of simple things. (P. 30)

Yeats's metallic bird at least did sing. Gray's singer, once poet of brawling tavernside and upland moor, now sits encased in ceremonial bronze, taunted by the tame park sparrows: "Sing! Sing! they say, and flutter with their wings." Art has been rendered impotent by Nature, which it can neither kill nor redeem.[59] No daisy chain makes the foul child fair. The gardener, an artist of sorts, executes his will on the daisies, laying them out in oblong beds (graves?). But their teeming vitality mocks his work, even as the birds mock the stolid figure of Burns, who "does not sing, he only wonders why/He is sitting there."

He is sitting there, of course, because he has fallen victim to popular acclaim—what Wilde once called the revenge of Caliban—an artist become prisoner of his art. Coming upon the statue at the very start of his poetic career, Gray obviously viewed "metal Burns" with a fatal skepticism.[60] With his proud Scots ancestry and humble background, Gray may well have identified with the actual poet, now so cruelly parodied by his apotheosis. Was Burns also to figure as another person in question, an image of the man Gray was to become, a kind of ghost of the future? Cold, hard, aloof, self-mocking: the qualities that characterize the statue—and the poem—came to be the words describing John Gray in later life, who also, ironically, by then lived in Scotland. From the perspective of age he came to realize his fate, which was to be not only the author, but also the offspring of his art: "Father Silverpoints" as the "Michael Fields" then called him. "The asphalt burns," yet fervent Rabbie Burns has cooled to metal. By analogy, Gray's own stated determination "to put more fire into your work than anyone else could ever find out" has cast itself into the rigid mold of the poem, which as "Poem" stands as a monument to his own impotence and the futility of his enterprise.

The poem is in any case only making explicit the self-parody of its subject: the statue of an idealized poet frozen at the moment of inspiration. A monument to its own contradiction of terms, it implies their ultimate rejection. Scotland was from henceforward to represent for Gray an abdication from poetry. In December 1893, ten months after this poem was published, Gray visited Edinburgh. There, in the window of a bookstore, he saw, as if in a dream, a book entitled *The Excellent Way,* from which he translated that great poem of Jacopone da Todi, "O love, all love above."[61] A few years later—having fled Wilde and shed "Dorian" Gray—as a seminarian in Rome he was to sign his letters "Jacopone." After his ordination, he declared that he was through with poetry: "And I/Yield to the strait allure of simple things." At the close, the poet abdicates from his poem to the more fruitful discipline of the world outside it, which was eventually to be the world of Father Gray, of Edinburgh, and the children of its foul slums.

It is odd that such an early poem should state so flatly the premises of its own destruction, except possibly when one considers how keenly Gray did seek to proceed by paradox and therefore, necessarily, by an almost conscious subversion. Here it is not solemn. "Poem" is in its way a fine piece of mischief, a half-playful, half-devastating critique of itself. It invited translation by the French decadent poet and friend of Gray's, Francis Vielé-Griffin.[62] And it invited such actual parodies as this one by Owen Seaman, significantly entitled "Disenchantment":

My love has sickled into Loath,
        And foul seems all that fair I fancied—
The lily's sheen a leprous growth,
        The very buttercups are rancid.[63]

There are times, indeed, in *Silverpoints* when it is hard to distinguish the actual parodies from the self-inflicted ones, the irony is so fierce and multidirectional. Ultimately, that irony not only sterilizes the emotions of the poem, but kills them off as well, leaving the verse with an inert quality, which led one reviewer to remark that Gray's "forced peculiarity of . . . language" has resulted in a "complete want of human passion, of human sensation; an oversweet, even sickly, elaboration. . . . It is the continual sickly-sweet atmosphere of his work that tires one so much, and yet without this Mr. Gray has nothing to give us."[64] Could this be Gray's version of the decadent "*faisandé*" style, the cloying stench of a decayed mode of expression? Certainly he aimed at a vigorous "decomposition" of a poem, if one may use that term to characterize his composition by cliché, inversion of stale conceit, or play of faded archaism. Probably it represents Gray's imitation of what he took, from Pater, to be the elaborate late Latin of Apuleius; the euphuism of John Lyly; the over-ingenuity of the Elizabethan sonneteers.

Gray's attempt to write English as if it were a dead language succeeds nowhere better than in his poem, "Crocuses in Grass":

Purple and white the crocus flowers,
        And yellow, spread upon
        The sober lawn; the hours
Are not more idle in the sun.

Perhaps one droops a prettier head,
        And one would say: Sweet Queen,
        Your lips are white and red,
And round you lies the grass most green.

And she, perhaps, for whom is fain
        The other, will not heed;

Or, that he may complain,
Babbles, for dalliaunce, with a weed.

And he dissimulates despair,
    And anger, and surprise;
    The while white daisies stare
—And stir not—with their yellow eyes. (Pp. 29–30)

After its excesses in Tennyson's "Maud" and its parody in *Through the Looking Glass,* the use of a cliché so utterly dead can only be called daring—or foolhardy. That deadness is useful; it lends the imagery the kind of flatness of a Japanese print; the metallic hardness of those stone-and-wire flowers which were to become so popular in the decade of art nouveau. It also gives the poem an excruciating preciosity, teetering between the sickly-sweet and the downright silly. Why did Gray do it?

He was taking risks, as he later confessed. He clearly intended to use a language exhausted through overuse, dying if not altogether dead. For him, it seemed to represent a kind of abstract language, one so purified of significance that it could be employed as part of a formal, even ritual, gesture. Perhaps it was his version of Mallarmé's injunction to "give a purer meaning to the words of the tribe." Nor are the social uses of cliché foreign to the orientation of *Silverpoints,* to its intent of charming, even of ingratiating itself through a recognizable style. Such use of cliché draws attention to the speaking voice, to the actual tonalities in which it is used, a strategy which again argues for Gray's use of his art for nonartistic ends: to impress his audience with a display of a certain sensibility, say, or a mastery of the precise nuance of mood. If accepted, if admired, it was because Gray's audience shared his understanding of poetry as one of the performing arts and perhaps as ironic comments on his posture as "Dorian" Gray.

That the poetry allowed Gray to experiment with other voices, to practice a kind of ventriloquism which in turn reflected his distrust of art is, however, only one of its virtues. Another, for which *Silverpoints* has in this century gained its reputation, was for its adaptation of new voices, particularly those from the French. For instance, the untitled poem, "Did we not, Darling," in which one corpse addresses another, draws its imagery from several novel sources: the conceit perhaps from Baudelaire—or from Emily Dickinson, the first English edition of whose poems was in Gray's possession.[65] But even more startling is its speaker: Pierrot, the melancholy idealist of Jules Laforgue who provides a couplet for Gray's epigraph to the poem.[66] From our perspective, the importation marks a milestone: for it is Laforgue's intonation that may be singled out as the most obvious precocity of *Silverpoints*, the most specific line of continuity between Gray's poetry and that of, say, T. S. Eliot.

So, while Gray's poems were written while under the influence of the French *symboliste* poets, several of whom Gray had met and whose work he had translated, he is by no means debauched by their "poisonous honey." Rather, he keeps his stylistic distance, taking his cue from the precarious self-mockery of Huysmans's hero, Des Esseintes, or from his own acknowledged master, Oscar Wilde. Both used exaggeration as a mode of escaping emotion, sterilizing it by its own excess. Both were masters of the mask and its clever ventriloquisms. Arguably, neither achieved a style of his own except by travesty of others; neither could be accused of sincerity. Their stylistic ingenuities allowed them to multiply their voices, but ultimately both proved empty performances—or, rather, performances that resonated because of their emptiness, turning mockery of others into self-mockery, performance into parody. And each, exhausting the logical possibilities of their method, arrived at its logical terminus: a dead end.

In these respects, Gray's large debt to early Huysmans and Wilde is obvious. Yet many of his contemporaries were of the opinion that he imitated the *symboliste* poets, Mallarmé in particular. Dowson's report about Gray's reading of verses "in the latest manner of French Symbolism" has already been noted, as has the *Silverpoints* review that names Mallarmé as "Gray's master."[67] Rather than evidence that Gray did actually imitate *symboliste* techniques, these remarks can be taken more as a commentary on the limitations of the nineties understanding of the *symbolistes* and, in particular, of Mallarmé's aesthetics. A look at Gray's translations of Verlaine, Rimbaud, and Mallarmé indicates that his own grasp of *symboliste* technique was in fact severely limited.

Silverpoints was thus not the child of the *symbolistes:* it was the offspring of Gray's own peculiar personality, which it also, paradoxically, helped to beget. The extravagance of its manner, its cultivation of surface values as a poetic strategy, the often whimsical quality of its self-mockery, is entirely its own. As an original experiment, it springs primarily from a preoccupation with stylization rather than style, thus becoming in the last analysis a kind of poetic cul-de-sac: "a sometimes beautiful oddity," as Lionel Johnson would call it.[68]

The Translations of Silverpoints

If Pound regarded the original poems of *Silverpoints* as a kind of curious mutation in the evolution of modern poetry, he left Gray's translations of other works out of his reckoning. They were—and are— crucial to its reputation for being relentlessly "new," for being at the very pitch of fashion. "One had in the late eighties and early nineties," wrote Victor Plarr, "to be preposterously French."[69] Gray's original poems (as we have seen) may have been at times preposterous, but they were not particularly French. The translations undeniably are. They also dominate the slim book, representing nearly half (thirteen of twenty-nine) of the poems. In fact, they were probably the first introduction for many of Gray's readers to the poetry of Rimbaud and Mallarmé, and among the first to Baudelaire and Verlaine.

In accounts of the 1890s, credit for this introduction is usually accorded to Arthur Symons for publishing, a year before *Silverpoints,* the first major collection of *symboliste* verse in *Silhouettes* (1892). Symons, however, limited himself to the translation of Verlaine. In comparison, Gray's poems cover an impressive range: from Baudelaire (three poems) and Verlaine (seven) to Mallarmé (one) and Rimbaud (two). If one may argue that modern poetry evolved in part through the discovery after the turn of the century by T. S. Eliot, W. B. Yeats, and Wallace Stevens, among others, of the *symboliste* poets and their disciples, then it is fair to say that John Gray here played a strategic if limited role.

Most of the translations of *Silverpoints* have distinctive merits; they also reveal distinct limitations. Gray entitled his translations "imitations" for a reason: he aimed at more than a paraphrase of the French. Rather than reproduce the original, Gray chose to transpose meter, for instance, into its English equivalent (largely, iambic pentameter); this tactic often improved on a more literal rendering. As we shall see, however, Gray's transposition takes a more drastic form in an apparently arbitrary deletion of whole lines and stanzas.

In most cases the reasons for such drastic editing remain obscure, but suggest several possibilities. Gray may have been persuaded of the unsuitability of certain lines and verses, as we have seen in Frank Harris's intervention over Rimbaud's "À la Musique" (see pp. 67f. herein). Or Gray himself may have removed passages he found in questionable taste, as in Baudelaire's invocation of his "Femmes Damnées": "O vierges, ô démons, ô monstres, ô martyres, / De la réalité grands esprits contempteurs . . ."[70] Such editorial strategies suggest a conflict between artistic audacity and fear of its consequence and the delicate compromises that sustained Gray's role as poet/dandy. For, if he genuinely felt revulsion at such lines, why translate the poems at all?

Not only did Gray translate them, but he also published them, mutilated, as if they were entire. Is there a parallel in the way he was living his life at the time: a pattern of flirtation, but not commitment? Or an analogy with this mode of translation, which leads toward key lines that are then suppressed? Certainly it defines the way Gray was to edit his past, leaving provocative hints in the form of certain letters, but apparently destroying key documents. In these instances, there appears an effort to subvert actual meaning, to reduce things to their formal elements—to decorative, if tantalizing, surfaces. Another possibility, which does not necessarily exclude the others, is that Gray simply lacked the poetic resources to translate *symboliste* technique into English, a failure typical of his generation of poets, but one perhaps also peculiar to Gray. We have seen his apologies for his poor French, for example, as well as his occasional lapses as a poet in his native tongue.

Yet these translations, both in their shortcomings and successes, offer arresting testimony to the mode in which the new French poetry was presented to its first English audience. Among the more remarkable can be numbered Gray's translations of Baudelaire. Of his contemporaries, Gray is the first to capture that austere precision which T. S. Eliot found so deficient in the translations of Arthur Symons.[71] The difference is apparent in the opening lines of their renditions of "Un Voyage à Cythère":

> My heart swung birdlike in its intense distraction
> And soared in the cordages, hung heavily by its grip:
> Under me swayed and surged the white-sailed ship
> Like a radiant angel filled with intoxication. (Symons)

> Bird-like, my heart was glad to soar and vault;
> Fluttering among the cordages; and on
> The vessel flew, under an empty vault:
> An angel drunken of a radiant sun. (Gray)

And the original:

> Mon coeur, comme un oiseau, voltigeait tout joyeux
> Et planait librement à l'entour des cordages;
> Le navire roulait sous un ciel sans nuages,
> Comme un ange enivré d'un soleil radieux.

Gray's muscular lines move with the tension of the original, entirely lost in Symons's flaccid (if faithful) paraphrase. Not only is Gray's poem admirable, but Symons may have pillaged it for his own closing lines.[72]

These stanzas suggest another reason for Gray's superiority as a translator of Baudelaire. Where Symons slurs over the sense of Baudelaire's "Hélas! et j'avais, comme en un suaire épais, / Le coeur enseveli dans cette allégorie," Gray acknowledges the logic of the imagery, its reasoning through analogy ("in that parable" as Gray translates). Gray's own proficiency at this kind of poetical logic, as opposed to the metaphorical development that he consistently ignores in, say, Mallarmé, is manifest in other original *Silverpoints* poems, most notably the conceits of "Heart's Demesne" and "To EMG."

The two other Baudelaire translations are for various reasons somewhat less successful. Impressive as far as it goes, Gray's "Femmes Damnées" is flawed by inexplicable excision precisely at the point where Baudelaire begins to work out his analogy. Is it possible that Gray did not grasp what the poem was about? After all, the holograph *Silverpoints* manuscript reveals that he originally translated this hymn to lesbianism under the title "Young Girls." For whatever reason, Gray's omission of the last two quatrains effectively disembowels the poem. Similarly, the failure of "A une Madone" is also hard to account for; could Gray not come to terms with its admixture of sexuality and religious terror? Or did the compression of the poem doom him, in English, to mere mediocrity?

If the translations of Baudelaire are striking even within these limits, Gray is at his most skillful with Verlaine. For various reasons, Verlaine proved the most adaptable of the modern French poets to English; his dreamy landscapes and verbal music were discovered with the shock of recognition by poets who looked to the Pre-Raphaelites, to early Tennyson, and to Keats as their masters.[73] Gray's own discovery may have been hastened by Symons; certainly Gray's progress from the disastrous rendition of "Beauté des femmes . . ." in *The Artist and Journal of Home Culture* (1890) to the very competent pieces of *Silverpoints* suggests that someone educated him to the techniques of Verlaine. One *Silverpoints* "imitation" in particular, that of "Un Crucifix," is masterly:

> A gothic church. At one end of an aisle,
> Against a wall where mystic sunbeams smile
> Through painted windows, orange, blue, and gold,
> The Christ's unutterable charm behold.
> Upon the cross, adorned with gold and green,
> Long fluted golden tongues of sombre sheen,
> Like four flames joined in one, around the head
> And by the outstretched arms, their glory spread.
> The statue is of wood; of natural size;
> Tinted; one almost sees before one's eyes

The last convulsion of the lingering breath.
"Behold the man!" Robust and frail. Beneath
That breast indeed might throb the Sacred Heart.
And from the lips, so holily dispart,
The dying murmur breathes "Forgive! Forgive!"
O wide-stretched arms! "I perish, let them live."
Under the torture of the thorny crown,
The loving pallor of the brow looks down
On human blindness, on the toiler's woes;
The while, to overturn Despair's repose,
And urge to Hope and Love, as Faith demands,
Bleed, bleed the feet, the broken side, the hands.
A poet, painter, Christian,—it was a friend
Of mine—his attributes most fitly blend—
Who saw this marvel, made an exquisite
Copy; and, knowing how I worshipped it,
Forgot it, in my room, by accident.
I write these verses in acknowledgement. (Pp. 31–32)

In French this is a relatively poor poem, loosely knit and sometimes flatly stated. But Gray met these difficulties, particularly the half-rhyme and run-on lines, by transposing the lengthy alexandrines into heroic couplets and varying the caesura so that the lines breathe with the rhythms of actual speech. The result is an immediacy entirely lacking in the original.

Verlaine is the only French poet whom Gray completely mastered; not even the language of the "Cythère" translation can match this sublime control. It is not surprising, therefore, that Verlaine's touch may be found everywhere in *Silverpoints:* in particular, in the play of internal rhyme, alliteration, repetition, and rhythmic variation deployed with such skill in this translation.[74]

From such a level of accomplishment, however, the limitations of Gray's other translations become clear. In neither his rendition of Rimbaud nor of Mallarmé did Gray succeed in conveying to his audience their unique—and revolutionary—qualities. The reason may have been that Gray did not entirely grasp them himself. The large gaps in the Rimbaud poem, "À la Musique," for instance, are not due

solely to a literary propriety based on Frank Harris's urging. De-
corum would not by itself have dictated Gray's excision, evident in
the holograph, of another tendentious verse:

> Flattening on the seat his rotund haunch
> A bourgeois with bright buttons Flemish paunch
> Fondles his overstuffed tobacco pouch
> Probably contraband one cannot vouch.

Another quatrain, even more savage, Gray did not even attempt,
again, not (it seems) on account of its sentiment, but because of the
difficulty of rendering Rimbaud's technique of radical personification
into English, as in:

> Des rentiers à lorgnons soulignent tous les couacs:
> Les gros bureaux bouffis traînent leurs grosses dames
> Auprès desquelles vont, officieux cornacs,
> Celles dont les volants ont des airs de réclames. . .[75]

As Gray also misses this technique in his translation of another line
("La notaire pend à ses breloques à chiffres,"), we may assume that he
was simply unable to find a way of wording it.

Originally, Gray had planned to translate all of *Les Illuminations,*
but the omissions in the Rimbaud poem, particularly the last, suggest
why he could not pursue this project.[76] In this difficulty he was not
alone. During the period until 1910 only seven translations were made
of Rimbaud's poetry in England and America. He was not, in fact,
widely translated until the 1930s. The reasons for such neglect are, as
this translation reveals, not merely those of taste and propriety, but
the problem of not having developed equivalent techniques.[77] Thus
Gray, in common with Symons, Dowson, and Wilde, was unable to
create a poetry at all comparable to that which he sought to imitate.
Yet he must be given due credit for his attempt, however tentative and
incomplete. Gray's "imitations" of "À la Musique" and a second
poem, "Sensation," are admirable as far as they go. As the author of
two out of seven Rimbaud translations published before 1910, Gray
must also be recognized for the precocity of his taste.

Yet, in the last analysis, one misses in Gray's versions the audacity of Rimbaud's technique. Set against the Baudelaire translations, these two poems seem tepid and stale. This failure to transpose what is, after all, a revolutionary poetic strategy is more distressing in his only translation from Mallarmé, "Les Fleurs." Here Gray unaccountably cuts out the crucial opening stanza—lines proposing the imagery from which the entire poem evolves—thus reducing the Mallarmé poem to a triviality and preciosity comparable with his own.

This small but critical failure explains a great deal about the course of Gray's career. He did not become a major translator of the *symboliste* poets, as did Symons, although he certainly had ambitions in that direction. The reasons for this are clear in the failure with Mallarmé: Gray resists here and throughout *Silverpoints* the notion of a poetry that evolves through imagery. The poems, both the originals and the "imitations," are cast into a discursive mode: simile rather than metaphor is the preferred vehicle; narrative or the extended conceit, the predominant form. This basic inability to grasp a technique which was, after all, crucial to *symboliste* poetry made it impossible for Gray to continue the line of discovery that Symons was to exploit with such success in the ensuing decade.

The Reception of Silverpoints

Gray had no sooner seen the publication of *Silverpoints* than he began to regret it. His uneasiness did not seem to have its usual origin in the vituperation of critics. Although there were a few scornful and snide reviews, two acquaintances, Richard Le Gallienne and Theodore Wratislaw, wrote perceptive and generally appreciative essays. Gray expected notices in *Nieuwe Gids,* "the engine of young Holland" as he called it, and an appreciation by Frank Harris for *The Times.*[78] Neither of these seems to have materialized, nor did reviews in the *Academy* or the *Athenaeum,* an odd omission since these two journals were sensitive to new literary publications and Gray had already contributed to the former. Even more odd is the silence of Harris's *Fortnightly Review,* which was to have released the translation of Rimbaud the preceding winter.[79] Critical appreciation, it appears, was limited to the coterie at which the poetry had been aimed, and among these circles and the society women which patronized them, *Silverpoints* became something of a *cause célèbre*.

Dowson wrote Gray of his "extraordinary and subtile pleasure" in "the wonderful little book. It is beyond my expectations even, in exquisiteness." Pater and Swinburne raised their voices to praise it; but in private conversation or letters, it seems, since no review of theirs can be tracked down.[80] In general, the same energies of fashionable gossip which had originally created "Dorian" Gray were at work with *Silverpoints*. Certainly the extraordinary physical appearance of the book, described at length in most of the reviews, did as much to impress London society as the poetry itself, which to most seemed rather imitative and labored. In these circles this dainty slim volume created a sensation, typified by Ada Leverson's remark that:

> There was more margin; margin in every sense was in demand, and I remember, looking at the poems of John Gray (then considered the incomparable poet of the age), when I saw the tiniest rivulet of text meandering through the very largest meadow of margin, I suggested to Oscar Wilde that he should go a step further than these minor poets; that he should publish a book *all* margin; full of beautiful unwritten thoughts, and have this blank volume bound in some Nile-green skin powdered with gilt nenuphars and smoothed with hard ivory, decorated with gold by Ricketts (if not Shannon) and printed on Japanese paper; each volume must be a collector's piece, a numbered one of a limited "first" (and last) edition: "very rare."[81]

And, inevitably, the vogue *Silverpoints* created was satirized in the taste of that silly society matron of *The Green Carnation,* Mrs. Windsor, who "though she read much minor poetry, and knew all the minor poets, . . . was not poetic, and she honestly thought that John Gray's 'Silver Points' were far finer literature than Wordsworth's 'Ode to Immortality,' or Rossetti's 'Blessed Damosel.' "[82]

The extreme design and mannerisms of *Silverpoints,* in short, caused it to be hailed fashionably as an epitome of "decadence"; the *Pall Mall Gazette* called Gray simply "le plus décadent des décadents."[83] In his choice of poems for translation as well as his affectations of style, Gray had gone to some pains to pursue this reputation.

But on the whole it overwhelmed any other critical appraisal of the book. As has been observed, Gray was ambivalent about this enter-terprise, as evidenced by the scrapping and bowdlerizing of certain poems and the rewriting of the *Silverpoints* contract. Within a fort-night of the book's publication, Gray wrote Pierre Louÿs of his break with Wilde. It may have been also at this time that Gray started his lifelong habit of buying up copies of *Silverpoints* to "immobilize" and destroy them.[84]

A review that reflects Gray's desire to have it both ways is Rich-ard Le Gallienne's, written a month after the poems' publication. To force *Silverpoints* into a stereotype, he wrote, relied on a vulgar misin-terpretation of "decadence" as being a "self-conscious arrangement of 'coloured' vowels or a choice for themes of disease and forbidden things generally." The "real core of decadence is to be found in its isolated interests," Le Gallienne continued: "Its effects are gained by regarding life as of but one or two dimensions." He concluded that "in spite of his neo-Catholicism and his hot-house erotics, Mr. Gray cannot accomplish that gloating abstraction from the larger life of hu-manity which marks the decadent."[85] The effect of this review, one of the earlier attempts to define the meaning of the term, was naturally to fix "decadence" and *Silverpoints* inseparably in the public mind.

An unsigned essay (actually written by Max Beerbohm) reveals how far things had gone in this direction. If Oscar Wilde had, it states,

lived in the days of Socrates he would surely have been impeached on a charge not only of "making the worse cause appear the better"—for paradox as a method is never acceptable to the many—but also of "corrupting the youth"; he would have been condemned, and would have drunk the hemlock under protest, and one of the corrupt—perhaps Mr. John Gray—would have written another *Phaedo* in his memory. Indeed, the harm that Mr. Wilde has done within a certain radius is incalculable. For the love of beauty for its own sake, which has absorbed his whole system and inspired everything he has written, is a very rare thing indeed. It is inborn and cannot ever be communi-cated. And thus the young men who have tried to reproduce not only the manner of "the Master" but his spirit also have, for the most part, failed absurdly.[86]

Although a humorous and benign satire, the essay shows the popular view of John Gray: a disciple and lover of Wilde's and one of the "decadents," the "corrupt."

Even when one takes into account the measures Gray employed to distance himself from Wilde, it appears he was of two minds about such sensation-mongering. Probably to a considerable extent, he wished to cooperate with, even exploit it. One cannot escape the impression that *Silverpoints* was, in part at least, a venture in bookmaking. Why else should such poor pieces as the birthday sonnet to Ellen Terry be included? Why else were the dedicatees so carefully chosen and complimentary copies of the book so generously pressed on influential people? Copies were sent to Terry; Alice, Princess of Monaco; Swinburne; Whistler, "who will show Mallarmé," as Gray wrote; Marcel Schwob ("the editor of *Paris* the only French daily") as well as to such personal friends as Dowson, Harris, Shannon, and— one should note—Gray's mother). Harris was also given copies to distribute for review.[87]

Thus, despite gestures of withdrawal, Gray clearly cooperated in creating his reputation as a poet of the new literary fashion, much as he had allowed himself to be introduced to society as "Dorian" Gray. Of course, the gap between what society women considered "decadent" and the analyses of the movement published in 1893 by Symons and Le Gallienne was very large. But, while Le Gallienne was scrupulously excluding Gray from the avant-garde, various artistic and social circles were taking him up. Gray preserved a great many of the letters of praise that flooded in from such people as the Princess of Monaco; from the "Michael Fields"; and from his own circle, Dowson and Sherard.[88] Of all these, Symons was the most attuned to Gray's consequent siege of remorse over what he was to refer to, in later life, as "the odious Silverpoints." Symons wrote to Gray, "I understand well enough your present feeling about it, but it is a book which will certainly be remembered as marking a certain hour of the day. Every line is packed; and in most books there is so amazingly little ore, when one looks into them."[89]

Silverpoints acted as a turning point in Gray's life: it marked the disillusionment with Wilde and with his role as Wilde's protégé; his introduction to Raffalovich and break with Wilde; his rejection of the role of "decadent" poet for that of translator, a role by which he would discover, during the next two years, a new language of faith. The poetry of *Silverpoints* represents a desperate attempt to find integrity, or, at very worst, to manufacture it, as a simulacrum for an inchoate, and therefore incoherent, self. Thus Gray's rejection of the book virtually at birth becomes thus nothing less than a rejection of himself. Its significance was not lost on the reviewer who wrote of *Silverpoints*, "As a collection the book is a failure. Mr. Gray is often clever and occasionally an artist; and on the whole, one may say that he is a young man with a promising career behind him."[90]

FOUR

❧ *The Prodigal Returns, 1893–1898* ❧

Holy Christ, upon thy cross of torture,
Deign to see the sinner at thy feet,
Ignorant, besotted,
Even in despair effete.

"Rosary of the Cross"
Holograph of *Spiritual Poems*
Dated 29 December 1893

However stumbling and confused, Gray's rejection of *Silverpoints* and of Wilde ended his career in paradox. Thus, in the opening months of 1893 one watches intently the disintegrating facade of "Dorian" Gray for a glimpse, beneath, of the "real John Gray." That moment never comes. Instead, during the period between 1893 and 1898 occurs what might be called an interlude between the acts. Of all the years of Gray's adult history, these are the most irretrievable: they come to us refracted through the more fully documented lives of Oscar Wilde, Aubrey Beardsley, and André Raffalovich, but in images that are fragmented and incomplete. Even the letters that survive this period are bland and noncommittal, sharpened only by the occasional note of bitterness. To watch this withdrawal behind the curtains is to entertain the possibility that there is actually no "real John Gray" who exists apart from his roles.

One might observe that one of the major public events of this period, the three Wilde/Queensberry trials in the spring of 1895, might themselves have persuaded Gray of the virtues of self-effacement. That is certainly so; but it goes deeper than that. Gray appears, in his poetry and prose as well as in his various intellectual preoccupations during this time, to be enacting a profound rejection of ego itself. His art, once the means by which he literally engendered himself, now becomes the instrument of an urgent quest for "authority, in the sense of spiritual knowledge."[1] His search leads him to experiment with supernatural dictation (through writing by "influx") and also, apparently, into the world of the occult. Gradually, both his friendship with Raffalovich, which became sublimated into a kind of religious vocation, as well as the practice of his art, became tools of this overriding need to find a final authority to which, in peace, he could at last submit.

Now the returned prodigal, Gray began to see in his assumption of the role of "Dorian" the belligerence of the apostate who cannot rid himself of the need for faith. Gray later analyzed his revolt, resembling that of Huysmans's hero, Durtal, as the route of the degenerated Romantic whose "keen quest of infamy being extra physical in some aspects, [becomes] a mode of inverted spiritism."[2] As such, Gray begins to see his history as "Dorian" as part of a spiritual progression: not merely as something to be expiated, but now also as the *necessarium peccatum* in the quest for God.

In the years between the publication of *Silverpoints* and his departure for the seminary, Gray made his life over. It is clear that this was largely a matter of will, a determination to mark the distance from his former life. Thus the "affair" with Raffalovich was transformed, not without pain and confusion, into a rare spiritual friendship sealed by their common conversion to Catholicism. Gray turned his aesthetic/decadent poetic mode into a poetry of private devotional exercise. But the seamark of these years is the death of Aubrey Beardsley, which marked, too, the death of "Dorian" Gray. At the last, Gray's efforts to turn all things to their spiritual use is fulfilled in his decision to give up his art and devote his life entirely to the Church.

The Friend

If Gray's life as "Dorian" Gray began with his introduction to Oscar Wilde, that of Father Gray may be dated from his introduction to André Raffalovich. It seems peculiar that Gray did not encounter Raffalovich sooner since both were part of the London Uranian literary demimonde. But of course, Raffalovich and Gray came from worlds so far apart as to be almost different planets.[3] Even when they did meet in

November 1892, the encounter was arranged. Apparently, Raffalovich in his role as critic had treated with some severity the prose styles of Wilde and Gray in an article under the heading of "Follies of the Week." Gray took exception and wrote a vitriolic published reply.[4] Not long afterwards, they were both invited to a literary gathering by Arthur Symons, who apparently thought that Gray and Raffalovich ought to know each other. When they met at Symons's rooms in the Temple, Gray was considerably abashed, uncertain as to how he might be received. To his surprise, Raffalovich was gentle and affable, and asked him to dinner the following week.[5]

From this date on, much of Gray's history to 1898 is available only through that of the energetic, gregarious Raffalovich. In mid-October of that year, Ernest Dowson wrote Victor Plarr: "This morning Gray who is finally leaving the Temple—quantum mutatus ab isto—fat but friendly, I fear incurably given over to social things—& about to take up his abode in Park Lane! This is sad." Forty-three Park Lane was not, as the footnote to this letter asserts, the residence of André Raffalovich, but a house leased to eleven residents a few minutes' walk from Raffalovich's house at 72 South Audley Street.[6]

In this confusion, however, rests a tale, for it was commonly assumed that Gray had become Raffalovich's lover, as the latter was by 1893 a well-known poet of the "Uranian" school and a familiar of the London homosexual underworld.[7] It appears that Raffalovich was in fact attracted to Gray and wished for such a relationship. Certainly the note of sexual jealousy over Gray's friendship with Wilde sounds clearly throughout Raffalovich's personal memoir of Wilde, with whom he had carried on what can only be called a flirtation.[8] Raffalovich began drawing back after Constance Wilde's "nice improper talks" remark, and over the months, distance turned to distrust, distrust to distaste. Eventually, after his public rejection of "the whole set," Raffalovich came to feel about Wilde that

everything he did or said annoyed me. He could do nothing right in my eyes. When I say he could do nothing right in my eyes, must this apply to the past as to the present? to his way, for instance, of always selecting the youngest in any company and talking to him endlessly, turning his head (as I said) for the mere pleasure of doing so, even though they were never to meet again. (Pp. 700–701)

Later, in one of his "scientific" articles on homosexuality, Raffalovich even went so far as to consider the jury's verdict against Wilde as justified, not so much on the grounds of the commission of homosexual acts, as on Wilde's *influence* on the society of young men around him.[9]

London gossip went further. Robert Sherard reports the speculation that Raffalovich had "avenged himself . . . on Oscar Wilde for one or two gibes about his personal appearance and his social success by breaking up a new friendship to which Wilde attached great value."[10] In any case, Raffalovich's bitterness, while certainly not based on moral grounds, acted as a catalyst in Gray's decision to break with Wilde. To all his acquaintances at the time, Raffalovich served the ultimatum: "You cannot be Oscar's friend and mine."[11]

Sexual feeling, sexual jealousy were at first certainly part of Raffalovich's feelings for Gray. Raffalovich later confessed as much, albeit obliquely, in a letter to Gray—then studying for the priesthood—which recalls their first meeting:

Still after all Symons the artist brought you and me together 7 years and 3 months ago. There was plenty of mental manure on which our fraternity could grow, n'est-ce pas, petit frère. And it has so thrived that I do not often bring into conscious thoughts how through eternity nothing I could ever do could quite atone for all I made you undergo. . . . It is curious that two human beings can get sure enough of each other not even to have to ask for forgiveness. . . .[12]

As the letter intimates, the friendship that sprang from the "manure" of sexual attraction in time became one of those rare relationships between two people of the same sex: one chaste, ennobling and dedicated to spiritual ends. Its archetype had already been set out by Raffalovich in his book, *Uranisme et Unisexualité; Étude sur Différentes Manifestations de l'Instinct Sexuel,* published in France in 1896. In this landmark publication, hailed by Havelock Ellis as being an early and important work on sexual inversion in England, Raffalovich argues that homosexuality is generally congenital rather than acquired, and therefore not a matter of moral responsibility.[13] He deplores, however, the "inferior" type of homosexual who gives into this appetite, while praising the "superior," who controls or even denies appetite for the sake of an intellectual and spiritual friendship.[14]

While some of these assumptions may seem dated, Raffalovich's emphasis on the quality of the relationship, rather than its orthodoxy, is enlightened. It also cautions against forcing the friendship of Gray and Raffalovich into some stereotype of inversion, although that relationship follows a pattern familiar in late Victorian "aesthetic" circles. The passionate friendship of Katherine Bradley and Edith Cooper, who wrote as "Michael Field" and who later became intimate friends of Father Gray, is another instance. As "Michael" nursed the younger "Henry" (as Edith was called) through her last illness, concealing from her the fact that she herself was stricken with the same disease, the true quality of that relationship becomes clear. A similar tragedy was suffered by Shannon and Ricketts when Shannon's fall down some stairs resulted in irreversible brain damage. When these two couples first met, in May 1894, Bradley confided in her journal, "These 2 men live & work together & find rest & joy in each other's love just as we do."[15] And in the pattern of their lives, Gray and Raffalovich confirmed their own friendship, which was to last forty-two years and end only by death. It is their capacity for tragedy, for nobility and permanence, which distinguishes these friendships from more transient homosexual affairs.

At first, it appears, Raffalovich was the giver, Gray, the taker, of affection. Already somewhat sexually anesthetized, Gray must have been emotionally numbed by the turmoil of late 1892, and in reaction he tried to distance himself. His attraction to the affectionate, solicitous Raffalovich made him not only question his attraction to Wilde, but also distrust feeling itself, a disenchantment powerfully stated in an unpublished short story, "The Yellow Princess." Here Gray tells the story of how the Princess, believing herself in love with one man, finds herself inadvertently returning the kiss of another. The second lover makes dust of the first; but she cannot love him for doing so. "That was eighteen years ago, and that is why she has never loved, never married, and why year by year she has grown more strange, more eccentric, more dull also, more suspicious of herself and of others, and why she has narrowed her life for fear of losing her freedom," Gray wrote.[16]

That Raffalovich loved Gray deeply is beyond question. "Oh, mon frère," he once wrote, "if I could pour myself out for you like water, I would."[17] His affection often took a practical turn. He gave Gray an assured income and a home. He entered into all of Gray's ambitions, at first artistic, then spiritual, entirely and without reservation. More than this, he created a world in which they could both find a place, a world outside the one that had bruised them both. Raffalovich, whose strong guttural accent marked him out as a foreigner, was the butt of anyone who indulged in a little xenophobia. His wealth provoked anti-Semitic gibes; his social ambitions, the snubs of those who considered him a *parvenu*. Even his appearance was against him: those who knew him considered his mobile, black, beady eyes and large mouth merely plain; others regarded him as so gloriously ugly that to call him plain would be an insult.[18] Like Gray, Raffalovich knew what it was to be an outsider at a time when the ranks of society were closed and when ostracism defined one as a kind of non-person. What he offered Gray might well be phrased in the proposal of marriage made by a character in one of Raffalovich's plays of this period:

We hate the world, you and I, a slanderous servant, an evil master. We can conquer together. You are unconventional. I am unconventional. Separate, we are at the world's mercy; together we are perfect strength. We can laugh at the world's unkindness. We can shut the door and be happy with silence and music, and beauty and friendship.[19]

Gray, the beloved, remained the beautiful, rather distant, and somewhat passive object of this intense affection. Raffalovich was inclined, as his letters to Gray show, to be effusive and sentimental in the Russian fashion. It seems that, under the pressure of this kind of emotional extravagance, Gray became spoiled and pettish. At the time (around 1893) Raffalovich's sister, Sophie O'Brien, regarded Gray as selfish, over-concerned for his own comfort, inclined to be greedy and not always polite. She thought Gray at first took Raffalovich and his generosity too much for granted.[20]

Under the circumstances, a romantic affair would have collapsed. Instead, the affection between them developed over the years into a kind of impersonal *caritas,* more like the unconditional love of a family. At the turn of the century, when Raffalovich wished to describe his relationship with Gray, he used the word "brother." It not only emphasized the Platonic nature of their friendship, but also Raffalovich's role as the older sibling; Gray's senior by nearly two years, he expressed his brotherly role by fussing about the details of Gray's health, both physical and spiritual, and all the minutiae of his daily life. "Brother" was also a convenient way of confirming Gray's adoption, not only by Raffalovich but also by Raffalovich's surrogate mother, the formidable Miss Florence Truscott Gribbell, who had accompanied him from Paris and who now acted as companion/housekeeper/trusted friend. Along with André, she fell into the habit of referring to John Gray as "our child" or "the dear child," and writing, in his absence, long chatty letters to him.[21]

Thus they became a family, and as the letters of the next few years reveal, it was as a family that Gray, Raffalovich, and to some extent, Florence Gribbell, discussed and arranged the future of Gray's two younger sisters, Sarah and Beatrice. They were to be educated at a convent school in Regensburg, Germany, a move presumably financed by Raffalovich. Their eldest brother would visit them there at least once a year, anxiously noting their progress. During the summer holidays, before she left for Germany, Beatrice joined her beloved brother John at Raffalovich's cottage in Weybridge, Surrey, where Gray would amuse her in various ways, such as performing tricks with static electricity (magic to her): "Indeed, in my small mind, all things were possible to this god who dominated my entire childhood," she wrote. Punting was a favorite pastime. Once, Beatrice reduced the god to helpless mirth by giving "full vent to [her] feelings" when a rainstorm overtook the party he had landed on a sandbank.[22]

Her account of these years has the element of an idyll. It was not simply the work of nostalgia. Gray had achieved a security which seemed almost absolute, in practical terms and in terms of human affection. It seemed a good time to embark on another kind of artistic enterprise. For two dandies, thrown together by circumstance, it is apt that Gray and Raffalovich should begin to build their new world together on the stage of private theatricals. There they could try out their new roles as writers, directors, and friends, shielded from the brutality of the world. During the next two years, 1894 and 1895, they jointly produced three plays.

The first was given privately on 17 April 1894 as part of an "At Home" for which Raffalovich rented the West Theatre, Albert Hall. It consisted of two one-act plays: one, "Sour Grapes," being described on the program as "A Masque, Written Entirely in Rhymed Couplets by John Gray"; and one by Raffalovich: "Black Sheep, A Pantomime Pastoral, with Spoken Prologue and Epilogue. . . . Concluding with a Dance."[23] Perhaps feeling them too precious even for an invited audience, Gray opened the program with what one guest described as the "Dynamiter's piece": "Etienne Rozenwaltoff," a rhymed monologue spoken by a foreign (Franco-Polish) anarchist, who confesses to killing for "fun."[24]

What could possibly have inspired this rough and rather violent poem? If intended to shock, at least it was timely. Gray was writing at the opening of the "black year" of anarchism in France. Although theoretical anarchism had been around Paris since the early 1880s and several of Gray's French colleagues, notably Félix Fénéon and Camille Pissaro, had been contributors to anarchist journals, theory had not issued in violence until almost ten years later. Then, between March 1892 and the upcoming summer of 1894, there were to be eleven major bomb explosions in Paris, the chosen method being tin cans filled with dynamite and nails. Indeed, less than a week after the "Dynamiter's" premiere, Fénéon himself had been arrested and charged with bombing the crowded, fashionable restaurant of the Hotel Foyot. Fénéon, who had admired in print the "intimate charm" of a previous bomb attack conducted by a friend (soon to be guillotined for his crimes), was arrested, held in prison for several months, but released after his trial in August, although his innocence has never been satisfactorily established.[25]

To all of this, Gray seems uncomfortably sympathetic, even though it is to his proxy in the poem, a "fine young fellow" wearing a white carnation, that the terrorist directs his hatred of the comfortable classes. It is nothing personal: his actions exhibit the cheerful neutrality of a force of nature. Nor would any other tone allow us to entertain the twisted logic of his version of class warfare. Gray knew his man. He was the rank outsider, in exile at home. But Gray is no longer able to accept the outsider's role as simply sacrificial. The poem is a poor one, an experiment that failed. But it marks a new direction; it is harder and colder and more violent than any of Gray's previous work; his grasp of the logic of hatred compels, and chills.[26]

In any event, the audience was not shocked. Perhaps they were unshockable, too upholstered by privilege and anesthetized by the sheer triviality of the "Masque" and "Pastoral" that ensued. In such a context, the "Dynamiter's piece" merely provided, one lady novelist confessed to Gray, "the masculine note . . . in the midst of the more fanciful & more tender pieces."[27]

This was merely a trial run. Gray and Raffalovich's real debut as playwrights did not come until nearly two months later. On 7 June, they launched their first collaborative project in the Prince of Wales's Theatre, Tottenham Court Road: a full-length melodrama entitled (tantalizingly) "The Blackmailers."[28] It was the first—and, as it turned out, last—public production of that or any other work by Gray and Raffalovich. The play was a debacle. Its plot was relentlessly repetitive, as a prominent review in *The Theatre* observed: "Blackmail is levied right and left; there is nothing but that in the play."[29] The final act reveals several other serious flaws. When, for example, the scoundrel, Hal Danger, is confronted by his outraged relatives, he turns from actual blackmail to moral blackmail, blaming his career on their hypocrisy. So predictable is the logic, even Hal's hysterical accusations fall dead from his lips.

That Gray and Raffalovich possessed no dramatic sense is, from these examples, painfully obvious. What might have saved the play was its timing. Among certain circles, particularly the homosexual/literary ones in which they both moved, it was known that, during the last two years, Wilde's dramatic successes had been paralleled only by his sexual excesses with extortionate, faithless boys who sought to blackmail him. These episodes can be dated from his involvement with Alfred Douglas, who, in the spring of 1892, initiated their affair when he sought Wilde's help in handling a blackmail threat over an indiscreet letter. From that date on, as in the play, blackmail was levied right and left, although it tended to be focused on their liaison. Gray and Raffalovich resolve their play by having its scoundrel seek solace with his "dear Hyacinth," a friend named Clyde, whom he trusts will offer him a haven in Paris (as opposed to his family, who wish to deport him to New Zealand). For those in the know, this ending may have been taken to allude to that infamous letter Wilde wrote Douglas in 1893 opening, "My dear Hyacinth."[30]

Given their disenchantment with Wilde, there must have been a temptation in this play to have put him on trial by proxy. But it is not so. As the influential critic, Clement Scott, was among those to complain, the play has no moral focus whatsoever. If anything, it seems to side with the scoundrel, Hal, who has the mechanical amorality of one of Wilde's dandies, without his wit or *élan*.[31] Could the authors' own divided loyalties have led to this dramatic falsity? to the accusations of bad faith which redounded upon themselves?

But even if the two playwrights had taken their revenge on Wilde here, the play would have been a disaster. The real fiasco was, apparently, its production, which was not their fault, the authors complained in an indignant reply to the critic of *The Theatre:* the play as given was only

a mangled and mutilated version of the first four acts. . . . It was only a consideration of honour which prevented us from withdrawing the play when we found to what a state it was being reduced from rehearsal to rehearsal. We saw scene after scene ruined by cuts, omissions, impoverishments and slipshod. It is no wonder that we refused to own the play by answering the kindly call of a disconcerted audience.

To this protestation, the critic replied with some justice, "that if authors choose to delegate their authority to unreliable people, or to resign their power of control, they have only themselves to thank for any mangling done on the theatre premises."[32] It may be said in mitigation that the distinction between amateur and professional management at the time was a blurred one. Yet certainly at this juncture in their lives, the very public failure of Gray and Raffalovich as serious dramatic artists had a critical effect. From this date on can be traced their retreat from a public audience and public themes and eventually, perhaps, from the artistic life itself.

Events were to confirm that direction. For the next two years, Gray lived a life of quiet obscurity. His name was not in the newspapers. He went to work and came home again. In the evenings, he worked on the translations which were, in 1896, to be published as *Spiritual Poems*. For Christmas 1894, he sent friends a little book of religious poetry, the first of his *Blue Calendars*. For those who had received, nearly two years previously, a copy of *Silverpoints,* the contrast must have been something of a shock. But, with few exceptions, we do not know their reactions, for very few letters exist from the years 1894–96. The reason is not far to seek. In the spring of 1895, England was in the grip of the Wilde/Queensberry trials. Gray was not the only one to burn any and all letters he could locate which might associate him with Wilde, and the gaps which do exist, such as in the correspondence with Louÿs, make it clear they were deliberate. Fear of rumor associating his name with Wilde's also prompted Gray to retain a well-known barrister, Frank Mathew, to attend the trials and to hold a watching brief on his behalf.[33] Gray's nervousness was not misplaced, for in the first trial, that of Queensberry, the leading counsel for the defense, Edward Carson, denounced *The Picture of Dorian Gray* as an immoral book. Gray's name, however, or any implication that he had been the original of Dorian, was not alluded to.

Indeed, it seems that during these months, when other friends and associates of Wilde left for Europe or laid low, Gray and Raffalovich affected a policy of noninvolvement and tried to live their London life as usual; a notable exception occurred when Raffalovich, in an extraordinary lapse of taste if not of judgment, attempted on one occasion to enter the Law Court's public gallery; he was turned back by a policeman, saying, "It is no place for you, Sir; don't go in."[34] As if to emphasize their indifference, Gray and Raffalovich published—and may have actually produced privately—two short dramas, "A Northern Aspect" and "The Ambush of Young Days," on 12 May, more than a month after Wilde was arrested and shortly before his first trial was to open.[35]

Two weeks later, however, before the verdict of the third and final trial was given, Raffalovich had discreetly taken himself off to Berlin by way of Brussels, where he was later joined by Gray and Florence Gribbell. There he arranged to be wired news of the sentence by his (and Wilde's) hairdresser. Raffalovich confessed that he heard of Wilde's sentencing to two years' hard labor with approval. "I could almost have said what Alphonse Daudet said to Sherard," he wrote; "'I admire a country where justice is administered as it is here, as is shown by to-day's verdict and sentence.'"[36]

Raffalovich was equally harsh in his article on the Wilde trials, "L'Affaire Oscar Wilde."[37] Appearing in a French journal only five weeks after Wilde's sentencing, it gained the dubious distinction of being the first of many accounts of the trials. Both its timing and its tone take revenge, and it is hard to remember, reading it, that Raffalovich was known as a kindly man, and a homosexual. But some of its vitriol was certainly inspired by the spectacle of Gray's suffering during the fall and winter of 1892, his self-recrimination during the trials. Thirty years later, Raffalovich tried to explain to a young friend disconcerted by his admission of "approval" for the verdict, "If you had lived through that time and seen at least one tortured victim as I did, and sinister shadows cast on whole tracts of human relationships, you would have understood my feeling. . . ."[38]

It is not known how Gray took the news. One story has it that Gray was walking up Coventry Street near Leicester Square one day when a stranger approached him, imparting a few words that were utterly devastating. Gray made his way to a nearby French church, Notre Dame de France, and knelt in prayer. A few minutes later, as it seemed to him, he noticed that it was dark and an old woman bearing keys came up to him to tell him that she was going to lock up. He had been on his knees all day.[39] Whether or not the words were about Wilde's sentence, the trials themselves marked a turning point in Gray's passage from moral confusion to moral clarity and self-castigation. His conscience, now fully awakened to a past which he had tried to deny, made him a "tortured victim" for the rest of his life. While Wilde finally accepted the verdict with fatalism but without guilt, Gray became both Grand Inquisitor and victim, finding relief from his own self-hatred only in the friendship with Raffalovich and in the stern perfection of his religious vocation.

"Authority, in the Sense of Spiritual Knowledge"

Gray's break with Wilde and with his past as "Dorian" Gray, although dramatic, obscures the continuity of his imaginative life. Increasingly, Gray was drawn to countries outside England, particularly France. From his first years as a writer, it was France, and not England, that Gray considered his spiritual home, France where he had experienced conversion, France as the source of a poetry which was to extend his range in the *Silverpoints* "imitations." England and its poets could not give him the words to articulate his inner life; he had to appropriate them elsewhere. From 1893 onwards, Gray ransacked the British Library for other poems, extending even beyond French to other tongues. Primarily medieval and mystical, these poems would form the body of *Spiritual Poems: Chiefly Done Out of Several Languages.*

That search for a language adequate to his condition, a language that is distinctly "other," mirrors Gray's search for an "other" self. In *Silverpoints,* the postures of frenchified decadence defined the persona of "Dorian" Gray. Likewise, the *Spiritual Poems* create the persona that was to emerge, years later, as Father Gray. In each case, the creation of this new self involved a radical rejection, not only of the "old" self, but of any assertion of self at all. In *Silverpoints,* the aesthete stands outside himself, coldly registering the precise nuance, the exact perception as it occurs. In *Spiritual Poems,* the convert anatomizes his suppliant and longing posture toward God. In each collection, the poet consciously submerges himself in the flow of subjectivity to the point where metaphors of erotic fusion become equally those of dissolution and death. Thus the very passivity of the poet becomes the condition of his poetry. Even the more experimental poems of this period underwrite this abdication of self. In their diverse ways, the *Blue Calendars,* "The Flying Fish," and "Leda" may each be taken as an attempt to use art as a way of comprehending the unknowable. Their method of composition, itself a rejection of ego, was designed to open a channel to the "other" and thus invest their creation with what Gray called "authority, in the sense of spiritual knowledge."[40]

In seeking "spiritual knowledge," Gray took the route that Yeats was to employ some years later, that of automatic dictation. Gray first became interested in the phenomenon through an introduction to James John Garth Wilkinson in January 1893.[41] A translator of Swedenborg, Wilkinson was also a student of Blake and a poet who imitated Blake's poetic method of inspired dictation. In an article for the 1893 *Dial,* Gray explored the nature of writing from "Influx," there explicitly identifying it as a "pentecostal" event, agreeing with Wilkinson that "writing from an Influx which is really out(-side) of your Self, or so far within your Self as to amount to the same thing, is either a religion or a madness. In allowing your faculties to be directed to ends you know not of, there is only One Being to whom you dare entrust them: only the Lord. Of consequence, before writing by Influx, your prayer must be to Him, for His Guidance, Influx, and Protection" (p. 23). It appears that Gray himself began shortly afterwards to compose by this means, producing poetry (as Wilkinson describes the process) without "premeditation or preconception" and "attended by no feeling, and by no fervour, but only by an anxiety. . . to observe the unlooked for evolution" (pp. 23–24). It is also probable that an initial falling-off of poetic achievement after *Silverpoints* might be the result of Gray's adoption of this method.

Every Christmas from 1894 to 1897, Gray sent friends a *Blue Calendar:* a small, privately printed booklet of religious poetry. Their mnemonic style suggests that they may have been written strictly by this method of composition and, specifically, as a form of prayer. Appropriately, many of them employ the traditional "tricks" of Ignatius Loyola (among others) for making the mind receptive to spiritual influence: repetition of words, meditation on scenes of Christ's life, even the use of the actual liturgy, as in the poem for May, 1895:

> Good Saint Mary fumbled deep,
> With a saintly gesture.
> In this bag (said she) I keep
> All the Infant's vesture.
> Ah Lord! how great is my reward.
> *My soul doth magnify the Lord.*

. . . .

Here be little cambric shirts,
Very small and slender.
Here the band His body girts,
Which is frail and tender.
So carefully must He be dressed.
Henceforth all nations call me blest.[42]

Although exaggerated here, the sentimental touch appears in many other poems of the *Blue Calendars,* particularly in the series of 1895 and 1896 which treat the life of Christ. Later, *Ad Matrem* (1904) and *Verses for Tableaux Vivants* (1905) betray the same self-conscious charm (which has no precedent in their models, the medieval religious lyric and traditional carol), but is there excused by their occasion: both were scripts for *tableaux* by the parish children. It is possible that Gray may have been working at this time toward a school of "naive" poetry, such as that inspired by Francis Jammes, a French religious poet with whom Gray was in correspondence after the turn of the century.[43] But even allowing for such an intention, few of these *Blue Calendar* poems are distinguished performances.

One key to their poor quality might be the difficulty encountered by the religious poet of finding images to depict spiritual events. Yeats came against this problem: at about the time of the publication of the *Blue Calendars,* he resolved to abandon the figure of Christ entirely, seeing its excessive spirituality as a threat to that "primitive faculty," that "impulse towards what is definite and sensuous, and an indifference towards the abstract and the general" which directs poetic power.[44] Less consciously, Gray sought the same corrective. One excellent poem of the 1896 *Blue Calendar,* "The True Vine," springs from mingled classical and Patristic allusions: Christ as the vine; Christ as the young Dionysus:

Another quells,
Another reins the leopards.
My portent tells
My story to the shepherds
Beside the wells.

The Prodigal Returns, 1893–1898

My face is tan.
My hair, my hair is golden.
None brighter than
My eyes were e'er beholden
By eyes of man.

I am the vine.
The cup is chiselled garnet
For garnet wine.
I am the vine incarnate.
The grape is mine.

With crown of bright
Green leaf and tender clusters
My head is dight;
Even as the starry musters
Adorn the night.

I am the vine:
The stock, the grape, the dresser;
In deed and sign,
The purple-footed presser
Of purple wine. [45]

The ease and imaginative unity of this lyric prompted "Michael Field" to observe, "The man works in religion as a worker in ivory—treats the things as lovely myths; but with a note of conviction a real classical student has, when he speaks of Apollo & the muses." [46]

From the style of the *Blue Calendars,* Gray's priorities are clear: they are instruments of spiritual purpose, just as the *Silverpoints* poems were in part an instrument of a social purpose. Beyond that which serves this end, Gray is not committed to any further artistic development. But outside the realm of religious poetry, Gray also begins to experiment with new material and new sources drawn, it appears, from the world of the occult.

This is, at best, conjecture, suggested by a new complex of interests in Gray's work. He begins to employ symbolism derived in part from reading Swedenborg and Böhme. He develops an abiding interest in the phenomenon of "second sight."[47] It is highly probable that Gray also began attending meetings of the London Theosophical Society—and even seances—in the company of Raffalovich.[48] One poem at least certainly originates in such experiences: "The Flying Fish," which appeared originally in *The Dial*.[49] Exactly thirty years later, when the poem was reprinted by Gray in *The Long Road*, Raffalovich published a short reminiscence, prefaced by part of the poem, in *Blackfriars*. Entitled "Parallels," it explicitly identifies several of the emblematic flying fish with different spiritualist practitioners.[50] Such "parallels" should come as no surprise. Gray was, after all, in the habit of alluding, however tangentially, to personal affairs in his work. Nor would such excursions into the occult be particularly idiosyncratic. One sees from Yeats's similar experiments that these preoccupations are a familiar pattern in the life of the nineties artist.

"The Flying Fish" is a remarkable poem; one critic, comparing it to *A Shropshire Lad* (also published in 1896) and "The Ballad of Reading Gaol," regards it among Gray's poems as "incomparably his finest."[51] Certainly it is a vivid, satisfyingly enigmatic fable told in swinging ballad style; even the sudden gaps, the roughness of execution, the touches of archaism become virtues in this form. Gray had found his subject at last in its emblem, the flying fish, like himself a creature caught between two worlds, driven by the "aspiration born of fear":

> Not to be one of the sons of air;
> To be rid of the water is all his prayer.
>
> All his hope is a fear-whipped whim,
> All directions are one to him. (P. 260)

Is this a comment, as Raffalovich's article suggests, on the desperate faith of spiritualism? Or on Gray's own desperation during this time, when all hope seemed "fear-whipped" and "all directions . . . one to him"?

Certainly other pieces during this period betray an uncertainty in Gray's artistic direction. From 1896 to 1898, he did a good deal of the poet's hack work, editing: he compiled collections of the poems of Sir John Suckling, Michael Drayton, and Thomas Campion in 1896; in 1897, of Henry Constable's poems and sonnets from early editions and manuscripts; finally, in 1898, the sonnets of Sir Philip Sidney. It was, Gray wrote Pierre Louÿs in January 1897, the kind of "humble and conscientious work, such as I take real pleasure in doing."[52] Over the same period, Gray's interest turned to German literature; he had, presumably, perfected his German while on his yearly trips to Regensburg to visit his two sisters, Beatrice and Sarah, now in a convent school there. This had an unexpected result; in December 1896, he completed a translation from the poetry of Friedrich Nietzsche, chiefly didactic and dithyrambic.[53] Gray had been persuaded to undertake this project by Dr. Alexander Tille, a lecturer in German language and literature at the University of Glasgow and a "furious Nietzschean" who had turned Glasgow into a center for the propagation of the Nietzsche cult.[54] Tille also acted as secretary to the Glasgow Goethe Society, and in this capacity asked Gray to collaborate with him in producing "a worthy English edition" of Goethe under its imprint. Gray's translation of "Satyros, or the Deified Wood-Devil" and the "Dramatic Fragment," "Prometheus," were published in 1898 as the initial volume of this series.[55] But these ambitious plans were abandoned when Tille's vehement pro-Boer sympathies made him so extremely unpopular that he could no longer continue his post in Glasgow; he returned to Germany in 1899.

Today, Gray's translations of the Goethe plays are credited as "excellent"; those of the Nietzsche, as "not excellent, but good."[56] But to Arthur Symons, writing anonymously in *The Athenaeum,* the translations were "a *tour de force*":

It is hardly possible to conceive of a more difficult task than that of rendering line by line, rhythm by rhythm, fault by fault, those gnarled and crabbed verses, which seem to have been written by force of will rather than out of any natural aptitude. They are full of a grim ingenuity, they are satires which hit downright blows, and in the English version hardly anything is lost of that straightforward crookedness which is their chief interest. Few translations into verse have ever been done with such fidelity, alike to the merits and to the defects of the original.[57]

Such excitement is merited: Gray's is part of the first major translation of Nietzsche into English. Yeats would read Nietzsche first in this edition,[58] an initiation that would have a tremendous impact on his poetic and philosophic development.

Gray, on the other hand, seems to have kept entirely aloof from Nietzsche's influence. Such neglect is unusual for so eclectic a writer, one so quick to domesticate the *symboliste* poets. Clearly this was a matter of choice: at this point in his life, Gray's missionary zeal was simply being redirected from the religion of art to the art of religion. And his uncertainty about the status of this art may be measured by a new cynicism about the significance of poetic statement. "I like immensely 'of summer I am very fond,'" Gray wrote Raffalovich in 1904; "I have often made a fool of myself in poetry groping after such effects. 'All do not all things well' fascinates me in the same way. Also 'Wie leicht er rollt um die Ecke.' Goethe, Majorie [?] & Campion all meant about the same—next to nothing."[59] This disclaimer notwithstanding, Gray had been consciously working toward exactly the same vacuum in the more derivative poems of *Silverpoints*.

Only Gray's "The Forge" seems to admit the influence of these new masters. But perhaps it owes less to Nietzsche's defiance or Goethe's Promethean quest than to Gray's own reclamation of his past. Directly, without shame, without apology, Gray renders a day at the Woolwich Arsenal as

> the arena wherein stubborn stuff
> With man locks strength; where elements dispute
> The mastery, where breath and fire bear blaze,
> Where sullen water aids, to quell the brute
> Earth into shape, to make it meek enough.

And this day is the type of many days.[60]

The power of such a poem might suggest that Gray was moving toward a more concentrated, muscular style. But such a judgment would be superficial, designed to picture Gray as a minor Yeats, who during these years transformed his deliquescent "aesthetic" manner into a potent, symbolic idiom. Exposed to the same revolutionaries, Gray overturned nothing; if anything, he went backwards. It is clear that in the series of *Blue Calendars* from 1895 to 1898, Gray was distancing himself from the experiments of *Silverpoints,* preferring now a poetry of moral order: employing allegory and fable rather than myth, emblem rather than symbol, the didactic over the evocative; and, in its models, embracing Spenser and Constable rather than Verlaine, Blake or Nietzsche.

One must turn to *Spiritual Poems* (1896) to find Gray's one concerted poetic effort to come to terms with the revolution in his own life. Written in the aftermath of the publication of *Silverpoints,* the *Spiritual Poems* are peculiarly private and personal in impulse. In terms of Gray's history, they may be read as responding to two distinct but related crises: first, his rejection of Wilde and the guilt suffered for that past which his association with Wilde came to symbolize, a guilt publicly represented in Wilde's own conviction and sentencing; and second, early in 1896, the conversion of André Raffalovich to Roman Catholicism.

Nothing had prepared Raffalovich's friends for this abrupt rejection of his native Judaism. Stories were told about it; perhaps William Butler Yeats is responsible for the most gorgeous nonsense. "According to Yeats, Gray and Raffalovich had gone cruising in the Mediterranean in a yacht which they had painted black and christened *Iniquity.* They put in at a small Italian port where some religious festival was in full swing; and there it was that their change of heart took place quite suddenly."[61] On Gray's part, it makes no sense at all. As we have seen, he had already become a Catholic six years before, in February 1890, and in some sense had been returning to his faith since the crisis of autumn 1892. But certainly something did happen to the two of them, privately but definitively; Yeats's story is true at least in regard to the spiritual drama of 1896, which had its lurid moments.

John Gray is the authority. Writing of Raffalovich only weeks after his death, Gray recalled,

His was a conversion *coup de foudre*. His friend from boyhood, Florence Truscott Gribbell, had, in the glory of her young fifties, been received into the Church. There was a 'ghastly row,' as the phrase of the day was; but the mettlesome youth soon compromised, watched Chère Amie to see that she did not injure her health through medieval penances, saw to her Friday menu, and started every Sunday from South Audley Street at a quarter to eleven to walk round the park. She might report at lunch who had preached or whom she had seen at Mass. No reply. Then, all but suddenly, André himself was a Catholic. No one can disclose how this came about.

But, Gray added, with "thoroughness which knew no exceptions he was soon conversant with Catholic devotions, Catholic ways."[62] Raffalovich's sister, Sophie, who had married an Irish Member of Parliament, William O'Brien, had taken the same step some six years previously, and offered much the same account.[63] But her story is almost as transparent as Gray's; neither makes any mention, for instance, of the Wilde trials, which certainly forced both Gray and Raffalovich to reevaluate their respective pasts. What both histories do make clear is that Florence Gribbell led the way for Raffalovich's reception into the Church on 3 February 1896, and that afterward, life was never quite the same again.

This was now Gray's family, and the pressure of their spiritual drama must have affected him, even though there are no public gestures, no letters which speak at this time of the state of his mind. What does remain is the early draft of *Spiritual Poems*. Gray had been working on these poems on and off for almost three years; the earliest piece is dated December 1893. In holograph, they confess their private nature. One draft of a poem, which Gray withheld from publication, describes his early childhood, his work at the Arsenal, and his growing ambition to "elbow me a place" in the world; it closes remorsefully, if enigmatically, "Ah, Lord! I thank thee for that chastening."[64] Several poems are spoken in the personae of "Godfrey" or "earth" and "Oliver" or "air"; they are certainly, in some sense, Raffalovich and Gray, respectively. The "Rosary of the Cross," also rejected from the final selection for *Spiritual Poems,* is Oliver's prayer:

> Holy Christ, upon thy cross of torture,
> Deign to see the sinner at thy feet,
> Ignorant, besotted,
> Even in despair effete. (P. 147)

In a published poem, "The Two Sinners," a dialogue between "God-frey" and "Oliver," each speaks his prayer in turn, one voice bound to the other by an agonizing sense of sinfulness.[65]

Although several of these poems were not published, they were carefully preserved, most in fair copy. They suggest that Gray, having difficulty in finding a voice for his own reawakened spirituality, instead sought to appropriate one. In this effort, he ransacked a wide body of religious poetry, quite eclectic in period, modality, and place of origin. Thirty-one of the forty are actually translations from Latin, Spanish, German, and French. Others are imitations. Why translate such a hodgepodge? Less, I believe, as a spiritual exercise than as a means of securing spiritual talismans which, for Gray, acquired great personal significance.

As a collection the translations are competent; some are excellent. Often, however, Gray tends to soften and elaborate what in the original is hard and fierce, as in his rendering of Jacopone da Todi's "O Love, all love above."[66] Here the poetry seems to swoon and languish:

> O Love, all love above,
> Why hast thou struck me so?
> All my heart, broke atwo,
> Consumed in flames of love,
> Burning and flaming cannot find solace;
> It cannot fly from torment, being bound;
> Like wax among live coal it melts apace;
> It languishes alive, no help being found;
> Seeking a grace to fly a little space,
> A glowing furnace is its narrow pound.
> In such a deadly swound,
> Alas, where am I brought?
> Living with death so fraught!
> O leaping flames of love! (P. 95)

"And so forth. The words had no special reference to her own condition at the time, probably none at all; yet such was the force of this unlooked-for revelation, she knew once for all and at the first glance that these words were meant for her." Thus Gray observes of the heroine of his story, "Light," who, prompted by a dream, finds her way to a certain bookstore and purchases an unknown book, first opening it to this poem of Jacopone da Todi's.[67] "Popery!," she thought, and slammed it shut (she was Chapel-Nonconformist); but it changed her life forever. For Gray too, the poem marked a milestone. It is reliably reported that Gray, while in Edinburgh in December 1893, was walking past a bookseller's window when a book of Jacopone's poems caught his eye. He bought it, and was so touched by certain lines that he decided to translate some of the poems.[68] Later he was to adopt the name of Jacopone as his own.

"All through, the phrases of the great Italian song [of da Todi's] filled her with terrible bliss, ecstatic terror" (p. 131), an emotional extremism shared with the heroine of "Light" by Gray in certain of the *Spiritual Poems* he composed himself. In one startling poem, "They say, in other days," Gray imagines "the Lover of the Dark Night's tryst":

> Saint John was folded in the hands of Christ.
> He lay upon their wounds, and wept the whole
> Of longing that was in his holy soul.
> Those molten hands were silent. And made speech:
> "Weep not for us, sweet Pity, lest thou teach
> "Us even greater sorrow than our own;
> "The angels weep not, nor doth Heaven make moan.
>
> . . . .
>
> And John was locked within the riven Side.
> The Wound said: "Sleep, beloved, and be calm;
> "I, in thy flesh, made wounds upon thee balm.
> "My torrent poured for thee; thou art my son;
> "I ached for this dear hour, my darling one. (P. 102)

This is not great poetry; nor is it, strictly speaking, original; but it is deeply felt. "I have invincible love of S: John of the Cross," Gray wrote Katherine Bradley in November 1908, "because, I suppose, he made a hole in the covering which I had woven about myself to hide me from God."[69] And, a month earlier: "I love him very much with a firm persuasion that I should now be in hell but for him. But I do not more than ask his intercession once or twice a day & take an extra glass of wine on November 24 & make fervent resolutions not to become a Carme[lite]." Bradley reported to her journal that Gray was thinking of becoming a Carmelite, but when asked if he could live on boiled cabbage for the rest of his life, discovered that he had no vocation.[70]

The extremism of the poetry, then, mirrors an extremism of feeling, a feeling that is prior to the poem; as Gray remarks of Saint John, "His love of God produces a literary quality in his expressions."[71] But Gray was never indifferent to literary effect, especially when it resembled that of Crashaw, whom both he and Raffalovich particularly admired. Such poetry (he remarked of George Darley's "The Bee") "stirs an old craving for the impossible in poetry—something to be got from words & images quite exterior to words & thought."[72] In taste he follows the lead of Huysmans's Des Esseintes, who relished the morbid excesses of late Latin poetry. Indeed, Huysmans told Raffalovich that he admired *Spiritual Poems*.[73]

Certainly they mark a step away from the charm, the somewhat over-refined prettiness of many of the *Blue Calendars,* even a rejection of it. In the grotesquerie of the Saint John poem one can see what Gray admired in the paintings of Grünewald, whom he used to think of as "a modern soul capable of wilful revolt against the sugared trash of the devotional picture." It might also be described as a revolt against art itself because—in a sense—the poetry no longer matters. "The odd thing [Gray remarked of the poems] is that the poetical interest is there by accident. S: John seems to regard them as a kind of aide mémoire."[74] Similarly, in *Spiritual Poems* Gray has come, ironically, to define the limits of poetry's usefulness as an "*instrument spirituel*": ultimately, the instrument must be abandoned for the real thing.

"Attouchement Divin"

Gray repented, and in repenting, renounced his past. Inwardly, he knew his spiritual conviction to be growing steadily, irresistibly; but outwardly it seemed to proceed by a series of shocks and revelations. Artistically, he seemed to falter; art increasingly became a means rather than an end, and when that end was finally clearly in sight, the means was rejected. The actual moment of decision crystallized around two events, one inner, one outer, so subtly connected that probably not Gray himself could disentangle them: the conversion of the dying Aubrey Beardsley; the moment his own heart consented to give itself to God.

Of the latter, Gray has left an intimate record in two stories written for *The Pageant:* "Niggard Truth" (1896) and "Light" (1897). With all of Huysmans's "deliberate rejection of symbol," Gray describes the effect of the *"attouchement divin."* To call it a spiritual crisis would be to misrepresent its nature, which resembled more a germ growing with irresistible force, so assuming the direction, so absorbing the attention, of its subject, that suddenly he is aware only of the fact that he *believes,* with not a trace in memory of how he passed from the somnambulance of everyday life to the anxieties of an awakening faith.[75]

Both are extraordinary stories; their mastery of the elusive course of spiritual growth is lost in summary or paraphrase. Unexpectedly, his subjects are very ordinary women. Harriet of "Niggard Truth" determines to marry her minister and finally, through her spiritual gifts, makes his career.[76] The smith's wife (never named) in "Light" finds she is being directed, in the middle of her stolid, strangely formal routine of housework, by an "inner voice."[77] It speaks to her in a chapel sermon; she is momentarily overcome by a vision. From that time on, ordinary experience is transfigured; her thirst for perfection dictates all her household duties, however menial; behind them there is an ecstasy of "tempestuous, chaotic prayer," until, at last, the inner voice takes possession of her entire consciousness. The smith, alarmed, calls a doctor, who predicts her death, although she is not ill. The village women whisper that she is raving; but as she dies, the smith at last perceives her holiness.

Gray's very tender, detailed description of the awakening consciousness of spiritual realities sets up one condition: that of absolute passivity. The final secret union with the "Divine Lover" brings about a death of the self and with it, almost as an afterthought, bodily death. Gray's search for "authority, in the sense of spiritual knowledge" ends in this vision of the enraptured heart.

Gray's own vision of this moment can be found in the twin poems, "Leda" and "The Swan" (1897).[78] He here affirms the continuity between the worlds of the visible and invisible that marks the reoriented consciousness. Unlike Yeats's "Leda and the Swan," there is no "sudden blow," and her mastery by the "brute blood of the air" is seduction, not rape. This Leda moves in a daze through an atmosphere of oppressive heaviness, the claustrophobia of the world which operates, like the jewel she wears, by the law of "exact similitude":

> All palpitant and dazed,
> Across the lawn doth Leda haste,
> To where the dreaming water lies;
> Therein to cool her mirrored eyes. (P. 83)

It is a vision of a world caught in the dream of Swedenborgian correspondences:

> The awful heavens burn
> Repeated in the hollows; yearn
> With ruddier purpose, to unfold
> The swelling destiny they hold.
>
> And, in a certain place,
> Suspended on the water's face,
> The doubled swans sit motionless,
> For ease against the summer stress. (Pp. 83–84)

Here, in this visionary paradise, the world of doubling and equivocal appearance that Gray confronted in "The Person in Question," appears the divine swan. There is no resistance; the swan recites the epilogue describing how Leda is lured into the pool:

Enticeth till her breast
Beyond the parapet doth rest;
Until a timid hand leans out
And folds his downy breast about. (P. 85)

And then, "The swan and Leda break/Triumphant the spreading lake,

Till sudden lightnings split
The burning sky, and empty it;
And raucously as eagles cry
An eagle screamed across the sky. (P. 85)

These Yeatsian anticipations drive home the difference between the two poems. In this breaking through the aesthetic trance of appearances there is no violence, no conflict, only a natural issue of events which has violent signs—a rending apart of the reflecting stagedrop of appearances.

Explaining his peace as a priest several years later to Raffalovich, Gray wrote:

Do you think there is an interesting psychological study to be made of the religious attitude of mind? . . . My own conversion in my mind nearly exactly coincides with the action of passing from a world of dreams to a world of *things*. *Thus* my ideal was the *inexact* (au fond) *now* it is the exact. I deliberately wanted desired things not as they were *but as I wanted them*. Now I want them *as they are*[.] All this is very badly expressed."[79]

Thus Gray haltingly described the passage from the world of fragmented mirrors of aesthetic perception, the world created in his own image, to that of *things* whose existence is simply accepted, the world beyond the deceptive projections of the ego. There is a sense of inevitability, too, about this perception; it seems less that Gray submitted to some outside force than that he acknowledged that his ego had been little more than egotism, an empty and perverse form of will.

At first, Gray's friends were not sure whether this new piety was not another elaborate pose. On receiving the first *Blue Calendar* in De-

cember 1895, Dowson wrote Gray praising its "rare, audacious, suc-
cessful—admirable" effects, particularly its "'Moyen-Age-fin-de siè-
cle'" flavor. Yet even Dowson (himself a convert) confided to Arthur
Symons some seven months later: "John Gray has sent me his new
book 'Spiritual Poems'. I can not determine whether his mysticism is
sincere or merely a pose—but I begin to think it is the former."[80] In
the mid-nineties, Rothenstein mentions in a letter how he saw Dorian
Gray wandering around Chelsea under the name of John Gray.[81] And
from Pierre Louÿs, who apparently had not written for two years,
came a shocked response to Gray's announcement in 1898 of his in-
tention to enter the priesthood:

Mon cher ami,
What does this extraordinary vocation mean and how can you think that
you have nothing more to say when you have just published the volumes I
have received? I understand that you are going to settle in Rome; happiness is
a hot-house plant which does not grow in our wretched countries. But why
become a religious there, even if you no longer wish to write?[82]

Whatever the inner events which led to Gray's decision, the cru-
cial moment arrived as the result of his friendship with the dying
Aubrey Beardsley. Two observations may be made about Beardsley's
relationship with Gray and Raffalovich. First, Gray once again ap-
pears as a shadowy figure; Beardsley's letters to him are strangely for-
mal. When Gray does appear, it is most often in the wake of Raffalo-
vich, in whose somewhat sentimental letters to Beardsley he called
himself "Mentor" and Beardsley, "Télémaque," in what Raffalovich
described as "affectionate playfulness."[83] In contrast, Gray's emo-
tional reserve seems almost bleak. A few have even found it ominous,
picturing Gray as a kind of ghoulish figure, hovering over the dying
Beardsley and, with Raffalovich's financial assistance, virtually black-
mailing the artist into entering the Roman Church.[84] In fact, the evi-
dence suggests that the plot should be reversed; it was Beardsley's
deathbed conversion which precipitated Gray's decision to give him-
self wholly to the religious life.

Their story begins several years before. In the spring of 1895,
Beardsley too had become a victim of the public hysteria over the tri-

als of Oscar Wilde. He was forced to leave his post as art editor of *The Yellow Book;* a few weeks later, unable to find other work, Beardsley turned to Raffalovich in desperation. Raffalovich recalls he had met Beardsley and his actress sister, Mabel, shortly before, and had no wish to see them again. Now, without notice, Raffalovich

found a strange visitor in the drawing room, near Gustave Moreau's Sappho. 'Mr Beardsley said he would wait,' I was told. He had travelled through the night from Paris. He was in a fix. His sister had suggested his consulting me. Could I advise, help? I heard his difficulty. We conversed amicably. He returned to Paris, and when he came back our intimacy started. . . .[85]

From that day in April 1895 onward, Beardsley's welfare, in all senses of the word, became Raffalovich's major concern.

In May, when Beardsley returned to London and to work, Raffalovich began to court him. "Of course, I admired him," Raffalovich wrote in old age; "he arrested me like wrought iron and like honeysuckle; hardness, elegance, charm, variety." He also confessed to delighting "in his fame, in his notoriety. Wherever we went he was gazed at. They sang about him at the Gaiety; Max [Beerbohm] caricatured him; strangers credited him with unfathomed perversity; acquaintances all recognised his simple boyishness."[86] There were invitations to lunch, to tea, to dinner, to the theater and the opera, invitations to join Raffalovich in Berlin. And gifts: chocolates, walking sticks, a sonnet, books, flowers from Bond Street's most elegant florist. When Raffalovich produced his tract on *L'Uranisme,* Beardsley saw it before publication, and Raffalovich read at least part of his "L'Affaire Oscar Wilde" to Beardsley from the manuscript.[87] Beardsley shared his distaste for Wilde and his taste for the unconventional. In a sense, Beardsley allowed Raffalovich to eat his cake and have it too: to enjoy the pleasures of notoriety and indulge his keen interest in the demimonde without paying the price in terms of respectability. He was, at last, a genuine patron; he relished the delicacy of his position.

That he conducted himself with consummate tact is clear. His financial help was often in the form of token commissions. Raffalovich wished his portrait made; it was planned, but never drawn. Beardsley was to have illustrated Gray and Raffalovich's "A Northern Aspect" and Gray's translation of Benjamin Constant's *Adolphe;* neither materialized. What Beardsley did provide was a frontispiece for Raffalovich's latest volume of poems, *The Thread and the Path.* But the publisher refused the magnificent, winged nude Amor on the grounds that it was hermaphroditic. Raffalovich liked it; Beardsley had read the poems correctly; but the book was finally published without.[88]

Beardsley's relationship with Gray was cooler, more clearly defined by their mutual admiration of their art. Gray wrote later of Beardsley, "One finds in the force of his inclinations an assurance of his genius."[89] For his part, Beardsley encouraged Gray to write. When a new magazine, *The Savoy,* was organized by Arthur Symons and a bookseller, Leonard Smithers, with Beardsley as art editor, he set out to persuade Gray to contribute. Gray submitted "The Forge," published in the April 1896 issue. In early July, after receiving *Spiritual Poems,* Beardsley wrote Smithers, "Gray has just sent me a copy of a new book of verses. They are *really admirable* & might be reviewed (I should have thought) in our monthly. I wish Gray was asked more frequently to contribute for us, he is one of the few younger men worth printing."[90] By September, Gray sent more poems to Beardsley, who again wrote Smithers, "I enclose Gray's poems. Please put them in No. 7. They are good" (p. 168). But *The Savoy* was beginning to fail. A week or so later, Beardsley pleaded, "For *goodness sake* put Gray in No. 7 or else I shall (all unwary) have put my foot in it" (p. 170). But the seventh issue, dated November, opened with the announcement by Arthur Symons of *The Savoy's* demise with the next issue, which was in fact to be written entirely by himself.

What these letters reveal is that Gray was actually only a peripheral member of that "Anglo-French" coterie composed of Conder, Dowson, Sickert, Symons, and Crackanthorpe, which gathered in Paris and dictated the style of the magazine.[91] Although Symons praised Gray's translations of Goethe and Nietzsche, there seems to have been some tension between him and Gray, as Gray himself admitted, years later, when he spoke of Symons "by me in the past, so much disliked & then liked."[92] Thus it was actually Beardsley who acted as Gray's advocate, seeking publication for him in *The Savoy,* even carrying his admiration to the extent of imitating one of Gray's best poems in his own "The Ballad of a Barber" (published in the July issue of *The Savoy*). Elsewhere, Gray's enthusiasms left their mark in Beardsley's acquaintance with Laforgue (turned to good use in *Under the Hill*) and in his taste for the more baroque elaborations of religious sentiment.

But for all this business of commissions and publications, enthusiasms and admirations, theirs was not a literary friendship. Raffalovich recalled that "my conversion in January, 1896, did not long precede his first haemorrhage of the lungs, 'and the cloud began to gather which meant death in the end.'"[93] By the end of January, Beardsley had stopped addressing Raffalovich as "Mentor," just as some months before, he had abandoned the use of "Télémaque" for himself. The scene had shifted. From this time on, Raffalovich, with Gray, was to be caught up in the drama of Beardsley's protracted death, which was about to enter its final act.

After the initial intimacy, Raffalovich and Beardsley had grown more distant over the period since 1895. Although he had frequent and dramatic collapses of health, Beardsley had been well enough to work. His letters to Raffalovich were often perfunctory, often merely polite. After January 1897, however, a new intensity enters the relationship. Gifts of chocolate and books, at least one gift of money, made their way to Bournemouth, where Beardsley had gone for his health. "Your sweet friendliness," Beardsley wrote somewhat dutifully, "helps me over such alarming difficulties" (p. 244). In February he wrote, "I am most envious of Joseph [Raffalovich's Swiss butler, who had converted, a little more than a year after his master], whose conduct of life puts no barriers in his way to the practical acceptance of what he believes in. . . . Do not think, my dear André, that your kind words fall on such barren ground. However I fear I am not a very fruitful soil; I only melt to harden again" (pp. 249–50).

When Gray and Raffalovich spent a few days in Bournemouth in February, Raffalovich arranged for Father David Bearne to visit Beardsley.[94] It was a brilliant choice. Bearne was not only a convert but a writer of boys' books; he and Beardsley hit it off immediately. Shortly after this visit, when Beardsley's mother confided in Raffalovich the distressing condition of their finances, Raffalovich proposed a regular monthly payment, so that she could remain with her son rather than seeking employment. Beardsley thanked him for such "wonderfully kind help . . . offered with so much intention and so much gentleness." In helping with "so much judgement," Beardsley wrote at the end of February, 1897, Raffalovich was helping "doubly" (pp. 255, 259, 260–61).

In early March, for the first time, Beardsley admitted he was dying. His doctor had recommended against going to London; Beardsley could read the signs. "I may not have many months now to live," he wrote a friend, the bookseller Leonard Smithers, days after teasing him about being "haunted . . . with visions of designing Jesuits" (pp. 269, 264). He was seeing more and more of Father Bearne; and as Raffalovich's solicitude began to justify the name of "brother," with which he now began his "kind letters," Beardsley began to cast out his spiritual doubts. Then, on 30 March 1897, Beardsley announced to Raffalovich, "Tomorrow, dear André, the kind name of brother you give me will have a deeper significance" (p. 287). The next day, Father Bearne received Beardsley into the Roman Catholic Church, an event which he called "the most important step" in his life. He was to die almost exactly a year later.

For the week previous to this event, Gray and Raffalovich had been at Beardsley's bedside. Later Gray recalled: "Fifteen months ago, in Bournemouth, he was thought to be dying: his whole appearance condemned him. Nevertheless he kept repeating: If I went to Paris, I would recover." Shortly afterwards, Beardsley and his mother travelled to London at Raffalovich's expense and then, with Raffalovich's doctor in tow, continued to Paris. "After arriving by some miracle at the Quai Voltaire," Gray recalled, "his expectations seemed to be realised. He made a recovery." At the end of April he was joined there by John Gray, Florence Gribbell, and Raffalovich, who were on their way to Touraine. They went to see him and discovered "numbers of people frequented his sickroom and spread hope there. For a short time even he regained the strength to handle his industrious pen."95 Beardsley welcomed Gray and Raffalovich warmly. "It's amusing to have them," he wrote his sister Mabel. "Yesterday we had a charming lunch party at Lapérouse. Rachilde [Madame Alfred Valette, critic and novelist] and some longhaired monsters of the Quartier were with us. They all presented me with their books (which are quite unreadable)" (p. 308). "It is like a dream that we lunched with Rachilde and her husband, and Mlle. Fanny and Alfred Jarry," wrote Raffalovich some thirty years later.[96] Raffalovich also attempted to arrange a meeting between Beardsley and Huysmans, but it appears this never came about.[97]

Beardsley did not alone exercise Raffalovich's patronage. It was on this visit, apparently, that Gray was also introduced to these literary celebrities and, at the elegant apartment of Madame Raffalovich, to several prominent figures of the political and scientific world.[98] Particularly valuable was the introduction to Thadée Natanson, whose brother, Alexandre, had organized the prestigious *Revue Blanche*. Since its founding in 1891, it had attracted almost every important contemporary artist: not only Verlaine, Mallarmé, and Laforgue, but also Cézanne, Gauguin, Toulouse-Lautrec, Bonnard, and Vuillard.[99] Since January of 1895, Gray's old friend, Félix Fénéon, had taken over the editorship. He immediately set out to persuade Gray to contribute, asking him if he could take up the position of London correspondent, which the journal desperately needed.[100] Yet, as is so often the case, Gray's contact with this journal was tangential. In June 1897 he published a short story there, "Daphné," which relates in creditable, if somewhat boring French, the story of a newly married wife, who discovers her distinguished husband in a pitiful state of madness, making little balls of lemon peel.[101] It may be taken as something of a triumph of Gray's "clinical" style.

In Paris, Beardsley's recovery was dramatic but brief. When the inevitable relapse occurred, he fled to Menton to die. Because his decision to enter the Catholic Church came after months of solicitous visits by Catholic priests and was preceded a month before by a pledge of regular financial support from Raffalovich—who also financed this trip to Paris—one of Beardsley's biographers claims that Beardsley was "bribed" into conversion.[102]

Such a view is merely crude. The actual case is both more complex and more harrowing. Beardsley, so weak he could not leave his bed nor, near the end, even move without help, turned to the Church to ease his terror of dying. All of this is perfectly orthodox; Beardsley had always felt a deep need to believe, and the circumstances of his conversion do no violence to the Church's claim that it teaches the

Christian how to die. The question is not whether Beardsley was "sincere" or "insincere"; it is rather what part Beardsley was to play in the psychological drama of Gray and Raffalovich.

Raffalovich's conversion, as he himself noted, was not long before Beardsley's first hemorrhage of the lungs; and sometime in 1896 or 1897 during the course of his dying, Gray came to the decision to enter the priesthood. The pressures a biographer might detect in Raffalovich's and Gray's eagerness to bring Beardsley into the Church are the psychological pressures exerted by two men who felt the necessity of ratifying their own actions. Beardsley was to become their symbol, their vindication; to some extent, Beardsley must have sensed and resented his role, for one finds in the letters of that last year a kind of ambivalence and duplicity toward Gray and Raffalovich. It should be said in extenuation that Beardsley certainly had a real affection for Raffalovich, and that the duplicity was probably the result of a set of conflicting feelings: embarrassment at his own helplessness, a mixture of relief and irritation at Raffalovich's obvious solicitude. Thus Beardsley was quite capable of writing, "How good you are to me, dear André, a brother in fact out of a fairy tale," while confiding to Mabel some months later, "If A.[André] is all right in January I need not get rid of them [i.e., Gray and Raffalovich] in any indecent haste" (pp. 343, 397).

By 30 November, a week after this letter, Gray resigned from his position as librarian in the Foreign Office. In the next month he left for a week's retreat with the Jesuits at Manresa House, Roehampton. Beardsley grew weaker throughout the first months of the winter but disguised his terror with a stoical, if pathetic, gaiety. Gray spoke of "his reputation for sweetness and resignation . . . during the martyrdom of his last eight days, those days of choking blood coughed up in torrents, and of painful attempts to cure."[103] Beardsley died on 16 March 1898 in Menton.

For *La Revue Blanche,* Gray wrote an "obituary memoir" prescient in naming Beardsley a "genius." As one could have expected, he defined Beardsley's artistic gifts precisely. But what Gray saw before others was that Beardsley would come to define not merely himself but an entire artistic period. He had an "astonishing flowering," Gray wrote:

In an instant he was famous. Music-hall writers adorned their verses with his name. Publishers anxious to make a fortune proffered their attentions. Women's dress conformed to his wish. Wagnerian concerts were thronged with his characters. As for himself, he did nothing but draw, unmoved, and was none other than Aubrey Beardsley.[104]

With Beardsley's death, that period came to an end. With it too died "Dorian" Gray: dandy, poet, decadent. Pierre Louÿs and Félix Fénéon unconsciously wrote Dorian's obituary when each separately reported to Gray that he had made his reputation in Paris as the importer of the fashionable new word, "smart," its triviality a fitting epitaph to his decade as dandy.[105] With the imprisonment of one friend, the death of another, the demise of the name and the image were complete. A confidante of Gray's later years recounts how Gray had told her of the hours after he received the news of Beardsley's death, wandering around Piccadilly aimlessly, murmuring to himself, "I must change my life. I must change my life."

And so with Beardsley's death, the ironic circle comes full turn as Gray, the lapsed convert, finds in Beardsley's conversion sanction for his own return to the Church. The cycle is completed in 1904 when Father Gray edits Beardsley's letters for publication. From these, Gray draws a parable of the discovery of faith through physical suffering. And this necessity of making "moral tales" out of his experience and symbols out of his friendships, present and past, becomes more pronounced as Father Gray begins to see his own history as one to be both rejected and expiated, as a "moral tale" in itself.

Such ambivalence toward experience is reflected in Gray's ambivalence toward his art. Gray kept in his library a copy of the *Pageant* in which was published "Niggard Truth," and to the end-papers two press cuttings had been secured. One described him as "interesting"; the other described his work as "silly, unsuitable, senseless, incompetent, affected, precious, laboured, ineffective and ignorant."[106] Gray relished such contradictions. But they also point to contradictions that underlie and undermine the artistic work of this period. If art is to be employed primarily as a route of access to the transcendent, then it is an instrument that must, logically, be abandoned with the discovery of the real thing: the spiritual instrument remains just that. If one finds new power in such poems as "The Forge" and "Leda," one may also see it mortified in the childlike, chastened voices of the *Blue Calendars*. These poems act as austere reminders that art is the handmaid of religion. In the end, Gray resolved the question of the value of such art—by rejection. Shortly before taking his final leave from London to study for the priesthood at Scots College, Rome, Gray announced to Pierre Louÿs that he would never write again.[107]

❧ *Father Gray: The Poet as Priest,* ☙ 1898–1921

> *He was a poet: but he might have been acclaimed a poet and he might have achieved what this world calls immortality. But he chose a higher and nobler immortality—more enduring and more glorious. The Poet gave way to the Priest. He made songs and sang as a poet: but it is the songs and the poems he did not sing that gave him his real, his royal, priestly greatness.*
>
> Father Bernard Delany
> Funeral panegyric for John Gray

On 28 October 1898 Gray entered the Scots College, Rome, to prepare for the priesthood. Officially he was still on leave from the Foreign Office, where his resignation did not come into effect until 30 November. But Gray left in early October, first travelling to Regensburg in Bavaria to visit his two younger sisters. On the eleventh he left for Rome, stopping briefly at Verona and Bologna, where he visited the tomb of St. Dominic. Once he reached Rome he went straight to the Scots College, in the Via Quattro Fontane.

Gray chose the Scots College on the advice of Monsignor Merry del Val.[1] A fellow student, Dominic Hart, thought Gray chose the College "out of abhorrence of 'Naughty Nineties' memories." He also recalls that it was said of Gray at the college that he was attracted by its uniform, the most picturesque in Rome: purple cassock, red cincture, and black *soprano* (or robe)[2]. That rings true; but Gray was, after all, of Scots descent, something he tended to emphasize more as the years wore on.[3]

From the first, Gray was set apart from the others at the college. He was, after all, at thirty-two, at least twelve years older than the other thirty students. For this reason, he did the shortened course of studies for "late vocations": three-and-a-half years rather than the usual six. Temperamentally, too, he was always to a certain degree aloof. Dominic Hart remembers that "apart from special occasions such as concerts, at which he used to sing songs, he did not have a lot to do with the rest of us. . . . There was always a certain remoteness about him, although he was, as we knew, very kind."[4] Perhaps because of his age or connections, Hart recalls, Gray was also permitted certain privileges denied the others: to go out "in black," for instance, rather than wearing the conspicuous college uniform, which also meant he could go out unaccompanied, normally against the rules. He did, however, have several special friends. He was close to Willie Mellon (afterwards Bishop of Galloway) whom he described as "'a solid mass of goodness,'" and to a younger student also named "John Gray," who went by his middle name, Alan, to prevent confusion. Hart also recalls that, as both Grays were good with their hands, it became routine that after dinner they "hived off to a lumber-room and did carpentry, plumbing, etc." thus saving the Rector, Monsignor Robert Fraser, many a lira.

This sounds as if Gray were neither a rank outsider nor unhappy. Yet Raffalovich's sister thought the new regime a trial to both Gray's temper and health, and it is clear that the latter did give Raffalovich concern.[5] Raffalovich did much to ease its stress. He sent food (packages of game, caviar, asparagus, and so forth, arrived almost weekly); wrote frequent letters; arranged introductions. Gray attended the occasional embassy dinner (where the husband of his friend, Lady Currie, was ambassador) and dined with several prominent churchmen. Raffalovich himself, together with Florence Gribbell, made prolonged visits to Rome to be with Gray. But this still did not mitigate the essential grind of the college. The Tridentine system by which seminaries were, until recently, conducted was authoritarian. Nine years previously, Frederick William Rolfe, alias Baron Corvo, entered Scots College also, to be expelled thence a year later on vague charges of unsuitability. He took his revenge in a partly autobiographical novel, *Hadrian the Seventh,* in which Rolfe/Corvo, now Pope, revisits "St. Andrews College." He recalls the ugly refectory and gaudy chapel, the library "where he had found impossible dust-begrimed books," and the large helpings of coarse food. His fellow students were "immature cubs mostly" or, more curtly, "savages," whose choice recreation was murdering stray cats: an act which encapsulated "the altogether pestilent pretentious bestial insanity of the place" which was his "homeless home."[6]

But whatever his trials, Gray was no Baron Corvo, whom he regarded as something between a legend and a joke.[7] Gray was at home, not in spite of but because of the college's authoritarian regime. This is clear from the reports he sent faithfully to Raffalovich in a correspondence that was to last for the next seven years, until Raffalovich moved to join Gray in Edinburgh in 1905. They are, with few exceptions, comfortable, even happy letters. From the first, Gray writes of an "ease & peace & satisfaction" which he takes as "indicative that I am in the right place & going the right road."[8] In November, for instance, he writes breezily of attempts to master the mandolin "out of pure wantonness" and to meet the Rector's request that he write the college song.[9]

In the same letter he details with obvious satisfaction the rigid schedule to which he is subject, a satisfaction, however, that did not extend to his studies. These elicited a new humility; he soon confessed to Raffalovich that "It is a fact that I have never had a moment of self complacency about my present work—and I lived largely on complacency once" (27 November 1899). Whatever the jolt to his self-esteem (the rapid lectures in Latin reduced him almost to despair), the quasi-monastic rule of the college appealed to Gray. Within it he found release from self-preoccupation, from personality, even from conscious thought. Of the healing power of complete submission to the Church, Gray wrote Raffalovich after two years at college that "now I am in such a confirmed & salutary state of mistrusting all my own thoughts & listening to what others have to say that I have practically no thoughts at all as I daresay you have found out. You always ask how I am & I say: never better" (5 March 1900).

Such buoyant well-being was punctured by occasional seizures of remorse. During his first year, Gray wrote Raffalovich:

On the 14th is the anniversary of my baptism. It will be, as far as I can make it so, a day of oblation and resolute resignation to the will of God. I suppose the longer I live the more tragic each anniversary of this day will become. I went through instruction as blindly and indifferently as ever anyone did and immediately I began a course of sin compared with which my previous life was innocence. The sequence of miracles which has brought me where I now am is beyond my comprehension. To contemplate it means to realise as much dread as security. (10 February 1899)

To this letter Raffalovich replied with characteristic compassion:

Mon frère, mon frère, be happy and well. Your past can be explained in this sense: that you were baptized because you were God's and had to come back from him. Think how many saints have been brought back from sins against the known truth: St. Andrew Cossini, B. Bernard of Scammaca, etc., etc., against a truth known and practised. (No date)

But Raffalovich's touching concern was never to ease Gray's remorse. As a priest, he was daily to work out what he saw as retribution for his own past. He sought also, with an urgency that went beyond even a priestly vocation, to save others from their own miserable history, as he himself had been saved.

The Uses of the Past

From the early years of his residence in Scots College, a pattern emerges from Gray's letters. It may be best defined as an overriding impulse to salvage from what he saw as the wreckage of the past his family, friends, and acquaintances: to save them through the only vehicle he knew, the faith of the Catholic Church. Marmaduke Langdale is a case in point. As previously noted, Gray's visit to the Langdale family in Brittany had been instrumental in Gray's discovery of religion. During the ensuing years, his friend Marmaduke turned out to be something of a black sheep. Never gainfully employed for any length of time, after the turn of the century he had taken up "any kind of hack work which would enable him to earn a few shillings." At this point his chronic alcoholism took a turn for the worse and, after a flirtation with taking holy orders, Langdale compounded the "despair of his very respectable [Catholic] family" by marrying the divorced wife of an Anglican clergyman.[10]

Gray tried to encourage his friend during that crucial period when Langdale was considering joining the Congregation of the Oratory of St. Philip of Neri, a congregation of diocesan priests living in community. By the end of 1899, however, Langdale had changed his mind, prompting Gray to write Raffalovich in exasperation, "and so you despair of Marmion. Why doesn't Fr. James tell him that if he doesn't work he'll go to hell. The silly ass has to be a Filipino. I should like to see him *in the novitiate*. The daily screw would bring the sense to the surface" (16 December). Three years later, Gray wrote to Langdale's sister, Fanny, about his friend's gradual drift from the Church and his "lamentable disregard for his health." Although Langdale had "suffered terribly," Gray wrote, "I advise you very strongly however to put a check on your impulse to make sacrifices on his account. A good deal of money has passed through Marmie's hands and so little remains to show for it. . . . Though you may think this a cruel point of view I hope never the less you will consent to be guided by it."[11] Certainly this was hard advice, but Gray accurately foresaw the inevitable outcome. In a letter written twelve years later, Gray chides Fanny:

Really if I were you I should not vex myself about Marmy. Pray for him and be ready in the last extremity to make sacrifices. He has a lot of good qualities mixed up with other things: but the truth is through all his craziness enthusiasm and suffering there is in him a profoundly selfish man. I like him both for the past & the present too & do not care a hang what he thinks about me. . . . He does not contrive pleasure for others. Don't think about the marriage. You can't influence him—or her. (30 September 1914)

When Marmaduke died in 1924, Gray consoled Fanny by saying, "Relations and friends have secured in Marmy what they would wish for themselves, a happy death. Such is the reward of prayer . . ." (22 May 1924).

The harshness of tone so evident in these letters springs from Gray's constant awareness of the alternatives. Even in Rome he did not entirely escape the past. In the first month of the new century, while walking with other students to Ara Coeli, he ran into Robert Ross with another group; "both parties looked at me as a bête curieuse," Gray reported to Raffalovich (January 1900). Certainly

"Dorian," transformed by the college uniform of purple, red, and black, must have made an arresting spectacle. On another occasion Gray, again walking in company, came upon "a large form planted as if to waylay him." It was Oscar Wilde. "There was complete silence," a close friend later reported, "but mockery dangled it."[12]

What emotional distance Gray had won from his past might be gauged by the manner in which he received news of the deaths of some of its principal players. Of Wilde's, perhaps only months after this encounter, there is silence, unless the letter was destroyed; Father Gray was known on rare occasions to advert to "poor Oscar," however. Of "poor Dowson's death," Gray remarked, "I used to like him very much & his poetry more if possible" (5 March 1900). Of Lionel Johnson's, Gray observed that it was a "funny case, it would be more so if one did not know that the man was as eccentric as he was . . ." (10 October 1902). His detachment, however, could not conceal his consciousness of a near escape, which made him exacting of himself. His own demand for spiritual perfection could also leave him angry and bitter over the waywardness of others and, finally, coldly indifferent if they persisted.

What might be called Gray's mission to bring others into the Church began long before he considered the priesthood and perhaps as early as his break with Wilde. Probably under the influence of her oldest son, Hannah Gray converted to Catholicism in 1893. Her three youngest children—Alexander, Norval and Beatrice Hannah (for whom Gray stood as godfather)—were brought up as Catholics.[13] As has been seen, Beatrice (or "Trixl," as Gray called her) and Sarah attended a convent school in Regensberg, Germany; Gray stopped regularly on his trips to and from Scots College to visit "my creatures," as he called them, visits Beatrice in her old age remembered as "unmitigated bliss." "Hansl," as she and her friends named Gray, was something of a pet of the nuns and was more or less given the run of the school. "He was known to assist at open-air needlework classes," she recalls, "and show off his skill at hemming with a child's thimble on his little finger. Once he even penetrated to the Junior's dormitory and gave the occupants affectionate goodnights."[14]

Yet Gray's obvious affection was tempered by anxiety, the pressure of which may be felt in the reports made to Raffalovich after each yearly visit. From his new residence in Scots College, Rome, Gray writes that "My sister Trixl's character shows no modifications. . . . Last April she was known to say: 'My brother has been gone three days. I am beginning to be a little cheerful again'" (13 October 1898). Gray could be cryptic, and this letter might be read as implying that Trixl felt her brother's departure so acutely that it took her three days to recover. Or it might suggest, despite her nostalgic reports of "unmitigated bliss," that "Hansl's" presence could be that bit oppressive; that view is borne out by the distinctly critical report Gray sent to Raffalovich almost exactly two years later, that Trixl, despite being "greatly improved in temper" and "a little more grown up, . . . remains however a decidedly low-comedy woman, and still takes no trouble to conceal or disguise her thoughts" (11 October 1900).

In retrospect, perhaps that pressure to shape her character was not only necessary but fruitful, for Beatrice Hannah became, after the turn of the century, Sister Mary Raphael of the Benedictine Order, which made its home in Princethorpe Priory, Warwickshire. Gray was to her much more than a good brother or even a second father; as Sister Mary Raphael later wrote: "I feel out beyond all human appreciation or otherwise of my brother. He fulfills a certain role in my life, which is too spiritual to be put on paper—and which outweighs all other aspects in value and importance."[15]

But where Gray succeeded in influencing his favorite sister, he found himself on at least one occasion meeting spirited opposition from his mother, who seemed to resent Gray's involvement with her younger daughters. In the autumn of 1902, almost a year after Gray had been ordained, Sarah set her mind on becoming the second wife of one Rear Admiral Arthur Roger Tinklar, for whom Gray had a high regard. Gray's mother, however, objected strenuously to the union, probably on the grounds of a large difference of age (Tinklar's two daughters were about the same age as the intended bride). Gray stepped in as mediator, attempting to reconcile mother and daughter. "Everything started as badly as it could," he wrote Raffalovich,

and towards evening my pent up feeling gave expression in such a violent form as I have never seen before. I thought it best to get Sarah out of her sight as soon as I could. . . . Poor Trixl begged me not to leave her with my mother but I persuaded her to stay though I could have wished to bring her with me. I left my mother in a calmer frame of mind this morning—Sarah says more pleasant than she has been since Christmas—and she & Sarah made peace at my instance. . . . (4 September)

Gray's perceptions of a necessity to save the children from the mother and hence, it seems, from the influence of the past, is implied in every line. Although it is not unusual for the eldest child to feel he must rescue the younger, in Gray's case this sense of mission was exacerbated by his distaste for the past, from which he regarded religion as the only hope of escape.

Accordingly, Gray became angry with his mother when she appeared to resist divine grace. A month after this scene with Sarah, Gray wrote Raffalovich:

. . . talking of my mother, she has been trying all she knows to make me unhappy, but hitherto without success. This day however, I hear that she is going to make a confession, the first since January; it is an amelioration for which I am devoutly thankful, for I said mass two days ago with a view of bettering the situation. . . . (3 October)

With Sarah married, Beatrice set on the path that eventually was to lead to a religious vocation, and with this "amelioration" of his mother's spiritual state, Gray had to some degree succeeded in rescuing part of his family from the conditions in which he himself had been brought up. That past he now regarded as if from a distance, and his mother's death six months later surely made him feel that he had left it even further behind.

Although he had not completed his full course of studies, John Gray was ordained on 21 December 1901 by Cardinal Respighi in the basilica of St. John Lateran, the cathedral church of Rome. A few months later he suffered a "thorough breakdown of health" and was advised to finish his theological studies at the University of Fribourg, Switzerland, in the belief that the climate might benefit him.[16] He was discovered to be suffering from a heart condition, although his letters from Scots College speak only of gout, neuralgia, and various minor ailments. But by September of the year he was deemed strong enough to take up his position as assistant curate at St. Patrick's in the Cowgate, Edinburgh.

It is possible that something of the same sense of mission he had shown toward family and friends prompted Gray to accept, as his first position, the poorest parish in Edinburgh. Was it a gesture of penance for his dandified London years? Or a gesture of concern for those born under conditions of poverty even more dire than Gray knew as a boy? Whatever the motive, we do know that Gray chose this course for himself; the rumor that the Pope, the Marquess of Bute, or some other prominent Catholic had prevented him from taking a position in England (because of his association with Wilde) is unfounded.[17] Gray had in fact from his earliest months at Scots College decided on such a plan. He sounded out the idea in a letter to Raffalovich, saying, "What do you think of my putting myself under the aegis of a Scots bishop when the time comes—with the view after ordination of working a year or two in a manufacturing town entirely among the hopelessly poor." He mentioned Dunkeld, Edinburgh, and Glasgow as good settings for such a venture, and asked Raffalovich to take the question into serious consideration: "You know we have often said it is *your* vocation we are struggling to set on foot. We are waiting to know what God will do with his lamentable subject and you are just as likely to hear as soon as I—or do you leave me to find out for myself?" (30 November 1898).

Father Gray

Gray's first pastorate had as its parish a district once the most desperately poor of Edinburgh, one originally settled in the mid-nineteenth century by the Irish brought over as cheap labor. Among its lodging houses and tenements every evil could be found. Tuberculosis, alcoholism, violence, and early death were daily encounters for the new curate. "There are ten thousand of us Catholics here in a very small compass," he wrote his niece, "and not a few of us drink; but on the other hand our faith is unbounded and we have moments of sorrow for our misdoings which a saint might envy."[18]

Despite the parish's harsh conditions, during his first year Gray expressed an eagerness and joy he had not known for years. Indeed, in many letters during the early months of his priesthood, Gray's enthusiasm for his job and the gratifying conviction that he had finally found his life's work contrast oddly with reports of the desperate misery of his parishioners. Shortly after assuming his duties he writes Raffalovich: "It is a very consoling life, what with the bad and the good. It is also full of surprises; every hour brings the news of a tragedy: as one goes out there are all sorts of people with all sorts of tales, in all degrees of drink, want and impudence" (29 September 1902). All that autumn the letters to Raffalovich, now visiting his family in Paris and travelling around the Continent with Florence Gribbell, remain assured and jubilant. Gray's efforts to save souls had never seemed more fruitful. "It is beautiful work," Gray wrote. "I don't want to exchange it for no matter what. It is all so simple: there are the open arms of God, and one has just to push people into them" (7 October). He no longer regarded illness, desperation or death merely as evil, but the occasion for the soul to find God. "It no longer needs an effort of my will," he confessed to Raffalovich, "for me to thank God when I hear a man is dead" (13 October 1902). A few days later, he sends Raffalovich an example of a routine pastoral visit:

I went the other night into a house of a couple belonging to us when there was a bit of a row going on. The wife 'had drink in her' as the phrase is here, and was by way of putting her husband out of his misery, to the screaming of five children ranging from a girl of eighteen down to nothing. My arrival quieted the storm and I bound them over as well as I could, while the combatants and the children tried to put the few things the room contained in their proper places. As I turned to go, almost immediately, I saw a small boy sitting in the middle of the floor, pen in hand, calmly going on writing on a small piece of paper, dipping his pen judiciously into a bottle of penny ink which was standing on the floor. I saw the woman the next morning, and learnt what I was very keen to know, what had been the instrument with which she was attacking her husband. It was the door of the oven. . . . She gave a very convincing account of the natural and acquired wickedness of her husband. Balzac could hardly have done it better. So we came to the euphemistic conclusion that there were many faults on both sides. Life is

like a dome of many-coloured glass—with most of the panes smashed.
(15 October 1902)

Gray's encounter with bedrock reality proved a relief. Visiting the
very sick, he writes that "the utter common sense of the hospital
charms, and after the years of *voulu* nonsense, looks like the very way
to God" (1 December 1902). Looking back, he recalls that once "I de-
liberately wanted desired things not as they were *but as I wanted them*.
Now I want them as *they are*" (18 March 1903). Being saved meant
literally being saved from himself, from a willful self-preoccupation
that had once led him into a nearly disastrous pursuit of pleasure.

Gray understood such acceptance of things "as *they are*" to be a
sign of salvation. One might find other signs in these letters: those of
joy and relief as well as new resources of humor. His faith gave him
security. It also gave him a role which was established, respected, and
useful—and one that legitimized his temperamental detachment.
Gray as priest could at one and the same time remain scrupulously
dressed, well-spoken, fastidious in every gesture—and still be accept-
ed in the rough neighborhoods of the Cowgate. He never felt he had
to become like his parishioners or live among them. In fact, he made
no effort to minimize the great distance between them, once describ-
ing the constraints between the priest and his people as "the great
wall of China" (6 January 1898). Gray returned to this image in a
poem of this time, "The Emperor and the Bird"; he had been moved,
he said, by an interest in the late emperor and empress mother
of China.[19]

What struck him was the priestly function of the emperor. In his
poem, the emperor comes to represent the exacting nature of the
priesthood, in contrast to the spontaneity of the spiritual life; the outer,
as opposed to the inner, man:

> Too sore upon a human frame: too great
> This heavy priesthood, royalty, immense
> Fatigue, the office of the exalted Bonze:
> Lonely, endeavourless, terrific state,
> From inattentive eyes too closely screened,
> In sombre courts of adamant and bronze,

Time polished and from age to age patined,
And quaking service all his recompense.

His sparrow, in the broad air, where he plays,
Delighted, in much light, with many a shrill
Contention, summoned, drops, a parachute:
By gardens and by devious covered ways
Sweeps silent, to the sacred hall addressed,
A satin flesh mailed mamelukes salute,
Wheels steadily to the Presence, preens his breast,
Waits gaily, back and forth, the sovereign will.[20]

The weight of office, that spiritual emperorship conferred with the priesthood, juxtaposed against the sparrow, delighted, free, which "wheels steadily to the Presence," defines an ambiguity in Father Gray, the double vision of the letters: joyous confidence within; apparent imperiousness without. In "the exalted Bonze," the figure of the Buddhist monk "from inattentive eyes too closely screened," one recalls the Father Gray of his later years: a face said to resemble an impassive mask; a priest described as cold, inscrutable, silent. Yet his aloofness was offset by an inner delight in his faith: it had the fine careless access of the sparrow, so unconscious of its commonness and triviality.

Both aspects were part of the "real" Father Gray. A friend of his later years, Father Edwin Essex, thought that Gray's distrust of his own emotions and their expression came from his idea of the priesthood, one so exalted that he kept himself on the tightest of reins. Gray also fought for a bitter self-control out of a lively fear of his past. Remarking on the appearance of coldness this habitual restraint created, Gray once told Father Essex, "I know what some folk think of me, but I just have to do it in self-defence. If I were to relax for a single moment, only God knows what might happen to me."[21] There are many stories of Father Gray's intuitive kindness, particularly toward his women parishioners. It was not kindness he intended to offer. He came to give spiritual aid, by means of the sacraments. But he would also scrub floors, mend fuses, give hard-headed practical advice. Above all, he made his parishioners feel that here was a man who had been through it all and could sympathize. Perhaps his role as priest is best summarized by Mary McMenemy, a resident of St. Patrick's parish for many years, who remarked: "Everybody said he was very proud, but he was awfully kind in the confessional."[22]

Other pictures show different extremes: that of the intolerably precious priest who organized a Toy Exhibition at Outlook Tower, Castlehill, Edinburgh in 1907; that of the humble, kindly man who came to know "everyone" on his summer holidays in Iceland and who, in Edinburgh, entertained the captain and crew of Icelandic fishing boats when they put into Leith.[23] Yet neither extreme is just; and in actual fact, one owes much to the other. Gray's interest in artefacts, for instance, grew from his first days at the Woolwich Arsenal. He understood that art could come from the folk; there is no contradiction in the once-exquisite poet writing, as a priest, an article on "Some Scottish String Figures."[24] Nor were his aesthetics of the Luddite stamp; he was one of the first to regard machines as a work of art. Not only did Gray like machines, he knew how to repair and run them, a talent that stood him in good stead both at college and in the Cowgate. While in Edinburgh he also found occasion to indulge a long-standing interest in the primitive, evident in such early short stories as "Loves of the Age of Stone" (1893) and "The Advantages of Civilization" (1894). After organizing a trip for some of the parish boys to see an exhibition of early weapons, he confessed to Raffalovich, "I scored a beautiful morning in the museum yarning with the subdirector, a bow and arrow man, the most purely selfish two hours I have spent in Edinburgh" (13 November 1902).

Yet for all his interest in the practical and the primitive, for all his grounding in the laboring classes, Father Gray was never a man of the people. He wrote to Raffalovich that, when meeting with the men of his parish, "from my desire to see the thing do the men good I become a little nervous, with a small temptation to diffidence. The 'men of the parish' are so vague, silent, mysterious, and yet they are very concrete all the same . . ." (10 March 1904). The note of respect was evident; he came to be respected in turn. It was not so much that Gray shared their taciturn and mysterious nature; he was accepted because he came with work to do, and he did it. In his years at the Cowgate, for instance, he set up, with Raffalovich's financial assistance, a hostel for illegitimate children. He also conducted a study of housing conditions and rents in the parish as well as of the working conditions in local industries.[25]

These years in the Cowgate were nothing if not exhausting. It was said of Father Gray that he soon began to be known in the parish as a priest who would go to places to which, even in daylight, the police would go in pairs, and that he would go no matter how late the hour or dirty the night.[26] It is not surprising, then, that Gray discovered he had little time for himself. He writes to Raffalovich:

To be a curate here is to feel like the Salisbury crags, a fixture; we do not get away. . . . The summer holiday is an abandonment of the people one has to look after, and the impression on return is . . . of beginning the whole thing over again, while in fact of course it is not so. I am hoping I am making for the time when I shall have my work well in hand, and at the same time be able to live a life for myself, and find scope for the hypothetical intellect I possess; work and a sort of half-piety, cemented together with bits of wasted time, make up the whole for the present, but experience will amend this. (16 November 1902)

At first much of his "spare" time must have gone into writing his sermons, which achieved a kind of fame in themselves. He was very self-conscious about them. "My sermon went off all right," he wrote Raffalovich. "Here of course we only hear what is wrong with our work; it seems the monotony of my voice drives to drink. In vain I tell them that the subject of Purgatory requires a monotonous voice. . ." (4 November 1902). When Raffalovich was planning a visit, Gray warned him: "Don't build expectations on hearing me preach. I prepare my sermons conscientiously, and I am not shy; the bizarrerie of my mind too sometimes keeps the congregation awake, but the rest is very uncertain" (11 May 1903). In later years, Father Edwin Essex described their technique:

His own sermons . . . were always in character with the man. "No matter where or how he begins," a listener remarked appreciatively, "the Canon always brings us in to the terminus." And that described his technique fairly enough. He could never be obvious, either in theme or phrasing, and from his opening statements it was impossible to deduce what was to be the trend of the sermon. Then very deliberately, in that quietly incisive voice, the Canon would proceed, using always the right word in the right place (second nature to him), until suddenly, often by wayside tracks of thought, the listener found he had been led to the essential point of the discourse.[27]

The sermons arose, naturally, from Gray's own reflections. A young man who once helped Gray to serve Mass, now Professor Geddes MacGregor, recalls the gist of one homily on the grandeur of the Mass in which Gray emphasized how no church, not even St. Peter's in Rome, no rite however grand, could be worthy of an event so stupendous. Father Gray's own great dignity at Mass was notable; he was a lesson in reverence, gravity, self-possession. On rare occasions, however, his own preoccupations took over and the reason for Gray's fear of relaxing his iron control over himself becomes evident. In one instance, in mid-sermon, Father Gray went suddenly off into a tirade about women who danced naked on a stage and sent men's souls to hell; this aroused a slight wave of astonishment in the congregation, so out of key was it with their pastor's usual tone.[28]

As part of his parish duties, Father Gray also found himself writing for a public again. These were the verses written "to accompany Tableaux Vivants (or Mimes) represented by the children of St. Patrick's parish" and were to be published initially as *Fourteen Scenes in the Life of the Blessed Virgin Mary* (1903). They may have arisen from his Thursday evening course of instruction on the parables of Jesus, which he was giving to the boys of the parish in the autumn of 1902. "I go at it the way which I believe in conscience to be the right way," he reports to Raffalovich. "Modernizing our blessed Saviour for all I am fit, dwelling on his cleverness and sharpness, and manliness, with perfectly reckless applications of local colouring, and when necessary I eke out the material with a little pantomime" (29 September 1902). The verses demonstrate many of the same qualities (which suit them perfectly for their purpose) as when Gray writes of Jesus:

> Joseph has taught Him how to use the plumb
> And spirit-level; bradawls, bits and brace;

He does not let Him use the axe, in case
He might chop off a finger or a thumb. (P. 204)

Unprepossessing as they were, these scenes proved quite popular and went, over the next three years, through two further editions.[29]

Despite his intense involvement in parish work during the first two years of his priesthood, Gray did eventually find a few hours of the day for his own work. But this work drew him, almost inadvertently, into the intellectual ferment within the Church which went by the name of "Modernism." In retrospect, one can say that "Modernism" was the occasion of the greatest crisis within the Church of Rome within the last hundred years, or until that unrest arising from the Second Vatican Council. Today, the *New Catholic Encyclopedia* defines "Modernism" as "a belief in an adaptation of the Church to what was considered sound in modern thought even at the expense of radically changing the Church's essence." This "new thought" gathered momentum after the turn of the century under Pope Leo XIII's liberal policies, but when Pope Pius X succeeded him in 1903, firm action against the "Modernists" seemed necessary. A series of papal decrees placed the work of many scholars, such as that of George Tyrrell, a member of the Society of Jesus in England, on the Index. Tyrrell had become a friend of Raffalovich, who followed all these developments closely, often reporting on them at length to Gray. By 1906, Tyrrell was to be dismissed from his order and excommunicated the following year. Indeed, so identified was Tyrrell with "Modernism," that when he died two years later, the movement in England was considered officially dead.

Years before the crisis reached its pitch, in 1902, Gray agreed to assist Monsignor Fraser, the rector of Scots College, in revising and correcting a translation he was making of a recent book on the Gospels by a French Dominican, Vincent Rose, professor of Scripture at the University of Fribourg, where Gray had known him. Gray regarded the exercise as "a means of forcing me into the rule of two hours work for the intellect in the day," as he told Raffalovich (15 October). By January 1903 he had worked through the first part; "I think it reads less like Scotch and Chinese than it did," he writes (6 January).

Meanwhile, he found himself drawn into the controversy and extended his reading. Within months he had concluded that "the 'silly man' Hegel, and his masters are at the bottom of the present crisis, though I don't thnink [*sic*] that anything but the forms is new" (27 March). He reflected that "it is consoling to think that the operation of submitting the scriptures to the historical method is passing so peaceably; it had to come, and there had to be a certain number of 'morts et blessés.'" And, he added: "Don't forget that this uproar may have for one good result to remind some of the good plodders that there is such a thing as scripture. I am often called a protestant by those who should know better—but I go on smiling" (15 April). Not that Gray was in any sense a "Modernist," although the intuitive grasp of spiritual reality possessed by the women in his short stories "Light" and "Niggard Truth" are imaginative versions of one aspect of the "Modernist" position, as are the "mystical" pieces in his *Spiritual Poems*. Perhaps for this reason—or perhaps out of sheer mischief—Gray many years later described the *Spiritual Poems* as "a lot of heretical rubbish."[30]

Gray submitted the finished translation, with which Raffalovich had occasionally helped, to George Tyrrell for final emendations. *Studies on the Gospels* by Vincent Rose, O.P., in the "Authorized English Version by Robert Fraser, D.D.," was published by Longmans, Green and Company toward the end of 1903. The year ended with reverberations from the past. A fire had gutted the publishers Leightons and Methuen; Gray reported that one of his books (*Spiritual Poems*) had been "burnt out. It was he [Leighton] too who cased *Silverpoints*," Gray continued, "and a pity he didn't burn that too" (9 December 1903). In January 1904 Gray announced that *Ad Matrem,* a revision of his scenes from the life of Jesus, would be out soon and he asked Raffalovich to buttonhole Arthur Symons for a review. Symons had the idea of turning it into a retrospective of Gray's work, to which Gray responded: "Arthur Symons might see his way to a serious article, if he were to take the present 'corpus' of my work. There is nothing in it but shame at any given point, but it has always had an aim, and that sometimes redeems even failure . . . " (22 March 1904).

By the autumn, Gray had become involved in another task

which became a means of reviewing—and revising—the past. During the spring and summer of 1904, he undertook to collate and edit for publication the *Last Letters of Aubrey Beardsley,* which appeared with an "Introduction" by the Reverend John Gray at the close of the year. Most of these were letters to Raffalovich, along with a few to Gray, which Beardsley wrote from the time of his first visit to Raffalovich's London house until his death in 1898. As editor, Gray expunged all proper names of those living and, at the insistence of the publishers, Longmans, Green and Company, most of the details of the "'horrors of consumption.' "31

Considering the many trivial pieces included—invitations to lunch, thank-you notes, and so on—the edition appears to be an obvious piece of bookmaking. What would inspire such an enterprise? Raffalovich later remarked that he and Gray decided to publish the letters to answer Roger Fry's description of Beardsley as "the Fra Angelico of Satanism."32 But other, more practical, considerations were also at work. It had been discovered that, after her son's death, Mrs. Beardsley was living in poverty; Gray directed Longmans to hand over all the proceeds of royalties to her.33 Meanwhile, as Raffalovich reported in some alarm to Gray, Madame Strindberg, the estranged wife of the playwright, had begun to collect Beardsley's letters and pictures, particularly the "distressing" ones, those erotic drawings that the dying Beardsley had telegraphed his publisher, Leonard Smithers, to burn, but which Smithers lied about destroying and later sold. Madame Strindberg ("Swindleberg," Raffalovich called her) now proposed to publish these; she was pressing Beardsley's sister, Mabel, for the German publishing rights. To make matters worse, Raffalovich announced, "Madame S. said she could not fit belief in God or the religious sense into Aubrey: his conversion to Catholicism, yes, but not a religious sense before he found he could not live" (9 October 1904).

Answering these charges was, then, at least one of Gray's purposes in publishing the letters. But rather than challenge Madame Strindberg's assertion about Beardsley's "religious sense," Gray vindicated it. With great force, he argues in his introduction that the realization that one is dying is an occasion when sickness seems to do what nothing else could. What appears to the observer is the gradual humiliation of the physical economy being accompanied by the proportionate emancipation of the spiritual. It is a spectacle so moving, the reduction of a coarse brute to a frank-eyed youth, the renascence of a gentle-souled factory-girl, supposed to have been long ago drowned in drink and gone for ever, from the wreck of a wild virago, that in the presence of it the words tuberculosis, cancer, and even the euphemistic G.P., cease to curdle the blood.

Of this transformation, observed at first hand among the rough people of the Cowgate, Beardsley's conversion offered the paradigm:

Aubrey Beardsley might, had he lived, have risen, whether through his art or otherwise, spiritually, to a height from which he could command the horizon he was created to scan. As it was, the long anguish, the increasing bodily helplessness, the extreme necessity in which some one else raises one's hand, turns one's head, showed the slowly dying man things he had not seen before. He came face to face with the old riddle of life and death; the accustomed supports and resources of his being were removed; his soul, thus denuded, discovered needs unstable desires had hitherto obscured; he submitted, like Watteau his master, to the Catholic Church.[34]

It was with this paradigm in mind that Father Gray angrily opposed Longman's effort to "clean up" the letters: "We are strongly of the opinion," he wrote the publisher, "that whatever there is of horror is vital to the interest of the letters, inasmuch as it serves to exhibit the moral victory of the sufferer & the power of divine Grace in him."[35]

But shortly after this protest, having come to "a better frame of mind about the ghastliness of some of the health details" (as he wrote Raffalovich on 6 October), Gray became fascinated with the book as a "literary curiosity." Certainly, he reflected, "it is unique in this, that never before have letters written with so remote an idea of subsequent publication been given to the public except in the interests of science, and only then I think as criminological documents . . ." (22 October 1904). There was also the possibility of a *frisson nouveau*, which Gray contemplated with a certain delight: "I anticipate a horrible explosion in the press," he wrote Raffalovich shortly after publication, "which we expect, having loaded the gun and applied the match" (18 December 1904).

The "explosion" did not materialize. But the edition of the letters did—slowly and subtly rather than abruptly—alter the public view of Beardsley. How this perspective changed may be indicated by a letter Henry James sent to Raffalovich several years later. He wrote thanking him for the volume of

Beardsley's letters by which I have been greatly touched. I knew him a little, and he was himself to my vision touching, and extremely individual; but I hated his productions and thought them extraordinarily base—and couldn't find (perhaps didn't try enough to find!) the formula that reconciled this baseness, aesthetically, with his being so perfect a case of the artistic spirit. But now the personal spirit in him, the beauty of nature, is disclosed to me by your letter as wonderful and, in the conditions and circumstances, deeply pathetic and interesting. The amenity, the intelligence, the patience and grace and play of mind and of temper—how charming and individual an exhibition! . . . And very right have you been to publish the letters, for which Father Gray's claim is indeed supported.[36]

In late November, several weeks before the Beardsley book was published, Gray fell seriously ill, suffering from an almost complete breakdown of health, clearly the result of the intensity with which he had thrown himself into his parish duties. Indeed, fears for his health had been expressed more than a year and a half earlier by his superior, Monsignor William Grady, the parish priest of St. Patrick's, who wrote of them to Raffalovich. Gray had responded, "I do not in the least resent being the object of solicitude, and I have not really the maniacal devotion to my work that is supposed, but I have abject fear of instability subjective or objective" (13 April 1903). It had been a period of strain. Shortly before Monsignor Grady's intervention, Gray's mother had died unexpectedly, on 4 March. As her first son, Gray was closest to her of all his family and her death was a blow. During the months before, he had also tried to do some of his own work, embarking on the translation of Father Rose's *Studies on the Gospels* and completing the text for the speaking tableaux which were to appear as *Ad Matrem*. In the next year, he was to publish the

Beardsley letters. Gray knew that the "strenuous life of the Cowgate" was taxing his reserves, observing to his sister Sarah that his work required "a lot of physical stamina . . . and as the life consists entirely in the work one does, the situation is serious."[37] But in the last analysis, it was not so much what the job required as what he required of himself, that nearly killed him.

The diagnosis was pneumonia. At first Gray was confined to bed. When his condition did not improve as rapidly as expected, his physician advised him to go to London. There Gray stayed briefly at Raffalovich's house before they left together for Rome. Raffalovich remained at Gray's side intermittently during the next six weeks of slow recovery. It was obviously a time for taking stock. Gray wished to remain in Edinburgh, but there was now a question of finding a parish suitable for him, since it had become clear his health would not allow him to return to the Cowgate. Gray later recalled that it was in Rome on 16 February 1905, during the visit of two friends—the Most Reverend James A. Smith, archbishop of St. Andrews and Edinburgh, and Gray's former rector at the Scots College, Monsignor Fraser—that he and Raffalovich raised the first formal suggestion that they should build a new Catholic church for Edinburgh over which Father Gray would preside.[38]

Such a plan was not merely expedient. It had a long gestation in what had evolved into their shared religious vocation. Raffalovich had once written Gray: "What matters most to me is our relation towards God, that you and I should do his will here, and be with Him for an eternity. That is the prize, the aim of all and everything, and our history, yours and mine, does point to such a scheme, to such a condescension of God's part" (no date). For a decade now, their relation to God had bound them together. They had sealed it in taking vows when, in October 1898, Raffalovich had joined the Third Order of St. Dominic, and Gray had followed his example a year later.[39] The Dominicans, as well as other religious orders, instituted a Third Order for lay people so that they might join in observing a modified version of the Order's rule. When he joined, Gray was studying for the priesthood; Raffalovich was also considering entering the priesthood, but was prevented by his health.[40] In a sense, then, Gray became a priest for both of them.

But now God's "scheme" seemed to demand more. Gray resigned his post at the Cowgate and returned to Edinburgh in May of 1905. He immediately began negotiations for a site and architect for the proposed new church to be built in the fashionable Morningside district of the city. Raffalovich financed the purchase of the site and building, but Gray would allow him to bear only a certain portion of the cost, as he felt parishioners would not consider the church their own unless they also contributed.[41] Also on Raffalovich's behalf, Gray purchased a substantial house within walking distance of the new church: Number 9, Whitehouse Terrace, where he would live with Raffalovich and Florence Gribbell from 1905 until the completion of the church and its adjoining priest's house in 1907. For Raffalovich had decided to move to Edinburgh. While he claimed that the climate better suited his health, the seriousness of Gray's past illness now made it inconceivable that Raffalovich should not live near him.

The foundation stone was laid in April 1906 and the church dedicated almost exactly a year later. Gray chose the architect himself: Robert Lorimer, later known for his work on the Scottish War Memorial. "There is . . . for the moment a violent set against Lorimer," Gray reported to Raffalovich, "but the chief complaint is that Lorimer is 'anglican,' which is vague. I do not see how his anglicanism is to affect me" (2 May 1905). Gray was clearly determined to ignore both the Catholics' and the Protestants' violent sectarianism in turn-of-the-century Edinburgh. And he was obviously able to work with Lorimer in such a way as to impose his own interpretation of the design.

Its plan was taken from that of the smaller primitive Italian churches.[42] Typically, the church and priest's house would nestle around a small, interior courtyard. The special ambience of St. Peter's immediately embraces those who pass through the gate. In contrast to the street outside, the courtyard is quiet and warm, the ochre-colored stone and brick and red-tiled roof capturing even the grey sunlight of Edinburgh, creating an atmosphere at once intimate and compelling.

As one enters the church, the mellow light of the courtyard vanishes; here the light is stark. It bounces off the bare white loggia that leads the eye up the lofty piers to the coffered roof of Oregon pine. Coming from the intimate scale of the courtyard, one feels immediately diminished, almost crushed by the height of the arches, the dark weight of the ceiling. Within the church proper one notes many mementos of Gray's Roman years—the replica of the ancient statue of St. Peter, for instance, and the copy of the Madonna of Santa Maria Maggiore in the Lady Chapel—which underline Father Dominic Hart's suggestion that the church was named St. Peter's "from Roman memories." But the interior justifies the other reason Hart suggested for its name: that it was so designated "because both St. Peter and John Gray—in his unregenerate days—had denied their Lord. This was for him a matter of infinite regret."[43] There is a terrible severity revealed here: not of mere style, but of first principle. When Raffalovich's sister, Sophie, asked once whether she could say goodbye to Canon Gray, then in the confessional, her brother rebuked her sharply: "We never speak in the church but of the things of God."[44]

Yet that bleakness and austerity, so much a piece of the architecture of the church, is at odds with the detail of its interior. There is a gorgeously carved baroque confessional, now relegated to a side chapel. Against the bare, whitewashed walls are paintings by John Duncan and Frank Brangwyn in the manner of the Pre-Raphaelites. The floor of the chancel is laid, lavishly, in rippled green/gray marble inset with small brass fish and elaborate wrought-iron serves for communion rail and baptistery gate. All were commissioned personally by Gray. And taken together all display an exquisite, if precarious, balance of the severe and the self-conscious, the simple and the florid: a rejection of the world juxtaposed with what one intimate described in Father Gray as a love of the sensuous so intense that it would scandalize a Manichee.[45]

If, despite some recent changes, the church still speaks of Gray's singular taste, the priest's house gives that taste its most complete expression. A friend of Gray and Raffalovich, Peter Anson, recalls its effect when he first entered the guest room in 1919:

Hanging on its walls were a few framed lithographs by Shannon and Ricketts. A heavy velvet-like fitted carpet added to the comfort. It was not until the following morning when the curtains were drawn back that I noticed the windows were very small leaded casements, filled with semi-opaque glass, through which the pale winter sunshine of Edinburgh hardly penetrated. The whole house was in a dim, mysterious, and elusive twilight. It was a world of half-tones: in fact it only needed an invisible gramophone playing Debussy or bits from Maeterlinck to make it quite perfect.

On the ground floor, Anson continues, was a small dining room. The large booklined study held a few comfortable green leather armchairs, and a businesslike desk. Gray's personality was revealed by the room and his wide interests by his books—works in Icelandic, much poetry and mystical theology, and costly illustrated volumes on sculpture, painting, and architecture. His austerely furnished bedroom was perhaps even more characteristic: the sheets on the narrow bed were of black linen.[46]

Installed as parish priest of St. Peter's in 1907, Gray served there until his death in 1934. His new world was curiously isolated from everything outside it, a perfect expression of his personality and love of the well-made artifact. When Raffalovich had moved to Edinburgh in 1905, he established a *salon* which over a period of almost thirty years became a kind of Edinburgh institution. Many passages in *Two Friends* describe Raffalovich's dinners: their stylized, rather dated manners; their carefully chosen company of academics, literati, and young artists; their conversations, kept in skillful play by Raffalovich. Moving between St. Peter's and these gatherings, which he attended faithfully for many years, Gray now circulated within a contrived, exquisitely artificial milieu, a whole world of ceremony and symbol which "Dorian" Gray had sought and momentarily lost. Gray himself put it another way when he observed to Raffalovich of the plans for St. Peter's, "I am sure the result will also be exceedingly beautiful; things really for once being remoulded nearer to the heart's desire . . ." (13 June 1905).

"Heretic Blood": Father Gray and "Michael Field"

Many histories were played out within this elegant setting; but they were for the most part backstage, hidden from the world. Few knew of Raffalovich's problems with his family or his finances; nor of his discreet patronage of such artists as Eric Gill and Cecil Wright, or his even more discreet acts of charity. Hidden too were Gray's efforts to help his own family and friends, as were the anxieties and grief he suffered at their illness or death. Outwardly, he seemed now the model of the respectable parish priest. He succumbed to that archetypal Scottish obsession, golf, to the extent that he confessed to a close friend that St. Andrews "competes with Jerusalem as a place I would choose to end my days."[47] In 1909, he founded the parish school of St. Peter's. He was elected a fellow of the Royal Anthropological Institute (a position he held from 1903 to 1915) and was to be one of the founders of the Edinburgh Zoological Park. Before the Great War shut down all travel to the Continent, he managed one extended trip in the summer of 1909 through Denmark to Sweden, this "wicked programme of movements" an indulgence in a personal pleasure trip.[48] He had also acquired a silver Skye terrier, appropriately named Tobias.

Surely with such credentials, which suggest a respectability bordering on immobility, none of his parishioners would have guessed that their cool, aloof Father Gray had embarked on a final, great intimacy. It was, as it had been with Shannon and Ricketts, a double friendship: with the aunt and niece, both poets, who wrote as "Michael Field." Katherine Bradley, the older by sixteen years, who went by the name of "Michael," had virtually raised "Field," or "Henry," born Edith Cooper, the daughter of Bradley's invalid sister. Both studied at University College, Bristol, where they were active in the debating society and an antivivisection group. In the 1880s, they made themselves into writers, working in such close collaboration that they would say, after the event, that they could not tell who had written what. Their literary production—twenty-seven plays, eighteen books of verse—was exceptional and well regarded. Lionel Johnson was their devoted admirer; Shannon and Ricketts, as well as Will Rothenstein, their lifelong friends. "Proud and aloof," as Rothenstein describes them, "they tended their minds as precious vessels prepared to receive all they held lovely, both in the physical and the spiritual world. They were the feminine affinities to Ricketts and Shannon with whose work they had fallen in love."[49] From their first meeting with the inhabitants of the Vale in May 1884, they acknowledged themselves as their doubles.

Gray should have encountered them there during the late eighties, but they did not meet then or later, even though "Michael

Field" wrote a letter in thanks for a copy of *Silverpoints*.[50] Eventually it was Ricketts who took matters in hand, introducing Gray to Bradley during one of his London trips in mid-January of 1906. She found him "rosy, inscrutable and kindly."[51]

When Bradley returned to their Richmond home to discover that their beloved chow dog, Whym Chow, was dying, it plunged her, however improbably, into spiritual crisis. Sometime later, in a startling, strange letter, Bradley gave an account of the moment in which she turned toward God. The letter suggests the complexity of her psychic drama and the primitive terror of the experience itself, both of which point to something essential in Gray's own experience. There is no possible way to relate Bradley's experience without sounding absurd, except in the context of her response to Gray's description of the corresponding moment in his own life.[52]

Dear Father Gray—
that is best—the search—light—in response—I will do all I can to aid—And now I am sending to you a little picture. It is a picture of our Bacchic altar— taken before we left our old home of Durdans, Reigate, in I think 1899. I said—we must have our Bacchic cub [Whym Chow] at the foot of the altar— & he obediently fell asleep there . . .—that day I met you at the Palace Jeu [Ricketts's house in the Vale], Tuesday 1906—I went home to learn my Chow was already in frenzy—(stricken of some awful brain disease). I nursed the little creature day & night—ready at once to part with him. . . . Vets, said I ought to give him a chance—till on the Sunday—for the bright eyes were growing blind & the little feet wandering in circles—that no gentle caress wd stop—I resolved to kill him. . . . It was in sacrifice—& indeed much for the sake of Love itself—& then,—through blunderings as pitiful as Goscommon's [Edith Cooper's then confessor, Father Goscommon]—I was nearly 5 hours seeking to quench that too sturdy life. . . . And no prayer was listened to—And I heard the cries of my little Whym—when after chloroform—he was being driven by the vet—for the final puncture—I *hoped* unconscious—

Then I came home, & took down the candles from the altar of the Trinity—& was left—oh—*a very brief while*—without God. Before Whymie was brought home to be buried at the foot of the altar of Dionysos in the garden—we were able to pray—& to ask God to accept that sacrifice—And

.presently—a month or two—after—at Rottingdean—I was quietly told of Heaven; that we three Henry, & Whymmie, & Michael were accepted—to reflect as in a dark pond—the Blessed Trinity—

It is our Mystery—*it is our secret*. In return for our blasphemy—Whymmie returned to us to be our guardian angel . . . & little living Flame of Love. He is a little Fellow, as Henry is my Fellow.

There! I have told you of my intercessor, as simply & bravely as you confide to me; & I shall never forget them(?)—the story of yours.

—I knew nothing of Sacrifice—till I offered one. It has been accepted. To my dear Henry the price was worse—for she loved him most—and from this I have learnt all I know of the Sacrifice in the bosom of the Trinity, and the search light you must cast—in on my *blasphemy*—and God rewarding *that*—so!

—There is nothing in my life worth talking about to God! I suppose it would be wrong to say—Would there were! I have had so sweet & noble parents—my nature lies all at unity with itself—vainly, as it seems to me(?) by happy instinct from the Seven Deadly Sins. There is deeply, heretic blood in me—and I pray—by penance—by all that . . . help—that I may be cleansed to receive the mysteries.

Pray for me—MICHAEL.[53]

This crucial drama occurred, as Bradley noted, immediately after her first introduction to Father Gray, although it was confessed to him months afterwards. In September 1906, the two women travelled to Edinburgh to visit Gray. Cooper, meeting him for the first time, recorded her impression in their journal thus: "The round little priest comes in quietly—as happy as a rose on a bow . . . greets Michael eagerly, bows to our hostess, . . . &, as with a pause of revelation & praise, he sees me beyond her & his eyes rest over me. A strange moment: the apprehension of the mystic & the approval of the man of the world at unison in that gaze." She refined her perception later, noting in him "the wild beast in a mystic," all more or less kept under control.[54]

The visit confirmed the "Michael Fields" in their interest in Catholicism, although no formal commitment had been made or, apparently, contemplated. Throughout that winter, Gray and Bradley corresponded with increasing frequency, Bradley demanding books and enquiring on points of dogma; Gray answering always by return. On

11 April 1907, Gray wrote inviting them to the dedication of St. Peter's. But before they were to start for Edinburgh, Cooper (apparently without telling Bradley) arranged for herself to be formally received into the Catholic Church. When told of Cooper's conversion, Bradley exclaimed: "But this is terrible! I too shall have to become a Catholic!"[55] Not that she had not been working in that direction herself; but what she feared most of all was that Cooper's decision would place a barrier between them. And so, on her journey to Edinburgh for the dedication, she determined not to leave the city without herself also being baptized a Catholic. In this Gray was unable to oblige her, but arranged for the ceremony to take place on 8 May, to be followed in January by her confirmation.

Such is the bare history of their conversions. Its real drama is played out in the decade of letters between "Michael Field" and Gray, in which, in Bradley's struggle with "heretic blood," is enacted Gray's own history of spiritual crisis and reconciliation. For Bradley, her turning to the Church was only the beginning of her acceptance of it; she was an instinctive rebel against all forms of coercion, however subtle. Being older and more forceful, she dominated her tall, pale "Fellow," her "Beloved," "Henry." And nothing else, not even their poetry, captures their personalities as do these letters, revealing them as scholarly, high-pitched, fervent, even reckless in their pursuit of the absolute. Once they had been part of the new "aesthetic" movement, friends of Browning, Meredith, and Yeats. Now, after the turn of the century, Bradley's letters, impulsive and often scrambled, are full of nostalgia for "those eighties, & their damnable aestheticism— there have been moments when I have . . . cursed it, & its lovely void." Although she admits that once "I did seek to flee," the older Bradley had gained enough perspective to appreciate "the work of those eighties & early Nineties—the good & vital work of Oscar— rising up from the folly—the good & the harm of Pater—your work—ours!"[56]

Because she shared this history with Gray, artistically as well as spiritually, she understood that quality in him which others missed, when she exclaimed to her diary: "It is almost appalling to find how strong the capricious dominion of the senses still is in this devoted servant of God. Oh! how our past is our tragedy."[57] She knew the intensity of his delight in the visible world; perhaps, too, his sensuality about food and drink, which made him a connoisseur of both, and his pleasure in flowers, which drove him to become a keen botanist. She also observed, as did Cooper, the iron control he exercised over his sensuous nature. In the completed St. Peter's, she acknowledged a reconciliation of the two: "Yesterday," she wrote Gray after its dedication, "how I rejoiced in our blessed church, & gave thanks it had been given to you to build it—surely in reparation—for all we were in deed or concept—in those years 85–95."

Thus Bradley was one of two people—Raffalovich being the only other—who not only recalled the past, but also asserted its persistence, as her nickname for Gray, "Father Silverpoints," suggests. Because of their shared history, she was able to turn to Gray as one who had survived the eighties and its "damnable aestheticism," and who understood implicitly its claim to freedom. Bradley declared herself free "by happy instinct from the Seven Deadly Sins," but she knew that the artist in her had "deeply heretic blood." Even before she was admitted to the Church, she feared it as an act that would sacrifice her hard-won autonomy, as an artist and also as a woman. For aid against her own rebellious nature, she turned more and more often to Gray:

My dear Father—

Of Lent—yes—I know you wd. not fail me. But I wrote to you when the great crisis of my life had come—when I had to give up my entire liberty, & abandoning every fastidiousness of choiceness & mood be . . . everyday with the Bread from Heaven.

I wrote to you, as my Father in God, to you, as perceiving how dimly I walk on the orders of things—. . . .

I know you did not understand I made appeal for help.

Bradley's difficulty came not only in submitting herself, but also in seeing God's grace at work in her past: "My terror is to *deny him in my past years*," she wrote. "I have received Him in Communion—He has sought me from a Child—and again & again I have forsaken Him & broken away in the great wave of 'Modernism' that swept over us in the eighties—Sometimes deliberately I have turned my lamp upside down." The great "Modernist" crisis of 1907 enacted publicly her spiritual dilemma. The difficulty lay in reconciling the assertion that "the Church *is the home of freedom*" with the expulsion of George Tyrrell from the Society of Jesus as the result of two letters he wrote to *The Times* criticizing the encyclical *Pascendi:*

My dear Father,
The Times of this morn. brings to me *very great trouble.* I deplore also extremely the letters (or rather the temper of the letters) of Father Tyrrell.

I maintain my right to criticise the encyclical letter. It has no claim to infallibility; & it is manifestly full of human temper, cleverness. . . .

The enclosed extracts this morning are far more serious. I am told that the Church *is the home of freedom.* And if today I purchased the reply of men on their defence, & considered what they need to say—I incur (officially) mortal sin—& may be excluded from the Sacraments of the Church.

But English Michael will read his Times attentively every morning. (Not all the Pope's horses nor all the Pope's men will keep him from the Times !!! & large extracts will surely be given from the defence. English Catholics fought for freedom against the Armada, & surely they will have to do this again.)

. . . If anyone has suffered from Modernism—I more. As you know, Father, I have cut it away from my life in so far as it could infect me.

Henry suffers worse than I—she suffers as a man when tight cords are drawn across his brain. We have very narrow priests here. . . .

Personally I take refuge in the Mass against schism—I seek every day to love his Church with Christ, as the Church he died for. . . .

Yet I feel that any day the most terrible of deprivations might be mine. Do give me help. I wish you had told me of this letter. *How does it affect you?* And how about the Church being the home of freedom? All this when every day we are growing profounder in our love to 'Sancta' [i.e., Mother Church]—our whole lives filled with happiness because of her.

Such amazement in my heart!
MICHAEL (5 November 1907)

Gray's reply to this letter has not been located, or it is possible, since the "Michael Field" letters were returned to Gray after their death, that it was destroyed. Those letters from Gray to Bradley which did survive address issues of dogma only on occasion, and then only cryptically.

Why this evasiveness? Partly, Father Gray's difficulty lies in the nature of the subject; partly in his instinctive sense for the privacy of Bradley's own experience: "I know—or think I know—well how it is, that any word I write reads irrelevant, intrusive as a stone in one's shoe," he wrote after one such discourse, shortly before Bradley was to appear in Edinburgh for the dedication of St. Peter's.[58] Instead, Gray advises on practical difficulties of the religious life and speaks of his own, particularly of his devotion to St. John of the Cross. As he grows easier with Bradley, he is apt to tell her about his own reading of the moment (for the most part literary rather than "spiritual") and about his own attempts to write again: "I am expiating: when I should have chosen things I cared for nothing but words: now things grind my face and I pine for words" (17 December 1907). He sends the "Michael Fields" his poem, "The Emperor and the Bird" (see pp. 192–93), with the comment, "It shows well how the remnants of my talent are limited—by the queer" (29 December 1908). He speaks to Bradley as poet to poet, remarking on effects he would like to achieve or those he admires. Only on rare occasions does he speak intimately of his own experience, as in that letter, now lost, in which he related his own moment of revelation in a Breton Church.

For Bradley's part, her letters (or, to be accurate, those from her which Gray chose to preserve) speak almost entirely of spiritual difficulties which became, under the pressure of the events about to overtake them, spiritual emergencies. For Bradley's was instinctively a protestant soul; obedience came hard to her, and her course was not to be an easy one in any case. Facing, perhaps, a familiar enemy, Gray threw his energy into strengthening Bradley in her struggle with herself. "Michael had the look, the laugh, and many of the thoughts of a child," Gray once said.[59] Certainly Bradley flung herself on the strength of Father Gray with a child's trust and impetuousness. His occasional obscurity or apparent harshness frightened both women. Once Bradley wrote, "Henry & I go on wondering about your last letter—we don't understand it: it seems like a vexed, angry arrival, & indeed we don't know where we have offended." Gray's habit of writing in aphorisms, it seems, worked against him. Again and again Bradley's letters repeat the accusation: "You put me into very hot temper last night—I could not understand your letter." On another occasion, she observed to her diary: "Monday and Tuesday filled with distracting letters from Father Gray. Not one of the simple sentences gives a simple meaning the meaning is scattered as the leaves of the pythoness."[60]

Despite this apparent obscurity, Father Gray was a rock of consolation during the tribulations the "Michael Fields" would face over the next few years. For some time Cooper had been frail, but on hearing of the death of her beloved sister, Amy Ryan, in February 1910, she collapsed. Gray wrote:

My dear Michael
The terrifying news. It is only a threat: the blow must not fall. I thank God that Henry will loyally use all the means of safety: and use good will—perfect will—to the same end. I am consoled by what you write of the long sleep. Michael has now a fine pact—to double the sollicitude [*sic*] which is already complete. . . . I shall make the solemn momento [*sic*]—immediately before communion—until all fear is past. (23 February 1910)

Bradley replied:

I read again & again the opening sentences of your letter. And also.— "I shall make the solemn memento immediately before communion—until all fear is past."—

Oh thank you.
this will steady me.
—Reprove & strengthen me: teach me how to behave to Henry.

MICHAEL

Weeks later is a journal entry in Bradley's hand: "I offered Divine Sacrifice for Henry's restored eyesight and Henry's restored wits."[61] But Cooper's state declined into mortal illness; in February 1911, she was discovered to have cancer. Cooper herself wrote Gray of that "Monday when the specialist was silent & I knew the worst," how she felt gripped by the "agony of a doom that reft Michael & me apart, who lived a bone-of-bone, a flesh-of-flesh life." Shortly afterwards, Bradley wrote to Gray, "The days are inconceivably terrible." She was nursing Cooper alone, with great tenderness and courage, for during this time she had learned that she too was suffering from the same disease. Bradley kept the fact secret except from Gray and her confessor, Father Vincent McNabb, and, rather than leave Cooper's side, refused an operation that might have saved her.

To Father Gray alone did she ask for help, or confess her terror. "Michael lies bleeding, & in the dust," she writes: "Help me more, Father, I have none save you to help." Who could be equal to such entreaty? There were the difficulties of distance; the pressure of work; the shortage of time. Gray apparently did not reply promptly, perhaps did not know what to reply. When he did at last write, his letters were, Bradley raged,

inexplicable. . . . O Poet of Silver-points, if you are back in that world of spleen, & pique—Michael, alas!—is only too able to follow you—to take revenges, & plan the most exquisite tortures but we have not so learned Christ!—When the great darkness of the spring fell on me—Henry's pain, & my injured health—I turned to you for help: and you cut all communication wires.

Unravel please, Inexplicable No. 2. Much as I desire to see you Father. It is not as a rosy riddle I would see you.

MICHAEL

In the end, Gray wrote, clearly and strongly. He visited. He prayed with and for Cooper and Bradley. Their suffering, and their redemption, marked forever the watershed between their shared past and shared present.

"I think constantly of you and Henry in your joy & suffering," Gray wrote Bradley at this time in the last letter to survive from his side of the correspondence:

Great is the Beloved who has chosen us. I feel much confusion under the sense of His goodness: and that I think produces the most quickening movements in my life. I ran about the world seeking the objects of my desires: and the longer they were unfulfilled increasing my demands. And when it was clearly of no use for me to continue kicking up the dust of the desert & there seemed nothing left but to hide myself & my failure without delay the heavens opened and the world revealed is so wonderful that it hardly surprised to meet Michael in the white robe of the redeemed. We never met in the desert. (13 May 1911)

Months later, a part of one of Gray's letters is copied into their private journal: "Michael, I join with great joy in thanking God for your birth. I have watched the day coming near. I hear with much gratitude about the sufferer and whatever consolations or mitigations are found: I wonder with deep sympathy, how you Michael, can keep the balance between attachment and detachment." In Bradley's hand the entry continues: "He speaks of a November visit and the opportunity to him most precious of sight with Michael and a word with her. Now *he* realizes her tragedy with fellow feeling and the intelligence of the heart."[62] In response, Bradley thanks him for the "strong words, so helpful to Henry & to me," resolving, "I will make a tremendous effort to overcome my hysteria. It grips me: it is cruel, edges of pain all about my body." She veers from terror to resolution and back again, pleading, "Teach Michael more of 'her part'." At the last, the help Gray was able to offer them is a tribute to the inner strength he found in his role as priest. "Father dear, what a bond that you love me," Cooper wrote a few months before her death. "It reminds me of the way, so intimate & powerful in [which] Whym Chow & I used to share our appreciation & love of Michael's self. Such a bond!" (12 June 1913).

Cooper died on 13 December 1913. At the funeral, Bradley suffered a hemorrhage; it was no longer possible to keep the truth from herself or others. Now ill and alone, Bradley turned once again to Father Gray to help her face her own great crisis. At first she rebelled at the Church's explanation of Cooper's life after death: of her being first in Heaven, then in Purgatory:

Father Gray comes. We have a solemn talk. I open up my grief at the Church's action—first speaking of my Love as among the Angels; then after a few weeks, in Purgatory. I tell him how this has checked me and use the simile of Henry landing in Australia and enjoying the kangaroos, and Henry still tossed on unknown seas. "Michael," he says, "you must accept this paradox." He always thinks of a dead friend as with God. The awful thing is for it to become possible to God, to have His desire and to be able to admit man into His presence. Father Gray makes me feel how awful God's task is. Yes: what I feel about Henry's being gone is aridity: it happens, He commands me to be sure, whatever suffering is before me, sufficient grace will be with me to meet that suffering.[63]

In the last months, Bradley moved from Paragon, Richmond, to a cottage near Hawkesyard Priory to be near Father Vincent McNabb, her confessor and friend.[64] In her last surviving letter to Gray there is a new control, but also a new fear of her "heretic blood":

Beloved & most faithful Father

I have been in mortal struggle. Forgive.

The wonder & joy of being summoned here to die among the Dominicans—the joy that Father Vincent wants me near him to be with him at the last, I have longed to write you of: you see, please God, I have left Paragon behind for ever.

—I am suddenly asked to die in a stuffy drawing room with a grand piano, & lusters & every form of vulgar & horrible detail.

—I am a little afraid of my brain giving way, & of turning blasphemer. . . .

—*Pray.*

And come & help me as soon *as you can.*

. . . I am humbly your child.

MICHAEL

Bradley died while getting ready for Mass on the morning of 26 September 1914, eight months after Cooper. Like her "Beloved," she had endured the pain of her last illness without opiates; and she remained steady in her faith. Ricketts, a beneficiary under her will, created a tomb for her of black-and-white marble. He asked Gray's help in designing the simple inscription, of Gray's invention: "United in blood, united in Christ."[65] The "Michael monument," as Ricketts called it, stands in the graveyard at Richmond.

Grouped around this central drama of the conversion and deaths of the "Michael Fields" are the histories of illness and deaths of Gray's family and friends. Gray apparently first heard from Bradley of Arthur Symons having been found at Bologna "mad and chained," as she describes him in her journal.[66] Having made his own enquiries about the situation, Gray replied:

It is as black a case as can be—so horrible: don't speak much about it, or you will learn details. I should think at first glance that the chain is a gloss that has slipped into the text. There are plenty of horrors with or without. 2 n. There is a little hope. The particular disease hitherto hopeless, has been treated in my madhouse by a physician a genius with much success. . . . The whole treatment is largely experimental; but I thought good to try what was possible for the poor soul by me in the past, so much disliked & then liked. (24 October 1908)

Symons had been incorrectly diagnosed as having general paralysis of the insane. Gray recommended Dr. William Ford Robertson, pathologist to the Scottish Asylums, who specialized in a serum treatment for this condition. On his own doctor's advice, however, Symons was taken to a private home run by a Dr. Griggin at Crowborough. Here Gray visited him, arriving with a book of Dürer woodcuts. "To assure the people, [to] be magnificent and leisurely," he writes of Symons to Bradley, "characterizes the disease." Gray further describes the interchange:

> What is your name sonny?
> Edward the Seventh,
> Ah, I am a priest,
> Yes. I shall soon be that myself. (11 November 1908)

From his visits, Gray was able to reassure the "Michael Fields" that Symons was receiving good care, and that his wife, Rhoda, was more than adequate to the task set her. In fact, Symons did eventually recover, to the extent that he was able to lead a normal life outside the mental hospital; but his writing never again achieved its former excellence.

During this time, too, Aubrey Beardsley's sister, Mabel, was mortally ill. "It is true," Gray wrote Bradley in 1908, "that Mabel Wright (AB's sister) and I are fond of one another."[67] She became another friend to see across death's threshold. Whenever Gray and Raffalovich could manage it, they would spend long hours with her in the nursing home, playing cards (although both men detested them) and amusing her as only she could be amused: Yeats named her as among those "who have lived in joy and laughed in the face of Death."[68]

Other blows fell. In 1911, Gray's younger brother Norval died. The difficult Alexander, who had at last settled down to a career as a military clerk in Africa and had married an African woman, died eight years later. Father Gray took in Alexander's two young sons for a short period and later supervised their schooling under the Dominicans at Hawkesyard.[69]

Period Piece

With the old intimate world so visibly and painfully dying around him, Gray did not seem to feel the First World War, whereas Raffalovich's letters are full of the deaths of young men. Raffalovich had also lost a good deal of his income, which had been invested in Germany and what was to become Czechoslovakia. There were, as one friend noted, curious economies, although Raffalovich would still have *gateaux* flown in from Sindar's or Rutenburg's in Paris for dessert. Yet he undertook the support of two young artists of merit, Cecil Wright and Eric Gill. During the war, Raffalovich and Florence Gribbell took the air raid warnings over Edinburgh calmly, but Gray with characteristic perversity complained after one air raid "that the people in the street made so much noise that you did not get the full effect."[70]

After the end of the Great War in 1918, Gray and Raffalovich came to be regarded as something near to anachronisms. "I know you like *period* individuals and I am distinctly *period*," Raffalovich confided to a young friend in 1931.[71] But even before the 1920s the pair must have seemed like cultural survivors from an earlier age. It was in this spirit that Gray was visited in September 1914 by Ronald Firbank, a minor novelist and convert to Catholicism. In meeting Gray, Firbank could reflect, he had at last completed his collection of living mementos of "the saint and martyr of homosexuality," Oscar Wilde.[72]

How Gray took to being "collected" is not known, for as Father Edwin Essex recalls, "it was seldom indeed that the Canon would open up on the personalities of the past." Even though Gray had been put "under obedience" to write about his acquaintances from the nineties, Essex considered that "it was asking too much of a man who had buried the past. Even the precious books that had survived the forgotten era were not allowed to show their faces on his shelves. Like so many naughty children they stood there—with their faces to the wall."[73]

But far from destroying his past, Gray came to embody it. One observer remarked of Gray's admirers and by implication the Canon himself, that

there was something as repulsive as attractive about all of them—a kind of hermetism that daunted, a ponderous *sic est & fiat* so alien to the late thirties and early forties—coupled with a ghostly delicacy/subtlety surviving from the Yellow Book—an epigrammatic skill in snubbing by implication—that to people of my generation as you might call it was incomprehensibly baffling, crushing and—you will hardly credit it—flirtatious.[74]

Such was the atmosphere of the priest's house. There, in monastic silence, a visitor would move through an unearthly gloom to confront Father Gray, who with the years had grown more formal, more ceremonious, more withdrawn. The house embodied his elusive personality, at once seductive and forbidding. In the library on the mantelpiece stood a statuette shrouded from head to foot. It seems that Gray had once asked Eric Gill to carve him a small statue of a man weeping for his sins; but when it arrived, it was found to be too 'fleshly' for exposure to the general gaze.[75] Should a curious visitor pick out one of the books whose spines were mysteriously turned toward the wall, it would without comment be gently lifted from his hand and replaced.[76]

And yet the atmosphere, oppressive to some, was imbued with the most hard-headed order. In Father Gray's house, a priestly colleague noted, everything went by rule. (Any failure put him out.) He had a special bath-towel which was like a dressing-gown, so that he could hop out of the bath and dry himself as he moved to his bedroom. For Mass he wore breeches under his cassock, so as not to spoil the crease of his trousers: of which he had seven pairs, one for each day of the week. After Mass and breakfast he dealt with as much of his correspondence as he could. (Once a month the arrears were tackled, and finished off.) His letters were like telegrams. Yet they were *written*. After that, his first task was to take holy communion to the sick of the parish.[77]

Those who lived with Gray during those occasions when they accepted his hospitality found that "the orderliness, regularity and punctuality of his life and household, his tranquil, tidy soul and all about him reminded one of the monastery, and Father John Gray the humblest, most studious and devoted monk in it."[78]

At St. Peter's, a visiting Dominican preacher each Sunday was the rule. Generally, the visitor arrived on Saturday, dining that night with Gray at the presbytery, usually saying the early Mass on Sunday morning, preaching at the sung Mass at which Gray was himself a celebrant, and again in the evening. After the High Mass, the visitor inevitably would be taken the short distance down the road to Whitehouse Terrace for the Sunday luncheons which, together with the Tuesday dinner parties, had become Raffalovich's Edinburgh version of his former London *salon*. There, beneath the magnificent portrait of his mother, Raffalovich's table would at one time or another include virtually every person of distinction within his considerable orbit. Noted academics, artists, and writers were invited as a matter of course; occasionally, there would be "a highly cultured Copt, a characteristically smiling Japanese, a Chinaman showing his interested audience the correct way of making tea."[79]

As the guest lists were ample evidence, Raffalovich no longer pursued his "lions." Many invited were young and obscure. "People were welcomed for their own sakes, for some gift of heart or mind which he alone may have been fine enough to discover," Margaret Sackville, a long-standing friend, who would herself preside over these gatherings in their final years, recalls. She valued the "curious delicacy" that dictated Raffalovich's taste in flowers as in friends, his genius for choice and arrangement, his sheer social artistry. "And all these guests, so ingeniously contrasted, were held together, enveloped, made one, by their host's watchful, interested, all-pervading personality," Sackville observes.

He was conscious of each individually, just as a conductor is conscious of each separate member of his orchestra. His admirable talk would flash, skim, dart, with the swiftness of a dragonfly, over the whole: turning from books to vivid personalities, with none of the awful creaking of cart-wheels which so often at British lunch-tables announces a change of topic! The conversational shuttlecock was never allowed to fall; or if it did touch earth for a moment it was soon in the air once more. Not even the clumsiest player could spoil the game.

Few who attended would forget to describe their host. Diminutive but sitting ram-rod straight, with impeccable white collar and clipped mustache, Raffalovich would follow the conversation with his quick black eyes, turning it one way or another with an adroit remark, or smiling at some sally with his beautiful smile, which would suddenly vanish as if it had been wiped off a chalkboard.

Presiding over these gatherings with practiced confidence, Florence Gribbell played her essential part in the Whitehouse Terrace household, and as Sackville observed, Raffalovich and Gray "considered her comfort and contentment in every detail: even seriously advising her on the choice of a new gown, and supervising her reading. Such solicitude was not officious but charmingly touching." As hostess of the Sunday parties, Florence Gribbell was, in Sackville's mind, "so *digne* (I can find no equivalent English for the expressive French word), so adequate in her behaviour."

As for Gray, Sackville remembered his considerable presence at those Sunday gatherings:

If André Raffalovich's conversation was quicksilver, the Canon's provided the solid foundation on which these airy improvisations might rest. A little remote, even, some might think, a little stern, anyhow austere, it is not without significance that his favourite travels were made in Iceland. He never talked at random, his judgment, always weighty and considered, was, without arrogance, final.

Father Gray was considered a kind of center of gravity to these proceedings. Despite his somewhat abstracted air, when he was appealed to in the course of a conversation, he "was always ready with the type of comment that seemed to make any further discussion of the matter superfluous."[80]

The gravity extended to the purpose of these occasions. They were not merely social pleasures; they were, as Gray once explained to Father John-Baptist Reeves, part of a mission. "Society," he said, "is something which God has built into human nature. It is the medium by which . . . Christianity circulates."[81] Raffalovich's and Gray's sense of society as vocation extended to every detail, including the care with which the food and drink as well as the conversation were chosen and supervised. By such attentions did exquisite taste express itself as a finely tuned moral sense. Recalling how Raffalovich would greet Gray, a guest observed: "Rooted, I felt, in an earlier generation, the high Edwardian handshake and slight formality of manner were of a different date. Always greeted by his host as an honoured guest (in spite of daily meetings), this special—some would think superfluous—courtesy belonged to the shape, the significance of Whitehouse Terrace hospitality." Others perceived its shape and significance as distinctly *fin-de-siècle*, so that, as another guest explains, taken all round, "it was rather like acting in one of Oscar Wilde's plays produced by Cecil Beaton in slightly off-period costume."[82]

"*Such* parties!" the young Hugh Walpole wrote Henry James. Walpole went regularly to Edinburgh, where his father was the Anglican bishop, and he had been invited to Mass at St. Peter's and dinner at Whitehouse Terrace. Rather than ritualized beauty, however, Walpole found offense. In his own life, religion and homosexuality had been kept rigorously distinct. In the friendship of Gray and Raffalovich, homosexuality had been sublimed into an ardent spirituality, perhaps leading Walpole to feel that their spiritual life was still, at this late date, immoral. Rather than spell out the complexities of his reaction after a service at St. Peter's, he wrote to James angrily of "immorality on stone floors." James's considerable sexual curiosity was piqued. He pressed for details. Walpole's further account still did not satisfy: "I could have done even with more detail—as when you say '*Such* parties!' I want so to hear exactly what parties they are. When you refer to their 'immorality on stone floors,' and with prayerbooks in their hands, so long as the exigencies of the situation permit of the manual retention of the sacred volumes, I do so want the picture developed and the proceedings authenticated," James wrote.[83] Whatever Walpole thought he witnessed, this is uncharacteristically heavy-handed for James. For who but he could better understand the bittersweet discipline of their relations? "Never for a moment did they appear to relax into the free and easy communication of old friends," one of their circle wrote.

Whenever they met, as they did almost daily, it was as though they had been parted for months. There was the same handshake, the same question and answer as to health and activities. The sight of them greeting each other, with what looked like a detached, impersonal interest, was a thing to marvel at. Their approach was so schooled, there was such an element of sweet restraint about it, that one found it hard to realise they had been intimate friends for so many years.[84]

Another friend confessed bafflement over an intimacy so profound that its only apparent expression was of ceremonial, somewhat over-elaborated formalities. "Of the friendship of John Gray and André Raffalovich it is difficult to write," confesses Peter Anson, who knew them both from December 1919, onward, "because it was so aloof and detached":

So far as the outside world was concerned it hardly existed. Their relationship—even after forty years—continued to be formal. Most Sunday evenings after a cold supper the front door bell would ring, and a few moments later the parlour-maid would open the drawing room door to announce 'Canon Gray.'

Had a complete stranger been present, his impression would have been that these two men were hardly more than acquaintances. André would jump up, bow slightly as he grasped the visitor's right hand, and say—almost in a tone of surprise: "Dear Canon, how kind of you to call!", or something to that effect. Then for an hour or so the conversation was as witty and epigrammatic as it had been at luncheon—possibly a little more intimate, but not much so. Then at 10 o'clock the parlourmaid appeared with a silver tray bearing whiskey, a siphon of soda-water, and cut-glass carafes of water and lemonade. "Dear Canon, will you be so kind as to serve the drinks?" And so, with further exchange of polite remarks, the typical Sunday evening came to an end, with more handshaking and bows.[85]

And yet, another friend asserts, for all this stiffness and ceremony, "one was immediately aware of the affectionate reverence each lavished on the other."[86]

The same discipline extended to other relationships. "Did anybody ever understand John Gray?" Anson once wondered. "When conversing with him one had the feeling that he was wearing a mask. At moments the mask was raised very slightly; but I can honestly say that never once in fifteen years that I continued to meet him was the mask removed. He remained inscrutable, enigmatic, shrouded in mystery, and it was largely because of this polished reserve that he was so fascinating."[87] Yet Gray's manner, which seemed increasingly to be out of touch with the new generation of the twenties and thirties, was not that of Ezra Pound's satirized nineties poet, M. Verog, "out of step with the decade/ Detached from his contemporaries,/ Neglected by the young." It merely deflected attention from a keenly modern sensibility which was, after seventeen years of silence, to find distinctive speech.

ABOVE: Beatrice ("Trixel") and Sarah Gray, two of Gray's sisters, c. 1896.

LEFT: John Gray, Sr., Gray's father.

BELOW: Beresford Square, showing the gates to the Royal Arsenal, Woolwich (1913?).

Furnace and steam-hammer in the foundry of the Royal Arsenal (c. 1910).

Ricketts & Shannon. Lithograph by William Rothenstein, 1897 (Fitzwilliam Museum, Cambridge).

"Dorian" Gray, 1893.

André Raffalovich, from a painting
by A. Dampier May, 1886.

ABOVE: André Raffalovich, in the garden of his summer house in Weybridge, Surrey.

John Gray, c. 1892.

André Raffalovich by Max Beerbohm.

BELOW: John Gray, Sophie
Raffalovich, André Raffalovich,
Florence Gribbell, and Georges
Raffalovich (?), c. 1896.

ABOVE: The Cowgate, Edinburgh, during Gray's lifetime.

RIGHT: The "Michael Fields": Katherine Bradley, above; Edith Cooper, below, from a miniature by Ricketts (Fitzwilliam Museum, Cambridge).

OPPOSITE: Katherine Bradley with Whym Chow.

St. Peter's Church, Edinburgh.

Interior of St. Peter's Church during Gray's lifetime.

OPPOSITE: John Gray on Skye, c. 1930.

Canon John Gray.

❧ *Father Gray: The Priest as Poet,* ☙
1921–1934

> *Pay the price. Prolong the search*
> *for, right or wrong, what pleases us.*
> *Listen; the patriarch of Uz*
> *is singing in the Temple Church.*
>
> John Gray
> "Audi Alteram Partem," *Poems* [1931]

Father Gray had apparently written nothing since he had sent his poem "The Emperor and the Bird" to the "Michael Fields" for Christmas 1908. He had not actually published anything of substance since 1905. The silence held until 1921, and, then, abruptly, was broken by a rush of essays and poems which were to continue until his death.

The long, dry season from 1900 to 1920: Gray was not the only poet to endure these arid years. Of the situation in the first decade of the new century, T. S. Eliot wrote: "I do not think it is too sweeping to say that there was no poet, in either country [England or America], who could have been of use to a beginner in 1908. . . . The question was still: where do we go from Swinburne? and the answer appeared to be, nowhere." Eliot himself confessed that the nearest he had come to "any living tradition" in poetry had been his reading, as an undergraduate, of the English poets of the nineties, who, he reminds us, culturally "were dead."[1]

Gray was doubly isolated—by his profession as well as by his residence in Edinburgh—from the poetic mainstream. As a priest, Gray felt a certain distaste for the poetic career of his youthful years, rejecting it as having "nothing in it but shame at any given point," even though "it has always had an aim, and that sometimes redeems even failure."[2] A poet who had known Gray in the nineties, Thomas Sturge Moore, once wrote to another poet who was collecting Gray's work in the thirties and forties: "I have always the idea that John Gray's conversion proved by no means a salvation[.] He once wrote to me that he had nothing left but 'the ruins of a talent.' The church seems to be determined [to] suppress even the ghost of that talent."[3] That impression is borne out by Father Bernard Delany's remarks during his funeral sermon for Gray, when he spoke of Gray as one who might have achieved acclaim as a poet. But "the Poet gave way to the Priest. He made songs and sang as a poet: but it is the songs and the poems he did *not* sing that give him his real, his royal, priestly greatness. . . . How many songs must die that the supreme song of self-dedication may live?"[4]

Certainly the perfection of Gray's self-dedication and not merely the demands of the priestly life kept him from writing poetry during this period. To a lesser extent, however, he was inhibited by actual physical isolation from the likes of such poets as Yeats, Eliot, Pound and others in London. Pound's influence was undeniable. "Pound did not create the poets," Eliot observed, "but he created a situation in which English and American poets collaborated, knew each other's works, and influenced each other."[5] Gray clearly understood the extent of his deprivation. At age sixty-four he wrote Edmund Blunden, "I am by age and infirmity, not to mention latitude, out of the movement, but I see [a] little poetry."[6]

Gray was also excluded, ironically, by virtue of past achievement, for the nineties poets, as far as the new generation was concerned, were indeed "dead." Even after publication of his "modern" poetry in the 1920s, Gray was placed in the uncomfortable position of ex-poet—or (even worse), following the domestication of Mallarmé, Rimbaud, and Laforgue after the turn of the century, a "precocious" poet. As if to drive the irony home, John Gray was "discovered" by a new generation of writers. In 1905, he received a letter from John Masefield requesting permission to use "The Flying Fish" and a poem from *Silverpoints,* "Wings in the Dark," for his anthology, *A Sailor's Garland*. Later, Gray gave permission for two original pieces from *Spiritual Poems,* "The Tree of Knowledge" and "On the Holy Trinity," to be republished in *The Oxford Book of Mystical Verse*. The nineties scholar and biographer of "Baron Corvo," A. J. A. Symons, privately printed "Sound," a poem suppressed from the *Silverpoints* holograph, nine years later, at the same time he reprinted six other poems from *Silverpoints* in *An Anthology of Nineties Verse*.[7] It was this selection that prompted Charles Ricketts to write Gray: "I thought you & Michael Field came out very well in the Verse of the Nineties. I found Dowson & Francis Thompson below their reputation."[8] Flattering though such attention may have been, it tended to type Gray's poetry as nineties productions just at the time when he was trying to work out a contemporary style.

Yet Gray did ultimately succeed, despite ecclesiastical duties, isolation, and labelling, in writing recognizably "modern" poetry. His physical isolation from London was crucial; but he was never entirely isolated intellectually. After thirty years in Edinburgh he had built up a formidable circle of literary friends and correspondents. Although he is never again part of a circle like the Rhymers' Club, Gray was in touch with the distinguished French poet, Francis Jammes; and with such established figures as John Masefield, Laurence Housman, Lady Gregory, Edward Martyn, T. Sturge Moore, W. P. Ker, Percy Lubbock, Sir Herbert Grierson (the editor of Donne), Roger Fry, and Herbert Read.[9] He and Raffalovich had an eye for talent, particularly among the young. Graham Greene recalls that during this period "it was the habit of Father Gray and Raffalovich to come to lunch" at Chipping Camden "when they used to make their yearly pilgrimage to Malmesbury. . . . It was always an amusing occasion."[10] Raffalovich first introduced Gray to many of these writers, initially through his contacts in Paris and London, later at his *salon*. "You are a guardian angel to me," Gray once wrote to him, "for without all these stimuli from without I should shrivel up intellectually at least if not also spiritually" (17 March 1904).

In the latter half of the twenties, when Gray once more began to publish a good deal, he also came to know several poets of the "Georgian school," which had its heyday during 1911–12: Edmund Blunden and Gordon Bottomley both became enthusiastic admirers of Gray's nature poetry. During this time, too, Gray was in touch with the "Yeats—Ezra Pound—Hauptmann Rapallo group" through a young artist friend, Desmond Chute. In the libraries of Gray and Raffalovich there is evidence of other sources of stimulation: they collected such writers as T. S. Eliot, Robert Graves, Aldous Huxley, D. H. Lawrence, Ezra Pound, Edith Sitwell and W. B. Yeats.[11] Thus all the evidence suggests that Father Gray was, in 1920, something more than a leftover from the nineties; that he was, at least, *au courant;* at best, he was intellectually if not actually involved in the current literary situation and with the work of contemporary writers.

Gray finally broke the long poetic silence with *Vivis* in 1922. It was hand-printed in an edition of seventy-five copies by Hilary Pepler, at his press in Eric Gill's artistic/religious commune at Ditchling, Sussex. As Gray wrote A. J. A. Symons, nothing was charged for the issue since it was "strictly for a small part of my own circle."[12] *Vivis* consists of a series of quatrains, highly condensed and self-contained; they may be taken as indicating some of the qualities of Gray's "modern" style:

OPTIMIST

Too simply I took
the world as stated;
where nothing is straight,
and little crooked. (P. 261)

PRELATE

The rest of you enjoy the earth;
and drink the light, and taste the feast;
while I lie quietly deceased;
ordained to be so from my birth. (P. 262)

Gray's use of this exacting form measures once again his sure sense of craft. In contrast to earlier poetry, the rhetoric is chastened and subdued; almost, at times, plain, with a new "patience and quiet honesty before the average data of human experience."[13]

That the data should be "average" at all distinguishes this poetry from the exotic experiments of the nineties. And yet this is no weak naturalist poetry in the Georgian mode; Gray is essentially "a fantast in search of a hard style."[14] Hardness is now a given in a new toughness of attitude and in a landscape that is undeniably Scottish—cold, bare, and subdued, its harshness mellowed by the gentle roll of hills, the rush of mountain streams, the fields of spring wildflowers. The preoccupations of these last decades of his life point toward Gray's great gift as essentially spatial; it expresses itself best in the actual architecture of St. Peter's, in the poetic structure of "On Aqueducts," in the vagaries of *The Long Road,* or the landscape of *Park.* The harmonies of space, Gray once wrote, console man "for the horror of living in time."[15] Within the ambit of his writing, imaginary and actual space are reconciled by a style matching in amplitude, firmness, and precision the paintings of Cézanne.

Poetically, the most extended example of this technique is *The Long Road* (1926), a series of short poems extended in manner and theme. These constitute, in part, a kind of diary of Gray's walking tours: an accumulation of episodes, imaginary and actual, over a number of years. Gray had always loved long tramps, and by the 1920s walking tours had once again become a large part of his life. When he first came to Edinburgh, he had taken to walks for the sake of his health; later he walked for its own sake. Pleasure would not always describe the motive. One friend recalls how, "one biting December, he set off alone to one of the highest districts in Scotland; and how his telegram reached us by the fireside at Whitehouse Terrace: 'Conditions delightful: Snow.'" Sometimes, another recalls, Gray would "leave his presbytery in the late evening and tramp through the night, reaching his destination at breakfast time."[16]

Many of his excursions took him to the rolling hills of Banffshire and Aberdeenshire, which, as Gray once explained, "were so much more 'satisfying' than the loftier and steeper mountains of the Central and West Highlands because their subtle God-designed curves resembled those of the human body." It was not the violent, but the tranquil in Nature that moved him, another acquaintance explained, and on at least one occasion, probably in 1914, Gray tramped around Iceland, where he came to "know everyone" and attempted to speak Icelandic.[17] On another, he set out with Father Dominic Hart on a walking tour of France.[18] Usually Gray stayed nearer home, however. Every summer, he spent two to three weeks in the Cotswolds and the West Country, his "holiday ground" as he called it. These holidays seem to have begun shortly after Raffalovich settled in Edinburgh and were to continue until his death. The routine was for Raffalovich to stay in Bath, at the Pulteney Hotel, while Gray made his headquarters at the Old Bell Inn, Malmesbury. Sometimes Gray would have a companion; a favorite was Norman Wright, a young man whose brother, Cecil, Raffalovich had helped financially in his artistic career. It is notable that, even with Gray's strenuous walking schedule, he found time to write letters—one very much in the whimsical mode of his longer essays of this period—to *The Wiltshire Gazette*. Then, on a given day, Raffalovich and Florence Gribbell would collect Gray in their chauffeur-driven car to return to Edinburgh, sometimes with a detour of a few days to London.[19]

In an essay on "Winter Walking," Gray stipulates the necessary equipment: sound hob-nailed boots, a Bartholomew's half-inch map and a "good conscience." During the course of this essay, Gray makes the case that "the essence of walking is spiritual . . . that it is a recovery of balance or of harmony. . . . The walker does many things, and something more; walking is life."[20] By just such metaphor Gray extends the significance of *The Long Road*. That this is the poem's intent is clear from the fragment of notes that Gray sent to his sister Beatrice.

1. The poem symbolizes life.

2. It charges the generality of men with two preoccupations: meals and death.

3. The monotony of life is varied with one excursion of the excursionist's own invention. . . .

4. The paragraph 'Along Wenlock Edge' is a march, not in space but in time, from 1 April to 31 December. The poem contains familiar, strange reflections on the nature of a road, an artificial river flowing both ways at once. . . .[21]

Gray's fourth item might apply as well to the entire opus. Constructed as an "artificial river flowing both ways at once"—surely his working definition of consciousness—the poem shifts back and forth between present and past, landscape and psyche, observation and rumination. Such is "'the road which ran with us'" that Gray invokes in his epigraph. The metaphor is echoed in the prolific river imagery and enacted in the long, loose catalogues in the manner of Whitman. If one may judge by the jumps in narrative and its strong, swinging rhythm, Gray probably composed most of the poem piecemeal while on his marathon walks.

The beauties of the poem are many, but two stand out: the moments of pure perception and the impetus that binds them. The perceptions are bound as such moments are to the moving eye: noted in their immediacy, they acquire a kind of portentousness, even as one observation is quickly succeeded by another. The technique creates the sense of being caught up in the rush of consciousness, as in Gray's catalogue of inns:

> The Magpie; the Chough;
> the Red, the Dun, the Dapple Cow;
> the Fish; the Boot and Shoe; the Plough;
> the Just in Time; the Barley Mow;
> the Woodcock; the Dove;
>
> the Plum Pudding; Wheel;
> the Merry Mouth; the Duck; the Fleece;
> the Apple, Oak and Cocoa Trees;
> the Hatchet Inn; the Compasses;
> the Bells by Rings and Eights and Threes,
> the Blue Bell, the Bell;
>
> and so on and so.
> But in the empire of the blest
> where inns are old and gala-dressed
> their signs are not among the least
> of things good to know.[22]

Such a catalogue by the sheer weight of detail creates an impetus that flows through the "Rivers" section, as in

> Rip ropple ho;
> it stumbles in a girlish fright,
> reflects the sun in pin-head light,
> and sweeps the stones it polished bright
> a long time ago. (P. 237)

Gray is often concerned, as he is here, with reproducing the actual sound and shape of a sensation, although the impression is always contingent on its movement, as in these lines in a motor car:

> Now hell's youngest son,
> the belching devil of the road,
> proceeding in the Burnley mode,
> and rolling to its pillion load,
>   is heard, seen and gone. . . . (P. 251)

The fine lines on migrating geese rely on the same principle of motion for their effect:

> The goose-gaggle's strength
> defined by cackling overhead
> of broods on Kebnekajse bred
> by one lithe bird a century led
>   in great shimmering length. (P. 252)

The image here, both musical and exact in visual terms, may owe much to Gray's long-standing interest in Chinese poetry. Years before Pound's *Cathy: Translations* (1915) found its way into the Gray/ Raffalovich libraries, Gray made several exquisite translations of poetry originally Chinese.[23]

But whatever their provenance, the verses of *The Long Road* stoutly declare their genre, belonging, in every line, to that great flood of literature written between the wars that has as its focus the spiritual journey. From Joyce's *Ulysses* (1922) to Auden and MacNeice's *Letters from Iceland* (1937), the traveler is no mere tourist, but a voyager: the experience not unique, but exemplary.[24] And like other works of this genre, Gray's poem assumes the same preoccupations— with specific names and spaces, with flora and fauna, with weather and meals. It has the disjointed, even undigested quality of actual experience. Sometimes the experience is too specific to escape its origins, or to make relation to the experience which comes next. Only in its latter sections does it find fusion of what it sees and what it finds.[25] But for all its slavery to circumstance, this particular journey

ultimately justifies its vision, which ends, appropriately, in a grave-
yard:

> The slow pollen showers.
> Blue geranium to my knee
> and scabiouses; chicory
> with wondrous eyes is watching me.
> O sweet God, the flowers.
>
> This green; sultriness;
> this swelling ecstasy of earth
> is rising to unruly worth;
> the clay were yet for length and girth
> a clean sober dress.
>
> To ends known, unknown,
> perhaps where summits of desire
> are touched by uncreated fire
> and joy is as a just man's hire
> the road passes on. (P. 255)

This is the achieved voice of the older John Gray: sober, precise,
mellow, alive to the beauties of the visible world. It is a voice that,
while it does not absorb entirely all autobiographical content, ulti-
mately subsumes larger influences to its tonalities. Its most apt praise
must have been that given by a friend of his later life, the poet Gordon
Bottomley. Although puzzled by a few allusions ("I haven't made the
leap yet, although your leaps are part of the delight"), Bottomley de-
lighted in the poem's "wayward beauties, its steady sharp vision, and
its immediacy."[26]

Gray's walking expeditions bore other fruit, notably the series of
essays published in *Blackfriars* from 1924 to 1934. Many of these spring
directly from, although they are not circumscribed by, a specific place.
"An Island Cloud-Factory" (1926), for instance, is about the light ef-
fects on Skye; Gray's excursion there was made more memorable when
he saved the life of his companion, Father Luke Walker, at great risk to
his own.[27] Another essay, "The Parting Guest" (1929), opens with a

meditation on the social intricacies of leave-taking. Although no names are mentioned, the piece ends with a vision of an actual farewell, that of Eric Gill and his family to their four-year home in Capel-y-ffin in the Black Mountains of South Wales.[28]

All the essays have as their bedrock specific, personal experience, but this only serves as a springboard for a rich contemplative excursion grounded at its close in some particular place and time. "Brokenborough" (1926), for example, leads the reader to reflect on what constitutes the most satisfying arrangement of buildings in a hamlet. For Gray, the question also provokes a larger aesthetic problem that arises when vision "attains a quality not obviously justified by the object." How does one balance such rapture with experience, so that the mind reaches equilibrium? In an "untouched expanse" it is easy, but "can any hamlet sanely satisfy?" By prolonged search, Gray meets at last the requirements of his own imagination in the composition of a particular Wiltshire village. "If, as we should, we take things for what they are," he concludes, "Brokenborough is to-day good, and may well remain so beyond our time."

In its intermingling of the meditative and the factual, the objective and the autobiographical, this essay might be taken as a type of all the others; on the whole they are distinguished by "the stamp of an unusual turn of mind and an easy, though never slip-shod, mastery of English prose style."[29] The essay on "Cyder" (1927), for example, opens with an odd turn: "Cider is vile stuff." The essays also disclose a mind keen and free of cant, as in "God-made and Machine-made" (1924), where Gray deplores not the machine, which is reckoned a benefit, but the loss of the small artistic touches that distinguish the handmade from the factory-made artefact. Similarly, in "Man's Visible Works" (1925) Gray attacks the notion that mankind's works violate Nature: "Permanent traces of man may be reasonable additions to subtler lines and surer colour: his dykes, his planting, houses, quarries, mills."

Two of the essays point toward a revived interest in word-play for its own sake, including the whimsical meditation on notices in "Trespassers will be Prosecuted" (1928) and a Joycean "Dialogue" (1928) which opens, "Have a norange." Proceeding by way of the *New English Dictionary*'s definitions and exemplars (from Dr. Johnson's liking for orange-peel in hot port to Robespierre's passion for oranges to Tennyson's suppressed poem), the "dialogue" closes with instructions on how to approach an orange: "Cut it through the equator, then across the poles: then imagine you are a meritorious negro." Nothing escapes Gray's keen sensibility: the design of his cracker; the horrors of a "mountain sandwich"; the lines of buildings and contours of hills; the exact genus and species of wildflowers; those "exquisite vehicles," the new motor cars, "yomphing" down the road at ten miles an hour.

It is hardly to be expected, then, that Gray should remain insensible to one literary phenomenon with which he was daily affronted: the hymn. Perhaps it was his Dissenter background which made him feel that the hymn needed to "be reconceived as a product of art; that is, skill." In "Hymns: A Suppressed Preface," Gray recalls a certain hymn at Scots College which "sent the blood to my head in indignation at this self-complacent trash." The hymn, he argues, "must be regarded as in its nature indivisible, consisting like other individuals of ends and a middle. . . . The result should rather resemble the call of a bird than a pattern of hotel wallpaper."[30] As its title confesses, this essay serves as a preface to Gray's own book, *Saint Peter's Hymns* (1925), which appeared a year before *The Long Road*. Taken as a collection, these meet the modest requirements made of them. They are merely good in the sense that their virtues are those of good workmanship; only one, "Speciosae et Delicatae Assimilavi Filiam Sion" surpasses this criterion.

During the mid-1920s Gray returned to translating, always the companion to his original work and sometimes its begetter. He turned into English a book of his favorite spiritual reading, the *Revelations* of Saints Gertrude and Mechtilde. The translation sold well; indeed, it may have been Gray's biggest commercial success, going through a second and third impression under the title of *The True Prayers of SS. Gertrude and Mechtilde*.[31] During this period Gray also undertook the editing of the *Annals of the Holy Childhood,* a journal that aimed to interest children in the work of Catholic missionaries in different parts of the world. Gray executed this work, as all other, with a sense of its possibilities and a standard of perfection. It is rare for this kind of journeywork to merit praise; Gray must have been gratified to hear from a friend, Father Bede Jarrett, the brilliant Prior Provincial of the English Dominicans, that "There is nothing so perfect as these [editions] of yours. They are a charm and a delight to me."[32]

Relieved now by his curates of much of the grind of parish work and secure in a world which satisfied equally his need for aesthetic delight and an assured affection, Gray found the resources for a final book, *Poems (1931)*, which serves to mark Gray's achievement of a distinctly modern voice. And yet it is also a voice in which one may trace continuities with the best of his nineties poetry, most evident, perhaps, in the opening "Ode," something of a *tour de force* in onomatopoetic technique:

> Empty the ears of every soft sound
> in the moss,
> in the air around;
> from the eyes
> banish the vision of repose,
> when the waters narrow and rise,
> with an action of fetched breath,
> and, rounded, plunge as to the hazard of death.
> Glassy column and sheet
> stand rigid at their fiercest speed;
> crash and explode at their feet;
> growl and churn;
> and climb the slippery stair;
> to return,
> and recede
> in skeins of incredible hair;
> around exhilarated, absent flesh
> hiss and swish afresh.
> A cool slide
> into a well-like, deep, tree-shaded pool;
> where a school
> of light and dark flecks play and hide.[33]

The virtue of these lines rests in a technical facility, a fluent verbal mimicry that Gray seems to have come upon on his own; there is no evidence that he had read James Joyce, although he would have known Proust, an enthusiasm of Raffalovich's. Still, these lines reveal less about "influence" than they do about the consistency of Gray's own poetic development; it is simply an irony of literary history that modern literature, particularly *Finnegans Wake* (1939), had at last caught up with Walter Pater's dictum that "all art constantly aspires towards the condition of music."

Although "Ode" was perhaps not entirely successful, especially in the sense that the technique tends to overwhelm its subject, it won enthusiastic praise from such figures as Edmund Blunden, who wrote Gray, "I shall not see truer and more imaginative poetry in my time."[34] Above all, it rings true; not only in exactness of observation—in a certain terse precision that was to become a Gray trademark—but in singular tonalities, particularly those (in the ensuing poems) that lie within the range from patrician distaste to sanative disgust. If a poem like "Audi Alteram Partem" recalls the studied ironies of T. S. Eliot's earlier poetry, the cantankerous turn is purely John Gray's:

> France you remember, Dominic,
> adjusted an accursed thing
> until it made a dead man sing.
> A queer, unnecessary trick.
>
>
> Caruso marred the cosy night
> until we bravely sued for peace
> to stretch our limbs again at ease
> and listen to the storm outside.
>
>
> The patient world revolving since,
> obedient to the charted speed,
> has brought to us the humble need
> of what when younger made us wince.
>
>
> We cannot be ubiquitous;
> nor longer yet suppress the wish

for past or ancient gibberish;
to let a jackass sing to us.

Do you refuse to be entranced
by some enchanted violin,
to seem to hear the waters dream,
to hear the notes a satyr danced,

because of scruples vaguely born
of griefs against united states,
and mechanisms dislocate,
and precious matter spoiled and torn?

Unwinding its concentric crawl,
a needle scrapes your epiderm,
methodically as the firm's
unnumbered patents foolproof all.

Pay the price. Prolong the search
for, right or wrong, what pleases us.
Listen; the patriarch of Uz
is singing in the Temple Church. (Pp. 277–78)

The poem, like so many of Gray's works, is highly allusive. Father Dominic Hart explains that "'France' was Father Samuel France, and 'Dominic' is myself. Canon Gray and I were France's guests at Haddington, and after dinner he played Verdi's *Aida* [starring Caruso] on the gramophone *ad nauseam* . . . until Canon Gray sought an excuse for bed."[35] It is a tribute to the skill of the poem—not merely the technical skill this time, but is wry reflections on the "price" paid in search for aesthetic satisfaction—that it survives these and other allusions to the private experience from which it originates.

The most successful poem of the collection is "Odiham":

Put his head
and anxious face
out of a car.

Seemed to have said:
Yell's the name
of this place;
seven, three, four.

Man addressed
tried to evince
interest,
as often before
and often since.
Said the name
of where they were
was Odiham.
Delighted, sir.

Fat, pale chap
seemed dissatisfied;
snatched a map
from those inside.
Engine tried
as much as it could
to drown the voices
with throbbing noises.
Man understood
him to say:
We know the way
to the south of France;
but Brodenham
is not in Hants;
we almost came
this way instead.

He said: I said
Odiham.
Odium: hatred.
Odi: I hate.
ham: ham.

239

A ridiculous name
in that point of view.

He said: Are you
then a Jew?

He said: No.

He said: Oh;
I thought I'd like to know;
but I can't wait. (Pp. 282–83)

Dry wit, innuendo, distaste: these are perfectly conveyed by the shorthand of the scene, one of those episodes from the life of the road. The fat tourist in the car is lost, cross, and impatient. He assaults the "Man addressed" (clearly Gray) with an unintelligible remark. Politely evincing interest, the Man replies that the name of the place is "Odiham," and, in return to a crescendo of non sequiturs, provides a little nonsense of his own in a false etymology: "Odium: hatred. / Odi: I hate." What he hates is clearly personified in the fat tourist, who does not listen, will not understand, and anyway does not have the time. It is a perfect, sharp satire of the encounter of modern with pre-modern individual, of yobbo with mandarin, of stupidity with style.

The poem's economy is matched by only one other piece in the collection: "Evening," of which the opening verses tell its quality:

We are just barbarians.
Our camp is vast.
The present camp and the past
show little variance.

For today we do
whatever we did
in times bysped
and the years ago.

240

All over the ground
is bewildering;
scarcely a thing
where it should be found.

Children and hens,
wherever they group,
all mixed up;
not without offence.

A true to the life
picture of us
ourselves, incongruous;
neither at peace nor strife. (Pp. 281–82)

The felicity here is a result of Gray's sure eye and ear as well as a willingness to experiment. Given this achievement, why were there not many more good poems in these last years? In part his poetic output was modest because Gray was now redirecting his energies into an extended prose work, which was to be published as *Park: A Fantastic Story* (1932). It is a singularly puzzling piece, but within this novella's difficulties of meaning and style may be discovered a clue as to why Gray did not continue this line of poetic development.

Park: *A Fantastic Story*

The stylishness of Gray's later poems does not pass for power. What feeling they have tends to be dissipated by the waywardness of *The Long Road* or exorcised by the contempt of "Odiham" or "Audi Alteram Partem." Too often Gray describes in order not to feel or allows the form to become formula. Often the poems are limited by the arbitrariness of personal anecdote. It was not always so. Once his poetry had been passionate; he had tried to put into it, he said, more fire than anyone would ever find out. But what had resulted had been a poetry of emotion so displaced that, to paraphrase Verlaine, when

Gray's heart should have been broken, he believed he was going mad. Putting the extremity of such poems as "The Barber" behind him, Gray began to cultivate a poetry of moral order, of restraint. He could not afford to let himself go; he was, as he himself realized, still in some ways a "person in question," a situation he recognized not in his poetry but in his prose. In "The Person in Question" Gray had gone in search of a person whom he recognized was "in some near or remote sense . . . *myself.*" Almost forty years later, still in quest of the self he had displaced, Gray wrote perhaps his most perfect and most exasperating prose work.

No one really understands *Park:* not Park himself, nor the reader, nor his creator. The fact itself should be grounds enough for tragedy. Consciously, the story is never presented as tragic, only as a problem, the kind of puzzle to which the reader is sure there is a solution but which is in fact insoluble. If anything, *Park* is about the misery of blank disorientation, of a white man lost in black country, lost to his time, lost to himself.

The plot is rather simple. The narrator, Dr. Mungo Park, a fifty-nine-year-old secular priest and professor of moral theology, is walking in the Cotswolds, Gray's "holiday ground." Somewhere along the Oxford Road, a strange psychic event takes place: "Mungo Park walked on in the belief, absurd as he knew it to be, that he had died."[36] He hears a long musical note, once, then repeated, then feels in his legs innumerable points of pain. "He tottered and fell. He had been well peppered. His last controlled thought was that the metaphor was good" (p. 2). When he comes around, he finds himself in the presence of a slight, powerful black man who takes him to a gamekeeper's hut.

Gradually, Park discovers he is the captive of a society ruled by black Catholic priests, the Wapami, which pursues an apparently utopian, pastoral existence in a region physically resembling the one Park was walking through. After many trials, his captors finally acknowledge Park as a priest, accept him into their society, enfranchise and ennoble him, although these acts bring him neither true recognition nor actual freedom. Then, abruptly, he awakens on the Oxford road, eastward from Burford, having suffered some sort of collapse. He is later assured by his doctor:

You were asleep, said he; it was not a faint. It was a short, deep sleep; and what you experienced was a waking state.

A short sleep, said Park.

But sleep is sleep, long or short.

And a long dream.

Somewhat more elaborate than is usual. (P. 108)

Much of the plot argues its origin in actual dream: its vividness, its peculiar but oddly logical leaps of scene and sense, its saturation by Gray's own tastes, aspirations, frustrations.[37] Especially the final inquiry into the narrator's true identity has all the conviction of nightmare. Such dreams may have been founded in reality. While Gray was still recovering from the collapse of his health in 1904, he was apparently treated with heroin.[38] In addition, while convalescing he had eagerly read H. G. Wells's *A Modern Utopia*. Gray's method in composing *Silverpoints,* of clapping two incongruous ideas together in his brain to let them "bake," may have been a factor in *Park*. Out of the coincidence of physical collapse, a psychotropic drug, and Wells's novel might well have come the recipe for Gray's novella.

Gray would write Raffalovich that he violently disagreed with Wells's premise, "the giant fallacy that the perfection of science is the solution of the human problem" (1 June 1905); in *Park,* the human problem is shown in fact to be insoluble, and the utopian society Gray initially proposes is soon revealed as flawed. Despite its technological sophistication, it has abandoned as much science as it employs; the internal combustion engine has to be explained to the Wapami, a people of the horse. A theocracy, it is also an empire kept in order by military force. For all its civilities, the society of the Wapami is impersonal, oppressive, and profoundly unreasonable. Its governance rests on suspicion; from his first appearance, Park is the subject of a formal commission of enquiry. In its concluding report, Park recognizes only a strange counterfeit of himself; and we, the reader, recognize an imposture of Father Gray.

But to explain the origins of *Park* is not to explain its significance; that lies elsewhere. In an essay on "Winter Walking" Gray says of walking that it is "an ambit in imaginary space, where sensation is fruitful and its fruit imperishable."[39] Park's walk leads us on just such an ambit within "imaginary space," which is at once, as his name implies, the compass of his own mind and the name of his estate. In short, what the story delineates is no less than a psychic map of the consciousness of John Gray.

The region described is pure space: it is timeless. Park's efforts to establish his age are greeted with ridicule; his insistence on chronological time, which is not recognized by the Wapami, is a major source of frustration. The country, Ia, is ringed by the unchanging hills, the flora and fauna that Gray so meticulously observed in his short essays for *Blackfriars*. In this world, the natural phenomena alone are unchanged from Park's more familiar world. Still England, it is an England transformed. Above ground, within its fields and hills, live the pastoral Wapami, a sophisticated/primitive society governed by black priests who observe the rituals of the Church and its seasons. Below ground live a race of rodentlike white men who inhabit the sunless tunnels of their former empire, tunnels and caverns constructed by a people who present an "intolerable paradox: mechanical construction & genius we cannot overpraise, with moral degeneration the most complete" (p. 38). In detail, as well as in status, this region parodies the nineties London of "Dorian" Gray, now literally an underworld and explicitly condemned as "decadent": a *fin de siècle* become a kind of *fin du globe*.

An alien to both worlds, Park is an uneasy familiar of each; his responses are a measure of his disorientation. Above ground, among fellow priests but denied the privileges of his office, Park finds society such torture that at times he fears going mad. His usual state of almost constant misery is mitigated only by the distraction of his friend, Dlar, the comforts of the liturgy, his daily bath, and the odd good meal. Although residing in the upper air, he is, as a white man, a true creature of the underworld.

Even before he knows of its existence, his dislocation is evinced by the dream of his first night: "He was in Westminster Cathedral and it was also a railway station of intolerable vastness & silence. . . . Park went down the line in his vestments looking for the sacristy and a third-class smoking compartment. He had lost his server and his railway porter" (p. 14). Later he is taken to a church that ministers to both worlds: arrestingly sumptuous, it is a "two-stage rotunda with a flattened dome" (p. 17). Park's view downward from its inner gallery recalls that from the dome of St. Peter's, an experience as dizzying and disorienting as that which Gray describes. Later, Park asks his guide the dedication of this church which unites lower and upper world. He is told, "The martyrs of Uganda": in actual fact, twenty-two African youths put to death between 1885–87 by the king of Buganda (as part of it was then called) for refusing to submit to his homosexual demands. Park replies only, "Benedictus Deus," but readers aware of Gray's own life in London during these years can note the aptness of the tectonics. If it is the Church that has united the two worlds, it is also the Church that has put Park, and by implication Gray, at such a vertiginous distance from that world and from his former self.

That distance is marked too by Park's day in the underworld. There is ease and delight in the old pleasures: the Reading Room of the British Library has become an enormous bookstore; the exotic books have their peculiar and intense gratification, as does the meeting with the great underworld scholar, Oli. But all is shadowed by repugnance, fear and a sense of profound alienation, for Park has, without knowing it, become acclimated to the upper air, a region that from the first has been defined by two words, "black" and "dead." The story opens with Park's puzzling belief that he had died, and he realizes he has drifted outside of chronological time: "I shall never be back in time, he groaned. I shall never be back in time. Every thought has two meanings. . . . 'Ever' is a property of time, & I shall never be back in time" (p. 13). After the first shock, there is a discovery, won from a dream, that, although he is white, he actually belongs to the world of black priests. "That is a strange thing, he thought; to dream a fact I did not know awake. I am black" (p. 15). Shortly afterwards, Park is provided with a companion/guide, Dlar, who confesses to a strange immunity:

No one, said he, is allowed to speak ill of me; the law protects me. I see, he said, that I puzzle you. I am one of the dead. It is a fiction; I am reckoned to be dead.

Drak [the native mispronunciation of "Park"] had it on his tongue to make a whimsical remark, but refrained. Dlar spoke in great earnest:

I have been condemned to death and reprieved.

Drak leaned forward.

I am in consequence regarded in many ways as though I had suffered the penalty I deserved. I am deprived of most of my civil and ecclesiastical rights; and also of many conveniences. I may not hunt, or have men-servants, or publish books. I cannot be a witness or a judge, or bring an action, or exercise a profession. But, on the other hand, no one may touch me either physically or morally: no one may sue me or send me samples or prospectuses, or ask of me alms or other favours; or, as I said, speak ill of me.

There must be some strange psychological consequences. (Pp. 31–32)

Dlar (it transpires) is deemed dead as punishment for a transgression in a previous life, which he lived under another name, Reni. In essence, Dlar is now directed "to try to behave in all ways" as though he were dead, "only awaiting the judgement" (p. 32).

As the narrative unfolds, Dlar and Park begin to emerge from its perplexities as ego and alter ego. Dlar, a black man, tells Park, "Drak, your skin is white, more's the pity; but you are black inside" (p. 39). This almost exactly mirrors a sentiment of Gray's own. As his sister Beatrice reports, Gray "was deeply interested in the black man (he was a keen anthropologist) and used to say, although he was a white man he was black inside, and foretold in a general way that the black man would rule." Whatever Gray meant by being "black inside," it is not too far-fetched to suggest a connection with his own name: that is, a white man who is actually black might appear to his public as Gray.

Almost exactly halfway through the tale, Park is granted new rights and privileges and a farm (called "Park"), and from now on, like Dlar, he is "for ever exempt from burdens fiscal, parliamentary and administrative. No one may cite him, sue him, ask favours of him or speak ill of him" (p. 54), a formula that echoes the one Dlar applies to the fictive dead. From this point on the narrator refers to both Dlar and Drak as "the dead men." What could this mean? The only possible answer is that Park, like Dlar, has entered upon some liminal existence which is neither of the living nor the dead. On the most superficial level, the words "black" and "dead" are the qualifications of Park and Dlar's priesthood, the black vesture of which is a mark of death to the world, and to Gray, specifically, a sign of the death of his former life. It is also, of course, a play with the sobriquet of the Dominicans, the "Blackfriars," in whose journal the novel was first published and with whose order Gray was affiliated; he once wrote the "Michael Fields" of his desire to be laid out, in death, in the Dominican habit.[40]

Gray makes the connection between black/death and the priesthood in a bitter quatrain from *Vivis*, "A Prelate":

> The rest of you enjoy the earth;
> and drink the light, and taste the feast;
> while I lie quietly deceased;
> ordained to be so from my birth. (P. 262)

From his "birth" as a priest, the priest is "ordained" to die; it is a tidy conceit. But the death of Gray's narrator is not merely a conceit. This death is suffered in *Park* as one suffers it in life: with whatever detachment and self-command one can muster; with whatever wit, however desperate. Gray read it as a Catholic: as a necessary death, the fruit of original sin, but also a death that should bring resurrection and life—and Park is duly wakened from the dead.

Stripping away the theology and considering only the psyche, there are cognate ways of reading *Park*. In its naked form, the experience bears an arresting resemblance to the features of a schizophrenic breakdown. The essential perceptions of the victim are the same: the conviction that the self has died; a journey into a strange psychic territory peopled by godlike figures; a sense that the victim, who must submit and be passive, as Park wills himself to submit, both suffers and at the same time controls and engineers the experience; the shift from chronological to 'eonic' time; the vivid experiences of obscure significance.[41] As in Conrad's *Heart of Darkness,* the symbolism of the character Park's exploration in Gray's novella suggests the exploration of the alien psychic territory of the unconscious. But the historical Mungo Park, a Scottish explorer of the late eighteenth century who set out to find the source of the Niger in Africa, never returned from his second attempt. He simply disappeared. If one accepts the hypothesis that a psychic breakdown is at least in part a search for a lost self, a pattern emerges from this strange narrative: Park's failure to "find" himself, to establish his true identity.

From the very beginning, Park had been subjected to some form of inquiry. "Do not let the fact distress you," he is told by a priestly official, "but it is as well for you to know that you are the cause of hideous excitement throughout the world. It is through no fault of yours; but the trouble is very great" (p. 7). Some time afterwards, Park learns that a commission has been set up; he is to be questioned, informally tried. There is a general sense of alarm and confusion: what are the charges, what is the object of the inquiry? He is subjected to a medical examination. The particulars describe the actual John Gray down to his four missing teeth (pp. 26–27).

The natives, however, remain unsatisfied. They refuse to accept Park's chronological age, as they are on "eonic" time. And aside from Park/Gray's own confusion as to whether he is alive or dead, black or white, is added the perplexity of names. Although Park is recognized as a priest, he is accused of being a missionary (p. 33). Later, when asked to explain his name, Park answers that "Mungo was the name of a saint. . . ." He does not add that Mungo was a saint of especial importance to the Scots, but he does explain that Park "as it happens means in my language an enclosed property" (pp. 43–44). To add to the confusion, during the course of the story, he is variously addressed as Park, Drak, and once as Dom Monaco Parek (p. 48). One is reminded of Gray's own series of names and nicknames and the fragmentation of self they imply.[42]

The commission's inquiries, both public and informal, issue in a long report, read to Park/Gray shortly before he awakens from his "experience":

P. the subject is a normal human being. . . . His body is complete, except that he has lost four teeth, unfortunately not replaced; slightly bald, good sight and hearing; intelligence fair; most of his reactions good.

He is presumed to be well educated according to some unknown system. . . . His knowledge of religion is wide and orthodox. Whatever other learning he possesses cannot, without injustice to the subject, be judged . . . but he may be safely described as a cultured man, for he responds to tests which only a cultured man could satisfy.

He recognizes at once the good qualities of buildings & other works of art, even showing at times some little refinement. He can draw; but only indifferently well. He is courageous, modest, perhaps diffident; he is bad tempered; he is truthful, with some power of dissimulation; but here allowance is due to his peculiar position. He has a sense of humour; and, among men he trusts (and his nature is affectionate), he is often vivacious.

He is not known to have any vices. (Pp. 94–95)

The report, exact in its notation of externals, is, as far as one can judge, exact also in its estimate of the inner Gray. Certainly his taste ran true, particularly in his eye for "buildings & other works of art." His courage had been proved at least once, in saving the life of Father Luke Walker. He could be bad-tempered, even (by his own admission elsewhere) violently so. He would evade a question rather than tell an untruth. His sense of humor, which Wilde praised publicly in "Dorian" Gray, as well as the affectionate nature that made him so vulnerable in that relationship, were for the most part buried beneath the public persona of Father Gray and were known only to himself and Raffalovich and to such as the "Michael Fields."

But when the report turns to a discussion of Park/Gray's origins, the facts are laughably distinct from Gray's actual history:

The subject was born about 300 years ago, in some remote community, probably mountainous, for mountains have a peculiar and exhilarating effect on the subject, unknown to the infidels. . . . He may have been a theocrat; for it is the firm opinion of all who have interviewed him that he is, as he believes himself to be, a priest; and the possession of a chronometer by a man found almost in rags is significant.

The supposition is that through some great misadventure, whether vicious & excessive indulgence (favoured), bereavement, crime, disgrace, fear of torture, or rash psychic experiment (extremely favoured), he came under the domination of a remote ancestral survival in his consciousness; so thoroughly that he acts, speaks, thinks, and remembers in the person of that ancestor.

This hypothesis offers the best suggestion of how he reached Ia & why he came hither. He would have been impelled to return to the place of his origin as indicated by his hallucination. (Pp. 95–96)

The report is read to Park/Gray, who is asked, "Filled with error, I suppose." Park replies, "Yes, sir; so far as I am competent to judge" (p. 97). What is reproduced is merely a simulacrum of Park/Gray: a mixture of hypothesis, invention, opinion, and fact.

And that is where the inquiry ends, as it did in life, for in actuality it was an analogue to the facade which Gray, as priest, presented as himself to others. His origins, his early life in London, and much of the history up to his arrival at Scots College remained a mystery to those who knew him or were subject to mystification. His veiled references to a "near escape" in the distant past, the traces of Cockney in an otherwise carefully modulated accent, his relationship with Raffalovich, and a thousand other details must have caused much speculation. The report of the commission in this novella might be taken as an objective correlative to the present enquiry into Gray's life.

That Park/Gray is unable to establish the nature of his true self at this juncture in the story is crucial, for without that recognition a complete reading of the narrative is lost. The definition of Park/Gray must remain an enigma, to be accepted simply on the level of appearances as a contrived puzzle whose meaning appears to be in the absence of meaning. One might go further and suggest that the simulacrum of Park/Gray so laboriously constructed by the committee of inquiry might be identified with Gray's public self, and that *Park,* even more than *Silverpoints,* concerns itself with its dramatization. However skillful the verbal experimentation of *Park*—and it deserves a reputation for skill alone—its main interest is thus ultimately biographical.

And here the results may be read as tragic. Is the frustration of Gray's search for the true identity of Park/Gray not itself a sign that he can no longer make a distinction between "mask" and the actual "inner" self? Is Gray's true self indeed lost to a merely artificial Park/Gray, an image of the "dead" self he dreamed he had become? Such a suggestion fits, uncannily, acquaintances' descriptions of Father Gray, in whom the mask of the exquisite dandy had hardened into the pose of the ecclesiastical mandarin grown "positively oriental in its false doors and booby-traps."[43]

That observer suspected he was being manipulated, a suspicion that Park shares in his own story. Park remains conscious that although he is the victim of a confusion of identity, it is a confusion that he has engineered himself, as the dreamer is the victim of his dream or the fantast of his fantasy. *Park,* it should be remembered, is subtitled "a fantastic story," and, reading it, I have a sense I have nowhere else that I am within the mind of John Gray, subject to all its preoccupations, all its quirks, not the least of which is a deliberate suppression of significance. Certainly there are passages that suggest the reader may be the victim of an elaborate hoax. In any case, we are left to make the connections and, like the commission of inquiry, to construct our own theories about Park. That he is a priest, that the mind at work is a Catholic mind, one takes as given. But ultimately *Park* has less to do with the nature of priesthood than with the nature of the imagination.

Gray said as much in reply to a letter of praise from Edmund Blunden. "Your astuteness has penetrated the whole matter," Gray wrote: "the man stumbling in his dream upon a chance of vengeance & the free expression of repressed ambitions, yet dogged all the time by the obstacles of his waking life."[44] These remarks refer less to specific episodes of the story than to its quality of mind. "Vengeance," for example, does not per se figure in the story, but may be taken as the work's representation of Gray's London world and its repellent inhabitants, some surely identifiable to his circle. There is also a strong probability that *Park* had something to do with the state of local clerical affairs in Edinburgh, and was a satirical comment on them.[45] "The free expression of repressed ambition" is exercised in Park/Gray's delight in the medieval/modern quality of the pastoral existence led by the Wapami; in their well-ordered theocracy; in their courtesy and love of beautiful artifacts, especially of books; even in their extraordinary diet. Park undergoes a meteoric rise from captive to landed aristocrat; although it is not established where he was born or who in fact he is, he is recognized as a man inherently noble.

But despite the "chance of vengeance & the free expression of repressed ambition," Gray depicts Park as "dogged all the time by the obstacles of his waking life." These are two, and related: the persistent inquiry into his identity and his subjection to a society which is unintelligible and arbitrary. Park is constantly engaged in wondering what "they" think of him; in the end he is forced to accept a relation to himself by means of his relation to "them." Above all else, this is the condition of his "death": they have defined his identity (whoever "they" are). It is for him to come to terms with it, to seek, as he does at the end, peace, and ask for the prayers due the dead.

It is a death that had been endured before. In the long-ago letter "Dorian" wrote Pierre Louÿs, Gray speaks of himself as consorting with the dead. "It is Folly and Calumny who keep me company," he wrote then. Likewise, Park is the cause of "hideous excitement" in Ia, and said to be notorious in the underworld. And within the perimeters of the novella, it is folly and calumny which triumph, in the sense that the protagonist is forced to accept an official and distorted version of himself. As a "tormented prisoner," Park is deprived of his priestly right to celebrate the Mass by his status as one of the "dead," a status perhaps like Dlar's, earned by past transgression. Yet there are compensations. With his bizarre guides and companions Park has entered into "the rich ground which hangs between Life and Death" which he is about to inherit: "I am going to enjoy my new estate presently," Gray had written Louÿs. That estate is *Park,* which he inhabits as Park, coming finally into the true heritage of his imagination.

Thus the tragedy of Park's death to himself may be ultimately qualified, as it may be in the case of John Gray. It may be that the mask had come to mark a distance between public and private so great that Gray himself felt he had lost touch with his actual self. It may be that, by default, he was forced to accept the public estimate of himself, whether as "Dorian" or Father Gray, however much he sought to avoid that fate. In Gray there is every evidence of a radical discontinuity between the inner life and the outer. The price of that discontinuity registers in the misery that saturates *Park.* But it may also be argued that Gray's mask was the very condition by which the inner self survived, and that it became the condition of its resurgence and its visible means of perfection.

Thus Gray's *Park* indeed sets out the parameters by which we may define his work: its richness as well as its restrictions rest within Gray's own self-preoccupation. He was himself, by this definition, his own most perfect artefact. But it is all probably said much better by that friend of Gray's later years, Peter Anson:

He remained inscrutable, enigmatic, shrouded in mystery, and it was largely because of this polished reserve that he was so fascinating. His face often reminded me of Leonardo da Vinci's famous painting of the Mona Lisa, and it would not be irrelevant to adapt Walter Pater's description of it to John Gray: "His is the head upon which 'all the ends of the world are come', and the eyelids are a little weary . . . He is older than the rocks among which he sits; like the vampire, he has been dead many times, and learned the secrets of the grave; and has been a diver in deep seas, and keeps their fallen day about him; and trafficked for strange webs with Eastern merchants . . . and all this has been to him but as the sound of lyres and flutes, and lives only in the delicacy with which it has moulded with changing lineaments, and tinged the eyelids and the hands . . . To burn always with this hard, gemlike flame, to maintain this ecstasy, is success in life."[46]

Having been, like the vampire, "dead many times," is not so much an acknowledgment of Gray's own death, spiritual or psychic, as a sign of the enduring vitality of the spirit. Wearing black, officially dead to the world, Father Gray did not lose his life; he found it with a fullness which the officially living could not comprehend.

❧[*Epilogue*]❧

On 4 February 1930, Gray was made a canon of the Diocese of St. Andrews and Edinburgh. He had long enjoyed the confidence of the archbishop, Joseph McDonald, but the canonry was also a mark of the esteem in which Father Gray was held by his fellow clergy. He had acted for several years as national president for Scotland of the Apostolic Union of Secular Priests; and from its institution he was the Catholic representative on the Scots Committee for Religious Broadcasting. Toward the end of the twenties he incurred new responsibilities as he was consulted increasingly by his archbishop, as well as by diocesan officials, on difficult and delicate matters of church business.[1]

They were new duties in a new decade. Now in the age of the motor-car, Raffalovich was still driven to St. Peter's in a landau or barouche, until, in later years, he compromised by taking the short trip in a taxi. Gray himself offered prayers every January for the soul of Verlaine on the date of his death, as he continued to do for all significant anniversaries of his life. There were some sad additions in these later years. In 1929, Charles Ricketts effectively lost Charles Shannon when the latter suffered irreversible brain damage in a fall. Ricketts himself died suddenly one October night in 1929, unattended. "Are we not dreadfully bereaved?" Gray wrote Bottomley, another ardent admirer; "death has seldom confused my mind more: for I feel a generation older than the impression my mourned friend made upon me."[2]

But it was the death of Florence Gribbell on 21 February 1930 that made the first momentous breach in Gray's small circle of intimates. Just two and a half weeks after Gray had been elevated to the office of canon, she died as she had lived, with dignity and presence of mind, attended to the last with great tenderness by Gray and Raffalovich. She had been a second mother to Raffalovich and at age eighty-seven was the last surviving link with his own family. But Florence Gribbell had become much more during the Edinburgh years in which she had ordered the household at Whitehouse Terrace and presided over Raffalovich's *salon*. Her place in Gray's affection was bound up in his own affection for Raffalovich; they had become nothing less than his family. "Our sorrow is very great," Raffalovich wrote their mutual friend, Norman Wright, "and I don't feel as if the pain would ever cease in this life."[3]

A few months later, in June 1930, as if to ensure his final appearance in the drama, Max Beerbohm travelled to Edinburgh to receive an honorary degree from the university and accepted Raffalovich's hospitality for five days.[4] Life continued much as it had, with Lady Margaret Sackville taking Florence Gribbell's place at the head of the table for Raffalovich's dinners. But at least one friend of Gray's thought that the Canon no longer had his heart in such festivities:

I was inclined to wonder now and then, especially towards the end of his life, if he still enjoyed meeting the guests at Whitehouse Terrace, interesting enough as they always were, hand-picked personalities in their own spheres. All of them the Canon could meet on equal terms; and André was his friend. But, as I glanced at him at table or in the drawing-room, I had a growing suspicion that their ways were no longer his ways, their thoughts and outlook no more his. I felt somehow that he had had enough, and I was right. In his closing years he was content to stay at home and eat his lunch with the curate. The time had come when he found it necessary to retreat into himself.[5]

It was perhaps this same instinct that his own life was drawing to a close that prompted Gray to make a last visit, in October 1933, to Scots College, Rome, as a guest of its rector, Monsignor Clapperton. Gray had maintained a lively interest in the college and its affairs; indeed, it was he who had been chiefly, if not entirely, responsible for the production of the history of the college which appeared in 1930. During his five-day visit, Gray was taken by the rector and students to spend a day at the college's villa in the Roman countryside. After lunch they all sang some verses of the song that Gray had written for the college more than thirty years before. The author was called for; with some hesitation, Canon Gray stood up and modestly disclaimed any credit, explaining that when he was a student the rector at the time, Monsignor Fraser, had said to him one day: "You write poetry, don't you? Well, write a song for the College," and "this," said Gray, "is the result."[6]

Gray "staggered" back to Edinburgh after the trip "so dazzled in October that I cannot remember to whom I have written my impressions," he confessed. "I went out deliberately taking as my rallying point Bernini, so far as the external Rome of my rapid visit was to render impressions; and came back justified."[7] In another letter, to his old friend Fanny Langdale, he alluded to the "great excitement" of his Roman visit.[8] He was writing to accept an invitation to the ordination of a nephew, Eugene Langdale, whose career Gray had followed with interest. The date of that occasion was to be 29 June, but by that date, Gray and Raffalovich were both dead.

On the morning of 14 February 1934—Ash Wednesday and the forty-fourth anniversary of John Gray's conversion to Catholicism—Raffalovich was found dead in his room by the maid calling with his early tea so that he could take the accustomed taxi to early Mass at St. Peter's. He had died in his sleep, peacefully; there had been no warning. The previous evening he had appeared in his usual good health and spirits, having attended a lecture by his friend Eric Gill, then staying with Gray.[9] But another friend, Charles Cammell, remembers thinking how frail Raffalovich had looked when he came to visit a few days earlier. Gray, summoned at the news of his old friend's death, took charge, giving Raffalovich conditional absolution and extreme unction, then returning to St. Peter's to say Mass after distributing the penitential ashes, signing each brow with an ashen cross and repeating, "Memento homo, quia pulvis es et in pulverem reverteris."

Gray never got over his friend's death. Father Dominic Hart remarked that he "seemed stunned by this loss, and for a while lost something of his mental balance. For instance, on the day after Raffalovich's death Canon Gray was making preparations for the funeral, and, as was his custom on big occasions, he telephoned to Raffalovich to seek his approval for the arrangements."[10] The funeral itself took place in Mount Vernon cemetery, outside Edinburgh, on a bitterly cold day. Gray officiated, standing in the cutting wind bare-headed and without a coat. It did not appear that he became ill as the result of this occasion; but such indifference to his own well-being became characteristic of his final months.

In June, a short appreciation of André Raffalovich by Gray appeared in *Blackfriars*. It spoke, although with great reticence, of Raffalovich's conversion to Catholicism; and of his personal qualities; in particular, his "natural kindness" and intelligence.

He read (though, indeed, exactly what he chose), meditated, discoursed and liked to be understood; and, without any human respect, he withdrew when he was not understood. Hence the vast and varied character of his acquaintance; his elastic memory; his facility with languages; the disquieting alertness of his mind. He liked hyperbole and family jokes; but he was never heard to employ an unnecessary expletive.[11]

On an afternoon in the beginning of June, the month that this tribute appeared, Canon Gray was discovered in his study, sitting half slumped over his desk, with his head between his hands. He had developed a fatherly affection for his young visitor, Margaret George, the daughter of his solicitor. She asked what was the matter with him; Gray replied that he was not feeling well.[12] The next morning, he was removed to St. Raphael's nursing home, where he was diagnosed as suffering from congestion of the lungs and pleurisy. On 10 June he seemed to have passed through the crisis and was sleeping better, but an abscess was found in his left lung, and the doctors decided to operate. Although the operation was successful, Gray's heart, never strong, gave out under the strain. He died on the afternoon of 14 June. Margaret George reports that he died "almost alone," but other accounts disagree. "He was quite conscious," his sister Sarah Tinklar later wrote, "& tried to join with the priests round his bed in saying the prayers for the dying. His last words were an act of contrition, & his last act to bow his head at the holy name of Jesus."[13]

St. Peter's was crowded for the office for the dead on the evening of 18 June and again for the Pontifical Requiem the following morning. The archbishop of St. Andrews and Edinburgh celebrated the Requiem, and the archbishop of Glasgow was present, as were the entire cathedral chapter of the diocese and, wrote Sarah, "Dominicans, Benedictines, Franciscans, Passionists & Jesuits, & of course all his sorrowful friends & parishioners." Sarah and her step-daughter, Coralie, were the only members of Gray's family present; his sister Beatrice, now Sister Mary Raphael, was prevented from coming by the rules governing her enclosed order. Gray was buried in the same cemetery as Raffalovich, in the section reserved for the clergy of the diocese. Afterwards, Sarah wrote to Frances Langdale, "I feel very sad & lonely without him, for he was more than a brother to me."

In the panegyric at the funeral Mass, a friend of the canon's, Father Bernard Delany, spoke of John Gray's "gift of vision and his power of giving rare expression to what he saw—all the instinct of his nature and the bent of his mind might have placed him, had he cared to use his gift, in the first rank of the literary history of the English tongue." Delany praised Gray's self-sacrifice in choosing "a higher and nobler immortality," the priesthood. "To me . . . he always seemed the ideal priest," Father Delany continued.

> A priest gives his heart to God and there were some people who were disconcerted by John Gray's ascetic reserve. He did not easily admit the outside world within the inner sanctuary of his soul. Yet those who knew him well knew a kindly, human priest with a depth of wisdom and sympathy, with the ready wit of a quick, lively mind, and the sense of humour that goes with humility. His was a keen mind, alert and always interested. He made no claim to scholarship yet his reading and learning were deep and wide—always directed by the apostolic zeal of the true priest.[14]

"He was a priest and a *great* priest," Father Delany concluded. And it was a conclusion which many who knew Father Gray would greet with a fervent "Amen." Even those who dissent from this view would acknowledge genuine respect for a man who had perfected his life by great effort and great sacrifice. But it is important to consider the nature of the sacrifice, and the cost to John Gray, a cost we can only know in part. John Gray himself insured that this would be so, by his cryptic answers to questions about his life, by his apparent "editing" of the records of that life. His destruction of key letters may have been merely a tactical diversion, one of those "false doors and booby-traps" that fill *Park*. It would be truer to say, however, that Gray's preservation of part of his correspondence constitutes on one level an act of priestly humility and on another a dangerous and even flirtatious jeopardizing of his own mask.

For the central fact of John Gray's life became the past he characterized as a "course of sin." Of what that past consisted must remain largely known only through the pressure it brought to bear on John Gray. He countered this pressure by silence or, at worst, circumlocution. Ultimately, his acute sense of the past was responsible for the perfection of his life as a priest and for the limits by which that perfection was made manifest: his aloofness, his distance, his refusal to be scrutinized and accounted for. To speak of John Gray's available self as a mask is to emphasize both these aspects: the fabrication of the ego into icon, by which it escapes the triviality of history; the suppression of those parts of the psyche which threaten the fabrication.

When one speaks of suppression, one does not mean rejection; quite the opposite. Wilde's Dorian Gray preserved his "secret" self as a portrait, secluded in an attic, where he visited it to note its record of his sinful deeds. Without these visits, the perfection of his life as a dandy, apparently untouched by either the moral or physical corruption of time, would become pointless. When, in the end, he felt he could no longer live with it, he stabbed it—killing himself. The transaction here between aging art and ageless life, in which the terms of history and object have become transposed, stresses the interdependence of the historical and symbolic self. John Gray, like his "dear Master," Oscar Wilde, created through his art a persona which he enacted as mask. His poetry, particularly his later poetry, at times achieved an independence from that mask, but it remained nonetheless highly allusive and personal in many respects. There is, in the last analysis, a failure of detachment which might be said to have arrested his artistic development. For although his poetry, and that of *Silverpoints* in particular, has the marks of the real thing, with few exceptions it misses being in the first rank of the minor poetry of its generation.

In his prose, however, Gray turns explicitly to the price exacted by the mask. "Dorian" Gray wrote of its bankruptcy in "The Person in Question," where his other self haunts him like an apparition. The hero of *Park,* in so many respects a simulacrum of Father Gray, is said to be "dead." Whatever the qualifications one may place on that death—and it offers itself as both a genuine death and as an entry into another state of selfhood, both richer and more circumscribed than that actually available—it remains the mode by which the protagonist must live in his world and implies the modality of Gray's life in the actual world. It is not surprising, therefore, that among the accounts of Gray's life are several reports of the appearance of the ghost of Canon Gray, "sitting in his old confessional, and getting up afterwards to go into the clergy house" of St. Peter's, Morningside.[15]

May his soul rest, at last, in peace.

❧[Notes]❧

Introduction (pp. 1–9)

1. Violet Wyndham, "Reminiscences, by Ada Leverson; I. The Importance of Being Oscar," *The Sphinx and Her Circle: A Biographical Sketch of Ada Leverson, 1862–1933* (London: Andre Deutsch, 1963), p. 105.

2. Father John-Baptist Reeves, taped reminiscences of Father Gray, made in conversation with Brocard Sewell, 19 March 1968.

3. Father Edwin Essex, "The Canon in Residence," Brocard Sewell, ed., *Two Friends: John Gray and André Raffalovich* (Aylesford, Kent: Saint Albert's Press, 1963), p. 154.

4. Essex, p. 155. Also mentioned by Katherine Bradley and Edith Cooper [Michael Field] in their unpublished journal, "Works and Days," 10 September 1909 [BM Add. Ms. 46799, f. 138], British Library Manuscript Collections, London.

5. "Introduction," *The Oxford Book of Modern Verse, 1892–1935* (Oxford: Oxford Univ. Press, 1936), p. xlii.

6. Peter Anson to Norman Wright, 28 January 1935, National Library, Edinburgh.

7. Published by Roger Lhombreaud, "Une Amitié Anglaise de Pierre Louÿs: Onze Lettres Inédites à John Gray," *Revue de Littérature Comparée* 27 (Juillet–Septembre 1953): 343–57.

8. John Gray, "The Person in Question" (Buenos Aires: Colombo, 1958). Published in a limited edition of forty numbered copies.

9. Brocard Sewell, Foreword, *In the Dorian Mode: A Life of John Gray, 1866–1934* (Padstow, Cornwall: Tabb House, 1983), p. viii.

10. G. A. Cevasco, *John Gray,* Twayne's English Author Series 353 (Boston: Twayne, 1982) p. 141, n. 2. Father Delany delivered Canon Gray's funeral oration: see "Sermon Preached at the Mass of Requiem for Canon John Gray," *Two Friends,* pp. 173–77.

11. Cevasco, *John Gray.* Apart from the cited publications, Cevasco also draws on Jerusha McCormack, "The Person in Question: John Gray. A Biographical and Critical Study" (Ph.D. dissertation, Brandeis University, 1973).

12. Letters which I first consulted in the Dominican Chaplaincy, Edinburgh, have since found their way to other collections; where possible, I have noted their present location.

13. Rupert Hart-Davis, ed., *The Letters of Oscar Wilde,* rev. ed. (London: Rupert Hart-Davis Ltd., 1963), p. 312.

14. Thus, letters or reminiscences are usually noted in their original form, for I have found that in publication they have quite often, either through error or intention, been subtly edited, in at least one case to suppress crucial evidence. See Roger Lhombreaud, "The Poetical Friendship of John Gray and Pierre Louÿs," *Two Friends,* and compare it with Lhombreaud's original article, "Une Amitié Anglaise de Pierre Louÿs: Onze Lettres Inédites à John Gray," *Revue de Littérature Comparée* 27 (Juillet–Septembre 1953): 343–57, which is true to the actual letters.

I have also preferred *Two Friends* to Sewell's later memoirs, as it presents actual reminiscence and seminal research upon which the later books have drawn.

15. "The Café Royal," *The Cafe Royal and Other Essays* (Westminster, England: Beaumont Press, 1923), p. 4.

16. Charles-Pierre Baudelaire, "The Painter of Modern Life: The Dandy," in *Baudelaire: Selected Writings on Art and Artists,* trans. P. E. Charvet (Hammondsworth, Middlesex, England: Penguin, 1972), pp. 420–21.

17. "The Person in Question," p. 19.

18. Inscription in Gray's hand of his translation of Paul Bouget's *A Saint and Others* (London: James R. Osgood, McIlvaine and Co., 1892) in the Wilde collection, Houghton Library, Cambridge, Mass.

19. Desmond Flower and Henry Maas, eds., *The Letters of Ernest Dowson* (London: Cassell and Co., 1967), pp. 182–83.

O N E. *John Gray* (pp. 10–52)

1. General Register Office, London. The eight other children were: Ada (Mrs. Pullen): b. 1868, d. 1945; Frederick William: b. 1870, d. 1961; William Thomas: b. 1872 (?), d. 1920; Emily (Mrs. Burbridge): b. 1875, d. 1950; Sarah (Mrs. Tinklar): b. 1877, d. 1950; Norval: b. 1880 (?), d. 1911; Alexander: b. 1882 (?), d. 1919; Beatrice Hannah (Sister Mary Raphael O.S.B.): b. 1887, d. 1963.

For further histories of these members of the Gray family, see Brocard Sewell, "John Gray and André Sebastian Raffalovich: A Biographical Outline," Sewell, ed., *Two Friends: John Gray and André Raffalovich* (Aylesford, Kent: Saint Albert's Press, 1963), p. 7.

2. Gray's birth certificate gives the date as 10 March, but Gray corrects it in this letter to Michael Field [Katherine Bradley], 20 January 1908, Henry W. and Albert A. Berg Collection, New York Public Library, New York.

3. Tape of reminiscences made for McCormack in May/June 1975 by Father John-Baptist Reeves, a close friend of Gray in his later years.

4. Mary Raphael Gray [Beatrice Gray], "A Sister's Reminiscences," *Two Friends,* ed. Sewell, pp. 100–05.

5. Brocard Sewell, *Footnote to the Nineties: A Memoir of John Gray and André Raffalovich* (London: Cecil and Amelia Woolf, 1968), p. 3.

6. Sewell, "Gray and Raffalovich," *Two Friends,* pp. 7–8.

7. Allan Campbell to Jerusha McCormack, 7 January 1985. The information in this paragraph is the result of Campbell's considerable research.

8. Marriage certificate of John Gray and Hannah Williamson, 13 June 1864. General Register Office, London.

9. Brocard Sewell, *In the Dorian Mode: A Life of John Gray, 1866–1934* (Padstow, Cornwall: Tabb House, 1983), p. 1.

10. Coltman to Brocard Sewell, 14 May 1984, Sewell papers.

11. Sewell, *Two Friends,* p. 8.

12. Gray to Raffalovich, 8 May 1904, Gray papers, National Library, Edinburgh.

13. Coltman to Jerusha McCormack, 26 April 1984, McCormack papers.

14. Mss. for both works in Gray papers, Dominican Chaplaincy, Edinburgh. The ensuing quotations are from manuscripts in this collection.

15. Father Edwin Essex, "The Canon in Residence," *Two Friends,* p. 152.

16. Gray to Louÿs, 3 December 1892. Quoted in Peter Vernon, "John Gray's Letters to Pierre Louÿs," *Revue de Littérature Comparée* 53 (1979): 98.

17. Gray to Sarah Tinklar, 31 January 1922, Brocard Sewell papers.

18. Gray to Francis Vielé-Griffin, no date, Beinecke Rare Book and Manuscript Library, Yale University, New Haven, Conn.

19. Gray to Raffalovich, 8 March 1903, Gray papers, National Library, Edinburgh.

20. Coltman to Jerusha McCormack, 27 August 1984, McCormack papers. According to the marriage certificate, Gray's mother was the daughter of a printer and so would have had book-learning in her blood. See n. 8 above.

21. Details of Gray's schooling here and below are taken from Sewell, *Footnote,* pp. 2–3. Letters from the headmaster of the Roan School, Maze Hill, Blackheath, to Brocard Sewell and Dr. Ian Fletcher both confirm the only known fact of Gray's later schooling, namely, that Gray applied for entry on 28 March 1878, and left the school at Easter, 1879. Sewell papers. As for the "Wesleyan" day school and the family's religious denomination, Beatrice could not confirm their Methodism. Still, Gray's admiration for the hymns of Charles and John Wesley and his sympathy with that sect suggests a possible connection. See also Brocard Sewell, *In the Dorian Mode,* p. 2. For Gray's knowledge of hymns, cf. his essay, "On Hymn-Writing"; of the practices of the sect, his short story, "Light."

22. Gray's brother Frederick's account, in Sewell, "Gray and Raffalovich," *Two Friends,* p. 8.

23. Gray to Louÿs, 24 November 1892. In Vernon, "John Gray's Letters," *Revue de Littérature Comparée* 53 (Janvier–Mars 1979): 97.

24. Holograph of *Spiritual Poems,* Gray manuscripts, National Library, Edinburgh. Bracketed material is my own; braces { } indicate passages cancelled in the original which have been, for the most part, reconstructed. The poem has been reprinted, without the reconstructed passages, by Ian Fletcher, ed., *The Poems of John Gray,* The 1880–1920 British Author Series 1 (Greensboro, N.C.: ELT Press, 1988), p. 149.

25. Gray papers, Dominican Chaplaincy, Edinburgh. Published in Fletcher, ed., *The Poems of John Gray,* pp. 72–77.

26. "The Forge," *The Savoy* 2 (April 1896): 85–86; reprinted in Fletcher, pp. 69–70.

27. Sewell, "Gray and Raffalovich," *Two Friends,* p. 8.

28. "The eternal dying of a summer day." Sewell, *Footnote,* p. 4, gives the

poem in incomplete form. A guess at the missing word, "centuries," is made by
Margaret Mary McAlpine, "John Gray: A Critical and Biographical Study," (M.A.
thesis, University of Manchester, England, 1967), p. 157. Reprinted in Fletcher,
p. 42.

29. Details of Gray's Post Office career given by F. Coates to McCormack, 17
June and 20 July 1970, McCormack papers.

30. According to the records, Edmonds joined in January 1880 (date of Civil
Service certificate, July 1880, Open Competition). He became a Lower Division
Clerk in the Savings Bank on 17 August 1880, and moved to the Confidential
Enquiry Branch, 16 January 1882, where Gray presumably first met him. Ap-
pointed Surveyors Clerk in August 1885, he died in 1894. (Coates to McCormack,
17 June 1970, McCormack papers.) The "Parent" letter is to John Gray, 28 October
1891, Gray papers, National Library, Edinburgh. The letter reads in part:

My dear Boy,
I got the books all right—Many thanks. Pour une nuit d'amour is curious—
very. I do not know if Thérèse Raquin was written first—but certainly Zola stands
alone in making horrors ordinary. I took that corpse down— Moi.

31. London University records. At this time, London University was only a
degree-granting institution. In 1858, all examinations (except for a medical degree)
were thrown open to all candidates irrespective of their place of education, thus
enabling such students as Gray to apply.

32. Edith Cooper, c. 8 January 1894, "Works and Days," journal of Katherine
Bradley and Edith Cooper [Michael Field] [BM Add. Ms. 46782], British Library
Manuscript Collections, London. See n. 79 below.

33. Rothenstein, *Men and Memories: Recollections of William Rothenstein,* vol. 1
(London: Faber and Faber, 1931), p. 173. Rothenstein, a painter, was later principal
of the Royal College of Art.

34. Rothenstein, *Men and Memories,* 1: 174–76.

35. T. Sturge Moore's notes in *Self-Portrait: Taken from the Letters and Journals of
Charles Ricketts, R.A.,* collected and compiled by T. Sturge Moore, ed. Cecil Lewis
(London: P. Davies, 1939), p. 14.

36. Frederick L. Gwynn, *Sturge Moore and the Life of Art* (Lawrence: Univ. of
Kansas Press, 1951), p. 19.

37. Gray, "Les Goncourt," *The Dial* 1 (1889): 10. Subsequent quotations are
from this source.

38. Gray, "The Great Worm," *The Dial* 1 (1889): 14–18.

39. Frank Liebich, "Oscar Wilde," a typescript reminiscence, Wilde L716M3
081 [191–?], William Andrews Clark Memorial Library, UCLA.

40. Rupert Hart-Davis, ed., *The Letters of Oscar Wilde,* rev. ed., (London:
Rupert Hart-Davis, 1963), p. 249. Hart-Davis details the work that Ricketts and
Shannon did for Wilde, p. 249, n. 2.

41. Hesketh Pearson, *Oscar Wilde: His Life and Wit* (New York: Harper Broth-
ers, 1946), p. 248.

42. "Modern Poetry," *Essays and Introductions* (London: Macmillan, 1961),
p. 495.

43. Gray to Michael Field [Katherine Bradley], 24 July 1907, Berg Collection, New York Public Library.

44. Gray to Félix Fénéon, 18 July 1890, Paulhan Archives, Paris. I have chosen to give this correspondence in translation, and not reproduce Gray's "painful" and often incorrect French.

45. This account of Gray's visit to Paris and his relationship with Fénéon is taken from Joan Ungersma Halperin, *Félix Fénéon: Aesthete & Anarchist in Fin-de-Siècle Paris* (New Haven: Yale Univ. Press, 1988), p. 170.

46. Gray to Fénéon, 20 July 1890, Paulhan Archives, Paris.

47. Gray to Fénéon, no date, Paulhan Archives, Paris.

48. Gray to Fénéon, 20 November [1890], Paulhan Archives, Paris. This translation is largely indebted to Halperin, *Félix Fénéon,* p. 170.

49. In April 1891, Lucien Pissarro announced that Fénéon, accompanied by Georges Lecomte, would soon spend a few days in London, but there is no record of their visit. Halperin, *Félix Fénéon,* p. 172.

50. Denys Sutton, "Neglected Virtuoso: Charles Ricketts and his Achievements," *Apollo* 83 (February 1966): 142.

51. John Rewald, ed., *Camille Pissarro: Lettres à Son Fils Lucien* (Paris: Editions Albin Michel, 1950), p. 190.

52. William Sutton Meadmore, *Lucien Pissarro: Un Coeur Simple* (London: Constable, 1962), p. 60.

53. Gray papers, National Library, Edinburgh, and John Gray Collection, John Rylands University Library of Manchester, England.

54. Gray, "Obituary: Dubois-Pillet," *Academy* 957 (6 September 1890): 205.

55. "Complaint," *Silverpoints* (London: Elkin Mathews and John Lane, 1893), p. ix, reprinted in Fletcher, p. 23.

56. Fénéon to Gray, 18 December 1890[?], John Gray Collection, John Rylands University Library of Manchester, England.

57. Fénéon to Gray, 20 August 1890, John Gray Collection, John Rylands University Library of Manchester, England.

58. Gray papers, National Library, Edinburgh.

59. Beinecke Rare Book Room and Manuscript Library, Yale University, New Haven, Conn.

60. Gray to Gordon Bottomley, 3 February 1933, papers of Roger Lancelyn Green.

61. Gray to Raffalovich, 1 December 1902, National Library, Edinburgh.

62. "The Cultured Faun," *Anti-Jacobin* (14 March 1891), pp. 156–57.

63. William Butler Yeats, *Autobiographies* (London: Macmillan, 1955), p. 302.

64. Notes sent to Brocard Sewell by James Langdale, Sewell papers. These are given in condensed form by Sewell in "Marmaduke Langdale," *Footnote,* Appendix I, p. 101. See also Edgar Jepson, *Memories of a Victorian* (London: Victor Gollancz, 1933), 1: 219, 222, 254.

65. James Langdale to Sewell, 7 February 1969, Sewell papers.

66. Gray to Fanny Langdale, 25 December 1908, James Langdale papers.

67. James Langdale to Sewell, 23 January 1968, Sewell papers.

68. Four letters from Lenoir to Gray are among the Gray papers in the Na-

tional Library, Scotland. Lenoir was very young, about ten, when they were written.

69. Georges Guitton, *Un "Preneur d'Âmes": Louis Lenoir, Aumônier des Marsouins, 1914–17* (Paris: J. de Gigord, 1922). Written on the envelope containing these letters, in Gray's hand, is the notation: "There is a question of the sanctity of Louis Lenoir."

70. James Langdale to Sewell, 23 January 1968, Sewell papers.

71. Gray to Fanny Langdale, 25 December 1929, Langdale papers.

72. Essex, *Two Friends*, p. 158.

73. Yeats, Introduction, *The Oxford Book of Modern Verse, 1892–1935* (New York: Oxford Univ. Press, 1936), p. x.

74. Huysmans, *Against Nature*, trans. Robert Baldick (Baltimore: Penguin, 1959), p. 87.

75. Pater, *Marius the Epicurean: His Sensations and Ideas*, (London: Macmillan, 1910), 2: 186.

76. Sewell, "Gray and Raffalovich," *Two Friends*, pp. 15–16.

77. Gray to Raffalovich, 10 February 1899, National Library, Edinburgh.

78. Gray to Raffalovich, 5 March 1900, National Library, Edinburgh.

79. "Works and Days," journal of Katherine Bradley and Edith Cooper, all except one written during their collaboration under the pen name "Michael Field," 1908 [BM Add. Ms. 46798, f. 202], British Library Manuscript Collections, London. During their lifetime, Bradley was known as "Michael," Cooper as "Henry," but friends referred to them as the "Michael Fields." To avoid confusion, I refer to them singly as Bradley and Cooper, and together as the "Michael Fields."

80. The remark about Shannon and Ricketts by Bradley is in "Works and Days," 9 July 1894 [BM Add. Ms. 46782] British Library Manuscript Room Collections, London.

81. The text for "Passing the Love of Women" is from Jacqueline Wesley, "Bibliographical Notes and Queries," *Book Collector* 39, no. 1 (Spring 1990): 115–17. Wesley quotes the poem from its holograph copy, which came into her hands by private sale. Previously, this holograph had been cited in the sale catalogue of Elkin Mathews, *Books of the Nineties* (1932, item 291) and was again offered for sale by Bertram Rota Ltd. (catalogue 62, 1939, item 287) before disappearing into private ownership. The version of the poem given by Ian Fletcher in the *Poems of John Gray*, pp. 43–44, is not from the holograph but from a typescript made from the holograph by John Gawsworth, who asked Father Gray whether he was the poem's author. Gray's chilly response: "I cannot remember ever having written a poem with the title *Passing the Love of Women*" (2 September 1932). Quoted in John Gawsworth, "Two Poets 'J.G.'," *Two Friends*, p. 170.

The remark on the poem's title, drawn from 2 Samuel 1:26, was made by Timothy d'Arch Smith, *Love in Earnest: Some Notes on the Lives and Writings of English 'Uranian' Poets from 1889 to 1930* (London: Routledge and Kegan Paul, 1970), p. 187.

82. Brian Reade, ed., Introduction, *Sexual Heretics: Male Homosexuality in English Literature from 1850 to 1900* (New York: Coward-McCann, 1970), p. 54.

83. D'Arch Smith, *Love in Earnest*, p. 60. See also pp. 17, 59–60, and 235–39 for information on Jackson and the contributors to his magazine.

84. T. W. G. W.[ratislaw?], "La Garde Joyeuse IX: 'John Gray,'" *The Artist and Journal of Home Culture* 14 (4 November 1893): 328–29.

85. Biographical information on Raffalovich is from Sewell, "Gray and Raffalovich," *Two Friends*, pp. 10–13 and Sewell, *Footnote*, p. 18–30.

86. Raffalovich's account of his family's circle of friends is given in an essay he wrote under the pseudonym of "Alexander Michaelson," "Giles and Miles and Isabeau," *Blackfriars* 9 (January 1928): 18–29.

87. Correspondence from these and other authors to Raffalovich may be found in the Gray/Raffalovich papers, National Library, Edinburgh.

88. Michaelson [Raffalovich], "Giles and Miles and Isabeau," p. 25.

89. Sewell, "Gray and Raffalovich," *Two Friends*, p. 13, n. 6.

90. For an account of Raffalovich's London salon, see Philip Healy, "Raffalovich and His Circle: Part One. London in the 1880s and '90s," *Book World* 25, vol. 3, no. 1 (February 1984), pp. 5–9.

91. *Letters of Oscar Wilde*, p. 173, n. 4. See also *The Picture of Dorian Gray*, ed. Isobel Murray (London: Oxford Univ. Press, 1974), pp. 7–8.

92. Hesketh Pearson, *Oscar Wilde*, pp. 216–17.

93. D'Arch Smith, *Love in Earnest*, p. 30 and p. 44, n. 107.

94. D'Arch Smith, pp. 30–31, p. 44, n. 108.

95. *Letters of Oscar Wilde*, pp. 172–73, and Michaelson [Raffalovich], "Robert Browning," *Blackfriars* 9, no. 95 (February 1928): 98, 99.

96. D'Arch Smith, *Love in Earnest*, p. 33.

97. Raffalovich to Charles Ballantyne, 21 May 1927, National Library, Edinburgh.

98. Michaelson [Raffalovich], "Oscar Wilde," *Blackfriars* 8, no. 92 (November 1927): 694–702. Raffalovich's account of Wilde in this paragraph is from this source.

99. Rupert Croft-Cooke, *Feasting with Panthers: A New Consideration of Some Late Victorian Writers* (New York: Holt, Rinehart and Winston, 1967), p. 209.

100. Liebich, "Oscar Wilde," p. 2.

101. Donald Hyde Collection, New York.

102. *Letters of Oscar Wilde*, p. 352.

103. D'Arch Smith, *Love in Earnest*, pp. 24–25.

104. Raymond Roseliep, "Some Letters of Lionel Johnson" (Ph.D. dissertation, University of Notre Dame, 1954), p. 109.

105. Brian Reade, "Introduction," *Sexual Heretics*, p. 35.

106. Charles Ballantyne of Edinburgh talked to me at length about John Gray and André Raffalovich. He also shared his opinions with Brian Reade, who echoes them in *Sexual Heretics*, pp. 34–35.

107. Charles Ricketts to John Lane, c. December 1892: "Gray (whom I sometimes see, about once every two years). . . ." Houghton Library, Cambridge, Mass. Ricketts's irony is not without motive; all the evidence is that Gray virtually deserted the Vale during the years 1891–98, although he returned to it

after his ordination, and kept in touch with Ricketts through letters and occasional visits.

108. "The Rhymers' Club," *Letters to the New Island,* ed. Horace Reynolds (Cambridge, Mass.: Harvard Univ. Press, 1934), p. 146.

T W O. *"Dorian Gray"* (pp. 53–102)

1. Rupert Hart-Davis, ed., *The Letters of Oscar Wilde,* rev. ed., (London: Rupert Hart-Davis, Ltd., 1963), p. 353.

2. On Wilde's foisting of the "Dorian" nickname on Gray, see Frank Harris, *Oscar Wilde* (East Lansing: Michigan State Univ. Press, 1959), p. 73. Gray was described as a "disciple" of Ricketts by William Rothenstein, *Men and Memories* (London: Faber & Faber, 1931), vol. 1 pp. 175–76. Described as Wilde's disciple by George Bernard Shaw in *Shaw: An Autobiography, 1856–1898,* ed. Stanley Weintraub (New York: George Braziller, 1969), p. 250, and by Max Beerbohm in "Appendix A: 'Oscar Wilde,'" *Max Beerbohm: Letters to Reggie Turner* (London: Rupert Hart-Davis, 1964), p. 290.

3. Horne was an architect, writer, and connoisseur (1864–1916). He "built the Church of the Redeemer, Bayswater Road, and from 1886 to 1892 he edited a quarterly magazine called the *Century Guild Hobby Horse,* in which he printed some of his own poems. Before the end of the century he went to live in Florence, where he wrote a biography of Botticelli (1908) and set up the Museo Horne in the Via dei Benci." Hart-Davis, ed., *Letters of Oscar Wilde,* p. 188, n. 3. For the Rhymers, see Karl Beckson, "New Dates for the Rhymers' Club," *English Literature in Transition* 13, no. 1 (1970): 37–38. For a rejoinder, see R. K. R. Thornton, "Dates for the Rhymers' Club," *ELT* 14, no. 1 (1971): 49–52.

4. Raymond Roseliep, "Some Letters of Lionel Johnson" (Ph.D. dissertation, University of Notre Dame, 1954), p. 109.

5. For the Mass incident, see the Reverend Dominic Hart, "Memories of John Gray," Helen Trudgian papers. Published, in a slightly altered version, as "Some Memories of John Gray by the Reverend Dominic Hart," ed. Brocard Sewell, *The Innes Review* 2 (1975): 80–88. On Johnson and the perambulator, see Father Edwin Essex, "The Canon in Residence," *Two Friends: John Gray and André Raffalovich,* ed. Brocard Sewell (Aylesford, Kent: Saint Albert's Press, 1963), p. 154. Information concerning the loss of the Johnson letters is from Father Anthony Ross, Dominican Chaplaincy, Edinburgh.

6. Desmond Flower and Henry Maas, eds., *The Letters of Ernest Dowson* (London: Cassell & Co., 1967), pp. 182–83.

7. Quoted in Karl E. Beckson, "The Rhymers' Club" (Ph.D. dissertation, Columbia University, 1959), p. 36.

8. The letter was addressed to "My dear Oscar" and signed, "Yours Ever, Dorian." Gray to Wilde, postmarked 9 January 1891, Donald Hyde Collection, New York.

9. *Silverpoints* (London: Elkin Mathews & John Lane, 1893), pp. 13–14. Reprinted in Ian Fletcher, ed., *The Poems of John Gray,* The 1880–1920 British Author Series 1 (Greensboro, N.C.: ELT Press, 1988), pp. 25–26.

10. This reading is indebted to Linda Dowling, "Nature and Decadence: John Gray's *Silverpoints*," *Victorian Poetry* 15, no. 2 (Summer 1977): 166.

11. Dowson to Arthur Moore, 20 March 1891, *Letters of Dowson*, pp. 189–90.

12. *Autobiographies* (London: Macmillan, 1955), pp. 166–67.

13. Katherine Bradley and Edith Cooper [Michael Field], "Works and Days," journal entry for 1907 [B.M. Add. Ms. 46796, f. 216], British Library, Manuscript Collections, London.

14. "The Rhymers' Club" (23 April 1892), *Letters to the New Island* (Cambridge, Mass.: Harvard Univ. Press, 1934), p. 143.

15. Introduction, *The Poems of Ernest Dowson* (London: John Lane, 1905), p. ix.

16. James G. Nelson, *The Early Nineties: A View from The Bodley Head* (Cambridge, Mass.: Harvard Univ. Press, 1971), p. 183.

17. Ernest Rhys, quoted in J. Benjamin Townsend, *John Davidson: Poet of Armageddon* (New Haven: Yale Univ. Press, 1961), p. 141.

18. Gray to Mrs. Maclagan, 9 February 1906, O'Connell Collection [box 3], Princeton University Library, Princeton, New Jersey.

19. Wilde was also a "permanent guest" of the Rhymers, but it is not clear what this status implied. For the most accurate listing of the membership of the Rhymers, see Townsend, *Davidson*, pp. 140–41 and also Nelson, *Early Nineties*, p. 168.

20. *The Dial* 2 (1892), p. 23; reprinted in *Silverpoints*, p. 6 and Fletcher, pp. 21–22. I give the later, and hence more definitive version here, as with the following poem, also originally from *The Dial* 2 (1892), p. 24 and also reprinted in *Silverpoints*, p. 5 and Fletcher, p. 21.

21. Cf. Ian Fletcher's seminal essay, "The Poetry of John Gray," *Two Friends*, pp. 50–69.

22. Gray to Pierre Louÿs, 6 January 1894. Peter Vernon, "John Gray's Letters to Pierre Louÿs," *Revue de Littérature Comparée* 53 (Janvier-Mars 1979): 104.

23. 15 January 1893, National Library, Edinburgh. Wilde dedicated a story to her in his *House of Pomegranates* (1891).

24. *In the Dorian Mode: A Life of John Gray, 1866–1934* (Padstow, Cornwall: Tabb House, 1983), pp. 55–57. "Opal" later became the unhappy wife of Lord Alfred Douglas.

25. *Black and White*, 1, no. 4 (28 February 1891): 125. Reprinted in Fletcher, pp. 42–43.

26. Karl Beckson, ed., *The Memoirs of Arthur Symons: Life and Art in the 1890's* (The Pennsylvania State Univ. Press: University Park, 1977), p. 56.

27. Beerbohm to Reggie Turner, 15 May 1893 [BMS Eng. 1098], Houghton Library, Cambridge, Mass.

28. Beckson, *Memoirs of Symons*, p. 56.

29. "Chancery Lane," *Post Office London Directory for 1891*. Gray shared this address (listed as nos. 61/62) with four other people.

30. Robert Sherard, *The Real Oscar Wilde: To be Used as a Supplement to, and in Illustration of "The Life of Oscar Wilde"* (London: T. Werner Laurie, n.d.), p. 337–38.

31. Essex, p. 154. The elopement story was an exaggeration. At the time she was engaged to the waiter, not the chef, and with her family's consent.

32. *Letters of Dowson,* pp. 207–08.

33. *Letters of Dowson,* p. 228. William Clarke Hall (1866–1932), barrister and later a distinguished metropolitan magistrate, was knighted in 1932.

34. Gray to Michael Field, [Katherine Bradley] 11 November 1908, Henry W. and Albert A. Berg Collection, New York Public Library.

35. For de Mattos as translator, see Edgar Jepson, *Memories of a Victorian,* vol. 1 (London: Victor Gollancz, 1933) pp. 225, 244. For Gray's trip to Holland, see *Letters of Dowson,* p. 214. Dowson writes to Gray (3 September 1891): "if you are not yet in Holland, come & see me. . . ."

36. "Translators' Note," *Ecstasy: A Study of Happiness* (London: Henry and Co., 1892), p. v. De Mattos eliminated Gray's name as translator in the 1919 editions, saying that there was "no true collaboration" and that Gray did not have the "original before him." Stephen McKenna, *Tex: A Chapter in the Life of Alexander Teixeira de Mattos* (New York: Dodd, Mead, 1922) pp. 128–29.

37. Reviews appeared in *Bookman* (December 1892), the *Academy* (4 February 1893) and the *National Review* (March 1893). The remark about Gray's English is given in an early draft of Sewell's *In the Dorian Mode;* source not given.

38. A. J. A. Symons, "The Diner-Out," *Horizon* 4, no. 22 (1941): 252.

39. *Letters of Wilde,* p. 320, n. 1.

40. Gray to Horne, July 1892. National Library, Edinburgh. Quoted in full with a companion letter of 10 August, by Margaret Mary McAlpine, "John Gray: A Critical and Biographical Study" (M.A. thesis, University of Manchester, England, 1967), p. 90.

41. Frank Harris, *Oscar Wilde: His Life and Confessions* (New York: Garden City Publishing, 1930), p. 86.

42. Harris to Gray, no date, Beinecke Rare Book and Manuscript Library, Yale University, New Haven, Conn. The two poems Harris refers to are "Les Demoiselles de Sauve" and "Poem," both of which eventually were published in *Silverpoints.*

43. Original lines from *Silverpoints* holograph, O'Connell Collection [MSS Bd], Princeton University Library, Princeton, New Jersey. Revised poem printed in *Silverpoints,* pp. 30–31, and reprinted in Fletcher, p. 36.

44. Alice, Princess of Monaco, to Gray, no date, National Library, Edinburgh.

45. National Library, Edinburgh; quoted by McAlpine, p. 90.

46. Pater is said to have praised *Silverpoints* in an unsigned review in *The Artist and Journal of Home Culture* 14, no. 161 (1 April 1893): 119.

47. Gray to Félix Fénéon, 14 April 1891, Paulhan Archives, Paris.

48. Marcel Schwob to Gray, postmarked 26 November 1892, quoted in Brocard Sewell, *Footnote to the Nineties: A Memoir of John Gray and André Raffalovich* (London: Cecil and Amelia Woolf, 1968), pp. 11–12.

49. Pierre Honoré Jean Baptiste Champion, *Marcel Schwob et son temps* (Paris: B. Gasset, 1927), p. 98. The date of the letter is not certain. Champion gives it as 1892, without specifying the month, but the context suggests January. For an account of Wilde's Parisian visit, see Richard Ellmann, *Oscar Wilde* (New York: Knopf, 1988), pp. 346ff.

50. Henry D. Davray, "Mallarmé as I Knew Him," *Horizon* 7, no. 41 (May 1943): 350. Although this memoir was written more than fifty years later, I find no reason to doubt its accuracy.

51. For a history of Sherard's relationship with Wilde, see Ellmann, *Oscar Wilde,* pp. 212–20 and passim.

52. Gray to Fénéon, 2 January 1891, Paulhan Archives, Paris.

53. Rothenstein, *Men and Memories,* I: 86, 93; see also Ellmann, *Oscar Wilde,* pp. 323, n. 26* and p. 350.

54. Sherard to Gray, no date, National Library, Edinburgh.

55. *Letters of Dowson,* p. 225. Barlas actually only fired a revolver near the Speaker's residence to express contempt for the House of Commons. He was arrested and later bailed out by Wilde.

56. Robert Harborough Sherard, *Twenty Years in Paris, Being Some Recollections of a Literary Life* (London: Hutchinson, 1906), pp. 353–56.

57. Holbrook Jackson, *The Eighteen Nineties: A Review of Art and Ideas at the Close of the Nineteenth Century* (London: Jonathan Cape, 1931), pp. 207–208. For an account of the cultural climate in which the Independent Theatre was born, see Allardyce Nicoll, "The Theatre," *A History of English Drama 1660–1900* (Cambridge: Cambridge Univ. Press, 1959), 5: 1–49. The Theatre's "first original production" was Shaw's *Widowers' Houses,* his first attempt to write for the stage. Details about the first two seasons of the Independent Theatre are taken from N. H. G. Schoonderwoerd, *J. T. Grein, Ambassador of the Theatre 1862–1935: A Study in Anglo-Continental Theatrical Relations* (Assen, Netherlands: Van Gorcum and Co., 1963), pp. 60–130; and from Anna Irene Miller, *The Independent Theatre in Europe, 1887 to the Present* (New York: Ray Long and Richard R. Smith, 1931), pp. 169–71.

58. "Note," *In the Garden of Citrons: Idyll in One Act by Emilio Montanaro,* trans. J. T. Grein (London: Henry and Co., 1892), p. 7. The *Star* review (6 February 1892) is quoted in Patricio Gannon, "John Gray: The Prince of Dreams," *Two Friends,* p. 108.

59. *Theatre: A Monthly Review of the Drama, Music and Fine Arts* 19 (January–June 1892): 146. Michael Orme [Mrs. Alice Augusta Grein], *J. T. Grein: The Story of a Pioneer, 1862–1935* (London: John Murray, 1936), p. 63. Schoonderwoerd writes: "I have found no evidence of this 'serious consideration,' except in an article by the Dutchman A. Teixeira de Mattos in *Dramatic Opinions,* a review of the piece 'from the proof sheets'" (p. 95).

60. Schoonderwoerd, p. 85.

61. "The Modern Actor," *The Albemarle: A Monthly Review* 2, no. 1 (July 1892): 20; reprinted in Sewell, *Footnote,* pp. 102–07.

62. Hart, "Memories of John Gray," Trudgian papers; see n. 5, this chapter.

63. *Artist* (2 January 1893), p. 8.

64. Quoted by Brian Daly, *Albert Chevalier: A Record by Himself* (London: John Macqueen, 1895), p. 123. No source or date is given; the review is also heavily edited.

65. From the papers of Helen Trudgian, who attributes it to a letter Gray wrote to *The Players* magazine, responding to its review of his lecture (9 February 1892), p. 184.

66. "Prologue," *London Nights* (London: Leonard C. Smithers, 1895), p. 3.

67. Beckson, *Memoirs of Symons,* p. 109.

68. Cyril Pearl, *The Girl with the Swansdown Seat* (London: Frederick Muller, 1955), pp. 208–209.

69. *The Players* (9 February 1892), p. 184, quoted in Gannon, *Two Friends,* p. 112.

70. *Letters of Ernest Dowson,* p. 223.

71. "To the Editor of the *Daily Telegraph*" (19 February 1892), in Hart-Davis, *Letters of Wilde,* p. 311.

72. *The Players* (9 February 1892), p. 184, quoted in Gannon, pp. 111–12.

73. "Mainly About People," *The Star* (6 February 1892), quoted in Gannon, p. 108.

74. Based on Miller's account in the *Independent Theatre,* p. 171. The other two plays were Arthur Symons's adaptation of a Frank Harris short story and William Archer's translation of Edward Brandes's *The Visit;* Schoonderwoerd, p. 114.

75. "Mainly About People," *The Star,* quoted in Gannon, p. 114. At Wilde's invitation, Louÿs and Shelley had attended the opening of *Lady Windermere's Fan* less than two weeks previously. See Ellmann, *Wilde,* p. 365.

76. *The Daily News* (London) quoted in Gannon, p. 114. In fact, Gray was experimenting with half-rhymes and visual rhymes (e.g., "feast" and "best"), a technique he was to develop further in *Silverpoints;* see typescript in the Lord Chamberlain's collection, British Library, London (Add. As. 53494). Published as *The Kiss,* with preface and notes by Ian Fletcher, by the Tragara Press, Edinburgh, 1983.

77. *The Players* (12 April 1892), quoted in Sewell, *In the Dorian Mode,* pp. 24–25.

78. *The Players,* n.d., n.p., among the Trudgian papers.

79. Quoted in Gannon, p. 108.

80. *Letters of Ernest Dowson,* p. 225.

81. Osbert Burdett, *The Beardsley Period: An Essay in Perspective* (London: John Lane, 1925), p. 165. Gray had a copy of this, the first edition, in his library, which suggests some sort of endorsement.

82. *The Star* (15 February 1892), quoted in Gannon, p. 109. Wilde's collaboration in the action against *The Star* is underlined by new evidence in the form of a letter from Ernest Poole of *The Star* newspaper to Oscar Wilde, dated 16 February 1892, which reads:

Dear Sir,

I enclose for your perusal a letter which I have lately forwarded to Mr. Gray's solicitor that you may see my anxiety to repair the wrong.

Yours faithfully,

ERNEST POOLE.

Oscar Wilde, Esquire

The text of the letter is given by Jacqueline Wesley, "Biographical Notes and Queries," *Book Collector* 39, no. 1 (Spring 1990): 117.

83. "The Drama of To-day," *Daily Telegraph* (12 February 1892), quoted in

Stuart Mason [Christopher Millard], *A Bibliography of Oscar Wilde* (London: Bertram Rota, 1967), p. 53.

84. The original version of "The Picture of Dorian Gray," *Lippincott's Monthly Magazine* (July 1890) spelled out the seduction of Dorian Gray by Lord Henry Wotton more explicitly. Wilde toned it down somewhat for its publication in book form in 1891.

85. *Letters of Wilde,* pp. 311–12.

86. There was, of course, the dinner party in early 1889; typescript reminiscence by Frank Liebich, Oscar Wilde papers, William Andrews Clark Memorial Library, UCLA. Further, Arthur Symons recounts how he was introduced by Wilde to "the future Dorian Gray" in what must have been late 1890, before the publication of *Dorian Gray* in novel form; Symons, *Memoirs,* p. 136. By the time Gray sent Wilde a copy of his poem, "Mishka," he felt sufficiently intimate to open with "My dear Oscar" and close with "Yours ever, Dorian."

87. Gray to Louÿs, 6 June 1892, in Vernon, "John Gray's Letters to Louÿs," p. 89.

88. *Anglo-American Times* (25 March 1893), reprinted in "Appendix A: Oscar Wilde by [Max Beerbohm masquerading as] An American," *Max Beerbohm: Letters to Reggie Turner,* ed. Rupert Hart-Davis (London: Rupert-Hart Davis, 1964), p. 290.

89. *Letters of Wilde,* p. 379; see also n. 2 above.

90. *A Study of Oscar Wilde* (London: Charles J. Sawyer, 1903), p. 53.

91. Symons, *Memoirs,* p. 136. For Symon's first meeting of Wilde, see *Letters of Wilde,* p. 276.

92. *Lippincott's Monthly Magazine* (July 1890): 75. In book form, (London: Ward Lock, 1891), p. 213. Sherard records his objections in *Bernard Shaw, Frank Harris and Oscar Wilde* (London: Greystone Press, 1937), pp. 154–55.

93. *Letters of Wilde,* pp. 263–64.

94. There are two letters from Ellen Terry among the Gray papers in the National Library, Edinburgh: one thanks him for his birthday sonnet (later published in *Silverpoints*); the other thanks him for *Silverpoints* itself. There are also letters from other more minor actresses: Mary Webster, Edith Chester and Florence St. John.

95. *Shaw: An Autobiography,* p. 250.

96. Review in *The Spectator* (26 November 1892), pp. 767–68. Attributed to Gray by Helen Trudgian, in whose papers a copy of it was preserved.

97. Copy from Wilde's library in the Houghton Library, Cambridge, Mass.

98. [January–March 1897], *Letters of Wilde,* p. 426. Here published in its entirety for the first time, this letter initially appeared in heavily edited form as *De Profundis* in 1905. This particular passage was not published during Gray's lifetime.

99. *Letters of Dowson,* p. 295.

100. Roger Lhombreaud, "Une Amitié Anglaise de Pierre Louÿs: Onze Lettres Inédites à John Gray," *Revue de Littérature Comparée* 27 (Juillet-Septembre, 1953): 344. Lhombreaud's article appeared in translation as "Arcades Ambo: The Poetical Friendship of John Gray and Pierre Louÿs," in *Two Friends,* ed. Sewell, pp. 120–33, but in a version that bowdlerized part of the text and one letter (that

mentioning the "whore-Club"). The following paragraph is indebted to Lombreaud's article in the *Revue de Littérature Comparée*, pp. 344–45.

101. To appreciate Gray's double-talk, the letter should be read in the original:

3 Plowden Buildings
in the Temple
Whitmonday 1892

Cher Monsieur Pierre Louÿs

Comme vous moy, vous congnois jà de nom de ce que m'y ay parlez Messire Oscar. Je puy vous franchemen parler sur les habitans des boys et des rivières de ce morne pays. Certes ils sont emplys de moutons et poyssons et aultres bestials dont le pluspart ne sont ni faunes ni nymphes nul n'ayant plus y besoingne. Venez chaussé le lumière ou de paille, vous serez le bienvenu. L'escolle est très paouvre à ceste heure. Notre Kit Marlowe est descendu soubz les ombrez suite d'ung mahlvays coup de dague à l'oeil. Cest entesté de Jehan Keatz n'a plus d'idée que de connoitre les fondes d'or et d'assier des soucys et des gazongz [.] Shelley est maintenant pêscheur de corails et Shakesper s'occupe à se feyre jouer. Voylà de nos nouvels dont n'a plus.

JOHN GRAY

Vernon, "Gray's Letters to Louÿs," p. 89. My translation is indebted to that of Michael Spiller in *A Friendship of the Nineties: Letters between John Gray and Pierre Louÿs,* ed. Allan Campbell (Edinburgh: Tragara Press, 1984), pp. 11–12.

102. 29 September [1892?], Vernon, pp. 93–94.

103. *Letters of Ernest Dowson,* pp. 271–72. I am indebted for the identification of "Kit Dowson" to Isobel Murray, "John Gray: The Person and the Work in Question," *Durham University Journal* (June 1984), p. 265.

104. André Gide, *Si le grain ne meurt . . .* (Paris: Gallimard, 1955), p. 332.

105. 15 June 1892, Lhombreaud, "Un Amité Anglaise," p. 345.

106. 15 June 1892, Vernon, "Gray's Letters to Louÿs," pp. 89–90.

107. 12 July 1892, 21 June 1892, Vernon, "Gray's Letters to Louÿs," pp. 92, 91.

108. *Letters of Wilde,* pp. 315–16.

109. 10 July 1892, Vernon, "Gray's Letters to Louÿs," p. 91.

110. Cyril Pearl, *The Girl with the Swansdown Seat,* pp. 208–09. Its license was revoked in 1894. For the Corinthian Club, see Douglas Ainslie, *Adventures Social and Literary* (London: T. Fisher Unwin, 1922), p. 142.

111. H. P. Clive, "Pierre Louÿs and Oscar Wilde: A Chronicle of their Friendship," *Revue de Littérature Comparée* 43 (1969): 369, and nn. 2, 3.

112. Clive, p. 367–77; also Vernon, p. 94 n. 25.

113. Lhombreaud, "Une Amitié Anglaise," p. 346. The passage about the "whore-Club" is cut, without notation, in Lhombreaud's version of the article, "Arcades Ambo," in *Two Friends,* p. 123.

114. Lhombreaud, "Une Amitié Anglaise," p. 347.

115. Vernon, "Gray's Letters to Louÿs," p. 92.

116. 16 July 1892, Vernon, "Gray's Letters to Louÿs," p. 92 and n. 17. The cousin was probably Frank Gray. Such badly hidden petulance over Gray's arrival shows how John Gray's sense of responsibility to his family is matched only by his irritation over their demands.

117. Lhombreaud, "Une Amitié Anglaise," pp. 347–48. The transcription of the date is almost certainly wrong: it should probably be 15 July.

118. 2 October 1892, Vernon, "Gray's Letters to Louÿs," p. 94 and n. 28.

119. Lhombreaud, "Une Amitié Anglaise," p. 348.

120. 10 October 1892, Vernon, "Gray's Letters to Louÿs," pp. 95–96. Following references are to this article.

121. 24 November 1892, Vernon, pp. 96–97.

122. John Gray died, aged 53, on 4 November 1892, at 2 Ripon Road in the presence of his wife. His occupation was listed as "wheeler"; cause of death, "cerebral atrophy." General Register Office, London.

123. 24 December 1892, Vernon, p. 99.

124. 27 and 28 November 1892, Vernon, p. 97.

125. 3 December 1892, Vernon, p. 99.

126. Hesketh Pearson, *Oscar Wilde: His Life and Wit* (New York: Harper, 1946), p. 186.

127. "The Person in Question" (Buenos Aires: issued privately in a limited edition by Patricio Gannon, 1958), p. 13. Subsequent parenthetical page references are to this text. "The Person in Question" is reprinted in Sewell, Appendix I, *In the Dorian Mode,* pp. 214–22.

Aside from its apparent allusions to Gray's relationship with Wilde, the following circumstantial evidence helps date the story as being circa late November 1892: (1) Written retrospectively, the story describes the course of a "fever," and with it, this hallucination, over the course of a year, from August to August. That Gray had been ill in early March 1891, and throughout the following months, may be established by his letter to Félix Fénéon of 14 April 1891 (cf. Chapter Two, pp. 71–72 herein) and by an anonymous correspondent who writes in October 1891. This illness came to a climax during the late autumn of 1892 in the physical and psychic breakdown evident in the letters to Louÿs and recorded in the journal of Bradley and Cooper (cf. Chapter Three, pp. 104–105); (2) The "friend" mentioned at the end of the story as offering to bring the narrator to a Jewish eating house closely resembles André Raffalovich—who also was referred to at times as a doctor because of his scientific interest in homosexuality. Gray did not meet him until 2 November 1892.

128. Walter Pater, *The Renaissance: Studies in Art and Poetry,* ed. Donald L. Hill (Berkeley: Univ. of California Press, 1980), p. 109.

129. Oscar Wilde, "The Critic as Artist," *Intentions* (New York: Brentano's, 1912), p. 176.

130. Arthur Symons, "The Café Royal," *The Café Royal and Other Essays* (Westminster, England: Beaumont Press, 1923), p. 4.

THREE. *Silverpoints* (pp. 103–45)

1. Minute by A. H. Oakes, assistant librarian, Foreign Office (Library Correspondence, PRO 366/392, 28 May 1896). Quoted in Peter J. Vernon, "The Letters of John Gray," (Ph.D. dissertation, University of London, 1976), p. 17, n. 9.

2. Gray to Pierre Louÿs, 15 June 1892, Peter Vernon, "John Gray's Letters to Pierre Louÿs," *Revue de Littérature Comparée* 53 (Janvier–Mars 1979): 89.

3. Sir John Tilley and Stephen Gaselee, *The Foreign Office* (London: G. P. Putnam's Sons, 1933), p. 144.

4. Gray's salary on transferring from the Post Office in 1888 was £95.00 (GPO Minute 14981). The *Foreign Office Lists* give the salary scale for a Second Division Clerk as being from £70 to £350 (in 1897); presumably Gray took up employment at about the £100 mark and then received annual £25 increments, bringing his income to the £200 figure for 1892.

5. On the price of rooms, see Vernon, "Letters of John Gray," p. 104, n. 2. The remark on starving was made to Katherine Bradley; see the journal kept by Bradley and Edith Cooper [Michael Field], "Works and Days," 1907 pt. 2 [B.M. Add. Ms. 46797 f.2], British Library Manuscript Collections, London. The worry over collectors is from Vernon, "Gray's Letters to Louÿs," p. 91.

6. Entry by Edith Cooper in "Works and Days" 1908 [B.M. Add. Ms. 46798, f.202.], British Library Manuscript Collections, London.

7. 24 December 1892, Vernon, "Gray's Letters to Louÿs," p. 99.

8. Vernon, "Gray's Letters to Louÿs," pp. 96–97.

9. 16 March [1893], Vernon, "Gray's Letters to Louÿs," p. 102.

10. H. P. Clive, "Pierre Louÿs and Oscar Wilde: A Chronicle of their Friendship," *Revue de Littérature Comparée* 43 (1969): 368. This account of Louÿs's relationship with Wilde relies substantially on Clive's work.

11. No date, but probably late June 1893. Roger Lhombreaud, "Une Amitié Anglaise de Pierre Louÿs; Onze Lettres Inédites à John Gray," *Revue de Littérature Comparée* 27 (1953): 352. For the dating of the letter, see Clive, "Louÿs and Wilde," pp. 375–77.

12. Rupert Hart-Davis, ed., *The Letters of Oscar Wilde,* rev. ed., (London: Rupert Hart-Davis, Ltd., 1963), p. 410.

13. I take the incident recorded by Martin Birnbaum in *Oscar Wilde: Fragments and Memories* (New York: J. F. Drake, 1914), p. 5, to be typical of the reaction of many of the young men Wilde befriended. He records how, when a young poet asked Wilde to refute the ugly rumors about him, "Wilde refused to discuss the topic and finally called to the driver: 'Stop to let this man out! I invited him for a drive, but he is not a gentleman!' "

14. Gray to Raffalovich, 30 November 1898, National Library, Edinburgh.

15. This alienation from a lost or elusive self which Gray records in "The Person in Question" is reflected with an eerie accuracy in the behavior of Wilde, at least one of the story's models, Gray himself being another. Among all Wilde's friends during this period there appears an increasing confusion as to who the "real" Oscar Wilde was, a confusion also evident among his contemporary biographers (Robert Sherard, Frank Harris, and Alfred Douglas), all of whom were

caught up in self-contradictions, irresponsible speculations, and even falsifica-
tions. Harris's *Oscar Wilde* (1930), for instance, is a notorious piece of yellow
journalism. Sherard and Douglas wrote of course out of self-defense. In *Oscar
Wilde and Myself* (1914) Douglas denies any improprieties in their friendship,
while saying at the same time that Wilde could not have been "mentally responsi-
ble" when he wrote "De Profundis" (p. 163). Sherard's *Life of Oscar Wilde* (1928)
goes further in saying that the discrepancy between appearance and reality in
Wilde's behavior must have been the result of "epileptiform," a kind of insanity
(p. 337). These examples can be multiplied in numerous other accounts.

Despite—or perhaps because of—the chaotic nature of these biographies, we
are presented with the history of the disintegration of a personality. They are not
purely the result of Wilde's own habit of keeping his friends in "moral-tight"
compartments and his own love of the factitious. The edition of his letters by Hart-
Davis documents the same increasing elusiveness of the "real" Wilde, his gradual
disappearance behind a facade of theatrical gestures and emotional posturings that
has, perhaps, its epitome in the long letter sent to Douglas from prison, available in
the Hart-Davis edition for the first time in its entirety.

For Wilde's treatment of his friends, see Hesketh Pearson, *Oscar Wilde: His
Life and Wit* (New York: Harper, 1946), p. 236. The history of the letter to Doug-
las is given in *Letters of Oscar Wilde,* pp. 423–24.

16. 12 July 1892, Vernon, "Gray's Letters to Louÿs," p. 92.

17. This account is indebted to R. K. R. Thornton, *The Decadent Dilemma*
(London: Edward Arnold, 1983), particularly the chapter, "Decadence as a Crit-
ical Term in England," pp. 34–70.

18. Arthur Symons, "The Decadent Movement in Literature," *Harper's New
Monthly Magazine* (November 1893), pp. 858–67.

19. This notorious attack on Wilde, probably written by Charles Whibley,
appeared in the *National Observer* of 6 April 1895. Reprinted, in part, in Thorn-
ton, *Decadent Dilemma,* p. 67.

20. *The Pall Mall Gazette* 56 (4 May 1893): 3.

21. Charles Ricketts, *A Defence of the Revival of Printing* (London: Hacon and
Ricketts, 1899), p. 18. Ricketts rejected the design proposed by Lane, offering his
own instead; Ricketts to John Lane, no date, Houghton Library, Cambridge,
Mass.

22. Violet Wyndham, "Reminiscences, by Ada Leverson: I. The Importance
of Being Oscar," *The Sphinx and Her Circle: A Biographical Sketch of Ada Leverson,
1862–1933* (London: Andre Deutsch, 1963), p. 105.

23. Frank Harris made an exception of "The Barber." *The Saturday Review*
75 (May 6, 1893): 493. Richard Le Gallienne, *Retrospective Reviews: A Literary Log*
(London: The Bodley Head, 1896), 1: 231.

24. Walter Pater's most eloquent defense of this idea may be found in "The
School of Giorgione," *The Renaissance: Studies in Art and Poetry,* ed. Donald L.
Hill (Berkeley: Univ. of California Press, 1980), pp. 102–22.

25. For information on the early years of the Bodley Head, see James G.
Nelson, *The Early Nineties: A View from the Bodley Head* (Cambridge, Mass.:
Harvard Univ. Press, 1971), pp. 6–35. Le Gallienne's comment is from *The Ro-
mantic '90s* (London: G. P. Putnam's Sons, 1926), p. 122.

26. This conflict would be exemplified in the rather comic battle for the Laureateship after the death of Tennyson in 1892. James G. Nelson writes in *The Early Nineties* that "The strenuous efforts which . . . leading literary czars of the hour made toward gaining the Laureateship for a young traditionalist poet like [William] Watson are indicative of a concerted effort in the early nineties to discredit and disarm young writers such as Symons, Gray, and Yeats, poets who were endeavoring to free English poetry from Victorian rhetoric and to search out a new path to the twentieth century" (p. 220). Who, today, reads William Watson? Yet he was not only read in his day, but held up as an example to the "decadent" poets of what they should be doing. Further, our realignment of the literary canon toward the more innovative poets also obscures the disagreements between them, as, for instance, in the Rhymers' Club, between those who advocated the "new" poetry of France (Arthur Symons) and those who wrote avowedly robust "English" poetry (John Davidson). To add to the confusion, Davidson went on to produce some of the more vigorously experimental poetry of the decade.

27. Thornton, pp. 188–200.

28. Gray to John Lane, 27 May 1892, Henry W. and Albert A. Berg Collection, New York Public Library; the first contract is in the Princeton University Library [MSS Misc. WIA-WIL], Princeton, New Jersey.

29. For the second contract see Bodley Head files; printed in Nelson, *Early Nineties*, p. 95. The second contract was highly disadvantageous for Lane; it is probable that Raffalovich was behind the scenes, guaranteeing him against loss. See Richard Ellmann, *Oscar Wilde* (New York: Knopf, 1988), p. 392.

30. *Silverpoints* holograph, Princeton University Library [MSS Bd: O'Connell], Princeton, N.J. Published more than thirty years later as *Sound: A Poem* (London: Curwen Press, 1926). Reprinted in Ian Fletcher, ed., *The Poems of John Gray*, The 1880–1920 British Author Series 1 (Greensboro, N.C.: ELT Press, 1988), p. 46.

31. Oscar Wilde, *The Picture of Dorian Gray*, ed. Isobel Murray (London: Oxford Univ. Press, 1974), pp. 134–35 and note, p. 245. With characteristic laziness, Wilde lifted the instruments' names from a passage in a museum handbook on exotic musical instruments. See also Isobel Murray, "John Gray: The Person and the Work in Question," *Durham University Journal* (June 1984), p. 262.

32. The Reverend Dominic Hart, "Memories of John Gray," Trudgian papers. Published in Brocard Sewell, ed., "Some Memories of John Gray," *The Innes Review* 2 (1975): 81.

33. *Silverpoints* holograph. "Song of the Stars" was first published in *Known Signatures*, selected and ed. by John Gawsworth (London: Rich and Cowan, 1932), pp. 54–56 and reprinted in Fletcher, p. 45. On Lane's request, see Gray to Lane, 18 June 1892, Berg Collection, New York Public Library. "By all means omit the 'Song of the Stars' from the Silverpoints. The publication will not take place until . . . September, I suppose."

34. Louis Couperus, *Ecstasy: A Study of Happiness* (London: Henry and Co., 1892), trans. A. Teixeira de Mattos and John Gray, p. x.

35. Walter Pater, *Marius the Epicurean: His Sensations and Ideas* (London: Mac-

millan, 1910), 1: 56. As the "golden book" of the period, see Thornton, *Decadent Dilemma,* pp. 91–92, 112–13.

36. "Translators' Note," *Ecstasy* pp. xii–xiii.

37. "On a Picture," *Silverpoints* (London: Elkin Mathews & John Lane, 1893), p. 21, and reprinted in Fletcher, pp. 30–31. All subsequent references to *Silverpoints* poems are to Fletcher, and page numbers will be cited parenthetically in the text. Gray invited Louÿs to see "the two best things Millais ever painted and probably therefore the finest modern pictures in existence" (among them, Millais's "Ophelia") on a trip to the Guildhall in June 1892. Gray to Louÿs, 15 June 1892, Vernon, "Gray's Letters to Louÿs," pp. 89–90 and p. 90, n. 5.

38. "Art and Ideas" [1913], *Essays and Introductions* (London: Macmillan, 1961), pp. 353–354.

39. Gray to Louÿs, 21 June 1892, Vernon, "Gray's Letters to Louÿs," pp. 90–91.

40. p. 23. The poem is called "inept" by Ruth Z. Temple, "The Other Choice: The Worlds of John Gray, Poet and Priest," *Bulletin of Research in the Humanities* 84, no. 1 (Spring 1981): 53.

41. "A Note upon the Practice and Theory of Verse at the Present Time Obtaining in France," *Century Guild Hobby Horse,* quoted in Thornton, p. 41.

42. "Works and Days," 1907 [BM Add. Ms. 46796, f. 216], British Library Manuscript Collections, London.

43. *Salome: A Tragedy in One Act* (London: Elkin Mathews & John Lane, 1893), p. 61.

44. Wilde had submitted the play to Louÿs to read and later dedicated it to him. Louÿs's letter to Gray is given in Lhombreaud, "Une Amitié Anglaise," p. 344. For an analysis of Louÿs's role in determining the final draft of the play, see *Letters of Wilde,* pp. 305–306, n. 1.

45. 18 February 1893, Vernon, "Gray's Letters to Louÿs," p. 101 and n. 57, same page. *Silverpoints* was actually published in the week of 4 March 1893; *Salome,* on 22 February 1893.

46. "Translators' Note," *Ecstasy,* p. xi.

47. Gray to Edith Cooper, 14 November 1909, Berg Collection, New York Public Library.

48. T. W. G. W. [Theodore Wratislaw?], "La Garde Joyeuse IX: 'John Gray,' " *The Artist and Journal of Home Culture* 14, no. 167 (4 November 1893): 328.

49. T. W. G. W. in "La Garde Joyeuse IX," p. 328. For Le Gallienne, see "Among the Brotherhood of Bards," *Graphic* 47 (8 April 1893): 383.

50. See Thornton, "Decadence as a Critical Term in England," *Decadent Dilemma,* pp. 34–70, and also Nelson, "The Bodley Head Poets: Poisonous Honey and English Blossoms," *The Early Nineties,* pp. 184–220, to which this discussion is particularly indebted.

51. Gray to Edmund Blunden, 21 July 1929, the Harry Ransom Humanities Research Center, University of Texas, Austin.

52. "Translators' Note," *Ecstasy,* p. xi.

53. Quoted by Olive Custance in a letter to an unidentified correspondent ("Lulu") in Brocard Sewell, *Footnote to the Nineties: A Memoir of John Gray and André Raffalovich* (London: Cecil and Amelia Woolf, 1968), p. 16.

54. A. G. Lehmann, *The Symbolist Aesthetic in France, 1885–1895* (Oxford: Oxford Univ. Press, 1950), p. 150.

55. "Mr John Gray writes before he has learnt to speak. He would sing before he is rid of stammering. . . . He is a lame man running before he can walk." Unsigned, *Saturday Review* (May 6, 1893), p. 493. Further, "to find his [Baudelaire's] wonderful language traduced into English that stumbles at every rhyme, and chokes with the least difficulty, is something more than can be borne with patience. . . ." T. W. G. W., "La Garde Joyeuse IX," p. 329. Ruth Z. Temple notes Gray's lack of lyric grace and verbal padding in her article, "The Other Choice," pp. 52–53.

56. Father Gray is identified as the fictive "Father Rosary" in Siegfried Sassoon's *Sherston's Progress* (London: Faber and Faber, 1936), p. 66, by James Darragh in a letter to Brocard Sewell, 5 July 1976, Sewell papers.

57. "Translators' Note," *Ecstasy*, p. x. Of this piece, one critic remarked: "Who translated Mr. John Gray's preface? Was it written in English and then handed over to a Dutchman?" Unidentified source, Trudgian papers.

58. "Translators' Note," *Ecstasy*, p. xi.

59. I am indebted here to the perspicacious analysis of the poem by Linda C. Dowling, "Nature and Decadence: John Gray's *Silverpoints*," *Victorian Poetry* 15, no. 2 (Summer 1977): 167.

60. Gray may have been present at the statue's unveiling by Lord Rosebery at the Victoria Embankment Gardens in 1884. Lord Edward Gleichen, "Robert Burns," *London's Open-Air Statuary* (London: Longmans, Green, 1928), p. 107.

61. The incident is recounted in "Light," *Pageant* 2 (1897): 122, which places the bookstore in Leicester Square, London. For the actual incident, see herein Chapter IV, p. 168. In the holograph of *Spiritual Poems,* Gray notes that his translation of Jacopone da Todi's "O love, all love above" was composed in Edinburgh on 18 May 1894.

62. Félix Fénéon to John Gray, 20 August 1890, John Gray Collection, John Rylands University Library of Manchester.

63. *The Battle of the Bays* (London: J. Lane, 1896), quoted in Thornton, p. 43.

64. T. W. G. W., "La Garde Joyeuse IX," p. 328.

65. *Poems by Emily Dickinson,* Mabel Loomis Todd and T. W. Higginson, eds. (London: James R. Osgood, McIlvaine and Co., 1891). The book, with Gray's bookplate, is now in the library of the Hawkesyard Priory, Rugeley, Staffordshire.

66. From "Figurez-vous un Peu," II, 17–18, *Poésies complètes* (Paris: Gallimard, 1970), p. 194. It originally appeared in *Des Fleurs de Bonne Volonté* (1890).

67. *The Letters of Ernest Dowson,* Desmond Flower and Henry Maas, eds. (London: Cassell and Co., 1967), pp. 182–83. The review is T. W. G. W., "La Garde Joyeuse IX," p. 328.

68. "Lionel Johnson," *Literary Essays of Ezra Pound,* ed. T. S. Eliot (London: Faber and Faber, 1954), p. 367.

69. Victor Plarr, *Ernest Dowson, 1888–1897: Reminiscences* (London: Elkin Mathews, 1914), p. 22.

70. Charles Baudelaire, *Oeuvres complètes,* ed. Claude Pichois (Paris: Gallimard, 1961), p. 114.

71. "Baudelaire in Our Time," *Essays Ancient and Modern* (New York: Harcourt, Brace, 1936), p. 19.

72. Ruth Zabriskie Temple, *The Critic's Alchemy: A Study of the Introduction of French Symbolism into England* (New Haven, Conn.: College and University Press, 1953), p. 141 and "Appendix A," pp. 322–25.

73. Temple, *Critic's Alchemy,* pp. 142–52, examines the importation of Verlaine's poetry by Arthur Symons, his special apologist in England, and the conditions which predisposed Symons to adapt some elements of Verlaine rather than others.

74. Symons isolated these as the technical details which constitute Verlaine's virtuosity in a review of *Bonheur* for the *Academy* 39 (18 April 1891): 362–63. See Temple, p. 146.

75. Arthur Rimbaud, *Oeuvres* (Paris: Mercure de France, 1952), p. 34.

76. Gray reported to Fénéon that his attempts to translate the "Illuminations" strongly resembled the poetry of Blake—with a bit of Walt Whitman. Gray to Fénéon, 14 April 1891, Paulhan Archives, Paris. See also Félix Fénéon to Gray, 8 May 1891 [?], National Library, Edinburgh.

77. For the various translations see G. Ross Roy, "A Bibliography of French Symbolism in English-language Publications to 1910: Mallarmé—Rimbaud—Verlaine," *Revue de Littérature Comparée* 34 (Octobre—Decembre, 1960): 645–59. This bibliography, although useful as a general overview of the English reception of these three French poets, is riddled with inaccuracies. In reference to Gray's work, the major errors are as follows:

Rimbaud: Roy lists Gray's "Charleville" (Rimbaud's "À la Musique") as the first translation into English. It is actually the second, the first being (as far as I can find out) T. Sturge Moore's translation of "Les Chercheuses de Poux," which appeared first in the 1892 *Dial.* The information that only seven translations of Rimbaud appeared in the period until 1910, I take to be correct.

Verlaine: Gray listed as third translator, with *Silverpoints* as first major collection of Verlaine's poetry in English. This inaccuracy is based on a misdating of Arthur Symons's *Silhouettes* (1892) which rightly holds that position (Roy gives as its date 1896).

Mallarmé: Entries correct as far as I can ascertain. Gray is listed as fourth translator.

On the difficulties—and consequences—of developing equivalent techniques, see Graham Hough, "Part I: Reflections on a Literary Revolution," in *Image and Experience: Studies in a Literary Revolution* (London: Duckworth, 1960), pp. 3–83.

78. Le Gallienne, "John Gray," *Retrospective Reviews,* pp. 229–32 (reprinted from a review of *Silverpoints* published in March, 1893) and T.W.G.W., "La Garde Joyeuse IX," pp. 328–29. On *Nieuwe Gids* and Harris, see Gray to John Lane, 4 January 1893, [MSS. Misc. GOR-GRA] Princeton University Library.

79. Frank Harris to Gray, no date, National Library, Edinburgh. Harris himself, however, did review *Silverpoints* for the *Saturday Review* 75 (May 6, 1893): 493, in a tone of disappointment. Only one poem ("The Barber") came up to the

binding; as for the rest, "Mr. John Gray has thrown down a bomb into poetical dovecotes that turns out on inspection to be merely a squib."

80. Dowson's comment [c. 27 February 1893] is in *Letters of Ernest Dowson*, p. 271. "Mr. Pater, Mr. Swinburne and Mr. Theodore Watts, have praised the 'Silverpoints' of Mr. John Gray. . . ." Unsigned review, "Art Literature," *The Artist and Journal of Home Culture* 14, no. 161 (1 April 1893): 119.

81. Wyndham, *Sphinx*, p. 105.

82. Robert S. Hichens, *The Green Carnation* (London: William Heinemann, 1894), p. 44.

83. *Pall Mall Gazette* 56 (4 May 1893): 3.

84. Brocard Sewell, "John Gray and André Sebastian Raffalovich: A Biographical Outline," *Two Friends: John Gray and André Raffalovich*, Sewell, ed. (Aylesford, Kent: Saint Albert's Press, 1963), p. 17. Also Father Edwin Essex, "The Canon in Residence," *Two Friends*, p. 155: "And he [Canon Gray] did all he could to withdraw from circulation his own first book of poems, *Silverpoints*, by destroying any odd copies he was able to buy up."

85. "John Gray," *Retrospective Reviews*, pp. 229–31.

86. The essay appeared about a month after *Silverpoints'* publication. "Appendix A: Oscar Wilde by [Max Beerbohm masquerading as] An American," *Max Beerbohm: Letters to Reggie Turner*, ed. Rupert Hart-Davis (London: Hart-Davis, 1964), p. 290. Reprinted from the *Anglo-American Times*, 25 March 1893.

87. Gray to John Lane, 4 January 1893, [Mss. Misc. GOR-GRA] Princeton University Library.

88. Gray preserved various letters to him, all undated, in the collection left to the Dominican Chaplaincy, Edinburgh, and now in the National Library, Edinburgh.

89. Gray to Edmund Blunden, 7 June 1930, Harry Ransom Research Center, University of Texas, Austin, and Symons to Gray, no date, National Library, Edinburgh. That this letter refers to *Silverpoints* is conjecture, but other remarks serve to date it circa 1893–94.

90. T. W. G. W., "La Garde Joyeuse IX," p. 329.

FOUR. *The Prodigal Returns* (pp. 146–81)

1. John Gray, "Garth Wilkinson," *The Dial* 3 (1893): 24.

2. John Gray, "The Redemption of Durtal," *The Dial* 4 (1896): 10.

3. Details of Gray's youth appear herein, pp. 10–21. Raffalovich's early biography can be found on pp. 44–46.

4. The article has not been found. Note by Helen Trudgian, Trudgian papers; cited by Brocard Sewell, *In the Dorian Mode: A Life of John Gray, 1866–1934* (Padstow, Cornwall: Tabb House, 1983), pp. 30–31 and 200, n. 33.

5. Sewell, *In the Dorian Mode*, p. 200, n. 34. Trudgian's informant was André Raffalovich's sister, Sophie O'Brien.

6. *The Letters of Ernest Dowson*, Desmond Flower and Henry Maas, eds. (London: Cassell and Co., 1967), p. 295 and n. 4, same page. "Park Lane," *The Post Office London Directory for 1895 (London)*. In December of 1896, Gray moved from

Park Lane to 92 Mount Street W., which is almost equally near Raffalovich's residence at 72 South Audley Street. See Henry Maas, J. L. Duncan and W. G. Good, eds., *The Letters of Aubrey Beardsley* (Rutherford, N.J.: Fairleigh Dickinson Univ. Press, 1970), p. 233.

7. Timothy D'Arch Smith, *Love in Earnest: Some Notes on the Lives and Writings of the English "Uranian" Poets from 1889 to 1930* (London: Routledge and Kegan Paul, 1970), pp. 29–34. That Raffalovich was indeed a familiar of the London homosexual underground is conjecture based on his detailed knowledge of its practices, which he displays in his treatise *Uranisme et Unisexualité: Étude sur Différentes Manifestations de l'Instinct Sexuel, Bibliothéque de Criminologie,* vol. 15 (Lyon: A. Storck, 1896).

8. Raffalovich wrote that Wilde "once talked to me for several hours about the more dangerous affections." Alexander Michaelson, "Oscar Wilde," *Blackfriars* 8 (November 1927): 698. Subsequent parenthetical page citations are to this text.

9. "L'Affaire Oscar Wilde," *Archives de l'Anthropologie Criminelle de Criminologie et de Psychologie Normale et Pathologique* (Paris) 10 (1895): 445. Reprinted under separate cover as *L'Affaire Oscar Wilde* (Lyon: A. Storck, 1895).

10. *Bernard Shaw, Frank Harris and Oscar Wilde* (New York: Greystone Press, 1937), pp. 90–91.

11. Michaelson [Raffalovich], "Oscar Wilde," p. 701.

12. Raffalovich to Gray, undated [c. February 1900], National Library, Edinburgh.

13. Havelock Ellis, *The Psychology of Sex: A Manual for Students* (New York: Ray Long and Richard R. Smith, 1933), p. 223.

14. Raffalovich, *Uranisme,* pp. 5–30.

15. "Works and Days," journal of Katherine Bradley and Edith Cooper [Michael Field], 22 May 1894 [BM Add Ms. 46782], British Library Manuscript Collections, London.

16. Gray papers, National Library, Edinburgh.

17. Raffalovich to Gray, undated [c. 1900], Gray papers, National Library, Edinburgh.

18. Sewell, *Footnote,* p. 26, and Sewell, "John Gray and André Sebastian Raffalovich: A Biographical Outline," *Two Friends: John Gray and André Raffalovich,* Sewell, ed. (Aylesford, Kent: Saint Albert's Press, 1963), p. 11. In fact, photographs of Raffalovich show an odd but interesting face, redeemed by its alertness and obvious intelligence.

19. *Roses of Shadow,* privately printed and not for general distribution (no printer's name, place or date), p. 13.

20. Sewell, *In the Dorian Mode,* p. 60.

21. These letters date from Gray's departure for the Scots College, Rome, in 1898. Gray papers, National Library, Edinburgh.

22. See Mary Raphael Gray, [Beatrice Gray], "A Sister's Reminiscences," *Two Friends,* pp. 100–105.

23. [Invitation] Gray to William Rothenstein, 29 March 1894, Rothenstein Collection, Houghton Library, Cambridge, Mass.

24. Gray papers, National Library, Edinburgh. Published in *The Poems of John Gray*, Ian Fletcher, ed., The 1880–1920 British Author Series 1 (Greensboro, N.C.: ELT Press, 1988), pp. 61–65.

25. Joan Ungersma Halperin, *Félix Fénéon: Aesthete & Anarchist in Fin-de-Siècle Paris* (New Haven: Yale Univ. Press, 1988), pp. 241–95.

26. The same understanding of hatred appears in an arresting, unpublished story of this time, "Their Mothers." Gray papers, National Library, Edinburgh.

27. [Mrs.] E. Lynn Linton to Gray, 18 April [1894], Gray papers, National Library, Edinburgh.

28. Allardyce Nicoll, "Late Nineteenth-Century Drama, 1850–1900," *A History of English Drama, 1660–1900* (Cambridge: Cambridge Univ. Press, 1959), 5: 390, 533. The final act survives in manuscript; Gray papers, National Library, Edinburgh.

29. *The Times* (8 June 1894), quoted in Sewell, "Gray and Raffalovich," *Two Friends*, pp. 20–21.

30. The letter, which fell into the wrong hands, proved a damaging piece of evidence at the Wilde trials. Richard Ellmann, *Oscar Wilde* (Knopf: New York, 1988), pp. 389–90, 393–94, 446.

31. *The Illustrated London News* (16 June 1894), pp. 766–68.

32. *Theatre: A Monthly Review of the Drama, Music, and the Fine Arts* 24 (1 July 1894): 37–38.

33. Sewell, *Footnote*, p. 35. Sewell received the information on Frank (Francis) Mathew in private conversation with Father John-Baptist Reeves. But no Francis Mathew appears in the list of solicitors and barristers presiding over the trial as given by the *Central Criminal Court Record*, vol. 122 (1894–95). A "watching brief" is a brief instructing counsel to "watch" a case.

34. Michaelson [Raffalovich], "Oscar Wilde," p. 701.

35. *A Northern Aspect. The Ambush of Young Days. Two Duologues by John Gray and André Raffalovich* (no place: no publisher, 12 May 1895).

36. On Raffalovich's removal to Berlin, see Beardsley to Raffalovich, 2 June 1895, *Letters of Beardsley*, pp. 89–90. His reaction to the Wilde sentence is in Michaelson [Raffalovich], "Oscar Wilde," p. 701.

37. *Archives de L'Anthropologie Criminelle* 10 (1895): 445–77. Some time later, this was issued under separate cover by A. Storck, Lyons. (See "The Check-List of Works of André Raffalovich," *Two Friends*, p. 188–89.)

38. Raffalovich to Charles Ballantyne, 13 November 1927, National Library, Edinburgh. Gray's suffering was made more acute by a subsequent rift with some members of his family. Heather Coltman reports that his brother William tore up John's photograph after the Wilde trials as a protest against the life he had been living. Coltman in conversation with McCormack, July 1989.

39. Sewell, "Gray and Raffalovich," *Two Friends*, p. 27 and *Footnote*, p. 43. Sewell had the story from the late William Muir, one of Father Gray's Edinburgh converts, to whom Gray apparently spoke freely about his private life. A similar incident occurs to Park in the novella of that name.

40. "Garth Wilkinson," *The Dial* 3 (1893) 1:24. Subsequent parenthetical page citations are to this text.

41. Wilkinson to Gray, 11 January 1893, National Library, Edinburgh.

42. "May 1895," *The Blue Calendar 1895: A Book of Carols* (privately printed and not for general distribution, 24 December 1894), reprinted in Fletcher, pp. 159–60.

43. Francis Jammes to Gray, 1913–30, National Library, Edinburgh.

44. "Swedenborg, Mediums, Desolate Places," *Explorations* (New York: Macmillan, 1962), p. 43.

45. "June 1896," *The Blue Calendar 1896: Twelve Sundry Carols* (privately printed and not for general distribution, 24 December 1895), reprinted in Fletcher, p. 174.

46. "Works and Days," entry by Katherine Bradley, 20 December 1894 [BM Add. Ms. 46782], British Library Manuscript Collections, London.

47. Gray, "Wilkinson," p. 23, n. 2., quotes the German mystic, Jakob Böhme, in the original. Gray's interest in second sight and spiritualism may be inferred from "The Person in Question" and "The Flying Fish" and from his encounters with such experiences not merely in the world of the occult, but (later) in the figure of Father Allan McDonald. For an account of Gray's visit to Father McDonald, see his letter quoted in John L. Campbell and Trevor H. Hall, *Strange Things: The Story of Fr. Allan McDonald, Ada Goodrich Freer, and the Society for Psychical Research's Enquiry into Highland Second Sight* (London: Routledge and Kegan Paul, 1968), pp. 305–307, 308.

48. Michaelson [Raffalovich], "Isis Unveiled," *Blackfriars* 9 (September 1928), 532–40.

49. *The Dial* 4 (1896): 1. Reprinted in *A Sailor's Garland,* ed. John Masefield (1906), *The Long Road* (1926) and Fletcher, pp. 255–60, from which the following page citation is taken. "Travellers' Tales," a fragment holograph from the collection of Donald Hyde, New York, is obviously a prelude to "The Flying Fish." Its mechanical style suggests that Gray was also experimenting here with writing from "Influx." Reprinted in Fletcher, pp. 44–45.

50. Michaelson [Raffalovich], "Parallels," *Blackfriars* 10 (January 1929): 779–85.

51. Robert Wells, "The Perils of Pietism," *Times Literary Supplement* (6–12 January 1989), p. 16.

52. Gray to Louÿs, 21 January 1897, Peter Vernon, "John Gray's Letters to Pierre Louÿs," *Revue de Littérature Comparée* 53 (Janvier–Mars 1979): 106.

53. These are poems Nietzsche did not choose to incorporate into longer prose works, such as *Joyful Science* or *Zarathustra.* They were published as part of a series in *The Works of Friedrich Nietzsche,* Alexander Tille, ed., vol. 10 (New York: Macmillan, 1897), "Poems," trans. John Gray.

54. Alexander Tille to Gray, 4 December 1896, National Library, Edinburgh. The letter confirms that Gray had completed his translation by this date. For Tille's role, see R. M. Wenley, "Nietzsche: Traffics and Discoveries," *The Monist* 31 (January 1921): 136.

55. Tille, Preface, *Publications of the Glasgow Goethe Society, II: Goethe's Satyros and Prometheus,* ed. A. Tille, trans. John Gray, (Glasgow: Glasgow Goethe Society, 1898). For the details of Tille's career at the University of Glasgow, I am grateful to the reference librarian there, Elizabeth G. Jack.

56. Bayard Quincy Morgan, *A Critical Bibliography of German Literature in English Translation, 1481–1927* (New York: Scarecrow, 1965), pp. 172, 360.

57. The date of the review is 7 March 1903. The review was of *The Dawn of the Day* by Nietzsche, translated by John Volz, published by Fisher Unwin. This volume also contained *A Genealogy of Morals,* which included Gray's translations of the poems, first published by Unwin in London in 1899. Raffalovich to Gray, 1 February (no year) speaks of "Arthur Symons revelling in your Nietzsche poems which he thinks excellent and he has written about them in the Athenaeum." National Library, Edinburgh.

58. Information from Denis Donoghue, editor of Yeats's *Memoirs.*

59. Gray to Raffalovich, 9 January 1904, National Library, Edinburgh.

60. *Savoy* 2 (April 1896): 97, reprinted in Fletcher, p. 70.

61. Sewell, "Gray and Raffalovich," *Two Friends,* p. 26.

62. "André Raffalovich," *Blackfriars* 15 (June 1934): 405.

63. Mrs. William O'Brien, "Friends for Eternity: André Raffalovich and John Gray," *The Irish Monthly* 62 (November 1934): 700–701. She added, "Had his health allowed, he [Raffalovich] would have been a priest." At about the same time as Raffalovich's conversion, his Swiss butler, Joseph Töbler, also became a Catholic. Sewell, "Gray and Raffalovich," *Two Friends,* pp. 12, 26.

64. *Spiritual Poems* holograph, National Library of Scotland, Edinburgh. The poem is partially reprinted as "Variations on Santeuil" in Fletcher, pp. 148–50. Subsequent parenthetical page citations are to this text.

65. Gray, *Spiritual Poems, Chiefly Done out of Several Languages* (London: Hacon and Ricketts, 1896), pp. 58–66. Reprinted in Fletcher, pp. 118–22. Subsequent parenthetical page citations are to this text.

66. Ian Fletcher, "Notes: *Spiritual Poems,*" *Poems of John Gray,* p. 314.

67. "Light," *Pageant* 2 (1897), 1: 128–29. Subsequent parenthetical page citations are to this text.

68. Presumably, Helen Trudgian got this information from Gray's sister. Draft of an unpublished biography by Trudgian, Trudgian papers.

69. Gray to Michael Field [Katherine Bradley], 24 November 1908, Henry W. and Albert A. Berg Collection, New York Public Library.

70. Gray to Michael Field [Katherine Bradley], 24 October 1908, Berg Collection, New York Public Library. The journal entry on Gray as Carmelite is in "Works and Days," [BM Add. Ms. 46798], British Library Manuscript Collections, London.

71. Gray to Michael Field [Katherine Bradley], 24 October 1908, Berg Collection, New York Public Library.

72. Raffalovich sent Beardsley, for instance, a copy of Crashaw. *Letters of Beardsley,* pp. 84–85. The comment on Darley is in Gray to Michael Field [Katherine Bradley], 3 August 1908, Berg Collection, New York Public Library.

73. Huysmans wrote to Raffalovich in 1896 that Gray's effort "est intéressante. Que n'en sommes—nous là, ici, en France, où la poésie religieuse ne se compose que de bas cantiques." The dating of the letter suggests *Spiritual Poems* as its subject, although it may have been one of the later *Blue Calendars.* Quoted in Roger Lhombreaud, "Une Amitié Anglaise de Pierre Louÿs: Onze Lettres Inédites à John Gray," *Revue de Littérature Comparée* 27 (Juillet–Septembre 1953): 354.

74. For Gray on Grünewald, see Gray to Raffalovich, 21 November 1904, Dominican Chaplaincy, Edinburgh. "Aide mémoire" is from Gray to Michael Field [Katherine Bradley], 29 January 1909, Berg Collection, New York Public Library, New York.

75. Gray, "The Redemption of Durtal," *The Dial* 4 (1896): 7, 9.

76. *Pageant* 1 (1896): 20–36.

77. *Pageant* 2 (1897): 113–34.

78. *The Dial* 5 (1897): 13–15. Reprinted as "Leda and the Swan" in Fletcher, pp. 82–85. Subsequent parenthetical page citations are to this text.

79. Gray to Raffalovich, 18 March 1903, National Library, Edinburgh.

80. *Letters of Ernest Dowson,* pp. 337, 372.

81. Letter from William Rothenstein, G. F. Sims Catalogue No. 25, item 245, quoted in Patricio Gannon, "John Gray: The Prince of Dreams," *Two Friends,* p. 110.

82. Lhombreaud, *Revue de Littérature Comparée,* p. 355.

83. Alexander Michaelson [Raffalovich], "Aubrey Beardsley," *Blackfriars* 9 (October 1928): 610.

84. The most explicit advocate of this view is Stanley Weintraub in *Beardsley: A Biography* (New York: George Braziller, 1967); see pp. 206–207, 213.

85. Michaelson [Raffalovich], "Aubrey Beardsley," p. 610. A regular allowance did not commence, however, until February 1897.

86. Michaelson [Raffalovich], "Aubrey Beardsley," p. 610.

87. Cf. Beardsley to Raffalovich, c. 11 May 1895, 15 May 1895 and December 1895–January 1896, *Letters of Aubrey Beardsley,* pp. 84–86, 109–10; also Miriam J. Benkowitz, *Aubrey Beardsley: An Account of His Life* (London: Hamish Hamilton, 1981), pp. 128–30 and passim.

88. *Letters of Beardsley,* pp. 86–90, 133, 210. In Gray's opinion the subject of the drawing was "a canting interpretation" of the first line of the book's opening poem. Quoted in Brian Reade and Frank Dickinson, eds., *Aubrey Beardsley Exhibition at the Victoria and Albert Museum* (1966), #555.

89. Gray, "Aubrey Beardsley," *La Revue Blanche* 16 (1898): 68. This translation was published as *Aubrey Beardsley: An Obituary Memoir* (Edinburgh: Tragara Press, 1980), p. 3.

90. *Letters of Beardsley,* p. 142. (Beardsley's suggestion of a review was not taken.) Subsequent parenthetical page citations to Beardsley's letters are to this edition.

91. See Thomas Jay Garbáty, "The French Coterie of the *Savoy* 1896," *PMLA* 80 (December 1960): 609–15.

92. Symons to Gray, no date, and Raffalovich to Gray, 1 February [no year], National Library, Edinburgh. Gray to Michael Field [Katherine Bradley], 24 October 1908, Berg Collection, New York Public Library. This is confirmed by the *Letters of Beardsley,* p. 142.

93. Michaelson [Raffalovich], "Aubrey Beardsley," p. 611. The quotation is from *Last Letters of Aubrey Beardsley,* John Gray, ed. (London: Longmans, Green, 1904), p. vi.

94. The account of Beardsley's conversion is indebted to Benkowitz, *Aubrey Beardsley,* pp. 172–76.

95. Descriptions this paragraph are from Gray's "Aubrey Beardsley," *La Revue Blanche,* p. 68, in the Tragara translation, p. 1 (see n. 89, this chapter).

96. Michaelson [Raffalovich], "Aubrey Beardsley," p. 613.

97. *Letters of Beardsley,* p. 302.

98. Gray preserved a calling-card from Edmond Perrier, naturalist, dated 29 April 1897, which enclosed other cards of introduction to notable figures of the scientific world. Gray also received cards from Thadée Natanson, Gustave Moreau, and several members of the French government. National Library, Edinburgh.

99. A. B. Jackson, *La Revue Blanche (1889–1903): Origine, Influence, Bibliographie* (Paris: M. J. Minard, 1960).

100. Fénéon to Gray, 9 January and 15 January 1895, John Gray Collection, John Rylands University Library of Manchester.

101. *La Revue Blanche* 12 (1897): 758–62. This piece as well as that on Aubrey Beardsley (see n. 103, this chapter) may have been translated into French for Gray.

102. Weintraub, *Beardsley,* pp. 206, 213. This view is stated more explicitly in a letter from Weintaub to the author, 24 January 1969. Brian Reade also talks about the "kindly talons" closing on Beardsley in *Aubrey Beardsley* (London: Studio Vista, 1967), p. 20.

103. "Aubrey Beardsley," *La Revue Blanche,* p. 70, in the Tragara translation, p. 6.

104. "Aubrey Beardsley," *La Revue Blanche,* p. 69 in the Tragara translation, p. 3.

105. Louÿs to Gray, 11 July 1899, Lhombreaud, "Une Amitié Anglaise," p. 356. Fénéon to Gray, 3 October 1898, John Gray Collection, John Rylands University Library of Manchester, England.

106. No. 209, *Catalogue 1: Anthony d'Offay, Books and Autograph Letters Mainly of the Eighteen-Nineties,* Gray papers, National Library, Edinburgh.

107. Lhombreaud, "Une Amitié Anglaise," p. 355.

F I V E. *Father Gray: The Poet as Priest* (pp. 182–224)

1. André Raffalovich to John Gray, no date, National Library, Edinburgh: "the Scots College was of your and Merri [*sic*] del Val's finding. . . ." Del Val was later made Cardinal.

2. Hart, "Memories of John Gray," Trudgian papers, p. 1; reprinted, somewhat altered, as "Some Memories of John Gray by the Reverend Dominic Hart," Brocard Sewell, ed., *The Innes Review* 2 (1975): 80–88.

3. As already pointed out, in later life Gray was known to refer punctiliously to England as "your country." Father Edwin Essex, "The Canon in Residence," Brocard Sewell, ed., *Two Friends: John Gray and André Raffalovich: Essays Biographical and Critical,* (Aylesford, Kent: Saint Albert's Press, 1963), p. 152.

4. Hart, "Memories," p. 2.

5. Mrs. William O'Brien [née Sophie Raffalovich], "Friends for Eternity: André Raffalovich and John Gray," *The Irish Monthly* 62 (November 1934): 701.

6. Frederick Baron Corvo [Frederick William Rolfe], *Hadrian the Seventh* (New York: Dover, 1969), pp. 239–43.

7. Gray to Raffalovich, 9 March 1901, National Library, Edinburgh: "Baron Corvo was one of us. There is a district legend of him, but you must have heard all the jokes. . . ."

8. Gray to Raffalovich, 1 November 1898, National Library, Edinburgh. All further correspondence between Gray and Raffalovich, cited parenthetically by date in the text, is from this source.

9. Reprinted in Ian Fletcher, ed., *The Poems of John Gray,* 1880–1920 British Author Series no. 1 (Greensboro, N.C.: ELT Press, 1988), pp. 85–86.

10. James Langdale to Brocard Sewell, no date, Sewell papers.

11. Gray to Fanny Langdale, 7 June 1902, Langdale papers. All further quotations from these letters are taken from this source.

12. "Works and Days," journal of Edith Cooper and Katherine Bradley [Michael Field], 1908 [BM Add. Ms. 46798 f. 202], British Library Manuscript Collections, London.

13. Brocard Sewell, *Footnote to the Nineties: A Memoir of John Gray and André Raffalovich* (London: Cecil and Amelia Woolf, 1968), p. 2, n.

14. Mary Raphael Gray, [Beatrice Hannah Gray], "A Sister's Reminiscences," *Two Friends,* pp. 101, 104.

15. Mary Raphael Gray to Helen Trudgian, 1962, Trudgian papers.

16. On the ordination, see Sewell, "John Gray and André Sebastian Raffalovich: A Biographical Outline," *Two Friends,* p. 28; on his health problems, Gray to Fanny Langdale, 7 June 1902, Langdale papers.

17. The rumor of the Pope's intervention is reported by Sewell in his essay, "John Gray and André Raffalovich," p. 28. According to Charles Ballantyne of Edinburgh, who knew both Raffalovich and Gray, it was said that Gray was prevented from preaching in London by the Marquess of Bute, a powerful Scottish Catholic.

18. Gray was writing his sister Sarah's new stepdaughter, Coralie Tinklar, 13 September 1902, John Gray Collection, John Rylands University Library of Manchester, England.

19. Edith Cooper, "Works and Days," [BM Add. Ms. 46798, ff. 203–04], British Library Manuscript Collections, London. The poem was originally sent to the "Michael Fields" on 29 December 1908; cf. Gray to Michael Field [Katherine Bradley] of that date, Henry W. and Albert A. Berg Collection, New York Public Library.

20. Found among the papers of the "Michael Fields," the poem was first published by John Gawsworth, in "Around My Shelves," *The Poetry Review* (January–February 1950), p. 22. Reprinted in Fletcher, p. 90.

21. Essex, p. 160.

22. Hart, "Memories," p. 5, and McMenemy, as reported to McCormack by Father Anthony Ross in conversation, April 1970.

23. Brocard Sewell, *Footnote to the Nineties,* p. 98.

24. *Man: Journal of the Royal Anthropological Institute* 3 (1903), item number 66, pp. 117–18.

25. Gray to Raffalovich, 7 and 13 October 1902, National Library, Edinburgh, and Sewell, *In the Dorian Mode: A Life of John Gray, 1866–1934* (Padstow, Cornwall: Tabb House, 1983), p. 100.

26. Moray McLaren, in an article in *The Universe* (26 May 1961), as reported in Sewell, "Gray and Raffalovich," pp. 28–29.

27. Essex, p. 162.

28. Sewell, *In the Dorian Mode,* p. 100.

29. First edition privately printed, 1903. Ensuing editions were *Ad Matrem* (London and Edinburgh: Sands and Co., 1904), and *Ad Matrem* (London: Catholic Truth Society, 1906). Reprinted in Fletcher, pp. 196–205, from which the preceding parenthetical page citation is taken.

Gray produced a similar set of poems the following year, to be published as *Verses for Tableaux Vivants* (London: privately printed, 1905).

30. Gray to Margaret George, 21 September 1925, upon presenting her with a copy of *Spiritual Poems.* Collection of Margaret George, Edinburgh.

31. Gray to Longmans, 21 September 1904, National Library, Edinburgh.

32. Alexander Michaelson [Raffalovich], "Aubrey Beardsley," *Blackfriars* 9 (October 1928): 614.

33. Gray to Longmans, 1 October 1904, National Library, Scotland.

34. *Last Letters of Aubrey Beardsley,* The Rev. John Gray, ed. (London: Longmans, Green, 1904), pp. vii, viii.

35. Gray to Longmans, 21 September 1904, National Library, Edinburgh.

36. Henry James to André Raffalovich, 7 November 1917, in *The Letters of Henry James,* Percy Lubbock, ed., 2 vols. (London: Macmillan, 1920) 2: 355–57.

37. Gray to Sarah Tinklar, 20 July 1904, papers of Brocard Sewell.

38. John Gray, *Saint Peter's, Edinburgh: A Brief Description of the Church and Its Contents* (Oxford: Basil Blackwell, 1925), p. 3.

39. Raffalovich took the name of Brother Sebastian and Gray, Brother Albert. Sewell, "Gray and Raffalovich," p. 33.

40. Mrs. William O'Brien [Sophie Raffalovich], "Friends for Eternity," p. 701.

41. Sewell, *In the Dorian Mode,* p. 113.

42. Gray once confided that it was actually after one that he and Raffalovich had admired from the window of his sickroom in Rome; statement by Kathleen O'Riordan, a parishioner of Father Gray's.

43. Hart, "Memories," p. 4.

44. Mrs. William O'Brien [Sophie Raffalovich], "Friends for Eternity," p. 705.

45. Walter Shewring, "Two Friends," *Two Friends,* p. 149.

46. Peter F. Anson, "Random Reminiscences of John Gray and André Raffalovich," *Two Friends,* p. 135.

47. Gray to Michael Field [Katherine Bradley], no date given, quoted in Sewell, *In the Dorian Mode,* p. 103.

48. Gray to Michael Field [Katherine Bradley], 10 June 1909, Berg Collection, New York Public Library.

49. William Rothenstein, *Men and Memories: Recollections of William Rothenstein,* 2 vols. (London: Faber and Faber, 1932) 1: 202.

50. Michael Field [Katherine Bradley] to Gray, 21 March 1893, National Library, Edinburgh. Gray had sent the copy with a covering letter to "Dear Sir," 3 March 1893 [Add. Ms. 45851] British Library Manuscript Collections, London.

51. "Works and Days" [BM Add. Ms. 46795, f. 38], British Library Manuscript Collections, London.

52. Gray's letters to the Michael Fields were returned to him by their executor, T. Sturge Moore, after their death. It seems that many of them—including this one—were destroyed. Edith Cooper refers to this exchange in her journal entry reviewing 1906; "Works and Days" [BM Add. Ms. 46795].

53. Michael Field [Katherine Bradley] to John Gray, no date, National Library, Edinburgh.

54. The hostess was a Mrs. MacDonald. Edith Cooper, "Works and Days" [BM Add. Ms. 46795, f. 172], British Library Manuscript Collections, London.

55. T. Sturge Moore, *Works and Days, from the Journal of Michael Field,* ed. T. and D. C. Sturge Moore (London: John Murray, 1933), p. 271. The book is composed of entries selected from the journal of the "Michael Fields" and from their letters (to Father Gray in particular), together with a commentary by T. Sturge Moore.

56. Michael Field [Katherine Bradley] to John Gray, no date, National Library, Edinburgh. All subsequent references to the Michael Fields's correspondence, most letters of which are undated, are to this collection.

57. "Works and Days" [BM Add. Ms. 46799, f. 144], British Library Manuscript Collections, London.

58. Gray to Michael Field [Katherine Bradley] 17 April 1907, Berg Collection, New York Public Library. All further references to correspondence from Gray to the Fields are from this source.

59. Mary Sturgeon, *Michael Field* (London: George G. Harrap and Co., 1922) pp. 38–39.

60. "Works and Days" [BM Add. Ms. 46796, f. 76], British Library Manuscript Collections, London.

61. Entry for 6 March 1910, "Works and Days" [BM Add. Ms. 46800, f. 49], British Library Manuscript Collections, London.

62. Entry for 27 October 1911, "Works and Days" [BM Add. Ms. 46801, f. 150], British Library Manuscript Collections, London.

63. Entry for December 1913, "Works and Days" [BM Add. Ms. 46803, f. 104], British Library Manuscript Collections, London. Gray's letters were not kept after February 1911.

64. *Works and Days,* p. 332, n. 1.

65. Charles Ricketts to Gray, no date, Beinecke Rare Book Room and Manuscript Library, Yale University, New Haven, Conn.

66. Entry for 27 October 1908, "Works and Days" [BM Add. Ms. 46798, f. 182], British Library Manuscript Collections, London.

67. Gray to Michael Field [Katherine Bradley], 1 July 1908, Berg Collection, New York Public Library.

68. Mrs. William O'Brien [Sophie Raffalovich], "Friends for Eternity," p. 703 and Alexander Michaelson [Raffalovich], "Aubrey Beardsley's Sister,"

Blackfriars 9 (November 1928): 675. Yeats immortalized Wright's grace and wit in the face of death in his "Upon a Dying Lady."

69. Gray to Fanny Langdale, 13 May 1920, Langdale papers.

70. Information on Raffalovich's financial difficulties is from taped conversation, Father John-Baptist Reeves. The information on importing desserts is from Charles Ballantyne, Edinburgh. On the financial support of Wright and Gill, see Raffalovich to Francis Wright, 1912–18, and Eric Gill to Raffalovich, 1914–20, both in the National Library, Edinburgh. For a discussion of Raffalovich's relationship with Eric Gill, see Fiona MacCarthy, *Eric Gill* (London: Faber and Faber, 1989), pp. 132–34 and Robert Speaight, *The Life of Eric Gill* (London: Methuen, 1966), pp. 72–73. Gray's complaint about the air raids is from Raffalovich to Melville Wright, 9 April 1916, National Library, Edinburgh.

71. Raffalovich to Charles Ballantyne, 7 June 1931, National Library, Edinburgh.

72. Firbank's biographers supplied the phrase, which mirrors Firbank's own view of Wilde. Gray and Raffalovich later appeared in two of Firbank's novels *Vainglory* and *Inclinations*. Brigid Brophy, *Prancing Novelist: A Defence of Fiction in the Form of a Critical Biography in Praise of Ronald Firbank* (London: Macmillan, 1973), pp. 274–75.

73. It is Essex who reports Gray's attempts "to withdraw [*Silverpoints*] from circulation" by "destroying any odd copies he was able to buy up." Essex, pp. 153–55.

74. Allan Neame to Brocard Sewell, 27 October 1964, Sewell papers.

75. Hart, "Memories," pp. 4–5.

76. Information from Father Anthony Ross, in conversation with McCormack, April 1970.

77. Hart, "Memories," p. 6.

78. Father Bernard Delany, "Sermon: Preached at the Mass of Requiem for Canon John Gray," Sewell, ed., *Two Friends,* p. 175.

79. Margaret Sackville, "At Whitehouse Terrace," Sewell, ed., *Two Friends,* p. 142, and the following quotation, p. 144.

80. Sackville, p. 146, and Essex, p. 165.

81. Father John-Baptist Reeves, taped conversation with Brocard Sewell.

82. Sackville, p. 146, and Anson, p. 137.

83. In Leon Edel, *Henry James, The Master: 1901–1916* (Philadelphia: J. B. Lippincott, 1972), pp. 407–408.

84. Essex, p. 156.

85. Anson, pp. 139–40.

86. Essex, pp. 155–56.

87. Anson, pp. 135–36.

S I X. *Father Gray: The Priest as Poet* (pp. 225–53)

1. "Ezra Pound," Walter E. Sutton, ed., *Ezra Pound: A Collection of Critical Essays* (Englewood Cliffs, N.J.: Prentice-Hall, 1963), p. 17.

2. Gray to Raffalovich, 22 March 1904, National Library, Edinburgh.

3. T. Sturge Moore to John Gawsworth, 21 March 1940, Reading University Library, England.

4. "A Sermon Preached at the Requiem of John Gray," Brocard Sewell, ed., *Two Friends: John Gray and André Raffalovich: Essays Biographical and Critical* (Aylesford, Kent: Saint Albert's Press, 1963), p. 175.

5. "Ezra Pound," p. 20.

6. Gray to Blunden, no date, Harry Ransom Humanities Research Center, University of Texas, Austin. The first page of the letter is missing, but an estimate of the date as October/November 1930, has been given by Peter J. Vernon, "The Letters of John Gray" (Ph.D. dissertation, University of London, 1976), p. 344.

7. For Masefield's request see his letter to Gray, 13 December 1905, National Library, Edinburgh. "The Tree of Knowledge" and "On the Holy Trinity" appeared in the *Oxford Book of Mystical Verse*, D. H. S. Nicholson and A. H. E. Less, eds. (Oxford: Clarendon, 1917), pp. 571–77. For "Sound" and the other *Silverpoints* poems see *An Anthology of Nineties Verse* (London: Elkin Mathews and Marrot, 1928). pp. 71–78. In his introduction to the latter book, Symons speaks of Gray's "Gallic elegance"; p. xx. A typical story of an attempt to collect Gray's nineties poetry by a young poet of the 1930s, John Gawsworth, can be found in "Two Poets 'J.G.'," *Two Friends*, pp. 167–72.

8. Ricketts to Gray, no date, Beinecke Rare Book and Manuscript Library, Yale University, New Haven, Conn.

9. Miscellaneous correspondence to Gray, National Library, Edinburgh.

10. Graham Greene to Jerusha McCormack, 13 October 1971. Greene described Raffalovich as a "sweet, cultured and most ugly Jew"; Raffalovich became a source for Eckman, an old Jew who had converted to Christianity in *Stamboul Train*. See Greene to his mother, 22 August 1932, quoted in Norman Sherry, *The Life of Graham Greene*, vol. 1: 1904–1939 (New York: Viking, 1989), p. 426.

11. Copies of the correspondence of Gray to Bottomley are in Sewell's private collection; the actual letters belong to Roger Lancelyn Green. Blunden to Gray, 1930–33, Special Collection, The University of Iowa, Iowa City. The Desmond Chute connection is in Raffalovich to Edward Playfair, 16 September 1930, "Letters of André Raffalovich to Edward Playfair," Brocard Sewell, ed., *The Antigonish Review* (Winter 1971), p. 56. The libraries of Raffalovich and Gray are described in Anthony d'Offay, *Books and Autograph Letters, Mainly of the Eighteen-Nineties* 1: Catalogue 1 (July 1961). Those listed here were originally in the Dominican Chaplaincy, Edinburgh, where a substantial number remain.

12. Gray to A. J. A. Symons, 6 May 1925 [Mss. Misc. GOR-GRA] Princeton University Library, Princeton, N.J. Reprinted in Ian Fletcher, ed., *The Poems of John Gray*, The 1880–1920 British Author Series 1 (Greensboro, N.C.: ELT Press, 1988), pp. 218, 234–66 (as noted). Subsequent parenthetical page citations are to Fletcher.

13. Ian Fletcher, "The Poetry of John Gray," *Two Friends*, p. 67.

14. "John Gray," *The Concise Encyclopedia of Modern World Literature*, Geoffrey Grigson, ed. (New York: Hawthorne Books, 1963), p. 151.

15. Gray, "Dods," *Blackfriars* 7 (October 1926): 640.

16. Walter Shewring, "Two Friends," *Two Friends*, p. 150; Father Edwin Essex, "The Canon in Residence," *Two Friends*, p. 163.

17. Peter F. Anson, "Random Reminiscences of Gray and Raffalovich," *Two Friends*, p. 140; Father John-Baptist Reeves, taped conversation with Brocard Sewell.

18. Hart recounts a 200-mile trek, "Memories of John Gray," Trudgian papers, pp. 7–8. It was by no means Gray's only walking tour of Europe.

19. Sewell, *In the Dorian Mode: A Life of John Gray, 1866–1934* (Padstow, Cornwall: Tabb House, 1983), pp. 187–88.

20. *Blackfriars* 6 (March 1925): 148–53.

21. Trudgian papers.

22. *The Long Road* (Oxford: Basil Blackwell, 1926), reprinted in Fletcher, p. 241. Subsequent parenthetical page citations are from this text. In the holograph manuscript, Gray divided the poem into different sections under different titles (such as "Rivers," below). Margaret George papers, Edinburgh.

23. Cf. his rendering of two Chinese poems, transliterated into German, in the course of his review of "A History of Universal Literature," *The Month* 407 (May 1898): 516, 517, reprinted in Fletcher, pp. 80–81, 86–87. The entire review reveals an unexpected intimacy with Chinese literature.

24. See Paul Fussell, *Abroad: British Literary Travelling Between the Wars* (Oxford: Oxford Univ. Press, 1980), particularly the chapter on "The Travel Atmosphere" and its analysis of literature of the road, pp. 50–64.

25. Ricketts to Gray, undated, Beinecke Rare Book and Manuscript Library, Yale University, New Haven, Conn.

26. Quoted in Sewell, *In the Dorian Mode*, p. 147.

27. As the story is recounted: Gray and Walker were making their way "along a steep slope of a mountain side with a hard rocky surface. Fr. Luke slipped on the rock and fell, then began to slide fast down the slope. As he slid he gathered momentum, and there was a nasty drop at the edge of the slope. The Canon, who was lower down, shouted to him to dig his stick into the ground. He tried but the stick broke and he continued to slide. The Canon simply sat down in his way. There was a hard collision and they both ended up on the brink, breathing hard and silently for some moments." This is said to have occurred some time in the 1920s, when Gray was about sixty. Father Reginald Ginns to Brocard Sewell, 24 January 1968, Sewell papers.

28. Speaight, *The Life of Eric Gill* (London: Methuen, 1966), pp. 72–73, 154, and MacCarthy, *Eric Gill* (London: Faber and Faber, 1989), pp. 132–33. Raffalovich had been acting as patron to Gill, who was a Dominican Tertiary. Gray visited Gill at Capel-y-ffin in 1924, perhaps to collect his nephew Norval, who regularly spent vacations with the Gills. Gray, much taken by Gill's experiment with an artistic/religious commune, may have drawn from it for his version of such a society in his novella, *Park*.

29. Alexandra Zaina, "The Prose Writings of John Gray," *Two Friends*, pp. 86–87.

30. Gray, "Hymns: A Suppressed Preface," *Blackfriars* 6 (October 1925): 579, 580. *Saint Peter's Hymns* (Kensington: Cayme Press, 1925) are reprinted in Fletcher, pp. 219–32.

31. *O Beata Trinitas: The Prayers of St Gertrude and St Mechtilde,* trans. John Gray (London: Sheed and Ward, 1927). This was reprinted in 1928 and again in 1936.

32. Jarrett to Gray, December 1933, quoted in Sewell, *In the Dorian Mode,* pp. 148–49. Gray was editor of the *Annals* from 1926 to 1933.

33. *Poems (1931)* (London: Sheed and Ward, 1931), reprinted in Fletcher, p. 269. Subsequent parenthetical page citations refer to this text.

34. Blunden to Gray, 16 February 1933; also Blunden to Gray, 28 April 1931, Special Collections, University of Iowa Libraries, Iowa City.

35. Hart, "Memories," p. 4.

36. *Park: A Fantastic Story* (Aylesford, Kent: Saint Albert's Press, 1966), p. 1. Subsequent parenthetical page citations refer to this text. The original was printed in a limited edition of 250 copies by Rene Hague and Eric Gill at Piggots, Buckinghamshire and published in London by Sheed and Ward in April, 1932.

Park was first published in four installments in *Blackfriars* 12 (November 1931): 682–95; 13 (January 1932): 45–51; 13 (March 1932): 158–63; 13 (April 1932): 231–42.

37. Trudgian, who had been in touch with Sister Mary Raphael [Beatrice Gray], considered *Park* to be the transcription of an actual dream. Sewell, *In the Dorian Mode,* p. 166.

38. Gray to Raffalovich, 26 May 1904, National Library, Edinburgh. The text is difficult to decipher.

The book itself explicitly suggests two sources: Mungo Park's *Travels into the Interior of Africa* (1799) and Herman Melville's *Typee,* incorrectly alluded to in the text as *Three Years [sic] in the Marquesas Islands.* Other literary sources are suggested by Bernard Bergonzi in his introduction to the 1966 edition of *Park* and by Zaina, "Prose Writings of Gray," pp. 95–96.

The following interpretation of Park is indebted to these two essays, as well as to Philip Healy's "Afterword" to his edition of *Park* (Manchester: Carcanet, 1966), pp. 109–27, and to Isobel Murray's perceptive review, "John Gray: The Person and the Work in Question," *Durham University Review* (June 1984), pp. 261–75.

39. *Blackfriars* 6 (March 1925): 151.

40. Quoted by Zaina, p. 95. Gray's sentiment echoes that of Blake's "The Little Black Boy." It is impossible to say whether Gray's opinion was entirely free from irony. Father John-Baptist Reeves recalls that Gray treated one of his African nephews, who was of mixed blood, "as an inferior being"; taped conversation with Brocard Sewell.

"'Si jamais je meurs' I should like to wear the habit and purple stole & have bare feet to look pitiable exposed to gaze upon the floor of S: Peter's." Gray to Michael Field, 7 November 1910, Berg Collection, New York Public Library.

41. R. D. Laing, *The Politics of Experience* (New York: Pantheon, 1967), pp. 128–45.

42. Besides "Dorian," Gray also signed letters as "Giacopone" or "Jacopone" to Raffalovich, and "Zifia Giovanni" and "Oheim" to his step-nieces. He earned the nicknames of the "Prince of Dreams" from Olive Custance, and "Father Silverpoints" from the "Michael Fields."

43. Alan Neame to Brocard Sewell, 27 October 1964, Sewell papers.

44. Gray to Blunden, 20 February 1933, Harry Ransom Humanities Research Center, University of Texas, Austin.

45. Sewell, *In the Dorian Mode,* p. 166.

46. Anson, *Two Friends,* pp. 135–36. Anson slightly misquotes this famous passage from Pater's *The Renaissance.*

Epilogue (pp. 254–60)

1. Sewell, *In the Dorian Mode: A Life of John Gray, 1866–1934* (Padstow, Cornwall: Tabb House, 1983), pp. 136, 162.

2. Gray to Gordon Bottomley, 9 October 1929, papers of Roger Lancelyn Green.

3. Raffalovich to Norman Wright, 8 April 1930, National Library, Edinburgh.

4. Beerbohm to Raffalovich, 17 June 1930, National Library, Edinburgh.

5. Father Edwin Essex, "The Canon in Residence," Brocard Sewell, ed. *Two Friends: John Gray and André Raffalovich: Essays Biographical and Critical* (Aylesford, Kent: Saint Albert's Press, 1963), p. 163.

6. Sewell, *In the Dorian Mode,* p. 182.

7. Gray to Bottomley, 1 December 1933, papers of Roger Lancelyn Green.

8. Gray to Fanny Langdale, 23 December 1933, Langdale papers.

9. Brocard Sewell, "John Grand and André Sebastian Raffalovich: A Biographical Outline," Sewell, ed., *Two Friends,* pp. 45–46, to which the following passage is also indebted.

10. Reverend Dominic Hart, "Some Memories of John Gray," ed. Brocard Sewell, *The Innes Review* 2 (1975): 9.

11. "André Raffalovich," *Blackfriars* 15 (June 1943): 406.

12. Margaret George, holograph of her memories of John Gray, National Library, Edinburgh.

13. Sarah Gray Tinklar to Frances Langdale, 20 July 1934, Langdale papers.

14. Father Bernard Delany, "Sermon: Preached at the Mass of Requiem for Canon John Gray," Sewell, ed., *Two Friends,* pp. 175–76.

15. Reported on different occasions, many years apart. To Sewell by Sister Mary Barbara, 18 March 1969; to McCormack in April 1970 by Father Anthony Ross, then director of the Dominican Chaplaincy, Edinburgh; more recently by Sewell, who had it from a "hard-headed elderly friend in Edinburgh," who reported several appearances of the ghost; Sewell to McCormack, 4 November 1980.

⁂[*Bibliography*]⁂

Primary Sources

I. MANUSCRIPT AND RECORD COLLECTIONS

Austin Texas. The University of Texas, Harry Ransom Humanities Research Center.
Cambridge, Mass. Houghton Library.
Edinburgh. The Dominican Chaplaincy, George Square.
Edinburgh. The National Library of Scotland.
Iowa City, Iowa. The University of Iowa Libraries, Special Collections.
London. The British Library.
London. Foreign Office Library.
London. General Register Office.
London. London University Records.
Los Angeles. The University of California, William Andrew Clark Memorial Library.
Manchester, England. The John Rylands University Library of Manchester, John Gray Collection.
New Haven, Conn. Yale University, The Beinecke Rare Book and Manuscript Library.
New York. Donald Hyde Collection.
New York. New York Public Library, Henry W. and Albert A. Berg Collection; Astor, Lenox and Tilden Foundations.
Princeton, N.J. Princeton University Library.
Private Collections: Papers of Margaret George, Roger Lancelyn Green, James Langdale, Jacqueline Paulhan, Brocard Sewell, Helen Trudgian.
Reading, England. The University of Reading Library.

II. WORKS BY JOHN GRAY

Gray's works are arranged chronologically by year, but within the year they are listed alphabetically, as it is not always possible to establish the month in which they appeared.

1889
"Les Goncourt." *The Dial* 1 (1889): 9–13.
"The Great Worm." *The Dial* 1 (1889): 14–18.

1890
"Obituary. Dubois-Pillet." *Academy* 957 (September 1890): 205.

"Sonnet: Translated from Paul Verlaine." *The Artist and Journal of Home Culture* 11 (1 August 1890): 241.

1892

Bourget, Paul. *A Saint and Others: From the French of Paul Bourget.* Translated by John Gray. London: Osgood, McIlvaine and Co., 1892.

Couperus, Louis. *Ecstasy: A Study of Happiness.* Translated by A. Teixeira de Mattos and John Gray with a "Translators' Note" by John Gray. London: Henry and Co., 1892.

de Banville, Théodore. *The Kiss.* Translated by John Gray. Performed by the Independent Theatre, 4 March 1892. Published in an edition by Ian Fletcher, Edinburgh: Tragara Press, 1983.

"Les Demoiselles de Sauve." *The Dial* 2 (1892): 24. Reprinted in *Silverpoints* (1893), p. 5.

"Dix Portraits d'Hommes par Paul Bourget." *Academy* 1061 (3 September 1892): 188.

"Heart's Demesne." *The Dial* 2 (1892): 23. Reprinted in *Silverpoints* (1893), p. 6.

"The Modern Actor." *Albemarle* 2 no. 1 (July 1892): 20–24. Reprinted: "Appendix II: The Modern Actor." Brocard Sewell, *Footnote to the Nineties: A Memoir of John Gray and André Raffalovich.* London: Cecil and Amelia Woolf, 1968, pp. 102–107.

"Parsifal: Imitated from the French of Paul Verlaine." *The Dial* 2 (1892): 8. Reprinted in *Silverpoints* (1893), p. 22.

"Note." *In the Garden of Citrons: Idyll in One Act by Emilio Montanaro.* Translated by J. T. Grein. London: Henry and Co., 1892.

1893

"Fiorenzo of Maggiolo." *The Butterfly* 1 (June 1893): 69–78.

"Garth Wilkinson." *The Dial* 3 (1893): 21–24.

"The Loves of the Age of Stone." *The Butterfly* 1 (July 1893): 142–51.

"Old Gouth." *The Butterfly* 1 (October 1893): 335–44.

"A Hymn Translated from the Italian of St. Francis of Assisi." *The Dial* 3 (1893): 31–32. Reprinted in *Spiritual Poems* (1896), pp. 54–57, and in *Blackfriars* 7 (December 1926): 781–83.

"Pacidejanus Victor." *The Butterfly* 1 (September 1893): 261–75.

Silverpoints. London: Elkin Mathews and John Lane, 1893. Reprinted: London: The Minerva Press, 1973.

1894

"The Advantages of Civilization." *The Butterfly* 2 (November 1894): 51–56.

The Blackmailers. Performed at the Prince of Wales Theatre, 17 June 1894. (Never published.)

The Blue Calendar 1895. A Book of Carols. London: privately printed, 24 December 1894.

Sour Grapes. Produced at the West Theatre, Albert Hall on 17 April 1894. (Never published.)

1895

The Blue Calendar 1896. Twelve Sundry Carols. London: privately printed, 14 December 1895. "November: The Ox," reprinted as "The Ox" in *Pageant* 1 (1896): 184.

Extract from an article on Albert Chevalier. Quoted in *Albert Chevalier: A Record by Himself.* London: John Macqueen, 1895, p. 123.

A Northern Aspect. The Ambush of Young Days. Two Duologues. Coauthored with André Raffalovich. London: privately printed, 12 May 1895.

"A Sonnet for March." *The Month* (March 1895): 428.

1896

"Battledore." *The Dial* 4 (1896): 34–36.

"The Beauties of Nature." *The Dial* 4 (1896): 15–17.

The Blue Calendar 1897. London: privately printed, 24 December 1896.

Fifty Songs. By Thomas Campion. Edited by John Gray. London: Hacon and Ricketts, 1896.

"The Flying Fish." *The Dial* 4 (1896): 1–6. Reprinted, with some changes, in *A Sailor's Garland.* Edited by John Masefield. London: Methuen, 1906, and in *The Long Road* (1926), pp. 31–38.

"The Forge." *Savoy* 2 (April 1896): 85–86.

"Niggard Truth." *Pageant* 1 (1896): 20–36.

Nymphidia and The Muses Elizium. By Michael Drayton. Edited by John Gray. London: Hacon and Ricketts, 1896.

Poems and Songs. By Sir John Suckling. Edited by John Gray. London: Hacon and Ricketts, 1896.

"The Redemption of Durtal." *The Dial* 4 (1896): 7–11.

Spiritual Poems: Chiefly Done out of Several Languages. London: Hacon and Ricketts, 1896.

1897

Collected Works. By Friedrich Nietzsche. Edited by Alexander Tille. Volume 10, *A Genealogy of Morals.* Translated by William A. Haussmann. *Poems.* Translated by John Gray. New York: Macmillan, 1897, pp. 233–89. Reprinted with identical titles, but changing volume 10 to volume 1. London: T. Fisher Unwin, 1899.

"Daphné." *La Revue Blanche* 12 (1897): 758–62.

"Leda." "The Swan." *The Dial* 5 (1897): 13–15.

"Light." *Pageant* 2 (1897): 113–34.

"Nietzsche as Poet." *Nietzsche as Critic, Philosopher, Poet and Prophet.* Compiled by Thomas Common. "Part 3. Nietzsche as Poet," translated by John Gray. London: Grant Richards, 1901, pp. 169–88.

"On the South Coast of Cornwall." *Pageant* 2 (1897): 82.

Poems and Sonnets. By Henry Constable. Edited by John Gray. London: Hacon and Ricketts, 1897.

"Saint Ives, Cornwall." *The Dial* 5 (1897): 12.

1898

"Aubrey Beardsley." *La Revue Blanche* 16 (1898): 68–70. Reprinted in *The Aylesford Review* 8 (Autumn 1966): 95–96. Translated as *Aubrey Beardsley: An Obituary Memoir*. Edinburgh: privately printed, 1980.

"Clair de lune," "Green," "Mon Dieu m'a dit," "Parsifal." *Bibelot* 5 (Feb. 1898): 74, 78, 80–82.

The Fourth and Last Blue Almanack 1898. London, privately printed, 1898.

"A History of Universal Literature." *The Month* 407 (May 1898): 512–24. Includes two untitled translations in verse by Gray.

Satyros and Prometheus. By J. W. von Goethe. Translated by John Gray. Edited by Alexander Tille. Glasgow: Glasgow Goethe Society, 1898.

Sonnets. By Sir Philip Sidney. Edited by John Gray. London: Hacon and Ricketts, 1898.

1903

Fourteen Scenes in the Life of the Blessed Virgin Mary. London: privately printed, 1903. Other editions: *Ad Matrem: Poems by John Gray*. London and Edinburgh: Sands and Co., 1904; and *Ad Matrem*. London: Catholic Truth Society, 1906.

"A Phial." *Venture* 1 (1903): 233–34. Reprinted as *A Phial*. Edinburgh: Tragara Press, 1954.

"Some Scottish String Figures." *Man: Journal of the Royal Anthropological Institute* 3 (1903), item number 66, pp. 117–18.

1904

Last Letters of Aubrey Beardsley. By Aubrey Beardsley. Edited with an introduction by John Gray. London: Longmans, Green, 1904.

"Saint Gregory the Great." *Downside Review* 23 (1904): 1.

1905

"A Pastor and Master: In Memoriam." *The Month* 106 (1905): 514–16.

Verses for Tableaux Vivants. London: privately printed, 1905.

"Via Vita Veritas." *Venture* 2 (1905): 62.

1906

"Wings in the Dark," "The Flying Fish." Reprinted in *A Sailor's Garland*. Selected and edited by John Masefield. London: Methuen, 1906, pp. 5, 18.

1907

"Introduction." Catalogue of an Exhibition of Children's Toys (held at the Outlook Tower, Castlehill, Edinburgh). Edinburgh: privately printed, 1907.

1908

"The Emperor and the Bird." Published by John Gawsworth in an unsigned article, "Around My Shelves," *The Poetry Review* (January–February 1950): 22. Originally sent to the "Michael Fields" for Christmas, 1908.

1912

"Children in thy presence met." *The Westminster Hymnal.* London: Burns Oates, 1912, no. 175.

"When in the crib so weak and small." *The Westminster Hymnal.* London: Burns Oates, 1912, no. 28.

1917

"The Tree of Knowledge" and "On the Holy Trinity." *The Oxford Book of English Mystical Verse.* Edited by D. H. S. Nicholson and A. H. E. Lee. Oxford: Clarendon, 1917, pp. 571–74 and 574–77. Reprinted: 1918, 1920, 1923, 1927, 1932.

1921

"Death." *Blackfriars* 2 (May 1921): 120.

1922

Vivis. Ditchling, Sussex: St. Dominic's Press, 1922.

1924

"God-made and Machine-made." *Blackfriars* 5 (November 1924): 451–57.

1925

"Hymns: A Suppressed Preface." *Blackfriars* 6 (October 1925): 578–81.

"Man's Visible Works." *Blackfriars* 6 (1925): 450–55.

On Hymn Writing. Kensington: Cayme Press, 1925.

Saint Peter's, Edinburgh: A Brief Description of the Church and Its Contents. Oxford: Basil Blackwell, 1925.

Saint Peter's Hymns. Kensington: Cayme Press, 1925.

"Speciosae et Delicatae Assimilari Filiam Sion: A Poem." *Blackfriars* 6 (January 1925): 41. Reprinted in *St. Peter's Hymns* (1925), pp. 34–35, and in *Poems (1931)*, pp. 34–35.

"Winter Walking." *Blackfriars* 6 (March 1925): 148–53.

1926

"Brokenborough." *Blackfriars* 7 (November 1926): 693–99.

"Dods." *Blackfriars* 7 (October 1926): 637–42.

"Excursion." *Blackfriars* 7 (February 1926): 80–85.

"Hymn to the Child Jesus." *Annals of the Holy Childhood* (February 1926): 5.

"An Island Cloud-Factory." *Blackfriars* 7 (June 1926): 370–75.

The Long Road. Oxford: Basil Blackwell, 1926.

"The Night-Nurse Goes Her Round." *Blackfriars* 7 (March 1926): 134. Reprinted in *The Long Road* (1926), p. 45.

Sound: A Poem. London: Curwen Press, 1926.

"Wings in the Dark," "Charleville." *Poetry of the Nineties.* Edited by C. E. Andrews and M. O. Percival. New York: Harcourt, Brace, 1926.

1927

"Allanwater." *Blackfriars* 8 (May 1927): 298–303.

"Baby-Clothes." *Annals of the Holy Childhood* (November 1927): 7.

"Cyder." *Blackfriars* 8 (August 1927): 499–504.

"Helichrysum." *Blackfriars* 8 (December 1927): 725. Reprinted in *Poems (1931)*, p. 17.

"The Lord Looks at Peter." *Blackfriars* 8 (April 1927): 238. Reprinted in *Poems (1931)*, p. 37.

"Mane Nobiscum Domine." *Blackfriars* 8 (May 1927): 280. Reprinted in *Poems (1931)*, p. 36.

"Nature-Morte." *Blackfriars* 8 (September 1927): 544.

O Beata Trinitas: The Prayers of St. Gertrude and St. Mechtilde. Translated by John Gray. London: Sheed and Ward, 1927. Reprinted: *The True Prayers of St. Gertrude and St. Mechtilde*, 1928 and 1936.

"October." *Blackfriars* 8 (November 1927): 688–93.

"Roxburgh." *Blackfriars* 8 (February 1927): 104. Reprinted as "Roxburghshire," *Poems (1931)*, pp. 24–25.

1928

"Charter Alley." *Blackfriars* 9 (January 1928): 30–34.

"Dialogue." *Blackfriars* 9 (May 1928): 304–308.

"Ils ont Heurtés Les Portes d'Or of Henri de Régnier." *Blackfriars* 9 (September 1928): 555.

"Lean Back and Press the Pillow Deep," "Complaint," "Les Demoiselles de Sauve," "Sound," "Mishka," "On a Picture," and "Crocuses in Grass." *An Anthology of Nineties Verse*. Selected and edited by A. J. A. Symons. London: Elkin Mathews and Marrot, 1928, pp. 71–78.

"Trespassers Will Be Prosecuted." *Blackfriars* 9 (March 1928): 164–69.

1929

"Birthday Wishes." *Blackfriars* 10 (February 1929): 847. Reprinted in *Poems (1931)*, p. 26.

"Ettrickdale." *Blackfriars* 10 (April 1929): 1016. Reprinted in *Poems (1931)*, pp. 22–23.

"The Parting Guest." *Blackfriars* 10 (January 1929): 786–90. Reprinted: "Appendix II," *In the Dorian Mode: A Life of John Gray, 1866–1934*. Padstow, Cornwall: Tabb House, 1983, pp. 222–26.

1930

"Audi Alteram Partem." *Blackfriars* 11 (May 1930): 310–11. Reprinted in *Poems (1931)*, pp. 18–19.

The Child's Daily Missal. Compiled by Dom Gaspar Lefebvre, and Elisabeth van Elewyck. Translated by John Gray. Lophem near Bruges, Belgium: Liturgical Apostolate, 1930.

"Evening." *Blackfriars* 11 (February 1930): 106–107. Reprinted in *Poems (1931)*, pp. 28–29.

"In North Iceland, 1914." *Blackfriars* 11 (September 1930): 558–59. Reprinted in *Poems (1931)* as "Poem," pp. 10–11.

"On Aqueducts." *Blackfriars* 11 (January 1930): 22–24. Reprinted in *Poems (1931)*, pp. 12–15.

1931

"Andante." *Blackfriars* 12 (January 1931): 33–34. Reprinted in *Poems (1931)*, pp. 32–33.

"Holy Communion." *Annals of the Holy Childhood* (February 1931): 1.

"Ode." *Blackfriars* 12 (April 1931): 237–43. Ode. Reprint from *Blackfriars*, 1931. Reprinted in *Poems (1931)*, pp. 1–9.

"Odiham." *Blackfriars* 12 (May 1931): 312–13. Reprinted in *Poems (1931)*, pp. 30–31.

Poems (1931). London: Sheed and Ward, 1931.

"The Kennet," "The Night Nurse Goes Her Round," "Compunction," "Enough of the World is Mine," "The Flying Fish (II)." *An Anthology of Contemporary Catholic Poetry*. Edited by Maurice Leahy with a preface by D. B. Wyndham-Lewis. London: Cecil Palmer, 1931, pp. 61–65.

1932

Park: A Fantastic Story. London: Sheed and Ward, 1932. Previously published in installments in *Blackfriars* 12 (November 1931): 682–95; 13 (January 1932): 45–51; 13 (March 1932): 158–63; 13 (April 1932): 231–42. Reprinted: *Park: A Fantastic Story*. Edited, with an introduction by Bernard Bergonzi. Aylesford, Kent: Saint Albert's Press, 1966; and *Park: A Fantastic Story*. Edited, with afterword by Philip Healy. Manchester: Carcanet Press, 1984.

"Sound" and "Song of the Stars." *Known Signatures*. Selected and edited by John Gawsworth (London: Rich and Cowan, 1932), pp. 54–56.

1934

"André Raffalovich." *Blackfriars* 15 (June 1934): 405–407.

1948

"On a Picture." *Fin de Siècle: A Selection of Late 19th Century Literature and Art*. Chosen by Nevile Wallis. London: Allan Wingate, 1948, p. 56.

1951

"Song of the Scots College, Rome." *Saint Peter's College Magazine*, Cardross (June 1951). Reprinted in Brocard Sewell, *Footnote to the Nineties*, pp. 113–14.

1953

"Voyage à Cythère," "Clair de lune," "Spleen." Ruth Zabriskie Temple, *Critic's Alchemy: A Study of the Introduction of French Symbolism into England*. New York: Twayne, 1953, pp. 322–23.

1954

A Phial. Edinburgh: Tragara Press, 1954.

1958

The Person in Question. With a note by Patricio Gannon. Buenos Aires: Colombo, 1958. Reprinted: "The Person in Question." *Antigonish Review* 1 (1971): 67–75; and "Appendix I: The Person in Question." *In the Dorian Mode: A Life of John Gray, 1866–1934.* Padstow, Cornwall: Tabb House, 1983, pp. 214–22.

1961

"Saint Christopher." *Frederick Rolfe and Others: A Miscellany of Essays.* Edited by Brocard Sewell. Aylesford, Kent: Saint Albert's Press, 1961, pp. 38–39.

1965

"The Barber," "Mishka," "Je pleurs dans les coins. . . ," "Lean Back and Press the Pillow Deep," "Sensation," and "Charleville." *Poets of the 'Nineties: A Biographical Anthology.* Selected and edited by Derek Stanford. London: Bajer, 1965, pp. 182–86.

1966

"On a Picture," "Poem," "A Crucifix," "Parsifal Imitated from the French of Paul Verlaine," "Femmes Damnées," "The Barber," "Le Voyage à Cythère," and "Mishka." *Aesthetes and Decadents of the 1890's: An Anthology of British Poetry and Prose.* Selected and edited by Karl Beckson. New York: Vintage, 1966, pp. 101–108. Revised edition. Chicago: Academy Chicago, 1981, pp. 101–108.

1967

"Voyage to Cythera," "To a Madonna," "Condemned Women," "Moonlight," "Green," "God Has Spoken," "Le Chevalier Malheur," "A Crucifix," "Parsifal," "Flowers," "Charleville," "Sensation," "Poem," "Mishka," "The Barber." *The Symbolist Poem.* Edited with introduction by Edward Engelberg. New York: E. P. Dutton, 1967, pp. 122–26, 149, 156, 157–60, 163, 177–78, 179, 240–43.

1968

"Appendix IV: Song of the Scots College, Rome." Brocard Sewell, *Footnote to the Nineties: A Memoir of John Gray and André Raffalovich.* London: Cecil and Amelia Woolf, 1968, pp. 113–14.

1970

"Lord, If Thou Art Present," "Les Demoiselles de Sauve," "Charleville," "Femmes Damnées," "Spleen," "Poem," "The Barber." *Poetry of the Nineties.* Selected and edited by R. K. R. Thornton. Baltimore: Penguin, 1970, pp. 110, 143, 173, 175, 178, 191, 206.

1983

John Gray: Five Fugitive Poems. Edited by Ian Fletcher. London: Eric and Joan Stevens, 1983.

1987

"Les Demoiselles de Sauve," "Wings in the Dark," "The Barber," "Mishka," "The Vines," "Poem," "Spleen," "Battledore," "'They say, in other days,'" "Tobias and the Angel," "The Flying Fish," "On the South Coast of Cornwall." *The New Oxford Book of Victorian Verse,* edited by Christopher Ricks. Oxford: Oxford Univ. Press, 1987.

1988

The Poems of John Gray. Edited by Ian Fletcher. The 1880–1920 British Authors Series, no. 1. Greensboro, N.C.: ELT Press, 1988.

Secondary Sources (Selected)

I. BIBLIOGRAPHIES

Anderson, Alan. "Bibliography of John Gray." In *Two Friends: John Gray and André Raffalovich.* Ed. Brocard Sewell. Aylesford, Kent: Saint Albert's Press, 1963, pp. 178–87.

Cevasco, G. A. "John Gray (1866–1934): A Primary Bibliography and an Annotated Bibliography of Writings about Him." *English Literature in Transition* 19 (1976): 49–63.

Fletcher, Ian. "Amendments and Additions to a Bibliography of John Gray." *English Literature in Transition* 22 (1979): 62–67.

McCormack, Jerusha. "Bibliography: Works by John Gray." In "The Person in Question: John Gray. A Critical and Biographical Study." Ph.D. diss., Brandeis University, 1973, pp. 262–68.

II. BOOKS, PARTS OF BOOKS, ARTICLES, AND STUDIES

Anson, Peter F. "Random Reminiscences of Gray and Raffalovich." In *Two Friends: John Gray and André Raffalovich.* Ed. Brocard Sewell. Aylesford, Kent: Saint Albert's Press, 1963, pp. 134–41.

Beardsley, Aubrey. *The Letters of Aubrey Beardsley.* Ed. Henry Maas, J. L. Duncan, and W. G. Good. Rutherford, N.J.: Fairleigh Dickinson Univ. Press, 1970.

Beerbohm, Max. "Appendix A: Oscar Wilde by [Max Beerbohm masquerading as] an American." In *Max Beerbohm: Letters to Reggie Turner.* Ed. Rupert Hart-Davis. London: Hart-Davis, 1964.

Benkovitz, Miriam J. *Aubrey Beardsley: An Account of His Life.* London: Hamish Hamilton, 1981.

Bergonzi, Bernard. "John Gray's *Park,*" *Aylesford Review* 7 (Winter 1965/Spring 1966): 206–15. Reprinted as "Introduction," *Park.* Aylesford, Kent: Saint Albert's Press, 1966, pp. i—xiii.

———. "John Gray," *The Turn of the Century: Essays on Victorian and Modern English Literature.* New York: Barnes and Noble, 1973.

Bradley, Katherine and Edith Cooper [Michael Field]. *Works and Days: From the Journal of Michael Field.* Edited by T. and D. C. Sturge Moore. London: John Murray, 1933.

Burdett, Osbert. *The Beardsley Period*. London: John Lane, 1925.

Cammell, Charles Richard. *Heart of Scotland*. London: Robert Hale, 1956.

Campbell, John L. and Trevor H. Hall. *Strange Things: The Story of Fr. Allan McDonald, Ada Goodrich Freer, and the Society for Psychical Research's Enquiry into Highland Second Sight*. London: Routledge and Kegan Paul, 1968.

Cevasco, G. A. *John Gray*. Boston: Twayne, 1982.

Croft-Cooke, Rupert. "Wilde, Gray and Raffalovich." In *Feasting with Panthers: A New Consideration of Some Late Victorian Writers*. New York: Holt, Rinehart and Winston, 1967.

Davray, Henry D. "Mallarmé as I Knew Him." *Horizon* 7 (May 1943): 342–53.

Delany, Father Bernard. "A Sermon Preached at the Requiem of John Gray." In *Two Friends,* ed. Sewell, pp. 173–77.

Dowling, Linda. "Nature and Decadence: John Gray's *Silverpoints*." *Victorian Poetry* 15, no. 2 (Summer 1977): 159–69.

Dowson, Ernest. *The Letters of Ernest Dowson*. Ed. Desmond Flower and Henry Maas. London: Cassell and Co.

Ellmann, Richard. *Oscar Wilde*. New York: Knopf, 1988.

Ellmann, Richard, E. D. H. Johnson and Alfred L. Bush. *Wilde and the Nineties: An Essay and an Exhibition*. Ed. Charles Ryskamp. Princeton, N.J.: Princeton Univ. Library, 1966.

Essex, Father Edwin. "The Canon in Residence." In *Two Friends,* ed. Sewell, pp. 152–66.

Farmer, Albert J. *Le Mouvement Esthétique et Décadent en Angleterre (1873–1900)*. Paris: Librarie Ancienne d'Honoré Champion, 1931.

Fletcher, Ian. *The Poems of John Gray*. The 1880–1920 British Authors Series, no. 1. Greensboro, North Carolina: ELT Press, 1988.

———. "The Poetry of John Gray," In *Two Friends,* ed. Sewell, pp. 50–69.

Gannon, Patricio. "John Gray: The Prince of Dreams." In *Two Friends,* ed. Sewell, pp. 106–19.

Garbáty, Thomas Jay. "The French Coterie of the *Savoy*." 80 (December 1960): 609–15.

Gawsworth, John. "Two Poets 'J.G.'" In *Two Friends,* ed. Sewell, pp. 167–72.

Gill, Eric. *Autobiography*. London: Jonathan Cape, 1940.

Gordon, D. J. "Aubrey Beardsley at the V. and A." *Encounter* 27 (October 1966): 3–16.

"Gray, John." *Foreign Office Lists: 1892–94, 1898*.

Gray, Mary Raphael [Beatrice Hannah]. "A Sister's Reminiscences." In *Two Friends,* ed. Sewell, pp. 100–105.

Grein, Alice Augusta [Michael Orme]. *J. T. Grein: The Story of a Pioneer 1862–1935*. London: John Murray, 1936.

Grigson, Geoffrey. "John Gray." In *The Concise Encyclopedia of Modern World Literature*. New York: Hawthorne, 1963, pp. 150–51.

———. "John Gray, Dorian Gray." *New Statesman* 65, no. 1676 (26 April 1963): 644. Reprinted in *The Contrary View: Glimpses of Fudge and Gold*. London: Macmillan, 1974, pp. 177–83.

Halperin, Joan Ungersma. *Félix Fénéon: Aesthete and Anarchist in Fin-de-Siècle Paris*. New Haven: Yale University Press, 1988.

Harris, Frank. *Oscar Wilde: His Life and Confessions*. New York: Garden City Publishing, 1930.

Hart, Reverend Dominic. "Some Memories of John Gray." ed. Brocard Sewell. *The Innes Review* 2 (1975): 80–88.

Hichens, Robert S. *The Green Carnation*. London: William Heinemann, 1894.

Jackson, Holbrook. *The Eighteen Nineties*. London: Jonathan Cape, 1931.

Le Gallienne, Richard. "John Gray." In *Retrospective Reviews: A Literary Log*. London: John Lane, 1896, pp. 229–32.

Lhombreaud, Roger. "Une Amitié Anglaise de Pierre Louÿs: Onze Lettres Inédites à John Gray." *Revue de Littérature Comparée* 27 (Juillet–Septembre 1953): 343–57.

———. "Arcades Ambo: The Poetical Friendship of John Gray and Pierre Louÿs." In *Two Friends*, ed. Sewell, pp. 120–33. An edited version of "Une Amitié Anglaise," in *Revue de Littérature Comparée*.

———. *Arthur Symons: A Critical Biography*. London: Unicorn Press, 1963.

McAlpine, Margaret Mary. "John Gray: A Critical and Biographical Study." Master's thesis, University of Manchester, 1967.

McCormack, Jerusha. "The Disciple: John Gray/Dorian Gray." *Journal of the Eighteen-Nineties Society* 5–6 (1975/76): 13–21.

———. "John Gray's Father and Father John Gray." *Durham University Journal* (December 1985): 113–20.

———. "The Person in Question: John Gray. A Critical and Biographical Study." Ph.D. diss., Brandeis University, 1973.

Meadmore, William. *Lucien Pissarro: Un Coeur Simple*. London: Constable, 1962.

Morgan, Bayard Quincy. *A Critical Bibliography of German Literature in English Translation, 1481–1927*. New York: Scarecrow, 1965.

Muddiman, Bernard. *The Men of the Nineties*. London: H. Danielson, 1920.

Murray, Isobel. "John Gray: The Person and the Work in Question." *Durham University Journal* (June 1984): 261–75.

Nelson, James G. *The Early Nineties: A View from the Bodley Head*. Cambridge, Mass.: Harvard Univ. Press, 1971.

O'Brien, Mrs. William [Sophie Raffalovich]. "Friends for Eternity: André Raffalovich and John Gray," *The Irish Monthly* 62 (November 1934): 699–706.

Raffalovich, Marc-André [Alexander Michaelson]. "Aubrey Beardsley." *Blackfriars* 9 (Oct. 1928): 609–16.

———. "Aubrey Beardsley's Sister." *Blackfriars* 9 (November 1928): 669–75.

———. "Edward Burne-Jones." *Blackfriars* 9 (March 1928): 152–59.

———. "Giles and Miles and Isabeau." *Blackfriars* 9 (January 1928): 18–29.

———. "Isis Unveiled." *Blackfriars* 9 (September 1928): 533–40.

———. "L'Affaire Oscar Wilde." *Archives de L'Anthropologie Criminelle de Criminologie et de Psychologie Normale et Pathologique* 10 (1895): 445–77. Reprinted under separate cover as *L'Affaire Oscar Wilde* (Lyon: A. Storck, 1895).

———. "Letters of André Raffalovich to Edward Playfair." Ed. Brocard Sewell. *Antigonish Review* (Winter 1971): 53–66.

———. "Oscar Wilde." *Blackfriars* 8 (November 1927): 694–702. Reprinted in Sewell, *Footnote to the Nineties*, pp. 108–22.

———. "Parallels." *Blackfriars* 10 (January 1929): 779–85.

————. *Uranisme et Unisexualité: Etude sur Différentes Manifestations de L'Instinct Sexuel*. Bibliothèque de Criminologie, vol. 15. Lyons: A. Storck, 1896.

————. "Walter Pater: In Memoriam." *Blackfriars* 9 (March 1928): 463–71.

Reade, Brian, ed. *Sexual Heretics: Male Homosexuality in English Literature from 1850–1900*. New York: Coward-McCann, 1970.

Roseliep, Raymond. "Some Letters of Lionel Johnson." Ph.D. diss., University of Notre Dame, 1954.

Rothenstein, William. *Men and Memories: Recollections of William Rothenstein*. Vol. 1, *1872–1900;* vol. 2, *1900–1922*. London: Faber and Faber, 1931, 1932.

Roy, G. Ross. "A Bibliography of French Symbolism in English-language Publications to 1910: Mallarmé-Rimbaud-Verlaine." *Revue de Littérature Comparée* 34 (October–December 1960): 645–59.

Sackville, Margaret. "At Whitehouse Terrace." In *Two Friends,* ed. Sewell, pp. 142–47.

Schoonderwoerd, N. H. G., *J. T. Grein, Ambassador of the Theatre 1862–1935: A Study in Anglo-Continental Theatrical Relations*. Assen: Van Gorcum and Co., 1963.

Sewell, Brocard. *Footnote to the Nineties: A Memoir of John Gray and André Raffalovich*. London: Cecil and Amelia Woolf, 1968.

————. *In the Dorian Mode: A Life of John Gray, 1866–1934*. Padstow, Cornwall: Tabb House, 1983.

————. "John Gray and André Sebastian Raffalovich: A Biographical Outline." In *Two Friends,* ed. Sewell, pp. 7–43.

————. "On Re-Reading 'Park.' " *Aylesford Review* 7 (Winter 1965/Spring 1966): 215–18.

————, ed. *The Aylesford Review. John Gray Commemorative Number* 4 (Spring 1961).

————. ed. *Two Friends: John Gray and André Raffalovich: Essays Biographical and Critical*. Aylesford, Kent: Saint Albert's Press, 1963.

Shewring, Walter. "Two Friends." *Blackfriars* 15 (September 1934): 622–25. Reprinted in *Two Friends,* ed. Sewell, pp. 148–51.

Smith, Timothy D'Arch. *Love in Earnest: Some Notes on the Lives and Writings of the English "Uranian" Poets from 1889 to 1930*. London: Routledge and Kegan Paul, 1970.

Speaight, Robert. *The Life of Eric Gill*. London: Methuen, 1966.

Sturgeon, Mary. *Michael Field*. London: George G. Harrap and Co., 1922.

Sutton, Denys. "Neglected Virtuoso: Charles Ricketts and his Achievements." *Apollo* 83 (February 1966), pp. 138–47.

Symons, Arthur. "The Café Royal." In *The Café Royal and Other Essays*. Westminster, England: Beaumont Press, 1923, pp. 1–4.

Symons, A. J. A. "The Diner-Out." *Horizon* 4 (1941): 251–58.

Temple, Ruth Zabriskie. *The Critic's Alchemy: A Study of the Introduction of French Symbolism into England*. New Haven, Conn.: College and University Press, 1953.

————. "The Other Choice: The Worlds of John Gray, Poet and Priest." *Bulletin of Research in the Humanities* 84, no. 1 (Spring 1981): 16–64.

Thorton, R. K. R. *The Decadent Dilemma*. London: Edward Arnold, 1983.

Vernon, Peter J. "The Letters of John Gray." Ph.D. diss., University of London, 1976.

———. "John Gray's Letters to Pierre Louÿs." *Revue de Littérature Comparée* 53 (Janvier—Mars 1979): 88–107.

Weintraub, Stanley. *Beardsley: A Biography*. New York: George Braziller, 1967.

Wells, Robert. "The Perils of Pietism." *Times Literary Supplement* (6–12 January 1989): 16.

Wenley, R. M. "Nietzsche: Traffics and Discoveries." *The Monist* 31 (January 1921): 133–49.

W[ratislaw?], T. W. "La Garde Joyeuse IX: 'John Gray.'" *The Artist and Journal of Home Culture* 14, no. 167 (4 November 1893): 328–29.

Wilde, Oscar. *The Letters of Oscar Wilde*. Ed. Rupert Hart-Davis. Fourth impression (corrected). London: Rupert Hart-Davis, Ltd., 1963.

———. "The Picture of Dorian Gray." *Lippincott's Monthly Magazine* (July 1890), pp. 3–100.

———. *The Picture of Dorian Gray*. Ed. Isobel Murray. London: Oxford Univ. Press, 1974.

Winckler, Paul A. "John Gray and His Times." In *Two Friends,* ed. Sewell, pp. 1–6.

Winwar, Frances. *Oscar Wilde and the Yellow Nineties*. New York: Harper, 1940.

Wyndham, Violet. "Reminiscences, by Ada Leverson: 1. The Importance of Being Oscar." In *The Sphinx and Her Circle: A Biographical Sketch of Ada Leverson, 1862–1933*. London: André Deutsch, 1963, pp. 105–23.

Yeats, William Butler. Introduction. *The Oxford Book of Modern Verse, 1892–1935*. New York: Oxford Univ. Press, 1936, pp. v–xlii.

Zaina, Alexandra. "The Prose Works of John Gray." In *Two Friends,* ed. Sewell, pp. 70–99.

Index

Continued from the copyright page:

Library, Yale University Library, New Haven, Connecticut, and the letter of T. Sturge Moore to "John Gawsworth" (Terence Ian Fytton), 21 March 1940, Reading University Library, Reading, England, all used by permission of their respective libraries and of Riette Sturge Moore.

Letters from John Gray to Mrs. MacLagan, 9 February 1906 (The O'Connell Collection, Box 3); to John Lane, 4 January 1893, and to A. J. A. Symons, 6 May 1925 (MSS Misc. GOR-GRA); holograph of John Gray, *Silverpoints* (MSS Bd: O'Connell); Oscar Wilde, *Notebook,* and Oscar Wilde and John Lane, contract for *Silverpoints,* 17 June 1892 (MSS Misc. WIA-WIL), published with permission of Princeton University Library, Princeton, New Jersey.

Letters from Félix Fénéon to John Gray and from John Gray to Charles Ricketts, to Walter Shewring, and to his step-niece, Coralie Tinklar, used by permission of The John Rylands University Library of Manchester, England.

Typescript reminiscences of Frank Liebich used by permission of the William Andrews Clark Memorial Library, University of California, Los Angeles.

Letters, memoirs, photographs, and other unpublished material in the files of Brocard Sewell, now in the Gray Archive, Dominican Chaplaincy, Edinburgh; and letters from Sewell to the author, used by permission of Brocard Sewell.

Photographs of John Gray, Sr., and of John Gray's sisters, and correspondence from Heather Coltman to the author, used by permission of Heather Coltman.

Cartoon by Max Beerbohm of André Raffalovich used by permission of Michael Maclagan and Sir Rupert Hart-Davis.

Photographs of St. Peter's Roman Catholic Church, Falcon Avenue, and the Cowgate, Edinburgh, used by permission of the Royal Commission on the Ancient and Historical Monuments of Scotland, Edinburgh.

Lithograph of Charles Shannon and Charles Ricketts by William Rothenstein, 1897 (P. 81—1943 [FMK 26573]), and pendant with miniature portrait of Miss Edith Cooper by Charles Ricketts (M. 3—1914 [FMK 11312]), used by permission of the Fitzwilliam Museum, Cambridge, England.

Photographs of the Woolwich Arsenal, Greenwich (the gates of the Arsenal opening onto Beresford Square [exterior], and the steam-hammer and furnace of the Arsenal [interior]), used by permission of the Greenwich Local History Library, London, England.

Letters from Edmund Blunden to John Gray (4 December 1930, 28 April 1931, and 16 February 1933) used by permission of the University of Iowa Libraries (Iowa City), and Claire M. Blunden.

Letters from James Langdale to Brocard Sewell used by permission of James Langdale.

Letters of John Gray to Gordon Bottomley, 1928–1934, used by permission of Richard Lancelyn Green.

Letter from Alan Neame used by permission of Alan Neame.

Letter from Graham Greene to the author used by permission of Graham Greene.

UNIVERSITY PRESS OF NEW ENGLAND
publishes books under its own imprint and is the publisher for
Brandeis University Press, Brown University Press, Clark University Press,
University of Connecticut, Dartmouth College, Middlebury College Press,
University of New Hampshire, University of Rhode Island, Tufts University,
University of Vermont, and Wesleyan University Press.

Library of Congress Cataloging-in-Publication Data
McCormack, Jerusha Hull.
    John Gray : poet, dandy, and priest / Jerusha Hull McCormack.
    p.   cm.
    Includes bibliographical references and index.
    ISBN 0–87451–533–5 (cl)
    1. Gray, John, 1866–1934.   2. Poets, English—20th century—
Biography.   3. Catholic Church—Scotland—Edinburgh—Clergy—
Biography.   4. Poets, English—19th century—Biography.
5. Dandies—Great Britain—Biography.   I. Title.
PR6013.R367Z73   1991
828'.809—dc20
    [B]   90–50906